Library of
Davidson College

United States Foreign Relations
1820-1860

United States Foreign Relations 1820 - 1860

by
Paul A. Varg

Michigan State University Press
1979

Copyright © 1979
Paul A. Varg
Library of Congress Catalog Card Number: 78-78245
ISBN: 087013-212-1
Manufactured in the United States of America

For Helen, again

Acknowledgments

The author owes debts to many scholars in the field of history of American foreign relations. Articles in learned journals and monographs analyzing developments in the particular period covered in this work are innumerable, and the authors too innumerable to mention except in the many footnotes that line these pages. As in the case of those scholars I have made every effort to exploit primary sources and to arrive at independent judgments not only because this is the duty of the scholar but because of the sheer pleasure of reading the original correspondence of participants.

I am especially indebted to two fellow historians, Paul Sweet and Lawrence Kaplan, who have read the manuscript with a sharp eye for both substantive errors and for style. Their many suggestions and questions have not only eliminated errors but have enriched the study. I am likewise indebted to my colleagues, Madison Kuhn and David Bailey, who read particular chapters close to their own fields of specialization and in friendly fashion needled me into further research and reflections upon my first interpretations.

University research grants facilitated the work but I am particularly indebted to the staff in the documents section of the library at Michigan State University. Eleanor Boyle's incomparable skill in locating pertinent materials long ago earned my admiration.

In addition I wish to thank Lyle Blair, Director of the Michigan State University Press. He represents a unique combination of the demanding editor, firm task master, and loyal friend.

Above all I am indebted to my wife whose patience while I labored at research was appreciated and whose typing of the manuscript and vigilant eye for awkward and unclear antecedents have been invaluable. In addition her many questions as to both clarity and interpretation added up to a delightful if wearing seminar. Without her assistance and encouragement this book would not have given me so much pleasure.

Contents

	Preface	xi
I	The Heritage from the Founding Fathers	1
II	The United States in the Atlantic Community, 1815–1860	20
III	An Assertive New Nation	43
IV	Anglo-American Rivalry	61
V	The United States and Europe, 1830–1842	75
VI	Trouble on the North American Frontier	94
VII	The Texas Question	118
VIII	Oregon: An Unnecessary Controversy	144
IX	War with Mexico	168
X	First Glimpses of World Power Status	195
XI	Anglo-American Rivalry in Central America	214
XII	Reaching for Forbidden Fruit	236
XIII	Adventures in the Pacific	257
XIV	Looking Backward on a Nation That Looked Forward	287
	Bibliography	295
	Index	303

Preface

In 1823 President Monroe stated that the United States would view any interference in the New World by European powers as unfriendly. This expression was little more than a hope, for the republic was not of sufficient stature to prevent intrusion. By 1860 the situation had changed dramatically. Both Great Britain and France had conceded United States dominance in North America. Barring any internal rupture in the republic, no longer was there need to fear European interference.

American foreign affairs during the years 1820 to 1860 are best understood in terms of the unleashing of forces transforming all western society. Great advances in technology, dramatic improvements in transportation, the rise of the factory system, the massive migrations of people, and the advent of modern banking and corporate enterprise greatly increased the importance of foreign relations throughout the western world. During the same years the emergence of new and vibrant nationalisms added to the tensions of increased economic rivalries.

The tremendous increase in international commerce brought with it various forms of imperialism. Contemporaries saw trade as the great civilizing agency, breaking down archaic societies, spreading new ideas, changing value systems, and sweeping away superstition. It was easy to believe that the western impact would benefit everyone. Thus, governments embarked on the opening of ports formerly closed, demanded security for their subjects in foreign lands, enlarged diplomatic and consular establishments, and called for stability and order in faraway places so that business might prosper. The importance of trade caused the United States to join in the race for markets, participate in the opening of China, lead the way in opening Japan, and energetically negotiate commercial treaties which included the most-favored-nation clause.

These developments gave a new vigor to expansionism. Russia took over territory extending to the Pacific Ocean and as far south as the Amur River. Great Britain incorporated additional territories in India into her empire, extended her jurisdiction to New Zealand, and placed herself in control of the Gold Coast in Africa. France acquired parts of North Africa and the Marquesas Islands in the South Pacific. The United States absorbed Texas and the vast territory west of the Louisiana Purchase including California, and annexed Oregon south of the 49th parallel. All four powers combined to intrude further in China and to seriously compromise that country's sovereignty.

Internal political struggles on the European continent led American observers to liken Europe to a volcano, and in Great Britain the movement for parliamentary reform and serious labor unrest led to bitter political struggles. The United States escaped political turbulence until the gigantic upheaval of the Civil War, but it experienced sharp conflicts rooted in sectional differences on issues such as banking, public lands, and the tariff.

The United States was not isolated from world developments but adhered to the policy of remaining neutral and uncommitted regarding the European alliance system. At the same time, it profited significantly and possibly escaped intervention in the Western Hemisphere because the European governments faced internal and external dangers that caused them to be conciliatory and restrained in relations with the United States. Nonetheless, Europeans viewed the rapid rise of the United States as dangerous and would have preferred to limit its growth and to establish a balance of power in the New World. American foreign policy, and more particularly the day-to-day conduct of foreign affairs, appeared erratic and unpredictable, while the inflammatory statements of congressional members, seeking to impress their home constituencies, struck Europeans as reckless and irresponsible, as well as portending future trouble.

The art of diplomacy combining restraint, patience, and respect for the interests of an adversary won few admirers among the American public. More often, these qualities were assumed to be evidence of weakness. The foreign service suffered from frequent charges in public print that the representatives rendered no useful service, that they were overpaid, and that they were contaminated by life in European courts. Too often the government was niggardly in paying its foreign representatives and withheld reimbursements for travel expenses or salary for the time spent in traveling to and from foreign posts.

Those charged with the conduct of foreign relations had to pay close attention to Congress and more particularly to what the Senate would approve in the way of treaties. At times Congress exercised a restraining hand, but at other times its demands went beyond what could reasonably be expected in negotiations with a foreign power. Frequently diplomats were embarrassed by speeches and committee reports from Congress aimed at satisfying the public's craving for patriotic affirmations and a bold stance. The speeches and reports received careful attention in the foreign offices of Europe and led to distrust. Congress, too, was responsive to the demands of special interest groups, large or small, and at times the executive branch was reduced to acting as an errand boy for business.

The United States had few experienced diplomats. John Quincy Adams and Albert Gallatin, who resided in Europe for extended periods, understood the workings of the concert of Europe and were familiar with the ways in which European foreign offices functioned. Other diplomats acquired a knowledge of foreign affairs while serving on congressional committees. The foreign service scarcely existed in 1820 but by the 1850s it was on the way toward becoming a professional body. By 1841 the nation had ministers in London, St. Petersburg, Paris, Berlin, Vienna, and Mexico City. Chargés, next in rank, were stationed at Madrid, Lisbon, Naples, Brussels, The Hague, Copenhagen, Stockholm, Rio de Janeiro, and in Peru and New Granada. By 1854 the number of legations had increased to twenty-eight. At only ten of these was the United States represented by a minister. Two legations were occupied by minister residents, fourteen by chargés, and two by commissioners. Ten also had secretaries of legation. In 1853 ministers plenipotentiary received a salary of $9,000, while ministers' salaries ranged from $4,500 to $6,000, and chargés' $4,500. The expense of living abroad and entertaining caused William Crawford, at an earlier date, to advise Martin Van Buren that "the salaries of our foreign ministers are so low that no one should accept an appointment for more than twelve months." The average annual cost of conducting the country's foreign relations in the twelve years ending in June 1853 was $304,683. New ministers were appointed with each change of administration, but lower posts were less subject to frequent change. In part, appointments were rewards for service to the political party in power, but considerable attention was also given to qualifications. Able men, such as Albert Gallatin, Edward Everett, and Louis McLane, received appointments and distinguished themselves as excellent diplomats.

In addition to sending its representatives to foreign lands, the United States scattered its navy on foreign seas. The navy was organized into seven squadrons—the West Indies, the African, the Mediterranean, the Brazil, the Pacific, the East India, and the Home Squadron. These included seven ships of the line. The navy's chief functions were to protect commerce, suppress piracy, and police the slave trade. Although the navy performed useful services, it was far from adequate had war come with Great Britain, and it was generally acknowledged that it could not have defended the coast nor prevented British seizure of Oregon or Hawaii. The United States also had a large merchant marine. It was always assumed that some of these ships could be converted into warships and that others would, as privateers, do great damage to enemy merchant ships. The weakness of the navy as a defensive weapon caused deep concern at times of crises in Anglo-American relations; also it was recognized that if the United States should annex Hawaii the islands could be taken by either Great Britain or France in the event of war. However, the navy did play a significant role during the Mexican War in blockading the Mexican coast, in assisting General Winfield Scott in an amphibious operation, and in seizing Mexican ports in California.

The author makes no pretension of plowing new ground. He can only assert that the subject is of sufficient importance to justify further examination. To the degree that this study differs from its predecessors it is in treating the forty years before the Civil War as one era and in its effort to place the diplomacy of these years in a world context.

Diplomacy is an art seldom if ever perfected, and individuals play an important role. The economic and political structures only partly predetermine what will happen. Within the political and economic framework, presidents, secretaries of state, and diplomats serve their nation state well or badly. Some bungle, misjudge, play the game with both eyes on personal advancement, or fail to take into account the vital interests and difficulties of adversaries. Others are judicious, skillful, imaginative enough to rise above *ex parte* argument. The complexity of the problems they face is seldom appreciated by an amiable public and almost never by an angry one. Few, if any, diplomats attain perfection but they usually deserve more understanding than they receive.

The author finds no overarching theory to explain what took place. The chief characteristic of both policy formation and the conduct of foreign affairs was the multiplicity of factors entering decision making. Of these the promotion of trade was the most basic, but rivalry with Europe, party struggles, the force of national pride, the prevailing ethnocentricity, and the idiosyncracies of leaders also shaped the course pursued.

National interest is the final guide in the formation of policy, but with different concepts of national interest at any one time inevitably disagreement arises. An even more fruitful source of argument and debate is how the generally accepted goal is to be achieved. Historians have engaged in heated controversy over Polk's handling of relations with Mexico, and few presidents have been accorded praise and blame in such generous doses. On the other hand, no historian has proposed that Polk's acquisitions be returned to Mexico. The critics only object to the way in which the territory was acquired. George Bancroft, the eminent historian who served in Polk's cabinet as secretary of navy, heartily agreed with Polk at the time. If Bancroft is to be harshly judged, it is also well to recognize that his historical studies did not immunize him to current waves of opinion, the excitement of a participant, nor the pleasure of having the approval of his colleagues. Historians dedicate themselves to objectivity, but like the ideals of diplomacy the goal is difficult to achieve.

Chapter I

The Heritage from the Founding Fathers

In 1803 a committee of Congress, buoyantly proud of the new republic, observed:

> The Government of the United States is differently organized from any other in the world. Its object is the happiness of man; its policy and its interest, to pursue right by right means.

"Princes," the report read, "fight for glory, and the blood and the treasure of their subjects is the price they pay. In all nations the people bear the burden of war, and in the United States the people rule." Jeffersonians could be cheerfully confident in the new order; their opposites, the Federalists, the disciples of Alexander Hamilton, could only sullenly meditate upon what they described as the ignorance and passions of the multitude. Both points of view were to endure.

The presence of unlimited resources in land, forest, and minerals favored the building of an acquisitive society in which banks, land speculation, shipping interests, foreign trade, and small manufacturing enterprises held sway. The rewards for innovation, improvements of mechanical devices, investments in land and new marketing and manufacturing ventures inevitably spurred rapid growth. In turn, politics became a contest among competing economic interests, and government became subservient to marketplace considerations in the promotion of a rapidly growing economy. In short, Whiggery with its emphasis on practical goals achieved a great ascendancy. Political rivalry was less a contest between the "haves" and the "have nots" than it was a contest among the "haves."

Almost infinite diversities existed. These ranged from a great variety of economic interests to differences in the cultural background among the immigrants and between them and the native-born. Most important were the economic differences. There was no one kind of farming; there were dairymen, corn and wheat growers, cattle ranchers, cotton planters. There was no one industry; there were wheat millers, textile manufacturers, ironmasters, railway entrepreneurs, shoemakers, and a host of food processors. There was no one business community, but rather a series of different entities. Financial interests and merchants in the port cities engaged in foreign trade had different points of view from the multitude of small manufacturing entrepreneurs, whose only concern was the home market. Many questions relating to foreign affairs touched these economic groupings in different ways, and often there was no common response.

Sectional and cultural differences added to the complexity. The southern states bent other interests to the preservation of slavery. The farmers and small businessmen of the Middle West had their own priorities. The Northeast was no less committed to protection of infant industries and commerce. In domestic affairs, in the years 1820 to 1850, a constant political bargaining between these sections developed, since each was dependent for success in politics on the support of another section.

Time and again sectional divisions took place on questions of foreign economic policy. Different economic groupings came into conflict over expansion, trade policy, and other issues. As a result foreign policy was shaped by developments in the outside world as well as by rival forces at home.

To add to the difficulty, those charged with the conduct of foreign relations had to consider less rational prejudices, deeply engrained attitudes, and tendencies of the public to become inflamed over issues that touched national pride or challenged long held values. From the heated forays of the critics of Jefferson and Madison in the years prior to 1812 down to the flood of moral indignation over Spanish atrocities in Cuba in the 1850s, administrators in Washington faced the danger of being overwhelmed by popular distempers.

These qualities of society and the nature of the political institutions confront the historian as he seeks to analyze the American position in the world in the first half of the nineteenth century. Foreign policy was often elusive, often in the midst of change, and always tinder in political party rivalry. However, in spite of the vicissitudes facing policymakers, united stands on particular issues and generally agreed upon objectives did make their way to the front. Both the processes by which these emerged and their implementation are central to this inquiry.

When the American envoys signed the Treaty of Ghent on Christmas Eve in 1814, thereby terminating the war with England, the most perilous era in the history of the nation's foreign relations came to a close. Ever since 1776 the country's future had been in jeopardy. The War for Independence pitted the new-born republic against the most powerful nation in Europe, one that enjoyed mastery of the seas and great financial resources. Only European rivalries saved the day. France, humiliated by defeat at the hands of England in the Seven Years War, cautiously sought to reverse the new balance of power by secretly assisting the rebels and by agreeing to a full-scale alliance in 1778. The long and costly war drained the French treasury, and by 1780 Foreign Minister Vergennes, alarmed by the prospects, entertained thoughts of accepting a Russian offer of mediation. Americans correctly perceived that in such a mediation their independence would be threatened, for the principles of *uti possidetis* would be applied and the British would remain in control of large parts of the republic. The republic would then be reduced to presiding over separated fragments of territory east of the Alleghenies. Fortunately, given this danger to the American cause, mediation by Russia was avoided thanks to George III, who rejected the offer. Finally, in October 1781 some 8,000 Americans and 7,800 French troops attacked the greatly outnumbered army of the British General Cornwallis whose route of escape by sea had been cut some days before when the French Admiral DeGrasse defeated a British fleet.

Perils of peace replaced perils of war in 1783. Victory allowed no pause for ecstatic reflections. Under the Articles of Confederation the looseness of the confederation permitted virtual autonomy of each state and negated any possibility of presenting a united front in foreign affairs. The founding fathers found this posture, which James

Madison termed imbecility, threatening to lay the country open to foreign exploitation. Shrewdly devised British orders-in-council limited American entry into the northern Maritime Provinces and prohibited American ships and important items of export from admittance to the British West Indies; these effectively placed the carrying trade in British ships, funneled exports, bound eventually for the continent, through the merchants of London and Liverpool. At the same time farmers of the southern states sank ever deeper into debt to British merchants. Members of Congress and leading merchants deplored the economic manacles that were reducing the new nation to an indentured status, while at the same time the British continued to hold their old fortifications in the Northwest. The American response in 1787 was the new Constitution, which effectively transferred control over foreign affairs to the new central government.

From 1789 to the ratification of the Treaty of Ghent in 1815 only brief periods of relative composure gave relief to the frequent, almost constant intrusion of vexatious issues of foreign affairs. Questions of foreign economic policy attached to basic domestic differences over the question of who should rule at home accelerated into polemical combat after England and France went to war in February 1793. Hamilton's Jay Treaty of 1795 sealed off the boiling political caldron by removing the most sensitive elements in the dispute. The British agreed to leave their posts in the Northwest, took the sting out of ship seizures by providing for compensation, opened the door slightly to American trade with the British East Indies; but it held firm on related questions of neutral rights on the high seas in wartime and excluded the Americans from the British West Indies except for ships of 70 tons or less, an opening so limited as to be deemed wholly unacceptable. In turn, the Americans compromised on the principle of "free ships make free goods," assured the British of payment of debts, and surrendered the favorite weapon of the Jeffersonians, the long-discussed discriminatory tax on British ships. The Jay Treaty reduced tensions but did not resolve long-term points of dispute.

The Quasi-War with France in 1797–1798 followed. The French Directory authorized privateering against American ships and treated American envoys with little less than insolence. Only with the return of peace in 1801 and termination of the 1778 treaty of alliance was equanimity restored.

The election of Thomas Jefferson to the presidency in 1801 inaugurated a period of growth. The acquisition of Louisiana in 1803 doubled the size of the national domain and catapulted the central government into a position of greater superiority as opposed to the individual states.

Jefferson dreaded war and at the outset of his presidency was prepared to subordinate principles of neutral rights to peace. The country needed time to grow and gain strength. The preference for maintaining a low profile soon eroded. Jefferson's constituency in the South and westward to the Mississippi was dependent for access to the sea by the rivers that flowed into the Gulf of Mexico, while the president himself lived in fear that the Floridas would, given the wars in Europe, fall into the hands of France. Spain, a feeble power, posed no dangers, but a powerful and aggressive neighbor such as France would force the new republic to wed herself to the British fleet.

In these circumstances Jefferson was incapable of maintaining an attitude of philosophical tranquility. His nationalism, leavened by a strong sense of mission, launched him on a program of expansion. He laid claim to West Florida as far east as the Perdido River on the grounds that this territory was a part of the Louisiana Purchase, magnified many times over the danger posed by two dilapidated Spanish forts in the extreme western part of the newly acquired territory, and held Spain guilty of failure to live up to an agreement to pay claims. Secretary of the Treasury, Albert Gallatin, pointed out the dubious quality of these charges, but Jefferson and Secretary of State James Madison pressed forward with an offer to purchase West Florida. Developments in Europe foiled their efforts. Other and more pressing concerns soon intruded.

After 1806 the Napoleonic wars in Europe were accompanied by developments ruinous to American foreign trade and humiliating to national pride. The shrewd French emperor, correct in his assessment that the British economy was dependent on access to foreign markets, set up the continental system. He commanded all ports across Europe that lay within range of his armies to exclude British ships. The British, in turn, issued an order-in-council on November 7, 1807, decreeing that neutral ships on their way to the continent must first stop in England and secure a license or they would be subject to seizure. Napoleon retaliated with the Milan decree. Any neutral ship submitting to the new British rule would be treated as having denationalized itself and would be subject to seizure on entering a continental port.

The Americans faced the limited options of submission, of adopting a policy of economic coercion, or of war. President James Madison dismissed the British assertion that their war with Napoleon made their measures necessary. With considerable justification, he attributed the British moves to jealousy of the rapidly growing American merchant marine. Extremists among his Federalist opponents, who saw an opportunity to gain party advantages, denounced the Republican policy as shameful obeisance to the French emperor. The American economy suffered severely, the country split into hostile camps, and Madison and his colleagues viewed the belligerents' arbitrary rulings on neutral trade as a challenge to American independence. Madison held that sovereignty extended to freedom of the seas; deprived of this freedom American sovereignty and independence itself were severely compromised. The crippling of the American economy, the blows to pride, and the frustrations induced by European dictates and severe domestic divisions exploded in war in June 1812.

Peace negotiations provided further instruction in the iniquities of European ambition. From July to December 1814 the American envoys at Ghent faced a complete stalemate in negotiations. Gradually the government in Washington had retreated from its fixed positions on impressment and neutral rights, but the British now demanded the creation of an Indian buffer state in the Northwest, one assured of virtual sovereignty, for it was to have the right to enter into treaties with Great Britain as if it were an independent state. Only when the British suffered military failures in North America in late 1814 did they retreat from this demand. The war closed without settling issues of neutral rights, but the long-held British aspirations to block American expansion in the Northwest came to an end.

From 1776 to 1814 Americans had benefited by European rivalries on several occasions, but they were more mindful of the fact that their weakness exposed them to dangers. In 1776 John Adams had warned that too close relations would reduce the republic to a mere puppet, danced on wires pulled by the cabinets of Europe. In 1801 Jefferson had warned against entangling alliances. The experiences

The Heritage From the Founding Fathers

since supported these admonitions. The close of the Napoleonic wars and the termination of the War of 1812 brought feelings of relief. Finally, the new republic could begin developing its own resources and turn its attention to the Floridas. British military operations within the Spanish-held territory during the recent war had placed the accent on the strategic importance of the coastal area on the Gulf of Mexico.

A new environment and remoteness from traditional Europe produced a new society. Well before the skirmishes with the British at Lexington and Concord a revolution took place. Transplanted institutions withered or took on new forms, and political terms acquired important new connotations. There was no aristocracy by right of birth, no one state church, no rigid social stratification; moreover, representative government had come to have a sharply different meaning than it had in the British House of Commons.

Americans cherished the differences. They minimized their European inheritance, exaggerating what was new. The youthfulness of the new society and the assurance bestowed by the abundance of land, forests, and streams led to a degree of bumptiousness, aggressive territorial ambitions, and adolescent effervescence that exaggerated the power of the new republic. The optimism was not misplaced. The sense of difference from the older societies of Europe was not illusory. This was a society of doers. A continent lay before them waiting to be developed. Given the promise of rewards to individual industriousness and the absence of a leisure class, it was inevitable that energy should characterize the new nation and that the same assertiveness should extend to the foreign policy.

Immigrants arriving early in the nineteenth century and the older settlers shared the conviction of uniqueness and the faith that the new land was endowed with a wealth unprecedented. A French settler in Pennsylvania, John Crevecoeur, replied in tones brimming with confidence to the question, "What Is An American?"

> He is arrived on a new continent; a modern society offers itself to his contemplation, different from what he had hitherto seen. It is not composed, as in Europe, of great lords who possess every thing, and of a herd of people who have nothing.

> Here are no aristocratic families, no courts, no kings, no bishops, no ecclesiastical dominion, no invisible power giving to a new a very visible one; no great manufacturers employing thousands, no great refinements of luxury. The rich and the poor are not far removed from each other as they are in Europe.[1]

In the next century thousands of European immigrants were pleased that the new land had no aristocrats before whom they had to bow. Lyman Beecher, Congregational minister in Litchfield, Connecticut, told his audience in New Haven in October 1812:

> No where beside, if you search the world over, will you find so much rich liberty, so much equality, so much personal safety and temporal prosperity, so general an extension of useful knowledge, so much religious instruction, so much moral restraint, . . .[2]

The sense of separateness from Europe did not delude them into illusory expectations of escape from man's dreary history. The leaders of the new society studied the ancient republics, seeking reasons for their decline.[3] They professed to find the same forces of destruction threatening America. The founding fathers were especially distrustful of power. In *The Federalist* Madison wrote:

> It may be a reflection on human nature, that such devices should be necessary to control the abuses of government. But what is government itself, but the greatest of all reflections on human nature? If men were angels, no government would be necessary. If angels were to govern men, neither external nor internal controls on government would be necessary. In framing a government which is to be administered by men over men, the great difficulty lies in this: you must first enable the government to control the governed; and in the next place oblige it to control itself.[4]

Protestantism, with its emphasis on the force of evil, strengthened the inclination to dwell on human avarice, pride, and lust. In a July Fourth oration in Boston in 1783 John Warren, leading doctor and surgeon, urged that everyone consider the fact that ancient republics had fallen upon evil days as a result of affluence. In gloomy tones he warned "that the principle of administration may be grossly corrupted, that the people may be abused, and enslaved under the best of constitutions, is a truth to which the annals of the world may be addressed to bear a melancholy attestation."⁵

This lamentation concerning man's propensity to do evil when entrusted with power had its counterpart in a widely prevailing querulous quality in foreign affairs. Perhaps it was part of the heritage from the Puritans of seventeenth century England. At least it was not new. The revolutionary generation demonstrated it in abundance as they found unworthy motives and dark scheming in each British move. Not all shared it, least of all Benjamin Franklin, but his colleagues in Paris, John Adams and John Jay, exhibited it to the point of distress in dealing with France. Adams noted in his diary: "Resentment is a Passion, implanted by Nature for the Preservation of the Individual. Man might suppress it but he ought to indulge it, to cultivate it. It is a Duty."⁶ Adams lived up to this duty, and along with many of his fellowmen expected the worst of nations as well as of individuals. The readiness to question extended itself to diplomacy. It served as a shield but also led to a refusal to take into account the legitimate interests of others.

The unilateralism that characterized American diplomacy owed even more to Jeffersonian political ideology. The guiding principles of republicanism gave rise to optimism. Faith in the people, confidence in the check and balance principle, the exhilarating view that freedom for the individual would result in an outburst of energy making the republic rich and powerful and its citizens enlightened concerning their own interests opened before the Jeffersonians a dazzling vista of a new era in human affairs.

Leaders recognized that dangers lay in the path to the achievement of these new political ideals, but they were determined guardians of the new ark of the covenant between the government and its people. Republicans and Federalists alike were uneasy about domestic developments but differed as to where the danger lay. The Jeffersonians saw a drift toward the insinuation of British practices whereby a small coterie of special economic interests held control through dominance of the legislative and executive branches. The reigning party, employing corrupt means, influenced the majority in Parliament. A wealthy mercantile aristocracy was, Jefferson thought, well on the way to ascendancy in the United States, thanks to Hamilton's National Bank and funding system. In 1791 he deplored the speculation of mercantile interests and lamented that capital was being held from productive enterprises and employed in gambling. The country, he feared, was being taken over by the "stock-jobbers" and "the rage of getting rich in a day" held sway. The only hope lay in "the augmentation of the numbers in the lower house, so as to get a more agricultural representation, which may put that interest above that of the stock-jobbers."[7]

Federalists had other fears concerning affairs at home. The ignorance of the populace, the demagoguery of Jefferson, and the triumphs of French infidelity threatened stability and law and order. The tyranny of ignorance beckoned behind the cloak of Jeffersonian republican principles. Cries of anguish from New England and the fears generated by the French Revolution created a political crisis in the 1790s.

Both parties were alert to dangers from abroad. In considerable degree these fears owed as much to the concerns about domestic affairs and the direction they were taking as they did to British or French provocations. Jeffersonians identified Federalism with admiration for the British system; Federalists saw republicanism as the American version of French Jacobinism. The popular agitation ran parallel to Hamilton's acceptance as a necessity, due to the need for capital, the bending of policy to assure good relations with England, whereas Jefferson and Madison saw in the continuation of British domination of American foreign trade the subordination of the United States and its reduction to the status of an economic colony.

Jefferson anticipated only inveterate hostility from Europe. The entrenched privileged classes could only wish that the republic would fail and thereby serve as an example of the futility of popular government. Jefferson welcomed the French Revolution and the Declaration of the Rights of Man. "I look with great anxiety for the firm establishment of the new government in France," he wrote, "being perfectly convinced that if it takes place there, it will spread sooner or later all over Europe." Its success is "necessary to stay up our own, and to prevent it from falling back to that kind of Halfway house, the English constitution."[8]

The failure of the French Revolution left the American republic standing alone, the only exemplar of the new political age. Jefferson considered it only a temporary setback. The irrepressible Virginia republican never lost faith that time would bring victory, and in the meantime the republican government in America would "be a standing monument & example for the aim & imitation of the people of other countries." He believed that the Europeans "will see, from our example, that a free government is of all others the most energetic" and "that the inquiry which has been excited among the mass of mankind by our revolution & its consequences will ameliorate the condition of man over a great portion of the globe."[9]

American nationalism embodied this sense of uniqueness and mission. In a world of dark despotism that rejected, as Americans saw it, the application of reason to politics and abjured the findings of science, the United States stood forth as the beacon of progress. This faith had as its corollary full confidence that republican principles had universal validity, and their eventual triumph was as inevitable as the rising and setting of the sun.

This sense of national mission dictated that American foreign policy should be dedicated to pushing back intrusions by strong European powers. European alliances could have no place in the New World. The long history of European imperialism hung over the new republic and instilled fear that the future would bring with it efforts to extend control over the Western Hemisphere. Herein lay a major impulse to expansionism.

Spanish possessions posed no immediate danger. However, Spain, in the words of Jefferson, was the most perfidious of nations and stubbornly resisted arrangements proposed by the United States. Spain's weakness and inability to resist the demands of her powerful neighbors posed the danger that her possessions would be transferred to France. In 1804 and 1805 Jefferson saw in the renewal of war in Europe and the rivalry of England and France an opportunity to bring about a happy resolution. An alliance with England limited to the objective of preventing French acquisitions impressed him as desirable, and he discussed it with his cabinet. Later he sought French aid in negotiations with Spain and persuaded Congress to appropriate $2 million for gaining Spanish assent to recognizing West Florida as part of the United States.

James Madison lived in fear that the Floridas would serve as a strategic area from which some powerful European nation could attack the United States. In 1810 he gave his approval to a revolt to be carried out by Americans living in West Florida, who favored annexation to the United States. Shortly after a miniature skirmish the Americans proclaimed the independence of West Florida. A few weeks later Madison, with congressional approval, annexed the territory.

Acquisition of the remainder of the Floridas was delayed until 1819, but the peril of powerful neighbors remained a basic concern of Jefferson and Madison throughout their administrations, and this fear was bequeathed to the next generation. The determination finally found expression in the Monroe Doctrine.

However, expansionism was not only a response to European imperialism; it had equally deep roots in land hunger and in the idea of mission. Frontier settlers and absentee speculators in land spilled over into border territories and served as advance heralds of annexation. The fact that these lands were uninhabited by white men and had not been cultivated conferred upon the United States the duty to acquire and develop additional territory. New territories would soon become states and would be assimilated into the federal union thereby extending republican principles and providing new opportunities for hard-driving farmers.

At times Jefferson was less concerned about adding to the territorial domain than he was in the spread of republican principles. Shortly after the acquisition of Louisiana he wrote to Joseph Priestley: "The *denouement* has been happy; and I confess I look to this duplication of area for the extending a government so free and economical as ours, as a great achievement to the mass of happiness which is to ensue." He was indifferent about the possibility that two confederacies, one Atlantic and the other Mississippi, might come into being. The new nation in the West, should it come about, "will be as much our children & descendants as those of the eastern . . ."[10] This idealistic attitude failed to survive, and later expansionists took delight in the republic extending from sea to sea and showed less and less interest in the spread of republican principles.

Faith in the beneficent effects of a free flow of commerce stood forth as a central tenet of American nationalism. It was rooted in the colonial experience in which the carrying trade constituted a major pillar of the economy. The War for Independence necessitated access to foreign supplies of war materiel from Europe. American representatives in Europe, John Adams, Arthur Lee, Silas Deane, and Francis Dana, went about explaining that access to the American market would make the countries on the European continent rich and powerful. Arthur Lee read Adam Smith's *Wealth of Nations* within weeks of its publication and found in it a presentation of the iniquities of mercantilism and was converted into a herald of free trade. Americans announced that an exchange of the superfluities of mankind would benefit all and that the interdependence of nations resulting from extensive trade would make war unthinkable.

At the close of the Revolution, trade revived slowly, with the British dominating the carrying trade. The inability of Congress under the Articles of Confederation to strike back served as a major force in the movement to revise the Articles. Southern fears of a strong central government rested on distrust of the merchants of the Northeast using the power of a stronger national government to serve their own interests at the expense of the South. By 1785 these fears gave way before a general recognition that the promotion of commerce was a national interest. This, in turn, led to the Constitutional Convention.

Confidence in the advantages that would flow from commerce was not limited to the merchants and shipping interests who had a direct stake. In 1783 John Warren, observed: "Commercial intercourse and connection have perhaps contributed more towards checking the effusion of blood, than all the obligations of morality and religion in their usual state of debility, could ever have effected."[11] Warren feared that a great inequality of riches followed the growth of commerce and that this, in turn, led to love of luxury, low morality and corruption, but he still was a supporter of commerce. In the first years of the newly created federal union the debates in Congress centered on the promotion of trade. Efforts to gain entry to the British West Indies enjoyed a high priority in all discussions regardless of party.

From 1789 to 1815 the American economy intertwined itself with that of Europe. The United States produced great quantities of raw materials, wheat, cotton, tobacco, rice, bar iron, naval stores, and lumber. An internal market had yet to be developed for any significant percentage of these products. During the same period the country depended on imports of manufactures. The value of exports increased from $19,012,041 in 1791 to $108,343,150 in 1807, while in 1804 American imports were valued at $75,316,937.[12] The great increase in exports from 1803 to 1807 owed much to the re-export of goods originating in the French West Indies. The wars in Europe cut off direct trade between France and her colonies, and the United States served as the carrier. From 1805 to 1807 these re-exports surpassed exports of domestic origin.[13] Foreign commerce became a vital part of the economy, a fact reflected in statistics on the growth of foreign trade and also in the prominence of foreign economic policy in the major political debates in the years 1789 to 1812. The fact that maritime grievances against England was the major cause of war in 1812 further underwrites the importance Americans attached to foreign trade.

Continental expansion and the search for markets became firmly imbedded in the outward thrust of the country. Pushed with energy by strong supporters in Congress these goals remained constants in foreign policy objectives.

The third component of American nationalism combined the elements of self-righteousness and moralism. This gave to American discussion of foreign affairs a distinctive coloring even if it had no significant influence on policy. It had its roots in the religious life of the nation and in the commonly held conviction that thanks to the nature of its government the United States was not only different but superior in terms of virtue to European nations. Whereas European nations faced constant danger of rivalry near at hand and therefore must be cautious and limit themselves to vital interests, Americans, isolated from the struggles of Europe, were freer to pronounce moral judgments on the right and wrong of every revolt, every alliance, and every government. This became a firmly entrenched habit in the course of the nineteenth century.

The propensity toward making moral judgments owed much to organized religion. Churches, which had occupied a central position in the colonial period, placed their stamp on their constituencies, on government, and particularly on education. A sharp decline in interest took place during the Revolution, but organized religion soon came to the fore again. In 1795 Timothy Dwight, president of Yale, launched an attack on the infiltration of infidel thought from France. He reduced the options facing American society to Christianity and infidelity. Revivalism soon became a major aspect of American life and helped to restore the churches to their former position of great influence. The revivals aimed at promoting moral virtue by putting an end to unbelief.

The Heritage From the Founding Fathers 15

The revivalists of New England turned from theological polemics to bolstering up society against the decline of morals. Intemperance, dueling, slothfulness in the face of iniquity, and the acquisition of wealth at the expense of the less fortunate permeated revival sermons. Lyman Beecher sounded the call to duty before his New Haven congregation in 1812:

> This exposition of public guilt and danger, is the appropriate work of gospel ministers. They are watchmen, set upon the walls of Zion to descry and announce the approach of danger. And if through sloth or worldly avocation, or fear of man, they blow not the trumpet at the approach of the enemy, and the people perish, the blood of the slain will the Lord require at their hands. Civil magistrates are also ministers of God, attending continually upon this very thing. It is their exclusive work "to see to it that the commonwealth receive no detriment." Indeed, every man, is bound to be vigilant and firm, and unceasing in this great work. And by sermons, and conversation, and tracts, and newspapers, and magazines, and legislative aid, the point may be gained. The public attention may be called up to the subject, and just apprehensions of danger may be excited, and when this is done, the greatest danger is past. The work is half accomplished.[14]

Revivalism soon captured the frontier churches. Men of the stripe of Peter Cartwright preached "hell fire and damnation"; their strategy was to play on emotions, fear, loneliness, the sense of guilt, and humor. As early as 1830 Calvin Colton, a clergyman, announced that revivals "have become the grand absorbing theme and aim of the American religious world—of all that part of it, which can claim to participate in the more active spirit of the age."[15] Revivalism resulted in rapid growth of church membership but, more important, it preserved and improved the status of the clergy in the community so that the word of the clergyman on social and political questions received a hearing. Alexis de Tocqueville, on his visit to the United States in 1842, observed: "There is no country in the world where the Christian religion retains a greater influence over the souls of men than in America."[16]

This aspect of American life did not make the United States more moral than other nations; it was no less concerned with self-interest than the European powers. However, it did inflate national self-righteousness and inculcate the habit of passing moral judgment on each and every development in foreign affairs. This habit sometimes led to sharp dissent from government policy; at other times it mustered popular support for actions dictated by the gaining of national advantage.

Organized religion held no monopoly in the application of moral sanctions. Jefferson and Madison established the tradition in the early national period. Their judgments rested upon their own understanding of nature's laws and interpretations of the law of nations. No two American statesmen were more alert to the interests of the republic nor more assertive in behalf of national interests, but they also believed that their actions coincided with the interests of mankind.

Neutral rights on the high seas were of prime importance to a nation heavily dependent on exports for its prosperity. Both Jefferson and Madison contended that these rights rested on moral principles and the law of nations. They held that the day would come when all nations would recognize that justice demanded that neutrals, who were in no way responsible for a war, should not have their rights abridged by more powerful belligerents. Current practice was an evil and an anachronism in an age of enlightenment. Madison, an authority on the law of nations, devoted a large part of his presidency to upholding the law on the high seas.

However, these practical statesmen were not prepared to sacrifice national interests. At the outset of his presidency Jefferson wrote to Robert Livingston, minister to France, outlining his views on free ships, seizure of contraband, and blockades. He defended the principle "free ships make free goods," declaring that belligerents had no right to seize contraband or to blockade the ports of the enemy. Having explained his reasoning Jefferson observed: "Indeed, it now urged, and I think with great appearance of reason, that this is general principle dictated by national morality; . . ." He wrote, "The doctrine that the rights of nations quietly remaining under the exercise of moral & social duties, are to give way to the convenience of those who prefer plundering & murdering one another is a monstrous doctrine; . . ." "Reason and nature," he concluded, "clearly pronounce that the neutral is to go on in the enjoyment of all its rights, that its commerce remains free, not subject to the jurisdiction of another, nor consequently its vessels to search, or to enquiries whether their contents are the property of an enemy, or are those which have been called contraband of war."[17]

Then came his more realistic judgment. As great in importance as these principles were, "yet in the present state of things they are not worth a war."[18]

In public office, responsibility presided over righteousness. Yet, outcries of moral indignation were common in American society, and they complicated diplomacy. Moralism gave a fervor to American nationalism that others found perplexing and strange. It was not unique to the United States. Nonconformist church groups in Great Britain exerted a similar influence on public foreign policy debates.

The strength of a country in foreign affairs and the posture it strikes is rooted in the nature and success of its economy. The presence of fertile lands ready to be cultivated, the generous public land policy, the wealth in minerals and lumber, and the access to markets of even remote areas offered rich rewards to people of drive and initiative. Greater growth lay ahead, but already in 1814 the wilderness of western Pennsylvania, Ohio, Kentucky, and Tennessee had given way to agriculture and industry. A writer for the *Niles Weekly Register* wrote concerning Ohio: "Let it be recollected, however, that about twenty years ago, this territory was a forest, in a state of nature, trodden only by wild men and wild beasts—the indian, the wolf, and the panther." Now, in 1814, it contained "at least 300,000 free inhabitants." The observer reported further: "The sturdy hand of honest labor has prostrated the forest and rich fields of grain occupy the spot where the bounding deer lately sported, or the hardy buffalo regaled on the luxurious productions of nature. How changed the scene!—the bustling town supersedes the indian village; the wood rattles with the sound of machinery—the rivers are covered with boats; the *yeo heave o* of the sailor is heard; and the mighty vessel, impelled by steam, takes place of the lonely canoe of the aboriginal inhabitant."[19]

By the close of the War of 1812 the country was a scene of bustling activity. The hard-driving population gained ever greater confidence in themselves and pride in their country.

The dire predictions of European travelers that the republic must break into fragments began to give way to friendlier estimates. In a review of Morris Birkbeck's *Notes on a Journey in America*, the writer informed the readers of the *Edinburgh Review* of the republic's great promise.

> It is impossible to close this interesting volume, without casting our eyes upon the marvellous empire of which Mr. Birkbeck paints the growth in colours far more striking than any heretofore used in portraying it. Where is this prodigious increase of numbers, this vast extension of dominion, to end? What bounds has Nature set to the progress of this mighty nation? Let our jealousy burn as it may; let our intolerance of America be as unreasonably violent as we please; still it is plain, that she is a power in spite of us, rapidly rising to supremacy; . . . In foreign commerce, she comes nearer to England than any other maritime power; and already her mercantile navy is within a few thousand tons of our own![20]

NOTES TO CHAPTER I

1. J. Hector St. John Crevecoeur, *Letters from an American Farmer* (Gloucester, Mass.: Peter Smith, 1968), p. 46.
2. Lyman Beecher, "A Reformation of Morals Practical and Indispensable. A Sermon delivered at New Haven, on the evening of October 27, 1812." Microcard copy of original in the Library of Congress (Utica, N.Y.: Merrell and Co., 1813), Sabin's Bibliotheca Americana, #4336.
3. For a discussion of the importance of classical authors' contribution to the thinking of the revolutionary generation of leaders see *The World of the Founding Fathers Their Basic Ideas on Freedom and Self Government*, ed. Saul K. Padover (New York: Thomas Yoseloff, 1960), pp. 30–33.
   See also James Madison "Of Ancient & Modern Confederacies," *The Writings of James Madison*, ed. Gaillard Hunt (New York: G. P. Putnam's Sons, 1901), Vol. II, pp. 369–90.
4. Padover, *The World of the Founding Fathers*, pp. 38–39.
5. John Warren, "An Oration, Delivered July 4th, 1783 in Celebration of the Anniversary of American Independence," quoted in *The Rising Glory of America 1760–1820*, ed. Gordon Wood (New York: George Braziller, 1971), pp. 55–56.
6. *The Adams Papers*, ed. L. H. Butterfield, *Diaries*, Vol. II (Cambridge, Mass.: The Belknap Press of Harvard University Press, 1961), p. 236.
7. *The Writings of Thomas Jefferson*, ed. Paul Leicester Ford (New York: G. P. Putnam's Sons, 1895), Vol. V, pp. 376–77.
8. Ibid., pp. 274–75.
9. Ibid., Vol. VIII, p. 8.
10. Ibid., Vol. VIII, p. 295.
11. Gordon Wood, *The Rising Glory of America*, p. 58.
12. Felix Flugel and Harold U. Faulkner, *Readings in the Economic and Social History of the United States* (New York: Harper & Brothers, 1929), pp. 118–22.

13. Ibid., p. 119.
14. Lyman Beecher, *A Sermon Delivered at New Haven, on the Evening of October 27, 1812* (Utica, N.Y.: Merrell and Camp, 1813), p. 12.
15. Calvin Colton, *History and Character of American Revivals of Religion*, pp. 5–6, quoted in Charles C. Cole, Jr., *The Social Ideas of the Northern Evangelists 1826–1860* (New York: Columbia University Press, 1954), p. 70.
16. Alexis de Tocqueville, *Democracy in America*, eds. J. P. Mayer and Max Lerner (New York: Harper & Row, 1966), pp. 268, 414.
17. *The Writings of Jefferson*, Vol. VIII, pp. 88–92.
18. Ibid.
19. *Niles Weekly Register*, May 28, 1814, Vol. VI, pp. 209–210, quoted in Flugel and Faulkner, eds., *Readings in the Economic and Social History of the United States*, pp. 130–31.
20. Review of Morris Birkbeck, *Notes on a Journey in America, from the Coast of Virginia to the Territory of the Illinois* in *The Edinburgh Review*, June 1818, pp. 120–40.

Chapter II

The United States in the Atlantic Community, 1815-1860

The fervent nationalism that prevailed after the close of the Napoleonic wars did not cut the ties to Europe. Economically and culturally the United States remained closely related to the Old World and to Great Britain in particular. British capital helped finance the building of roads, canals, and railroads. Immigrants from Ireland, Germany, and England provided the desperately needed labor supply. European technology and science contributed to the growth of industry, the advancement of medicine, and knowledge of the physical and biological world. European philosophers, poets, and novelists provided the intellectual fare of the American reading public. Contemporaries acknowledged these ties.

The United States, many observed, differed from Europe only in its political institutions. Political change was underway in Europe. The triumph of free institutions appeared inevitable, but the older society of Europe remained tied to the past in ways not true in the United States, where traditional institutions had never gained a hold. Vested interests in Europe persevered in perpetuating the landed aristocracy, the state church, the military, and remains of feudalism, but these interests were fighting a losing battle. The same liberalizing forces at work in the United States operated in Europe, and these would inevitably triumph.

Aside from the difference in political systems, society in western Europe and the United States was in most respects the same. The family system, the legal order, the economy with its emphasis on private property, individual enterprise, and the responsibility of the state to promote economic growth, the value system with its emphasis on individual worth, and the general acceptance of basic Christian tenets meant that in everyday life people on both sides of the Atlantic shared common daily experiences and concerns. Consequently, the literature of Europeans and Americans could be read by each other without having to surmount barriers to understanding.

During the post-Napoleonic era the middle class in both America and Europe triumphed. This triumph first occurred in the United States, but signs of its coming to power in Europe appeared clear. Alexis de Tocqueville, in his *Recollections*, wrote of the predominance of the middle class in France:

> Master of everything in a manner that no aristocracy has ever been or may ever hope to be, the middle class, when called upon to assume the government, took it up as an industrial enterprise; it entrenched itself behind its power, and before long, in their egoism, each of its members thought much more of his private business than of public affairs; or of his personal enjoyment than of the greatness of the nation.

Men engaged in commerce, doctors, scientists, and lawyers had a common bond in their devotion to inquiry, for in their constant pursuit of truth in their particular sphere they became conditioned to accept nothing on the basis of authority and to go beyond tradition in their investigations. Liberty was synonymous with inquiry, and the advance of the middle class gave life to the spirit of liberty.

This cultural and economic interdependence obviously did not create a utopian western brotherhood. Nation states remained in an adversary relationship, whether located on the same continent or separated by three thousand miles of ocean. The United States, like its European counterparts, had its own set of interests and was at least equally endowed with pride and self-assurance. It wisely perceived that, given its underdeveloped state, entanglements in the European balance of power system involved dangerous commitments and such involvement would inhibit its freedom in the Western Hemisphere. This purely pragmatic approach was a matter of strategy rather than a policy of isolation. At the same time American foreign policy focused much more on developments and interests in Europe than on South America or Asia. This was even more true regarding relations of people to people as opposed to relations of government to government. And the former was more important in American foreign relations in the nineteenth century than the state-to-state relationship.[1]

Economic ties surpassed all others in importance. This becomes clear when the emergence of an American national economy is viewed, not as an isolated phenomena but as an integral part of the rapid increase of commerce and industry in the entire western world.

Prior to the War of 1812 the American economy to a large extent was local in nature and at most regional, with roughly ninety percent of the population agricultural. Farms produced largely for local markets and the farmers' own families. The major exceptions to this highly local characteristic were in the southern states, where tobacco, rice and, after 1790, cotton were produced for a foreign market. There were also significant exports of meat, especially from the Middle Atlantic states, and both fish and lumber from New England. Industry, even more than agriculture, produced almost wholly for a local market.

The emergence of a national economy by 1850 stands out as one, if not the most important, development in the antebellum period. Foreign markets and foreign sources of both manufactures and capital played an important part. The sharp growth of national economies in western Europe paralleled their American counterpart, and their growth contributed to the expansion of both agriculture and industry in America. In turn, the European economies shot upward, in part because of the stimulus from this side of the Atlantic.

Cotton fiber provided the first cord binding the two continents together. Cotton exports constituted 39 percent of the value of all exports during the years 1816 to 1820. By 1840 cotton reached 63 percent of the total. By 1860 1,700 million pounds, valued at $200 million, were exported.

The phenomenal growth of the South, thanks to cotton cultivation, promoted two new features in the American economy. The concentration on cotton created a demand for foodstuffs. The Mississippi River and its tributaries offered cheap water transportation so that the developing agriculture of the Northwest had ready access to the rapidly growing population in the South. Some part of this food surplus also found its way from New Orleans to East coast cities, but the South provided the larger market.

The burgeoning of cotton exports made available abundant supplies of foreign exchange. This, in turn, opened the door to the purchase of European manufactures and to the borrowing of European capital, both so essential to American economic growth.

A vast program of internal improvements soon augmented the natural waterways between the upper Mississippi valley and the South. The rapid growth of western population created a need for roads and canals. Roads were largely constructed by local governments, but roads that were intersectional required the support of the federal government. The first of these, the National Turnpike, reached Columbus, Ohio, in 1833 and Vandalia, Illinois, in 1844. After the War of 1812 attention was focused chiefly on canals, because of the cheapness of water transportation. The Erie Canal, connecting the Great Lakes and the Hudson River, opened in 1825. It remained the one truly intersectional canal, but scores of others were built along the East coast. Other extremely important canals crisscrossed Ohio, Indiana, and Illinois. By 1850 it is estimated that the country had 3,700 miles of canals. Most of them were constructed prior to the panic of 1837. Chester Wright, well-known economic historian, summed up the results:

> This development hastened the westward movement; it widened the markets for the products of every region, thus furthering specialization and division of labor, increasing trade, and augmenting the productive capacity of the nation; it helped break down the local or provincial economy of many sections, hastened the growth of a national economy, and helped to increase trade that was international in scope.[2]

The availability of canal transportation made it possible to ship wheat to New York and then to world markets. This promoted an increasing concentration on wheat in the West. By 1860 wheat exports were valued at $19,500,000, ranking second to cotton. Much of this increased wheat export was a result of the repeal of the

British Corn Laws in 1848. The rapid expansion of wheat production, in turn, spurred interest in linking the Middle West and the East by railway. But construction was delayed by the economic depression of 1843–1847. Not until the 1850s did the long trunk lines become a major factor in the hauling of grains and meats to market. In 1857, for the first time, railways carried a larger tonnage of freight than the Erie Canal.[3]

The growth of manufacturing rivaled the expansion in agriculture. Economic historians differ as to the date of take-off but generally agree that it took place between 1820 and 1840.[4] In 1820 only $50 million was invested in manufactures; by 1860 the investment totaled one billion. The manufacture of textiles led the way. Prior to the introduction of the power loom in 1814 manufacturing was largely limited to the making of yarn, with weaving being carried on in homes. The power loom was not adapted to the manufacture of woolens until the 1830s. By 1860 manufacturing consumed some 423,000,000 pounds of cotton, as compared to an estimated 5,000,000 pounds in 1790. In terms of capital invested, number employed, or net value of product, cotton manufacture was the country's leading industry in 1860.

During these same years, 1820 to 1860, other industries, small arms manufactures, woolen manufactures, iron manufactures, and textile machinery experienced only a slightly lesser growth. By 1859 manufacturing employed 1,311,246 people, and the value of the items produced totaled $1,855,862,000.[5]

This rapid growth of the economy prior to the Civil War would not have been possible had the United States been isolated from the Atlantic community. A considerable part of the technology was imported. The European market for cotton, wheat, flour, and meat provided access to European capital. Many manufactured items necessary to the new economy, such as railroad rails, tin plate, and iron, came from Europe. British capital, in particular, played a major role in the building of roads, canals, and railways. This fact is widely recognized by economic historians.[6]

These ties were not incidental or casual; the American economy was but one sector of the larger Atlantic economy. To a considerable degree the old mercantilist policy of the European states gave way to greater freedom of trade. After the Napoleonic wars both England and France relaxed trade restrictions. The United States did embark on a program of protective tariffs for manufactures, but by the 1840s there was a return to a low tariff policy. The net result was a relatively free exchange of commodities. American imports averaged annually $56,749,000 from 1821 to 1830, rose to an annual average of $104,139,000 in the next decade, and mounted to a high annual average of $267,871,000 in the 1850s. In 1850 imports of cotton manufactures were valued at $20,781,000. Wool manufactures, next in importance, were valued at $19,621,000.[7] In 1850 total imports were valued at $144,376,000. Of these, $108,638,000 came from Europe.[8] One economic historian concludes that in no other period did international trade play a greater role in the American economy.[9]

Foreign investments in the United States, particularly those of British origin, helped make possible the building of roads and canals and other private business enterprises. The House of Baring, in London, concentrated its attention on the United States in the decades prior to the Civil War. An American, Joshua Bates, occupied a leading position in the firm's London office, and Thomas Wren Ward represented the Barings in the United States. Ward, described as a man of "honesty, conscientiousness, and intense pride in the good name of Baring Brothers and Company," served the firm with great energy and remarkably fine business judgment.[10] The Baring firm worked closely with the Bank of the United States.[11] In 1817 the Bank of the United States sent John Sergeant to London to negotiate with the Barings. Sergeant made a contract providing for the Barings to furnish approximately $3,100,000 in specie.[12] This relationship continued, and the bank and Barings engaged in large-scale operations in the 1830s. The company greatly expanded its operations in the United States after 1830, helping to finance not only trade with England but also American trade with China. By the close of 1831 almost forty American firms had been granted automatically renewable importing credits, and Barings financed almost all dry goods operations.[13]

No final accurate estimate of the amount of foreign capital that found its way to the United States is possible. Stuart Bruchey, basing his conclusion on the statistics assembled by Douglas C. North, estimates the figure to be $500,000,000.[14]

Foreign purchases of securities issued in the United States were attractive because they yielded a high return. Again, precise figures are not available. In the 1830s the greatest amount was in state bonds issued to pay for internal improvements.[15] One economic historian estimates that from one-half to three-fourths of the state bonds were held in Europe.[16] State bonds held the lead, but foreign investors also placed their funds in American corporations, banks, and railroads.[17] This amount increased rapidly in the late 1840s and early 1850s.

In 1853 the House of Representatives called on the secretary of the treasury to provide information as to "the aggregate amount of federal, state, city, county, railroad, canal, and other corporation bonds, stocks, or other evidences of debt, held in Europe or other foreign countries." In his report the secretary stated that there were $190,718,221 bonds outstanding in the states, and of this total $72,931,597 was held by foreigners.[18] The amount of bonds outstanding of city governments totaled $93,280,518, and $21,462,322 was held by foreigners.[19] Foreigners held $6,688,996 in stocks and bonds of banks.[20] They held only a negligible $378,172 in the securities issued by insurance companies,[21] but they held $36,125,172 in railroad bonds.[22] The secretary of the treasury placed the value of all stocks and bonds held by foreigners at $222,225,315.[23] He acknowledged that his statistics were not complete and, as we have seen, scholars have recently estimated the indebtedness to be twice that amount.

The dependence on Europe for the supply of labor was greater than its dependence on capital. The great wave of immigration did not take place until after the Civil War and only reached its peak in the first decade of the present century, but the earlier European migration attained significant proportions. Conditions prevailing in Europe at the close of the wars provided the impetus. By 1817 the greatest migration in human history was underway. In that year the number of new arrivals approximated 30,000—20,000 from the British Isles, 8,000 from Germany, and 2,000 from France.[24]

Immigration to America, as Marcus Hansen pointed out, was closely related to a series of economic developments in the nineteenth century. This is not to say that the emigrés were motivated wholly by economic considerations, for many factors influenced individuals who made the momentous decision to leave the Old World, with economic motives playing the greatest role.

However, the broader economic developments, rather than individual motivation, must be accorded first attention. These included the business cycle with its periodic ups and downs, the swelling of Europe's population ever since 1700, the flood of democratic political ideas among the masses after Napoleon's downfall, the growth of commerce between the New and Old Worlds with its attendant increase in public information, and, extremely important, the availability of transportation. The ships that carried the bulk products—such as cotton, tobacco, flax, and naval stores—to Europe served as immigrant passenger lines on the return voyage.[25] The industrial revolution led to a decline of agriculture, the increased dependence of Ireland on successful potato crops, the increased population in some German states accompanied by ever smaller land holdings and increases in rural indebtedness. All stimulated the great migration.

In the decade of the 1850s some 2,600,000 immigrants arrived, and by 1860 there were more than 4,000,000 foreign-born inhabitants. England, Ireland, and Germany contributed by far the larger numbers. The census of 1850 reported 961,719 Irish in the United States. Ten years later the Irish numbered 1,611,304. In 1832 ten thousand German immigrants arrived; in 1834 seventeen thousand came; in 1837 some 24,000; and from 1845 to 1860 the total reached 1,250,000.[26] By 1860 there were nearly six hundred thousand who had been born in England, Scotland, or Wales.[27]

The European migrants contributed on a large scale to the breaking of new lands in the Middle West, to the construction of internal improvements, and to the building of industry. The Germans and the British migrated to the West in large numbers. By 1850 the western states that produced the bulk of agricultural products, excepting cotton and tobacco, had large percentages of foreign-born: Illinois, 13.22; Michigan, 13.82; Ohio, 11.15; and Wisconsin, 36.25.[28]

The Irish often found work in the building of roads and canals. In 1818 3,000 Irish were employed on the Erie Canal. Carl Wittke, eminent immigration historian, concluded: "There was hardly a canal built anywhere in the United States before the Civil War without Irish labor."[29] Irish also constituted a majority of the workers constructing the railroads in the East and Middle West. To a large degree the Irish population in New York, Boston, and Chicago were engaged in construction.

A considerable portion of immigrants, more particularly those from the British Isles, provided the labor in the new industries. Rowland Berthoff's *British Immigrants in Industrial America* tells the story of the important role the British played as entrepreneurs, skilled artisans, and laborers in both the cotton and woolen industries in New England. Lancashire calico printers "filled 'English Row' in Lowell," and English and Scottish superintendents and craftsmen were prominent in the new mills in Lawrence, Fall River, and New York.[30] British miners by the hundreds worked in the anthracite regions of Pennsylvania, outnumbering all others, and other British immigrants worked in large numbers in the lead mines of Wisconsin and the copper mines of Michigan.[31]

Irish and German immigrants frequently encountered strong prejudices, and the nativist movement of the 1840s called for restrictions. Others, more mindful of the contribution the immigrants were making, welcomed their coming. In 1841 one of these friendly observers wrote:

> Looking at what has already been done by the aid of the foreign labor, the great public works of our cities, our canals, railroads, and indeed every enterprise of physical power, and seeing what yet remains to be accomplished before this continent can have fulfilled its destiny, the interruption of immigration would be an actual decree against improvement, —a ban on civilization,—a fiat for the perpetual existence of the wilderness, and for the everlasting establishment of savage life.[32]

European immigrants constituted the major tie between the United States and Europe. The thousands of letters they wrote to their friends and relatives who remained in their native country, the scores of foreign language newspapers with their reports of happenings in the Old World, and the churches and fraternal organizations with their preservation of traditional attitudes and customs made of the United States a kind of European pudding stone.

Ties to the mother country injected a new element into political life. The immigrants became ardent advocates of republican rule and often the staunchest supporters of territorial expansion. They also brought with them, especially in the case of the Irish, abundant prejudice toward one or another country in Europe. Some viewed Canada as the prospective hostage for striking out for freedom for Ireland from British rule. American political leaders catered to the foreigners. In the election of 1852 presidential candidates for the first time made a bold bid for the foreign vote. General Winfield Scott, the Whig candidate, praised the Irish and Germans for their bravery in the Mexican War; on Sundays, during the campaign, he attended Catholic mass in the morning and a Protestant service in the evening. The Whigs buttressed these efforts to capture the Irish vote by labeling the Democratic support of a low tariff as mere kowtowing to the British.[33]

Americans made a practice of announcing the superiority of their political institutions and held fast to the faith that republican ideals would eventually triumph everywhere, but they also frequently expressed pride in their British political heritage. The Glorious Revolution and the Bill of Rights of 1688 stood forth in this inheritance as deserving of eternal gratitude.

Law was central in this transplanting of British and European institutions. In the course of the nineteenth century American legal developments, like so many others, were to influence British law, but Americans remained indebted to the British for a considerable part of their legal structure, particularly for the common law. It was by no means inevitable that it should be so. Jeremy Bentham, the British philosopher and advocate of codification of the laws, enjoyed a strong following in the United States early in the nineteenth century. But well before the Civil War the influence of four great American jurists, Kent, Story, Shaw, and Gibson, brought about the victory of common law. An earlier strong advocate, Peter S. Du Ponceau, eminent French immigrant who achieved fame as a lawyer, had pushed vigorously for the continued adherence to the common law. He had written that the argument scarcely needed development for it was a self-evident principle: "We live in the midst of the common law; we inhale it at every breath, imbibe it at every pore; we meet it when we wake, and when we lay down to sleep . . ."[34]

Philosophy and literature flowed freely from Europe to America. Only the most modest of beginnings of an American school took place in either of these branches in the years prior to 1850. A lively interest in the writings of Europe and the art treasures of the Old World provided the intellectual fare. Those who read and those who wrote for American journals acknowledged that they must look to Europe. As late as 1849 a writer for the *North American Review* observed: "It may not be our destiny to produce a great literature, as, indeed, our genius seems to find its kindliest development in practicalizing simpler and more perfect forms of social organization. We have yet many problems of this kind to work out, and a continent to subdue with the plough and the railroad, before we are at leisure for aesthetics."[35] The note of apology, found so frequently in the journals of the day, reflected the readiness to embrace the European works. The relatively new country, busy in clearing a continent, could take pride in Washington Irving and James Fenimore Cooper and the eminent historians, William Prescott, John Motley, and George Bancroft, but Europe remained the major source for serious readers.

The historian of American magazines, Frank Luther Mott, observed that something more than Fourth of July oratory was required to make an American literature.[36] Strident nationalism characterized the decades after the War of 1812. Periodical editors never tired of pleading for an original American literature, one that would foster a love of republican institutions and native values. Spread-eagle orators decried the dependence on foreign books. Scores of magazines, most of them short-lived, took pride in publishing native writers, but the quality of the productions rendered them largely ephemeral. With a few exceptions, European writers continued to dominate until approximately 1850. American magazines of the period imitated English magazines in both form and content.[37] More important, in the judgment of Mott, "it was British literature that was chiefly read in America."[38]

The general readiness to turn to Europe owed much to the qualities shared by American and European societies and to the fact that the changes taking place in philosophy, poetry, religious thought, and political and economic thinking were not confined by the boundaries of any one country. Americans, Englishmen, Scots, Germans, and Frenchmen confronted the same questions of epistemology, religious belief, the role of the state in the economic sphere, and the relationship between the state and the individual. The issues arising out of new scientific discoveries, the instability of old political institutions, and challenges to religious authority evoked lively debate. The thoughtful reading public sought answers in an atmosphere where old certainties were lost, while at the same time promise of a new day beckoned.

The absence of international copyright agreements promoted free exchange of new forms in fiction and poetry and examination of new philosophical teachings. Americans freely published European works without compensating the original publishers or the authors. The result was a flow of books at low prices. The benefits to the American public were substantial; the effect on American authors was equally injurious. Publishers found it more profitable to print the works of well-known Europeans who did not have to be paid than they did American authors, most of whom were not yet known.

Europe offered a fare of sufficient variety to arouse a warm reception by one or another school of thought in America. Parties of Whiggish persuasion took delight in the Manchester school of economics, in Sir Walter Scott, and in Henry Peter Brougham. Transcendentalists delighted in the writings of Thomas Carlyle, Samuel Taylor Coleridge, and Victor Cousin. There was no one intellectual tie between the continents but rather a large aggregation of links of groups of like-minded.

The nature of the cultural relation was less one of dependence than one of sharing. Several American writers—Washington Irving, James Fenimore Cooper, Nathaniel Hawthorne, and Edgar Allan Poe—were read abroad. A much greater number of Europeans met with enthusiastic response in the United States, among them Sir Walter Scott, William Wordsworth, Lord Byron, Victor Cousin, and Fredrika Bremmer, prior to 1840, and Charles Dickens and Alfred Tennyson later. The exchange reflected the fact that literary tastes, popular interests, and new themes, styles, and philosophical concepts were common to countries on both sides of the Atlantic.

The *North American Review*—in terms of literary quality, truly professional literary criticism, and awareness of significant new developments in science, education, and philosophy—was easily the foremost journal of the day. It served as the wellspring for serious readers anxious to be informed of the latest findings and the new currents in literature. During the first twenty-five years of its existence the *North American Review* was almost exclusively devoted to what was taking place in the sphere of learning overseas. Gradually American contributions in science, medicine, and literature came to occupy a larger place. In 1840 the editor noted the trials of the early years and acknowledged that formerly "lower efforts" in literature had "to suffer great discouragements, when, in consequence of community of language, they are brought at once into comparison with the best productions of another highly cultivated society. So it has been, however, in these twenty-five years," he explained, "that, even had we been disposed to exclude foreign works from consideration in these pages, we should have had little cause to complain of any deficiency of grist for our critical mill." Earlier, he observed, "we could scarcely find American books to notice" but "now the difficulty is to keep up with the press."[39]

Theological controversy and the relation of morality to revealed religion attracted more readers than questions of epistemology. No philosopher of any note appeared on the scene until late in the century, but European philosophers received wide reading. Prior to 1825 John Locke's *Essay on Human Understanding* was the standard textbook used in virtually every American college, but the Scottish philosophers then took over. Of these, Dugald Stewart, and more particularly his volume entitled *The Philosophy of the Active and Moral Powers of Man* became popular. Stewart's writing was introduced as a textbook at Brown in 1825, at Yale the same year, and at Dartmouth in 1838. In a letter to Coleridge in 1829 James Marsh reported: "The works of Locke were formerly much read and used as textbooks in our colleges; but of late have very generally given place to the Scottish writers; and Stewart, Campbell and Brown are now almost universally read as the standard authors on the subjects of which they treat."[40]

Locke's disciples eventually promoted a skepticism that repelled American readers, but the Scottish philosophers offered escape from this uncongenial result. The *North American Review* devoted fifty-four pages to a review of Stewart's book. The writer found fault with some of Stewart's analysis and described him as lacking in originality and exhibiting a "somewhat limited power of thinking," but these shortcomings were gladly forgiven. The reviewer took delight in the fact that Stewart's writings were "inspired throughout by the purest and most amiable moral feelings" and he had "breathed into all his works the kind, gentle, social, and benevolent spirit." Stewart "teaches us to believe in virtue and brings the celestial vision before us in full loveliness and beauty, so as to engage our affections in her favor."[41]

Jeremy Bentham's philosophy of utilitarianism received much attention and also gained many adherents in America. William Paley, eighteenth century Brisish philosopher, likewise a utilitarian, did much to popularize utilitarian ideas on questions of morals. His treatise, *Natural Theology*, was widely used in the academies of the day.[42] Richard Hildreth, editor and historian, extended Bentham's influence by presenting a system of ethics based on science.[43] His ideas ran counter to prevailing opinion. Hildreth proposed to apply the scientific method. He bitterly attacked the religious base of morals as one perpetrated by a combination of the state and the clergy. In an analysis for the *North American Review*, a hostile writer attacked Hildreth "for conveying the most licentious sentiments in morals and theology." Morals, argued the reviewer, "are intrinsic and essential qualities of actions,—eternal and unchangeable, though the heavens fall." The moral laws, he asserted, are the laws of God.[44] The controversy in which Hildreth and his contemporaries joined had its parallels in Europe, where the writings of the utilitarians offended the clergy and religious believers in general.

Americans found the writings of Sir Walter Scott and William Wordsworth congenial, and reviewers praised their moral purity. Although not uniformly so, purity was the first measuring rod of most American literary critics. Lord Byron did not receive general acclaim in large part beacuse the writer's private life did not conform to conventional standards.

In the early decades particularly, and especially in the South, the most popular writer was Sir Walter Scott. He also enjoyed a following in New England where, in 1832, the author of an article in the *North American Review* entitled "English Literature of the Nineteenth Century," wrote: "Scott's greatest glory, however, arises from the superior dignity to which he has raised the novel, not by its historic, but its moral character, so that, instead of being obliged, as with Fielding's and Smollett's, to devour it, like Sancho Panza's cheese-cakes, in a corner as it were, it is now made to furnish a pure and delectable report for all the members of the assembled family."

By 1840 Charles Dickens gained the greatest acclaim. American readers, a contemporary reported, were so eager to obtain his novels that the interest was best described as "general and intense." The novels were republished in every form of newspaper, weekly, and monthly periodical.[45]

The appearance of *The Pickwick Papers* jolted the editors of the *Southern Literary Messenger*. The low social status of Dickens' characters and the absence of sterling moral qualities did not make them fit for a novel. In the next issue the editor told of the readers' response to his indictment and expressed astonishment that his remarks aroused "a host of enemies, by whom a shower of puny missiles have been launched against us." He dismissed Dickens as a panderer to the new and vulgar tastes, but Dickens more than survived the attack. Dickens far surpassed Scott, his only rival in literary popularity. By 1842 Dickens' early novels were read all over America; when he toured the country in that year, he was welcomed everywhere as a great hero. In the first issue of *Harper's New Monthly Magazine* in June 1852, two of the three short stories were by Dickens, and in 1852 the same magazine published *Bleak House* and *Little Dorrit*.[46]

Scholars in American literature whose special interest is transcendentalism have pursued with vigor the inquiry into the origins of the movement. The indebtedness of the transcendentalists to Coleridge and Carlyle is well established. What they owed to German philosophy, more particularly to Immanuel Kant, is difficult to ascertain. It has been proposed that Ralph Waldo Emerson owed little to Kant other than the term "transcendental." However, Theodore Parker, who read German, professed that he was indebted to Kant for his method of inquiry and for the beliefs that there are, beyond the purely rational, attributes of consciousness that provide intuition of the divine, of the just and right, and of the immortal.[47] Victor Cousin, French philosopher, also helped by putting Kantian philosophy into more popular and readily understood language. However, American transcendentalism was not purely an imported

European body of thought. It owed much to earlier religious thought in New England, to the sterile quality of early Unitarianism, and was also a reaction to the emergence of a business-dominated society.[48]

Like many hackneyed phrases, the saying "Science recognizes no national boundaries" contains a major element of truth. Long before the period under consideration a community of science arose in Europe and the practitioners eagerly exchanged information by correspondence and publications. The British colonists belonged to this community. European researchers eagerly sought specimens of plant life, animals, and minerals; and collections of these, forwarded by colonial naturalists, preceded and, for a long time, surpassed those in North America. John Bartram, Pennsylvania naturalist, corresponded with the Swedish botanist, Carolus Linnaeus, along with other distinguished Europeans.[49]

Medicine, more than any other sphere in colonial science, looked to Europe. From 1749 to 1812, 139 Americans received their medical training in Edinburgh. Other Americans, too, belonged to the scientific societies in that city. There was a constant flow of books, periodicals, and specimens to English scientific societies in the last decade of the eighteenth century.[50]

It was in Europe, the home of the enlightenment, that the important scientific discoveries took place, but the spirit of the age extended to America. European scientific thought had an important impact on men such as Benjamin Franklin and Thomas Jefferson. The naturalists in the New World concentrated on assembling collections. Scientific work, well into the nineteenth century, adhered to the Baconian concept of science, as a system of classification. Taxonomy wholly dominated all investigation.[51]

In the 1840s and 1850s American scientists took significant steps forward, although classification continued their chief pursuit. These strides included an increasing professionalization, the emergence of important organizations, and the establishment of institutions dedicated to encouraging inquiry and to publication of findings. Many early scientists carried on investigations as an avocation. For instance, Nathaniel Bowditch, the astronomer and authority on navigation, worked as an officer in insurance companies in Boston;

William C. Redfield, an early meteorologist, devoted most of his time to steam engineering. Many pursued studies in more than one area. Benjamin Pierce, at Harvard, was primarily a mathematician and secondly an astronomer. Edward Hitchcock, professor at Amherst, lectured on chemistry, geology, mineralogy, and zoology. After 1830 the great growth of knowledge and increasing complexity of each field ruled out both the amateurs and generalists.[52] Without exception, after 1830 the leaders in science were specialists in one field: Benjamin Silliman in chemistry, Louis Agassiz in zoology, Asa Gray in botany, James Dwight Dana in geology, and Joseph Henry in physics.

Scientists eagerly promoted lyceums and associations. No less than 107 societies were formed between 1785 and 1845; the next twenty years added 318. Many of these were ephemeral, but several became permanent and played major roles. The most important of these, The American Association for the Advancement of Science, began in 1848. The membership included more than 300, among them every leading scientist of the day. The annual meetings of the association provided scientists the opportunity to exchange information. When they met in Albany in 1851, 134 papers were presented.[53]

The excitement of opening the door to nature's mysteries injected a drive to get on with the work and to find funds to support research. The author of a contemporary account of the annual meetings declared: "Though no prophecy reveals what the future may have in store, it is still the confident anticipation of reason, that new wonder-workings will not cease to flow from the *cornucopia of speculative and experimental science.*"[54] The National Academy of Science, organized in 1862, became a chief promoter of what one of its founders, Joseph Henry, called "abstract science," and its highly selective membership eventually became the chief authority on problems of social policy.

The founding of the Smithsonian Institution in 1846 marked the first milestone of the development of a center supported by the federal government. A long and heated controversy preceded the vote by Congress. Much of this debate arose because the advocates of one group favored establishing a college, with another group intent on founding a national library. A fourth dimension was added by congressional members who opposed national support on states' rights grounds or simply because they had a measure of contempt for most intellectual endeavors. The act of Congress did not resolve all the attendant disputes, but the appointment of Joseph Henry as director of the Smithsonian gave assurance that the promotion of science was to have highest priority.

Government support for science at the state and federal levels came as a direct response to practical needs and only incidentally as a result of an interest in pure science. Both levels of government helped finance the 21 surveys of states that resulted in the mapping of the country and the location of important mineral deposits. The greatest achievement, however, related to the high seas. The Wilkes Expedition, under the direction of the navy, spent four years, 1838 to 1842, exploring the coasts of South America, Antarctica, the Central Pacific Islands, and the west coast of North America. The primary interest was in oceanography, but the expedition also collected astronomical and magnetic data. The findings filled twenty-four volumes and constituted "the largest scientific treasure in the country."[55]

One historian of American science describes the condition of American science prior to 1860 as "vigorous adolescence." In the previous decades the scientists decried dependence on Europe and called for an "American science." These men shared fully the broadly held nationalistic sentiment that the United States must be second to none in every phase of achievement.[56] However, the very volume of the protests against American inferiority was in itself acknowledgment of European leadership. Histories of the branches of sciences, including those written by American scholars, confirm the view that American scientists did not make any significant breakthroughs or present new generalizations revolutionizing a field of investigation.[57]

Necessity rather than preference dictated dependence on Europe. In writing his highly successful *Elementary Treatise on Mineralogy and Zoology* in 1816 Parker Cleaveland had no choice but to draw on English, French, and German writers. In an address before the Lyceum of Natural History of New York in 1826 James E. De Kay, after noting the increased interest in scientific undertakings, reported that many mineralogists in America "have enrolled themselves in the School of Mines at Paris." He also stated that a European geologist, Maclure, had come to the United States to study rock formations and had written a report entitled " 'Observations on the Geology of the United States,' a bold outline, sketched by a masterly hand, and replete with the most valuable and interesting information." Botany, said De Kay, "had fared better in this country than the sister sciences" but had neglected important areas. Zoology had received less attention than the other sciences, and few works had been published in the United States. He ruefully observed that a great obstacle "to the advancement of science in this country, is the want of books, cabinets, and scientific apparatus in general."[58]

The reviewer of "De Kay's Address" believed that progress was underway. The Boston Atheneum had secured funds enabling it to procure "entire sets of the Transactions of the Royal Societies and Academies of Sciences in London, Edinburgh, Dublin, Paris, Petersburg, Berlin, Turin, Göttingen, Stockholm, Copenhagen, Madrid, and Lisbon."[59] The *North American Review* observed that the diffusion of scientific knowledge could not be achieved "without easy access to the labors of the learned in other parts of the world; and every lover of science in this country, . . . , has had occasion to know and lament the obstacles, which have hitherto obstructed such access; . . ."[60]

In the decades ahead the problem of access was in considerable part solved, and the advances in science in Europe became known in America after only a brief lapse of time. The Smithsonian Institution, thanks to Joseph Henry, traded publications with European societies and assisted by handling customs clearances and, on occasion, providing free transportation for imports of publications.[61] When the work of science excited popular interest, publishers readily reprinted the book. Less than a year after the publication in London of Charles Darwin's *Origin of Species*, it was reprinted in New York. Darwin sent copies to some of his friends in America, including Louis Agassiz, who promptly denounced it as atheism and made a public issue of it. Asa Gray wrote a review and forwarded a copy of it to Darwin, who found it admirable. On both sides of the Atlantic Darwin came under attack from organized religion and from men who held strongly to the theory that the evidence of harmony and design in nature offered proof of a creator. Benjamin Pierce, the Harvard scientist, during his visit to Oxford in 1860 heard a debate on the question between the bishop of Oxford and Thomas Henry Huxley. He found the bishop eloquent "and the slippery character of the divine was apparent in all his argument." Darwin was delighted to learn from James Dana that his book had promoted "warm discussions" in the United States.

That the American reading public should have been so heavily indebted to Europe is, of course, not surprising. More important than the indebtedness is the fact that the United States was a part of the Atlantic community. Differences among the member states of this community were present and important; and many of the conditions in the New World, such as the political system, the abundance of land, and the presence of a large immigrant population gave to American society a degree of distinctiveness, but similar degrees of distinctiveness existed among the nations of western Europe. Yet western Europe constituted one civilization tied together by a common culture. The United States shared this culture. It was an integral part of the western world.

The United States remained politically peripheral to Europe. The Congress of Vienna created the concert of Europe, and the relations among European states rested on the assumption of a high degree of interdependence. The actions of any of these nations, including the internal political and economic happenings, were a matter of deep concern to each of the others. This gave rise to sharp rivalries but also to collaboration when the national interests of two or more states coincided. The United States, on the other hand, dealt solely with relations between itself and the other nation and steadfastly declined to enter into commitments in relation to existing arrangements in Europe. It remained firmly neutral regarding European conflicts. In this sense only was it outside of the Atlantic community.

NOTES TO CHAPTER II

1. The examination of economic ties, of immigration, and of the sharing of philosophy, literature, and science lead to the conclusion that the United States was a member of the Atlantic community. In our analysis of these ties the aim is not to demonstrate that Europe influenced America or vice versa. Both are correct assumptions, but both lie beyond the scope of our concern. Nor are we intent, in a spirit of nationalism, on demonstrating achievements

in the American sphere or of focusing attention on development of increased economic strength and the advancements in philosophy, literature, or science. These have occupied the time and energy of innumerable specialists in these fields. The focus here is on relationships and on the common sharing that go to make up a community.

2. Chester W. Wright, *Economic History of the United States* (New York: McGraw-Hill Book Company, Inc., 1941), p. 336.

3. Paul H. Cootner, "The Role of the Railroads," *Journal of Economic History*, Dec. 1963, p. 499.

4. Stuart Bruchey, *Roots of American Economic Growth 1607–1861, An Essay in Social Causation* (New York: Harper & Row, 1965), p. 76.

5. *Statistical Abstract of the United States*, 1941, p. 845.

6. See J. G. Williamson, "International Trade and United States Economic Development: 1827–1843," *Journal of Economic History*, Sept. 1961, pp. 372–83; Carter Goodrich, *Government Promotion of American Canals and Railroads, 1800–1890* (New York: Columbia University Press, 1960); Douglas C. North, *The Economic Growth of the United States* (New York: Prentice-Hall, Inc., 1961), and same author's "International Capital Flows and the Development of the American West," *Journal of Economic History*, Dec. 1956, pp. 493–505; Dorothy Adler, *British Investments in American Railways* (Charlottesville, Va.: University of Virginia Press, 1970); Leland Jenks, "Railroads as an Economic Force," *Journal of Economic History*, May 1944, pp. 1–20; Kenneth L. Brown, "Stephen Gerard, Promoter of the Second Bank of the United States," *Journal of Economic History*, Nov. 1942, pp. 119–48; Frank Thistlewaite, *The Anglo-American Connection in the Early Nineteenth Century* (Philadelphia: University of Pennsylvania Press, 1959); and, of course, the classic in this field, Ralph W. Hidy, *The House of Baring in American Trade and Finance, English Merchant Bankers at Work* (Cambridge: Harvard University Press, 1949).

7. *Statistical Abstract of the United States*, 1941, pp. 527–31.

8. Ibid., p. 540.

9. Williamson, "International Trade and United States Economic Development," *Journal of Economic History*, Sept. 1961, p. 375.

10. Hidy, *The House of Baring in American Trade and Finance*, p. 100.

11. Ibid., p. 112.

12. Brown, "Stephen Gerard, Promoter of the Second Bank of the United States," *Journal of Economic History*, Nov. 1942, p. 145.

13. Ibid., p. 102.

14. Bruchey, *The Roots of American Economic Growth*, p. 133.

15. Adler, *British Investments in American Railways*, p. 10.

16. Ibid., p. 9.

17. Dorothy Adler cites Representative Garland's statement in the House of Representatives in 1830 in which he estimated that, in addition to state bonds, Europeans held $24 million in securities, principally in banks. A House report in 1843 referred to $28 million in the stock of the United States Bank and $9 million in the securities of the Farmers' Loan and Trust Company, the Commercial Bank of Vicksburg, and New Jersey's Camden and Ambay Railroad. Adler, *British Investments in American Railways*, p. 10.

18. Report of Secretary of the Treasury James Guthrie, Senate Executive Document 42, 33rd Cong., 1st Sess., Serial 698, pp. 4–5.

19. Ibid., p. 10.
20. Ibid., p. 31.
21. Ibid., p. 35.
22. Ibid., p. 50.
23. Ibid., p. 53.

24. Marcus Lee Hansen, *The Atlantic Migration 1607–1860 A History of the Continuing Settlement of the United States* (New York: Harper & Row, 1961), p. 90.

The United States in the Atlantic Community, 1815-1860

25. For a full account of the transportation problem see Hansen, *The Atlantic Migration*, Chapter VIII.
26. Carl Wittke, *We Who Built America The Saga of the Immigrant* (Cleveland: Press of Western Reserve University, 1964), pp. 131 and 187.
27. Thistlewaite, *The Anglo-American Connection in the Early Nineteenth Century*, p. 25.
28. *Statistical View of the United States*, 1850, p. 61.
29. Wittke, *We Who Built America*, p. 131.
30. Rowland Tappan Berthoff, *British Immigrants in Industrial America* (Cambridge: Harvard University Press, 1953), p. 31.
31. Willis Frederick Dunbar, *Michigan: A History of the Wolverine State* (Grand Rapids, Mich.: Erdmans Publishing Co., 1965), p. 353.
32. "The Irish in America," *North American Review*, Jan. 1841, p. 214.
33. Wittke, *We Who Built America*, p. 160.
34. Review of Peter S. Du Ponceau, *A Dissertation on the Nature and Extent of the Jurisdiction of the Courts of the United States*, *North American Review*, July 1825, p. 138.
35. "Nationality in Literature," *North American Review*, July 1849, p. 209.
36. Frank Luther Mott, *A History of American Magazines 1741–1850* (New York: Appleton and Company, 1930), p. 392.
37. Ibid., p. 393.
38. Ibid., p. 397.
39. "Recent American Literature," *North American Review*, Oct. 1840, p. 486.
40. *American Transcendentalism An Anthology of Criticism*, ed. Brian M. Barbour, "John Locke and New England Transcendentalism," by Cameron Thompson (South Bend, Ind.: University of Notre Dame Press, 1973), pp. 84–85.
41. Review of *The Philosophy of the Active and Moral Powers of Man* by Dugald Stewart, *North American Review*, July 1830, p. 216.
42. William Martin Smallwood and Mabel Sarah Coon Smallwood, *Natural History and the American Mind* (New York: Columbia University Press, 1941), p. 251.
43. Richard Hildreth, *Theory of Morals An Inquiry Concerning the Law of Moral Distinctions and the Variations and Contradictions of Ethical Codes* (Boston: Charles C. Little and James Brown, 1844).
44. Article entitled "Hildreth's Theory of Morals," *North American Review*, Apr. 1845, pp. 393–403.
45. Review of *American Notes for General Circulation*, *North American Review*, Jan. 1843, p. 213.
46. "The Copyright Law," *The Dickensian*, Winter Number, 1940–1941, pp. 40–42; ibid., "World's Best Seller," Spring Number, p. 56; ibid., Winter Number, 1948, "Dickens in American Magazines," p. 51.

Frank Luther Mott estimated that by 1940 more than two million copies of the *Christmas Carol* had been sold in America, over a million copies of each of nine other Dickens' novels, and over a half million of seven others.

47. Barbour, *American Transcendentalism An Anthology of Criticism*, "The Minor Transcendentalists and German Philosophy," by Rene Wellek, p. 113.
48. Ibid., "From Edwards to Emerson," by Perry Miller, pp. 76–77.
49. Smallwood and Smallwood, *Natural History and the American Mind*, p. 33.
50. Ibid., p. 79.
51. George H. Daniels, *American Science in the Age of Jackson* (New York: Columbia University Press, 1968), p. 63.
52. Russell Nye, *Society and Culture in America 1830–1860* (New York: Harper & Row, 1974), pp. 246–47.

53. "The American Association for the Advancement of Science," *Putnam's Monthly Magazine*, Sept. 1853, p. 320.
54. Ibid., p. 324.
55. For an excellent account of this expedition and the debates it provoked see A. Hunter Depree, *Science in the Federal Government A History of Policies and Activities to 1940* (New York: Harper & Row 1957).
56. For an interesting discussion of this popular topic in the years after the War of 1812 see George H. Daniels, *Science in American Society A Social History* (New York: Alfred A. Knopf, 1971), Chapter VI "Science in Free Society."
57. See, for instance, Aaron J. Ihde, *The Development of Modern Chemistry*. (New York: Harper & Row, 1964) and Henry M. Leicester, *The Historical Background of Chemistry* (New York: John Wiley and Sons, Inc. 1956).
58. "De Kay's Address," *North American Review*, July 1826, pp. 204–205.
59. Ibid., p. 207.
60. Ibid., p. 210.
61. Depree, *Science in the Federal Government*, p. 88.

Chapter III

An Assertive New Nation

In the words of a prominent historian, the industrial revolution opened a new age of promise. "It also transformed the balance of political power, within nations, and between civilizations; revolutionized the social order; and as much changed man's way of thinking as his way of doing."[1] The new American republic experienced the full impact of the change. Free of the retarding influence of a landed nobility, leavened by the generally accepted rule that social standing was dependent upon acquisition, and possessed of the hope made ebullient by the presence of unrivaled natural resources, the American people struck out to take advantage of the new opportunities.

Many of those opportunities were linked to foreign markets and maritime shipping. The abundance of agricultural produce far surpassed domestic needs and the ever-increasing production jibed nicely with the rapid growth of Europe's population and the expanding of industry in England. A long tradition of seafaring provided the backdrop for an amazing growth of the merchant marine. Americans enjoyed many advantages in shipbuilding and in the operation of ships. Lumber was far cheaper than in England and France. Taxes were lower. And American shipowners cut operating costs by employing smaller crews, and food for the men was cheaper than in Europe. The extensive coastline—the trip from New Orleans to New York equaled one-third of a transatlantic crossing—made coastwise trade a major enterprise. This was restricted to American vessels. The monopoly served as a subsidy. Merchants, shipowners, and the growers of cotton, tobacco and, to a lesser extent, the farmers, looked to the government to promote their interests and to guard against the setting up of hostile barriers by competing nations.

England, of course, set the pace in industrialization, the search for foreign markets, and the promotion of the shipping industry. The manufacture of cotton goods led the way. By 1837 the cotton textile industry consumed 366 million pounds of cotton. The products sold in all parts of the world. The amount exported surpassed home consumption by a third.[2] The iron industry in England experienced almost as phenomenal a growth. The output of pig iron more than doubled between 1806 and 1825.[3] The coming of the steam engine increased the use of coal, and the 11 million tons used in 1811 doubled by 1830 and doubled again by 1845.[4]

France, as the defeated nation, offered a sharp contrast to postwar England. Aside from the able bureaucracy created by Napoleon, which continued to function after the fall of the empire, instability characterized the period. Louis XVIII, ugly in appearance and so fat that he could not rise from a chair without assistance, understood that there could be no return to the ways of the old regime. He was honest and well-intentioned but lacked political wisdom. Even had he possessed great talent his lot would have been difficult, since factions rather than organized and responsible political parties contributed to instability, fear, and distrust.

Economically France faced enormous difficulties. The interest charges on the internal debt in 1814, not including those accumulated by Napoleon, amounted to 63 million francs.[5] At the close of the war France was forced to pay the costs of the allies' armies of occupation, and after Napoleon's return it was assessed an additional 700 million francs to meet the cost of defeating the emperor a second time.[6] Payments to the allies after the final peace treaty approximated 1,540 million francs, including the cost of the renewed war. This was not the end, for private debts due to foreigners were binding under the treaty. Claims flowed in from across Europe, and these were finally settled by an agreement with the allies in 1818. France agreed to pay a lump sum of 265 million francs.[7] This tremendous debt was financed in considerable part by costly foreign loans.

The problem of debt almost fully occupied the time of French Restoration governments at the expense of promoting foreign trade.

The economy did not fail to prosper, but it was not a period of expansion. A large part of industry remained satisfied as long as it dominated the home market. The slowness of enterprise in introducing new machinery and continued adherence to the older handicraft modes of production assured high quality of textiles, but French industries were unable to compete with British goods in foreign markets. Whereas the British zealously sought out foreign markets and made every effort to please different tastes and also provided easy credit, the French were content to remain at home.[8]

The reasons for this industrial difference between England and France have been the subject of considerable historical writing. David S. Landes places emphasis on the freedom of the British, the readiness of the nobility and gentry to enter business, and the advanced state of the banking structure. On the continent the prestige of large landholding, the high cost of credit, and familial nature of much business enterprise had the effect of delaying the industrial revolution.[9] However, there was a rapid closing of the gap after 1830.

The United States experienced a burgeoning similar to that of Great Britain. Agriculture and manufacturing multiplied many fold in the four decades after 1820. Foreign trade expanded. The total value of imports and exports in 1821 was $127 million; in 1860 it was $762 million. The American merchant marine experienced phenomenal growth, ranked second only to the British; and British shipping interests saw in it a threat not only to their nation's economic well-being but to British naval supremacy. Due to lower construction costs and lesser expenses in providing crews, American vessels were able to charge lower freight rates than those of any other nation. The result was a near monopoly of the carrying trade from and to American ports. Statistics for the twelve months following September 1828 showed that American tonnage entering American ports totaled 872,949 tons, whereas all foreign tonnage amounted to only 130,721 tons.

Immediately upon the close of the War of 1812 the United States adopted a policy of reciprocity, admitting vessels of foreign nations to American ports on the same conditions as American vessels, providing the foreign nation admitted American ships on the same basis. The act of 1815 was supplemented in 1817. Under this act vessels of foreign nations engaged in indirect trade were excluded if that nation did not admit American ships to the indirect trade. This legislation represented an effort to gain admittance to the indirect trade with the West Indies. The policy of free competition regarding shipping was pushed. A series of commercial treaties embodying the principle of this legislation were negotiated with several European countries. Great Britain and France sought to contest the Americans, and the rivalry furnished the cause for lengthy, difficult, and cutthroat diplomacy.

Upon his arrival in Paris as minister, Albert Gallatin reported that American trade faced serious difficulties. At the close of the war French shipping was a nullity, but it had "recovered with unexampled rapidity." Americans continued to have a superiority in maritime affairs but only temporarily. The French tariff and the extra duties and charges on commerce with the United States injured American shipping interests. In a letter to the secretary of state on October 26, 1819, Gallatin reported "American vessels are daily withdrawing from the trade and if the evil is not corrected, the whole of commerce between the two countries will soon be carried on almost exclusively in French vessels."[10] He discussed the problem with the French foreign office one month later. Although the existing system struck Gallatin as intolerable, he did find the French ministry friendly though not responsive to his complaints. He received no reply to his inquiry for two months; when the response came, it was so negative that he concluded that France would do nothing unless the United States took countermeasures. French shipping interests were strongly opposed to any negotiation that looked to equality.[11]

In the spring of 1820 Gallatin placed before the minister of foreign affairs another major grievance. Goods shipped in American vessels paid higher duties than specified in the official tariff, and American ship captains also paid high port charges. Under French law the role of interpreter to the captain of a foreign ship was delegated to a ship broker. These brokers made a practice of levying higher charges than called for by the tariff law and defended the practice on the ground that foreign ships took more time. Gallatin found that at Le Havre these brokers extorted fees more than double those fixed by the tariff.[12] Gallatin also protested the local charges laid on American vessels, pilotage and brokerage fees that were "sometimes heavy and always vexatious."[13] In his correspondence with the French government he predicted that continuation of these practices would throw all trade between the two nations into French vessels, thereby compelling the United States to resort to higher countervailing duties, a development that could only cause injury to the extensive commerce between the two countries.[14]

The inequality under which Americans labored caused Congress to take drastic action the final day of the session in May 1820. The new law placed a duty of $18 a ton on French vessels. Gallatin would have preferred a tax of an amount that would equalize conditions. The French viewed the act as hostile and amounting to an exclusion of French goods.[15] On July 29 the French retaliated with a duty of 90 francs per ton on American ships.

Gallatin was distressed by the hasty action of Congress. Not only was the tax too high but the new duty was made effective immediately. Secretary of State John Quincy Adams explained how it was originally intended to make it effective October 1 but this would have required an amendment and this, in turn, would have postponed action for several months. Adams had favored a tax of $12. He noted: "The call for the law from the merchants was loud and urgent, and the committee as usual sympathized with the feelings of their constituents."[16] The effect of the American tax was that French ships lay idle.

In September 1821 the negotiations were transferred to Washington at the request of France. President Monroe offered to make concessions and Secretary of State Adams sought to convince the French minister, Hyde De Neuville, of the desirability of a convention based on reciprocity. Neuville showed little interest and also sidetracked the negotiations by tying them to the question of Article VIII of the Louisiana Purchase Treaty. He maintained that this article provided that France was entitled to most-favored-nation treatment in the ports within the territory of Louisiana. Adams was equally adamant in denying the French contention. However, negotiations were completed, and the new commercial treaty was signed on June 24, 1822. It spelled out in a precise manner the limits of discrimination on French vessels in American ports and on American vessels in French ports.[17] The treaty was to be in effect for two years and to continue if not terminated by one of the parties. It proved satisfactory to both and remained in effect throughout the decade.

The benefits to be gained by both in terms of cordial relations were, however, nullified in part by a lengthy controversy over the issue of spoliation claims filed by Americans for losses suffered at the hands of the French during the wars of the French Revolution and the Napoleonic wars. In 1816 France pleaded that the indebtedness imposed on her by the victorious allies made it impossible for the government to assume a new debt. Time and again French officials appeared favorably disposed and did not question the justice of the American claims. However, the tone changed by 1822 when Viscount Montmorency pleaded that the Council of Ministers preferred to await the outcome of the negotiations on commercial questions, whereupon Gallatin promptly denied that there could be any connection between the claims issue and the question of trade and that "the prosperous situation of the French" now made the original plea for postponement wholly invalid.[18]

The conclusion of the commercial convention provided the occasion for the minister of foreign affairs to propose a negotiation of the claims, but this offer was tied to the condition that differences between the two countries regarding Article VIII of the Louisiana Purchase Treaty be included.[19] Gallatin saw in this stipulation an excuse for further delay. On one occasion Neuville announced that France could easily take back Louisiana. A conversation with Neuville and the minister of foreign affairs in November 1822 caused sharp irritation. Both men argued that the present French government was not bound to pay the American claims arising from Bonaparte's aggressions.[20]

The total amount of these spoliation claims was $6,005,648. Many claims were filed by insurance companies that had insured the ships destroyed or confiscated. For instance, the Insurance Company of North America filed a claim for $479,350; and the Insurance Company of the State of Pennsylvania, for more than $500,000.[21] Scores of other claims were typically for a few thousand dollars.

John Quincy Adams, as secretary of state under James Monroe and later as president, dedicated himself to the promotion of national interests, and he saw these not from the perspective of immediate crisis but from a long-range viewpoint. In the summer and early fall of 1823 he worked vigorously on instructions to be sent to Richard Rush in London and Henry Middleton in St. Petersburg. These defined what *ought to be* and presented a carefully prepared case of argumentation, precisely the kind of challenge that elicited Adams' complete dedication. When Adams read these to President Monroe and the members of the cabinet, John C. Calhoun and William H. Crawford advised that England would never agree. Adams admitted the same and noted in his diary, "My plan involves nothing less than a revolution in the laws of war—a great amelioration in the condition of man. Is it the dream of a visionary, or is it the great and practicable conception of a benefactor of mankind? I believe it is the latter; and I believe this to be precisely the time for proposing it to the world. Should it even fail, it will be honorable to have proposed it."[22]

Adams approached his responsibilities as secretary of state in the spirit he exhibited summer afternoons while swimming in the Potomac. Invariably he chose to swim against the tide and exhausted himself by never touching bottom during the two hours he allotted to this exercise. The tide was more effective in impeding his forward movement than were his colleagues who lacked both his persistence and wide knowledge of European affairs. He was an expert given to thinking in terms of broad policy and the future, an architect rather than a mere artisan in the field. Monroe scarcely garnered the smallest grain of admiration from his secretary of state, but Adams also had the good judgment to graciously defer to his chief. Deference, however, did not stand in the way of his protecting his public reputation. In late November 1823, after lengthy discussion of the message he proposed to send Tsar Alexander, Monroe asked Adams to delete significant parts. Privately Adams told the president that while he was a subordinate agent there also rested upon him as head of a department a peculiar responsibility, "one resting upon each head of a Department for the papers issued from his own office," and this, he explained, was his motive "for wishing to retain a paragraph . . . containing the soul of the document."[23] Monroe yielded.

Adams was deeply aware that cabinet members were heads of departments first and only secondly members of the cabinet. Each enjoyed prerogatives in the sphere over which he presided. Adams captained foreign relations, and his fellow cabinet officers did not seriously challenge him. He also abided by the rule that only the president could overrule him.

The spring and summer of 1823 passed quietly with no crisis in foreign relations. Adams devoted most of his time to preparing for negotiations with Great Britain. Most disturbing was the French invasion of Spain, but this action apparently evoked no fear that if France succeeded in Spain the Holy Alliance would undertake to restore Spanish control in South America. The question of Cuba did provide cause for discussion. The war in Europe opened the possibility that Great Britain, in return for assisting Spain against France, might be compensated by a transfer of Cuba to her possession. This made President Monroe extremely nervous, and at a cabinet meeting on March 17 he proposed to offer Great Britain a mutual promise not to take Cuba. Adams and Calhoun opposed the proposal, and Adams noted in his diary that it was one of many ways the United States could be plunged "into the whirlpool of European politics."[24] The note tapped the roots of his deepest convictions.

In a meeting with Stratford Canning, the British minister to Washington, Adams again had occasion to make known his views of relations with Europe. Adams spoke of the British withdrawal from the Quintuple Alliance and Great Britain now "waived the principles which were emphatically those of this country, and she disapproved the principles of the alliance which this country abhorred." This, Adams believed, provided "a suitable occasion for the United States and Great Britain to compare their ideas and purposes together, with a view to the accommodation of great interests upon which they had heretofore differed."[25] Some days later, on June 17, Stratford Canning told Adams that these earlier observations led him to believe the secretary was "desirous of considering it as a proposal to Great Britain for an alliance with the United States." Adams abruptly replied that it was not.

On another occasion Adams staunchly set forth the view that the New World was no longer open to colonization. A Russian ukase of 1821 had laid claim to the Pacific coast as far south as the 51° parallel and barred foreign ships from the waters 100 miles off the coast. Although the Russians in 1822 suspended their ukase, they continued to defend the claim. Adams, deeply interested in this question, made an extensive study of the Russian argument that this territory was rightfully theirs because of prior discovery. By July 1 he observed: "I find proof enough to put down the Russian argument; but how shall we answer the Russian cannon?"[26] In a conversation with Baron Tuyll, minister of Russia, concerning this

Northwest question, Adams told him "that we should contest the right of Russia to *any* territorial establishment on this continent, and that we should assume distinctly the principle that the American continents are no longer subjects for *any* new European colonial establishments."

The question of supporting the Greeks in their revolution against the Turks arose at a cabinet meeting on August 15, and once more Adams' basic approach came to the fore. Secretary of War John C. Calhoun exuded confidence in the Greeks and showed admiration for them, but he did not enter into the question as to whether aid to Greece was a matter of national interest, nor did he make reference to relations with Turkey. Secretary of the Treasury William Crawford said less but appeared ready to assist the Greeks. Adams dismissed their observations as "all sentiment" and told Monroe he did not think "quite so lightly of a war with Turkey."[27]

Adams, it is clear, held a series of fixed positions prior to the crisis produced in the fall of 1823 by the arrival of a series of dispatches from Rush in London. These related immediately to the French invasion of Spain in 1823 for the purpose of putting down the liberal revolution and restoring the Bourbons to control. In August, George Canning aggressively entered into discussions with Rush, proposing that England and the United States join hands in a declaration that they were opposed to intervention by the Holy Alliance in behalf of Spain's restoration of control over her colonies in Latin America. Canning, in the early meetings, stressed the urgency for prompt action. Rush thought of going ahead on his own but concluded he could not risk doing so unless Great Britain was prepared to grant diplomatic recognition to the new republics. Canning assured him that this would come in due time but that a number of considerations made such a step inappropriate now.

At first glance the Canning proposal appeared to present an opportunity to join hands with the supreme naval power of the Atlantic in calling a halt to ambitions of continental monarchies to effect the triumph of the monarchical principle over republican principles in the New World.

The principle of noninvolvement in European affairs, although often enunciated, was as yet far from a fixed principle. Hostility toward the Holy Alliance and the prevailing fear of the combined despotisms of Europe might set aside earlier caution. Now, it appeared, England was ready to stem the tide of reaction. Administration and congressional leaders, in spite of popular Anglophobia, were well informed about the more recent breeches in the Quintuple Alliance and British departure from the continental alliance.

Fears of a move by the Holy Alliance to crush the triumph of republican principles in the New World were unchecked by any realistic appraisal of continental politics and the forces that would inhibit the Holy Alliance. At the time few, perhaps only John Quincy Adams and Albert Gallatin, possessed the necessary information. These two men felt no alarm.

Actually, there was no serious danger. The reactionary rhetoric of French ultraroyalists, the solemn pontifications of Alexander I of Russia, and the pleas of Ferdinand of Spain, while honest expressions of their desire to crush the revolutionary spirit everywhere, posed no danger. Internal restraints, though less visible, were real. Alexander traveled almost constantly to inspect his troops, fearful that the dread disease of revolt might infect his forces. Joseph de Villèle, prime minister in France, absorbed in solving France's extremely difficult financial problems and in manipulating the several factions in the Chamber of Deputies to prevent antiroyalist forces from strengthening their position, stood opposed to overseas adventures.[28] Metternich, never sympathetic with the ambitions of Ferdinand of Spain, was determined to avoid alienating the British and splintering the Quintuple Alliance by insisting on the suppression of revolts in South America.

Historical documentation now makes clear that there was no possibility of intervention in South America, but it was less clear to Americans in 1823. Secretary of State John Quincy Adams denied that the Holy Alliance would come to Spain's assistance. The information he acquired from American ministers abroad, together with the understanding he had acquired of the politics of the major powers during his years in Europe, caused him to reject the popular view of the Holy Alliance as ready to embark on a crusade to restore Spanish control.

Upon his return to New York in June 1823, Gallatin wrote to the secretary of state informing him of a discussion he had had with Chateaubriand prior to his departure from Paris. He had explained the American position to the French foreign minister in frank terms. The United States had not interfered in Europe even in questions connected with South America, "although their wishes were not doubtful." Gallatin stated that he had every reason to believe the United States "would not suffer others to interfere against the emancipation of America." If France should assist Spain in reducing the colonies to their former yoke or attempted to take possession of one of them, Gallatin warned "that the United States would oppose every undertaking of this kind and that it might force them into an alliance with Great Britain." He informed Adams, "Mr. Chateaubriand answered in the most explicit manner that France would not make any attempt whatever of that kind or in any manner interfere with the American question." Gallatin added that he had spoken in the same manner to the Russian minister in Paris.[29]

Adams was well aware that the British opposed intervention in South America by the continental powers. Great Britain, with her growing trade with Latin America, had much at stake, and in the conferences of the Quintuple Alliance consistently opposed proposals to aid Spain in regaining control. The British had not granted recognition to the new republics but had sent special agents to serve as consuls. The messages from Rush in London testified further to British concern.

Yet, in the crisis of the late months of 1823 it was not an established fact that the Holy Alliance would not intervene nor even that Great Britain alone would go to war, if necessary, to prevent intervention. What might take place was still an open question, and members of the administration and Monroe himself offered different opinions. Calhoun asserted with vehemence that the troops of the European powers would land any day in South America; and when word arrived in November that the French had wiped out all resistance in Spain, he appeared even more certain. Adams argued that there was no danger.

Questions closely related to the Canning proposal also demanded attention in November and December 1823. How should the United States respond to the tsar's message, received October 16, announcing that the tsar would not receive any agents of the new governments in South America and expressing approval of the United States for pursuing a neutral course in the war between Spain and her colonies, even though granting them recognition? Was the tsar warning that if the United States departed from this course of neutrality Russia would support Spain?[30] And how should the United

States respond to the recent Greek plea for recognition and assistance? There was a strong popular feeling of sympathy for the Greeks, which could easily lead to moves in Congress to bring about support in one or another form. Finally, there was the question of what the president should say to Congress in his annual message.

Others have traced in detail the discussions that took place in the cabinet, the points made by Calhoun, the views expressed by Monroe, the impact of the letters received from Jefferson and Madison in response to Monroe's requests for their opinions, the editing of the diplomatic dispatches and the president's message.[31] Adams' memoirs are almost the only source for what took place in cabinet discussions, and Adams was far from unbiased in reporting the remarks of Calhoun and Crawford, who were his rivals in the coming presidential contest.

Adams emerges from his memoirs as the professional expert on foreign affairs, who easily parried off those who disagreed with him. His overriding aim was to avoid any involvement in European affairs and at the same time not to open the door to European, including British, intrusion in the affairs of the New World. The former was of even greater importance to him because he feared nothing more than that his whimsical colleagues and countrymen would in some feverish outburst entrap themselves in the maze of Europe's rivalries. Moreover, he avoided laying before the cabinet his overall aim of emerging from the discussions with a continental policy that would let Europe go its own way free of intrusion, while at the same time discouraging European powers from intruding in the New World. He did explain this to Monroe, but he did not reveal it to the cabinet. Had he laid before the cabinet the full scope of his overarching design, his colleagues would have found it easier to challenge him. Monroe, sympathetic to the Greeks and favorably inclined toward Canning's proposal, was watchful but not assertive, and was scarcely prepared to repudiate his secretary of state and thereby usher disarray into his administration in his last year in office.

Adams quietly, yet firmly, slipped through each piece of his grand design. He appealed to Monroe's feelings against giving the appearance of taking a position subordinate to England,[32] had no difficulty in winning the assent of those present to his proposal that the United States, quite independently of England, assert its position to Russia and France,[33] easily won approval of both his proposed oral and written communications to Baron Tuyll—although Calhoun and also Gallatin, who was consulted, objected to making the statement so bold as to imply censure of the tsar[34]—and repeatedly used British unwillingness to grant the South American republics recognition as a foil for refusing to accept Canning's proposal. No one challenged this argument, although at various times Calhoun and Monroe favored joint action.

What was Adams' real objection to Canning's proposal? He assumed that Canning had some hidden self-interest. He confided to his diary:

> The object of Mr. Canning appears to have been to obtain some public pledge from the Government of the United States, ostensibly against the forcible interference of the Holy Alliance between Spain and South America, but really or especially against the acquisition to the United States themselves of any part of the Spanish-American possessions.[35]

Adams injected this into the discussion, but Calhoun, and Jefferson in his letter, held this price of self-denial to be no objection.

Adams had another objection which he did not express until the cabinet meeting of November 26. William Wirt, attorney general, asked whether the American public was ready or prepared to support a war to protect South America. Adams immediately raised this to a question of first importance, claiming that it had given him great concern.[36] He had, he said, himself brought up this question earlier in the deliberations. Could the administration make such a commitment without congressional approval? Wirt raised the same question.[37] Calhoun differed. A joint declaration would probably prevent war but if war came, as he thought it would, the public would support the war.[38] Adams replied at length. While he did not believe the Holy Alliance would go to war simply to aid Spain and while the allies would find it difficult to agree on partition of the colonies, if they did, the powers on the European continent would find themselves wasting blood and treasure in a hopeless cause. Also, before this took place England would intervene and be victorious. But, Adams explained, Canning could not commit England to war and neither could the executive branch of the American government.[39]

Having pierced Calhoun's argument that going along with the

Canning proposal offered security, Adams returned to the central objection. This was not the occasion for taking a public stand alongside of Great Britain; it was in fact the reverse. The United States now had the opportunity to avow that it stood part from Europe and that this stand rested on the differences in political principles which guided governments in Europe and in the United States. These differences did not imply that the two were on a collision course. In fact, acceptance of the differences plus the avowal that the United States would not meddle in European affairs offered the republic the advantage that should hostility come it would not be a result of American, but rather of European initiative.[40]

Adams had written the paragraphs on foreign affairs for the president's message and included was the noncolonization principle. This elicited no contrary opinion. It was Monroe's remarks to the effect that the nation confronted a crisis, that republican principles were under attack, and France and the Holy Alliance had unjustly put down liberalism in Spain that evoked debate.

Adams took strong exception. The remarks Monroe proposed would provoke severe reaction on the continent, for it came close to defiance. Moreover, the American public would object to any hint of dangerous adventure. In a private conversation with the president, Adams urged that it would be a serious mistake for him to alarm the public and the president should prefer to have his administration appear, as it had been, the friend of peace.

The message to Congress set forth three principles. Monroe stated that the monarchical system of Europe was essentially different from that of America, and the United States would consider "any attempt . . . to extend their system to any portion of this hemisphere as dangerous to our peace and safety." Likewise, any attempt on the part of European powers to interfere with already independent governments in the New World would be viewed "as the manifestation of an unfriendly disposition toward the United States." Monroe set forth as a corollary that the United States would not interfere in the internal affairs of Europe. The president also included a statement of Adams' favorite noncolonization principle.

Adams' communication to Baron Tuyll included the no-transfer principle. The United States "could not see with indifference, the forcible interposition of any European Power, other than Spain, either to restore the dominion of Spain over her emancipated Colonies in America, or to establish Monarchical Governments in those Countries, or to transfer any of the possessions heretofore or yet subject to Spain in the American Hemisphere, to any other European power."[41]

On November 29 Adams sent off instructions to Rush as to the reply to Canning. The reply avoided any promise of a joint declaration but expressed agreement with the principles Canning had drafted. Rush was advised that should any emergency arise that seemed to call for a joint declaration he was to refer it to Washington for action.[42]

The president's message to Congress on December 2 was received with general public approval. The British chargé in Washington, Henry U. Addington, reported to London:

> The President's Message to Congress seems to have been received with acclamation throughout the United States. Although naturally commented on in detail according to the political prepossessions and views of each individual, it has enjoyed, as a whole, unqualified approbation. The explicit and manly tone, especially, with which the President has treated the subject of European interference in the affairs of this hemisphere, with a view to the resubjugation of those territories which have emancipated themselves from European domination, has evidently found in every bosom a chord which vibrates in strict union with the sentiments so conveyed.[43]

The policy so laboriously shaped by Adams did meet with public favor, but it did not square with the power the United States could or would exert. In drafting the program for neutral rights Adams noted that he was sowing a seed for the future. He never spoke of the Monroe Doctrine in this fashion, but he may well have conceived of it as such.

The message sacrificed preciseness for affirmations. It created a myth that enjoyed the sanctity of appeal to the Scripture. The generalizations it provided became symbols which future statesmen employed in lieu of more rational assessment of questions confronting them. Was the noncolonization principle to apply to all of North and South America? Was the United States to assume the role of guarantor of government by republican principles throughout the New World? What was the definition of the internal affairs of Europe? Was it assumed that a country so closely tied to European markets and sources of capital could safely ignore shifts in the balance of power on that continent? Was American "national interest" to be equated with American hegemony in the Western Hemisphere? The message lent itself to an interpretation giving an affirmative answer to each of these questions.

The record of presidential administrations and of Congress during the years after 1823 demonstrated a wide gap between the presumptuous dicta of the message and practice. Indeed, John Quincy Adams had no confidence in the new Latin American republics, questioned the wisdom of having granted them recognition so soon, and procrastinated in appointing diplomatic representatives to these governments.[44] When Monroe amended the draft of a message to Rush in late November to read that the United States would "throw no impediment in the way of an arrangement between Spain and her ex-Colonies by *amicable negotiation*," Adams insisted that the United States must first be assured "of equal favor with the most-favored nation."[45] Adams had his eye on commerce with South America rather than the political future of these governments.

It is significant, too, that Adams would have much preferred to limit the message to points made in earlier ones, adding only a statement of the noncolonization principle.[46] Monroe's message was not of Adams' choosing; but confronted with the president's request, Adams could only hope to channel it along the lines of his own stance.

At the time of the message moves in Congress violated the injunction against involvement in the affairs of Europe. The *North American Review* in October 1823 published an article by Edward Everett pleading for support of the Greeks in their war for independence from Turkey.[47] Daniel Webster corresponded with the author, discussing with him how best to promote the cause in Congress. Concerning Monroe's message, Webster observed that it had taken "pretty high ground as to *this Continent*" while at the same time exhibiting fear of appearing ready to interfere in the concerns of Europe. "This does not weigh greatly with me," he wrote, "I think we have as much Community with the Greeks as with the inhabitants of the Andes, & the dwellers of the Vermillion Sea."[48]

Support for the Greeks reached sizable proportions in January 1824. Webster led the way with a speech on January 19, claiming that the American people looked for action and held that there was nothing to fear in the way of giving umbrage to the Holy Alliance.[49] Nothing came of Webster's efforts, in considerable part because Monroe objected that Congress was interfering with the prerogatives of the executive.

In the two years, 1824–1826, neither the president nor Congress applied the Monroe Doctrine in strict or rigid manner. The United States in May 1824 granted diplomatic recognition to Brazil, although it was ruled by a monarchy. In August 1824 Adams made clear to Colombia that he did not object to the employment of Spanish troops in the New World. Monroe, in that same year, held that the Latin American republics were free to govern as they pleased. The United States, far from assuming responsibilities in South America, abstained. The Monroe Doctrine was not evoked by name until the presidency of James K. Polk, and did not become an integral part of public thinking until the 1850s when American concern over British activities in Central America caused a minor crisis.

NOTES TO CHAPTER III

1. David S. Landes, *The Unbound Prometheus* (Cambridge: Harvard University Press, 1969), p. 41.
2. Ibid., p. 42.
3. Ibid., p. 96.
4. Ibid., p. 97.
5. M. D. R. Leys, *Between Two Empires A History of French Politicians and People between 1814 and 1848* (New York: Longmans, Green and Co., 1955), p. 30.
6. Ibid., p. 71.
7. Ibid., p. 93.
8. Arthur Louis Dunham, *The Industrial Revolution in France 1815–1848* (New York: Exposition Press, 1955), pp. 382–83, 385, and 389.
9. Landes, *The Unbound Prometheus*, pp. 128–33.
10. Albert Gallatin to the secretary of state, Papers of Albert Gallatin, Oct. 26, 1819. Library of Congress Microfilm Copies, Roll 32.
11. Ibid., Jan. 20, 1819.
12. *American State Papers Foreign Relations*. Vol. V, p. 24.
13. Ibid., p. 33.
14. Ibid.
15. Gallatin to the secretary of state, July 31, 1820, Gallatin Papers, Roll 33.
16. Ibid., Adams to Gallatin, Sept. 15, 1820.
17. *American State Papers Foreign Relations*, Vol. V, pp. 222–24.
18. Ibid., p. 309.
19. Ibid., p. 311.

20. Gallatin to secretary of state, Nov. 13, 1822. *Gallatin Papers*, Roll 35.
21. *American State Papers Foreign Relations*, Vol. V, pp. 392–93.
22. *Memoirs of John Quincy Adams comprising portions of His Diary from 1795 to 1848*, ed. Charles Francis Adams (Philadelphia: J. B. Lippincott & Co., 1875), Vol. VI, p. 164.
23. Ibid., p. 212.
24. Ibid., p. 138.
25. Ibid., p. 152.
26. Ibid., p. 159.
27. Ibid., p. 173.
28. For an excellent analysis of the European scene, see Ernest May, *The Making of the Monroe Doctrine* (Cambridge: Harvard University Press, 1975), Chapter 3, "Foreign Politics."
29. Gallatin to Adams, June 27, 1823, *Gallatin Papers*, Roll 35.
30. Samuel Flagg Bemis, *John Quincy Adams and the Foundations of American Foreign Policy* (New York: Alfred A. Knopf, 1950), p. 384.
31. See Bemis' biography of Adams and May's *Making of the Monroe Doctrine* for these detailed accounts. See Dexter Perkins, *A History of the Monroe Doctrine* (Boston: Little, Brown, rev. ed., 1955). This book continues to excel other works on the subject.
32. Adams, *Memoirs*, VI, p. 178.
33. Ibid., p. 179.
34. Ibid., p. 180.
35. Adams, *Memoirs*, Vol. VI, p. 177.
36. Ibid., p. 202.
37. Ibid., p. 205.
38. Ibid., p. 206.
39. Ibid., p. 208.
40. On November 27, in a private meeting with President Monroe, Adams explained his approach in full. *Memoirs*, pp. 211–12.
41. Bemis, *John Quincy Adams and the Foundations of American Foreign Policy*, p. 395.
42. Ibid., p. 396.
43. *Britain and the Independence of Latin America, 1812–1830*, ed. C. K. Webster (London: Oxford University Press, 1938), Vol. II, pp. 508–509.
44. Adams, *Memoirs*, Vol. VI, pp. 197, 233.
45. Ibid., p. 193.
46. May, *The Making of the Monroe Doctrine*, p. 211.
47. Review of *The Ethics of Aristotle*, ed. A. Coray, *North American Review*, Oct. 1823.
48. *The Papers of Daniel Webster*, ed. Charles M. Wiltse (Hanover, N.H.: Dartmouth College by the University Press of New England, 1974), vol. I, p. 339.
49. *Annals of Congress*, 17th Congress, 1st Session, Vol. 2. pp. 1094–1100.

Chapter IV

Anglo-American Rivalry

The Monroe Doctrine pronouncement in 1823 took place during a long and bitter conflict with Great Britain over trade with the British West Indies. It was on this issue that the two nations approached collision. The commercial treaty with Great Britain of 1815 provided for free and equal access to each other's ports except for British ports in the West Indies. Given the historical importance of this trade to American shipping and the fact that the West Indies and the United States produced goods that were in demand by each other, the British restriction appeared intolerable and unnatural to Americans.

Since 1815 Parliament and Congress had engaged in a push-and-pull contest for advantageous arrangements. American ships were permitted to carry certain commodities to Bermuda, and then British ships transported these to the West Indies. In 1818 Parliament opened the ports of St. John, New Brunswick, and Halifax, Nova Scotia, to commodities needed in the West Indies. Frustrated by British policy, Congress in 1820 closed American ports to British ships coming from British colonies and the importation of colonial produce unless shipped directly from the colony producing them.

These restrictions worked a hardship on the planters of the West Indies and, with the support of advocates of free trade in England, they succeeded in having Parliament open a list of enumerated ports from which American and other foreign ships were permitted to carry certain specific goods directly to the port of the country whose flag the ship was flying. In return the United States again opened its ports to British ships coming from the colonies. However, what at first appeared to be an agreeable cessation of commercial warfare turned out to be the entryway to a more difficult conflict.

On the ground that Great Britain levied lower tariff duties on products entering a British port from another port in the empire, the United States levied higher tariff and tonnage duties on goods imported in foreign ships.[1] This difference soon widened into a gulf, with neither side prepared to compromise.

What appeared to be amenable to negotiation escalated into a heated controversy. Fear and pride combined to generate adamancy. From the British point of view the contest involved maritime supremacy. The United States merchant marine rivaled the British. It dominated the carrying trade between the two countries; if American ships were to be permitted to enter the West Indies free of all restrictions, there was reason to fear, from the viewpoint of powerful British shipping interests, American capture of the whole of the transatlantic carrying trade.

American shipping interests, no less powerful in the national councils, clothed their vested interests in terms of the laws of nature, humanitarianism, and national security. John Quincy Adams, first as secretary of state and later as president, watched the developments with a vigilance nourished by distrust and even hatred. In a letter to President Monroe in 1818 he decried the British monopoly, pointing to the fact that only when one of the frequent hurricanes wrought havoc in the West Indies, bringing destruction and starvation to the population, were American ships permitted temporary entry. For the United States to refuse, on these unhappy occasions, to rescue the inhabitants would be inhumane. Yet, the British measures compelled the United States to retaliate in defense of American interests. Adams wrote: "By the laws of nature, no society can be justifiable in adopting measures toward another state, which may compel the latter to retaliate, in self-defence, by measures incompatible with humanity; yet such is the character of the intercourse permitted by several of the European nations between their colonies in the West Indies and the United States."[2]

This righteous tone flowed not only from Adams' distrust of the British but also his aversion to colonies as a blot on the history of mankind that added up to a blasphemy of the exalted principles of the right of a people to govern themselves. New England shipping interests were no less adamant than Adams in seeing free entry as a natural right and they, like him, maintained with confidence that free trade was dictated by the dependence of the islands on agricultural produce from the United States.

At a public meeting in Merchant's Hall in Boston in January 1822 resolutions were adopted supporting the policy of the American navigation acts of 1818. The policy had assured Americans of the opportunity of entering into fair competition with rivals. The Committee of Commerce in the House of Representatives responded with a strong endorsement of the free trade policy. The British aim, the report charged, "was to destroy the equality of navigation" established by the Convention of 1815 and "to obtain a monopoly in favor of British vessels." If the American laws of 1818 and 1820 were to be repealed, British vessels would supplant American ships in the ports of England and other European nations. Should the British government succeed in carrying out her policy, "it would give her the ascendancy over every nation in every market of the world." In words reminiscent of James Madison's speech before the House in July 1789, the committee warned that national security rested on a strong merchant marine, "the nursery of seamen," making possible a powerful navy.[3]

From February to July 1824 Richard Rush, the American minister in London, met with Colonial Secretary William Huskisson and Stratford Canning, of the foreign office, to discuss the question of commercial relations and other important issues. Twenty-six sessions of earnest debate failed to reach a single agreement. The British repudiated the American contention that the United States should pay no higher duties or port charges than ships carrying goods from one British colony to another. This trade, the British asserted, was "no other than a part of the coasting trade" and the Americans enjoyed "a like advantage on their side."[4]

This was the crux of the controversy. Americans rejected the British system of imperial preference; the British insisted on maintaining it. Yet, the British recognized that trade with the United States was important to the West Indies in respect to the availability of American produce at low prices and to access to the American market for disposal of sugar and molasses. The trade was at least of equal importance to the American agricultural interests, who looked to the British West Indies for a market, and to northern shipping interests. Neither side could afford to be content with the abolition of the trade.

However, the question reached an apparent point of no return in 1825. Parliament, in an act of June 27 and another of July 5, 1825, opened the West Indies ports to any nation willing to meet certain conditions. These laws impressed John Quincy Adams, now president, as ambiguous; even a year later the new secretary of state, Henry Clay, advised Albert Gallatin that the meaning of these laws remained to be determined by experience. Clay believed that they did open the ports to foreign nations and with no higher duties than those imposed on the same goods coming on British vessels. One restriction remained. Foreign vessels were restricted to direct trade between the country to which it belonged and the British colony. The United States did not insist on the right to participate in the trade between the colony and Great Britain but did require that American vessels be free to go from the colony to other foreign countries. President Adams asked that the British give evidence of having surrendered the system of imperial preference and also that American vessels be free to go from the colonies to foreign ports. When the United States did not agree to reciprocate the British concessions by opening American ports to British ships coming from the West Indies, the British withdrew the offer and issued an order-in-council closing off all further negotiations with the United States on this question.

Gallatin's instructions called for a settlement of a number of different issues: the West Indies trade question, the opening of the St. Lawrence River to American shipping, a division of the Oregon territory at the 49th parallel, and a resolution of the long controversy over the Maine boundary question. Adams' ambitious goals, at a time when the outlook for a settlement of an even modest degree was doubtful, placed the veteran diplomat at an almost hopeless disadvantage.

In June 1826 the administration had appointed Albert Gallatin to serve as minister to London to continue the negotiations. Adams held Gallatin in high regard, but the two men were of different molds. Adams wrote instructions calling for a rigid stand on a set of desired objectives, a rigidity induced in part by fear that the Senate would refuse to approve a treaty that provided less. Gallatin approached the negotiations in a spirit of compromise. He, too, could be firm and zealous in his defense of national interests, mastered every question to the last detail, and was also infinitely patient and understanding of the adversaries' problems. He protested at length that the instructions he received did not jibe with his own understanding of what he had been told earlier, and he viewed the proposal to negotiate the question of opening the West Indies as untimely and an obstacle to success on other points. Having made his complaint, he set out to master the details of each of the questions to be discussed and adhered to his instructions.[5]

A series of factors operative in 1826 made his task difficult. Monroe's message with its noncolonization principle created ill-feeling in England, for it appeared not only presumptuous but gave evidence of dangerous American ambition. In the midst of the negotiations, Charles Hughes, Jr., stationed in Brussels, who had many acquaintances in England, wrote to Gallatin concerning the sources of British distrust. The British, he said, were disappointed in Gallatin's appointment, believing that as a former ally of Jefferson he shared his anti-British views. They likewise saw in John Quincy Adams evidence of increasing hostility. But, wrote Hughes, nothing had upset the British more than Monroe's noncolonization principle, which they viewed as arrogance and one that the United States lacked the power to sustain.

> I know that no speech, or act of ours, since our commencement, grated more ire, or gave a greater shock to British pride, than that phrase of Mr. Monroe; I know, to use the words of a great British [sic], there was not a man in the British Councils, whose blood did not tingle at his fingers' ends on reading that proposition of Mr. Monroe.[6]

Undoubtedly, there was considerable truth in these estimates of Hughes.

Gallatin, in a letter to Clay on December 20, attributed the British position on Oregon to their determination to protect the interests of the Northwest Fur Company, to national pride, and to resentment aroused by Mr. Monroe's message. He wrote:

> Not only from them, but from several other distinct quarters it is certain that that pride was sorely wounded by that fact of the late President's message, which declared that America was no longer open to European colonization . . . This was no

doctrine, and was considered dictatorial, and as hinting too, with no favorable intentions to the existing British Colonies.[7]

Gallatin also attributed the change in atmosphere since 1818 to the rapid growth of American shipping, causing the British to view the United States as a rival to be feared.[8] Some weeks later, in a letter to John Quincy Adams, Gallatin attributed part of the coolness to the British having read Adams' letters to Rush when they were printed by the Senate.[9] The letter of instruction of July 22, 1823, included one of Adams' more flamboyant declarations.

> It is not imaginable that, in the present condition of the world, *any* European nation should entertain the project of settling a *colony* on the Northwest Coast of America; that the United States should form establishments there, with views of absolute territorial right, and inland communication, is not only to be expected, but is pointed out by the finger of nature, and has been for years a subject of serious deliberation in Congress.[10]

Adams' letter set forth the noncolonization principle. This language could only challenge British pride and lend strength to the idea that the overbearing new nation required a lesson in restraint.

Other developments contributed to the hostile spirit shown by Canning and Huskisson during their first meetings with Gallatin. England was in the midst of a serious business recession, and the shipping interests blamed Huskisson, who had relaxed controls over colonial trade. He was assailed from all sides as a theorist, an accusation Gallatin did not accept. Gallatin, who did not have any hope of the British opening the West Indies at this time, took Huskisson's domestic difficulties into account. Another disturbing factor was the appearance of a bristling report by the Baylies committee in the House of Representatives. Baylies, a violent enemy of John Quincy Adams, voted against Adams in the electoral college on the ground that he was morally unfit. The report dealt with the Oregon question, denied all British claims to the territory, and placed severe censure on the British. The report read:

> Great Britain adopts no plans of policy from caprice or vanity; her ambition is developed in a system of wise and

sagacious projects, to check, to influence, and to control all nations, by means of her navy and her commerce; in prosperity and in adversity; in peace and in war, she has pursued this grand design, with an energy and perseverance, which does infinite credit to her political sagacity and foresight.[11]

Damning the British with charges of ambitious deviltry, the Baylies committee contended that England was determined to control the waters of the Pacific so as to "enable her to control the commerce and policy of Mexico, Central America, and South America." This report so upset Foreign Minister George Canning that in a conversation with Gallatin he said that he viewed it as almost tantamount to a declaration of war.[12]

Canning learned that, prior to leaving for London, Gallatin confided to Senator Samuel Smith that he would have preferred more lenient instructions on the Northwest boundary question. Canning did make use of this within the British cabinet.[13] It is also true that Gallatin was not, at the time of receiving his instructions, wholly convinced that the United States had much of a case aside from the fact that John Jacob Astor had established a settlement at the mouth of the Columbia.[14] Gallatin may well have changed his mind after further study. At any rate he demonstrated superb skill and also determination when the Northwest boundary question came before the representatives of the two governments.

Party rivalry, never more tense than during Adams' administration, contributed further to undermining the negotiations. The issue of discriminating duties was not one on which all sections of the country agreed. In the spring of 1826 the Senate Committee on Commerce considered a petition from Baltimore merchants calling for the abolition of discriminatory duties on British ships. The merchants held that Great Britain having opened the trade of her colonies, the United States should abolish all discriminatory duties on British vessels.[15] Samuel Smith, of Maryland, spoke in favor of the petition. He contended that the tax fell on the agriculturalists. Farmers were in need of aid that could be given them. He decried the failure to take advantage of the British act of 1825, and accepted the preference granted to goods shipped from one part of the empire to another as wholly reasonable. In the course of his remarks he gave high praise to Huskisson:

That great man and his colleagues form the most able, the most wise, and the most useful administration that has ever existed in Great Britain—they are doing great good to commerce, great and useful service to the nation, and opening the eyes of the world to the advantages of free trade.[16]

The committee cited the prohibitory duties laid by the United States on certain imports. Those engaged in shipping, mostly northerners, the report stated, focused all of their attention on navigation but "the South is primarily interested in a foreign market and care little whether their produce is carried by the ships of one or another nation."[17] The debate resulted in no action, but several southern senators supported Smith.

The question came before Congress again in the spring of 1827. In the House, George McDuffie of South Carolina led the attack on the president for failure to respond to the act of Parliament of 1825. He spoke in favor of a bill which he described as renouncing, "by a legislative declaration, the indefensible pretension" that the United States cannot accept any preference given to products of one part of the British empire on entering another British port.[18] The southerners failed to have their way; but, of course, the British negotiators, well informed of the division in Congress, held a stronger hand.

Shortly after his arrival in London Gallatin received word of the British order-in-council of July 27 suspending all American trade with the British West Indies. A more discouraging beginning could scarcely be imagined. Gallatin saw it as offensive; Canning defended it as consistent with the act passed by Parliament the previous year. Gallatin countered that the cutting off of the trade would be more injurious to Great Britain than the United States.[19] For the next several weeks both parties marked time explaining past actions, and no progress was made. Gallatin concluded that the British had determined to leave the United States no options except forgoing the trade or accepting British regulations.[20] In September Canning sent Gallatin a peremptory communication on the subject bristling with challenges and hostility. Gallatin had acknowledged the British right to control the trade or even prohibit it, but Canning distorted what Gallatin had said. Gallatin refrained from citing past injuries. His aim was to remove the problem from the realm of legislative recriminations and to make it a matter of a mutually advantageous treaty settlement. Gallatin ignored Canning's irritating letter and simply noted that it was full of "ingenuity and cleverness but it is altogether argumentative, containing nothing important or new."[21] Clay found Canning's letter offensive and stated that the United States had entered into the discussion in a conciliatory spirit and did not object to British insistence on maintaining imperial preference.[22] Nothing came of the exchange on the colonial trade, and Gallatin merely commented that after an experiment for two more years the British would probably yield.

Before proceeding Gallatin asked if he had the president's permission to discuss the Northwest question, given the failure on the trade question. He was instructed to go ahead, and negotiations were resumed on November 15. As was to be expected, both sides made much of rights based on prior discovery and exploration, and here the British had arguments at least as strong as those of the United States.[23]

Gallatin found the early discussions of the Oregon question desultory but by November 25 he also noted some improvement in tone. Huskisson had said "that it would be lamentable that, in this age, two such nations as the United States and Great Britain should be drawn to a rupture on such subject as the uncultivated wilds of the North West coast."[24]

To the surprise of Gallatin the British position had changed since the negotiations of 1818. Canning, Huskisson, and Addington now based their claims on occupation, pointing to the prior existence of a series of small settlements along the coast. Having set this forth, they moved forward to an interpretation of the Nootka Sound Treaty of 1789 and proceeded to argue that this settlement, now a matter of international law, opened the entire Pacific Northwest to the trade and settlement of all nations. That treaty, the British contended, extinguished prior Spanish claims based on discovery and accordingly rendered the United States' contention that it had acquired Spain's rights by the treaty of 1819 meaningless. The British stated that they made no claim to exclusive sovereignty; only the United States claimed exclusive sovereignty.

This approach accorded with British interests. They readily stated that they had no plans to colonize the area. As Gallatin explained, the British were responding to the powerful Northwest Fur Company, which needed a period of years to exhaust the fur resources. The British plenipotentiaries made it appear that it was the United States that was presumptuous and the aggressor.

Gallatin held that the proposal ran counter to the interest of the United States. It was an effort to undermine the American claim and to prevent the establishment by the United States of a territorial government.[25] The British proposed that the convention of 1818 be renewed subject to an amendment specifying that neither nation would assume or exercise any right of exclusive sovereignty or dominion. This would have barred the United States from organizing a territorial government, precisely the major purpose of Canning. Gallatin promptly informed the British negotiators that any change in Articles II and III of the 1818 treaty would have to be referred to the president. Presenting the American side, he disputed the British claim of prior discovery, argued that historical precedent in North America provided the basis for claiming the lands directly west of earlier grants of land by the Crown, held that it was inevitable that Oregon south of the 49th parallel would be settled by Americans, and contended that the Nootka Sound Treaty was only binding on the parties to it.[26] He wrote to Secretary of State Henry Clay that he would strive to have the treaty renewed without change. In March he received a reply. The president rejected the British proposal.

Before the close of the year the attitude of Canning and Huskisson became more cordial. Gallatin's refusal to respond to unfriendly provocations and his quiet but persistent pursuit of the main objectives won the confidence of the British opposites who had viewed the United States as hostile and unreasonable. Gallatin, himself, attributed the change to Canning's concern that continued Spanish interference in Portugal, while the French still dominated Madrid, could end in a war. Canning discussed the problem in frank terms with Gallatin. Gallatin, in turn, fearing that if war should take place the British would be tempted to seize Cuba, discreetly affirmed that of course neither the United States nor Great Britain could permit a maritime power to take the island. Canning replied that England already had too many colonies. Gallatin's efforts to have Canning make a forthright commitment failed, but after Gallatin mentioned the possibility of independence for Cuba Canning "said the subject was worthy of consideration and that he would certainly attend to it."[27]

Some further desultory discussion with Canning on the trade question took place in late January, but both wisely avoided letting this issue come to the fore. Canning stated that it was wiser to focus on what was negotiable and then in one of those rare instances when he permitted a note of congeniality, observed regarding the two countries: "The ties of common origin, laws, and language must always form strong bonds of National Alliance between them. Their respective interests, well understood, harmonize together as much as their feelings."[28] Gallatin welcomed the new tone but remained pessimistic on reaching agreements. Part of his gloom was due to the part played by Addington, whom he found "extremely unmanageable." Addington was the chief spokesman on boundary questions.

Delay ensued because of the change in the British government in April and the illness of both Canning and Huskisson. Clay continued to push the trade question, but Gallatin held out no hope. Huskisson was under bitter attack, and more recently the shipowners of Hull aggressively opposed any arrangement with the United States.[29]

In that same month of April Gallatin worked hard on the Maine boundary question. He was convinced that the United States was absolutely right in its claim, but he also feared that the British would exploit the reference in the Treaty of Paris to the "highlands" as the boundary. There were no elevations worthy of the term and, in fact, there were some slightly higher elevations that the British would cite whose location accorded with British claims. Gallatin held that the central question was the line drawn by the Proclamation of 1763 and this was the line that the treaty of 1783 referred to.[30]

Not until June 1827 did the negotiators make significant progress. At the beginning of that month all questions remained to be decided. Gallatin found the British haggling over minor points and seeking to circumvent his decisions by new phrasing. On June 5 he wrote to Clay concerning the Maine boundary question: ". . . I am obliged to dispute every inch of the ground to prevent any undue advantage being taken."[31] On June 19, in a discussion of the Oregon question, the British plenipotentiaries raised once again the proposed stipulation to prohibit any actions based on exclusive jurisdiction. This time they sought to have it inserted in the Protocol, thereby imposing their own interpretation.[32] By this time it had been tentatively agreed to renew the Commercial Convention of 1815, but the British insisted that an article must be added prohibiting the levying of a higher duty on rolled than on forged iron. This was a matter of some importance because at the time England alone exported rolled iron, and a higher duty on it was seen as discriminatory.[33] Gallatin rejected the proposed article and then a move to have it included in the Protocol. These same points were introduced again by the British at a meeting on June 26.

It was during these June days that Gallatin won the debate over Oregon, but it should also be said that Canning and Huskisson demonstrated a conciliatory spirit. The two British men were worried about what the United States might do in the way of creating a territorial government and establishing fortifications. Gallatin turned the discussion to the Convention of 1818. That agreement, he explained, aimed only at preserving freedom to trade and settle. It did not bar military posts, nor did it exclude the setting up of territorial government as long as these did not interfere with free trade. He went on to explain that the Northwest Fur Company constituted a law enforcement agency for all Britishers in the area and that the company's stockades were tantamount to fortifications. The United States did not and could not achieve these ends through a private monopoly. Therefore, it would not forego the right for the government to take measures assuring peace and security. The British, at this time, showed concern that developments in the future in Oregon could create conflict, which must be avoided. Gallatin pointed to the success of the Convention of 1818 and contended that it provided security against future disturbances.[34] The British now gave way to a renewal of the earlier Convention without any changes.

Finally, on June 28, the negotiators were ready to sign the conventions upon which they had finally agreed. The Commercial Convention of 1815 was renewed. The Convention of 1818 providing for joint occupation was extended with only one change. Each party could terminate the treaty after due notice, whereas the previous agreement provided for ten years. Negotiations on the Northeast boundary question continued until September 29. This convention provided that the question should be submitted to arbitration by a third party and specified the maps to be submitted to him. The vast accumulation of documents compiled by commissioners in the past was to be withheld because it was anticipated no sovereign of a third nation would be willing to undertake the task of analyzing it.

The ten months of negotiating appear, at first glance, to have ended largely in stalemate. The falsity of this impression is readily apparent when either the absence of any efforts to negotiate or a breakup of the negotiations is contemplated. On both the British and American sides popular passions had risen to the danger point, and a chain of legislative recriminations and charges of a very intemperate character portended a drift toward conflict at the worst and unprofitable controversy at best. The negotiations did not wholly dissipate the clouds, and continued rivalry perpetuated the sensitivity of two peoples made proud by their achievements.

The negotiations did have results that contributed to peace. It was now clear to Americans, at least those in high office, that Great Britain, as Gallatin phrased it, "does not seem indisposed to let the [Oregon] country gradually and silently slide into the hands of the United States; and she is anxious that it should not, in any case, become the cause of a rupture between the two Powers."[35] The renewal of the Commercial Convention prevented a trade war in which each would have engaged in retaliating discriminatory acts. Beyond these benefits was the even more important clearing of the air of misunderstandings and mutual censures inspired in part by domestic political considerations.

NOTES TO CHAPTER IV

1. The act of Congress of March 1, 1823, provided that the president had the authority to abolish any discriminatory duties on port charges when he had proof that the British levied no higher duties or port charges on American vessels and produce "than upon British vessels or upon the like goods, wares, and merchandise imported into the said colonial ports from *elsewhere* . . ." Adams affirmed that the term "elsewhere" included other ports within the British empire. Thereupon, Stratford Canning, in a letter to Adams, on May 17, 1823, stated that "Such being the intention of the act, it is vain for the present, to enter upon any discussion of the question . . ." *American State Papers Foreign Relations*, Vol. V, p. 522.

2. Secretary of State John Q. Adams to the president, March 17, 1818. *Annals of Congress*, 15th Cong., 1st Sess., Vol. I, pp. 275–76.

3. Report of the Committee of Commerce, Mar. 15, 1822. *Annals of Congress*, 17th Cong., 1st Sess., Appendix, pp. 2228–90.
4. *American State Papers   Foreign Relations*, Vol. V, p. 567.
5. Albert Gallatin to Henry Clay, June 29, 1826. *Gallatin Papers*, Roll 36.
6. Charles Hughes, Jr. to Gallatin, Dec. 10, 1826. *Gallatin Papers*, Roll 37.
7. Ibid., Gallatin to Clay, Dec. 20, 1826.
8. Ibid., Gallatin to Clay, Sept. 22, 1826.
9. Ibid., Gallatin to Adams, Oct. 17, 1826.
10. 19th Cong., 1st Sess., Appendix, p. 31.
11. Report of Baylies Committee, May 15, 1826, 19th Cong., 1st Sess., Report 213, pp. 20–21.
12. Gallatin to Clay, Nov. 27, 1826. *Gallatin Papers*, Roll 36.
13. See Frederick Merk, *Albert Gallatin and the Oregon Problem* (Cambridge: Harvard University Press, 1950), pp. 61–64.
14. Gallatin to James Barbour, June 30, 1826. *Gallatin Papers*, Roll 36.
15. *Annals of Congress*, 19th Cong., 1st Sess., Part I, p. 576.
16. 19th Cong., 1st Sess., pp. 455–62.
In the debate that ensued Martin Van Buren delivered a lengthy speech, favoring the elimination of discriminatory duties when the British were ready to do justice. He used the occasion to reprimand the administration and to demand firmness with the British. "We have," he said, "to contend with an adversary deeply versed in the arts of diplomacy, and every way competent to discern the intentions of those whose interests may come in competition with her own.", pp. 469–83.
17. Ibid., pp. 577–85.
18. *Annals of Congress*, 19th Cong., 2nd Sess., Part 3, pp. 1515–17.
19. Ibid., Gallatin to Clay, Aug. 19, 1826.
20. Ibid., Aug. 28, 1826.
21. Ibid., Gallatin to Clay, Oct. 12, 1826.
22. Clay to Gallatin, Nov. 14, 1826. *Gallatin Papers*, Roll 37.
Clay, in a letter to Gallatin on October 12 had already made the point that the United States was willing to "yield the point that the British Government may retain the monopoly of the carrying trade between the parent country and her Colonies." At this stage the British held out on negotiating the question preferring to make it a matter of legislation. See Clay to Gallatin, Oct. 12, 1826, pp. 778–81; Clay to Edward Everett, Oct. 19, 1826, pp. 804–805; and Clay to James Lloyd, Oct. 21, 1826, in *The Papers of Henry Clay*, eds. James F. Hopkins and Mary W. M. Hargreaves (Lexington, Ky.: The University Press of Kentucky, 1973), Vol. V.
23. For a contrary view, see Merk, *Albert Gallatin and the Oregon Problem*, pp. 66–68.
24. Gallatin to Clay, Nov. 25, 1826, *Gallatin Papers*, Roll 36.
25. Gallatin to Clay, Dec. 5, 1826, *Gallatin Papers*, Roll 37.
26. Gallatin to Clay, Dec. 22, 1826, *Gallatin Papers*, Roll 37.
27. Copy of Gallatin's remarks at conference on Dec. 19. *Gallatin Papers*, Roll 37.
28. Ibid., Canning to Gallatin, Jan. 27, 1827.
29. Ibid., Gallatin to Clay, Apr. 21, 1827.
30. Ibid., Gallatin to Enoch Lincoln, Apr. 27, 1827.
31. Gallatin to Clay, June 5, 1827, *American State Papers   Foreign Relations*, Vol. VI, p. 673.
32. Ibid., June 20, 1827, p. 675.
33. Ibid.
34. *American State Papers   Foreign Relations*, Vol. VI, p. 680.
35. Ibid., Gallatin to Clay, Aug. 10, 1827, p. 694.

Chapter V

The United States and Europe, 1830-1842

In February 1833 the American chargé d'affaires in London, Aaron Vail, had a long interview with Prince Lieven of Russia. The two men discussed the recent commercial treaty negotiated by their respective governments. Prince Lieven observed that the principle of equality and reciprocity in the treaty "would, in fact, be nominal, and throw all the advantages on the side of the American ship owner." The Russians, he said, could not compete. Vail then wrote to Secretary of State Edward Livingston:

> In this opinion, which I believe no longer excites surprise in the United States, Prince Lieven is far from being singular in Europe. The superiority of our merchant marine and mercantile skill is brought home to the conviction of the people and Statesmen of this country by the increase of our tonnage and the monopoly which from the unavoidable course of things, falls into our hands wherever anything like fair and equal terms are extended to us. Besides the advantages within the reach of our commercial people, there are other causes growing out of the unsettled political state of Europe, which contribute not a little to secure a preference to our flag when not excluded by prohibitory regulations.[1]

The advantages that the United States enjoyed in shipping were also present in the production of cotton, tobacco, and other produce. These advantages combined to make unequal the effects of the most-favored-nation policy, which presumably provided for equality of commercial opportunity.

Economic growth depended on foreign markets and this, in turn, was inextricably tied to the interests of shipowners, merchants, and the growers of cotton, tobacco, rice, and other products, creating a national interest that enlisted every administration in its service. The United States remained largely isolated from South America and Asia but never from the great markets of Europe. Vigilance in protesting every foreign measure that interfered with trade became standing practice. The seeking out of additional opportunities became a duty that no administration could neglect.

Other difficulties often loomed larger, but representatives abroad served as watchdogs of this commercial interest. In 1840 and 1841, in the midst of a serious crisis with Great Britain over border disputes and the slave trade, the American minister, Andrew Stevenson, carried on a vigorous campaign to have Great Britain place imports of American rice on the same favored basis as imports of African rice. Edward Everett protested strongly against discrimination suffered by American merchants in New Zealand. During his long tenure as minister to France, Lewis Cass devoted most of his time to protesting against the French government monopoly of the tobacco trade. The monopoly provided a large percentage of government revenue and, given the financial difficulties of the government, this revenue was of major importance. Nevertheless, Cass never ceased to argue that the tobacco raised in France was inferior and that the monopoly placed imports of American tobacco at a great disadvantage. These observations are not intended to deny the historian's premise of multiple causation. Foreign policy was not the exclusive product of concern for markets, but this concern was a major force in the 1830s.

And trade, inevitably a two-way channel, elevated the American market to first rank among all the foreign markets of England and France. This gave the United States a leverage in its dealings.

Free to launch new and ever larger enterprises, as unbound as Prometheus from government regulations, and free from the stifling influence of a hereditary aristocracy, middle-class America embarked on converting unlimited and unrivaled natural resources into a productive economy. That economy depended upon foreign capital and foreign trade, and the first axiom of foreign policy was to lend a helping hand to commercial expansion.

Furthermore, freedom from threats by powerful neighbors enabled the government to channel its energy into the development of commerce. It was not so with Great Britain and France, close allies beginning in 1832, who had to give thought to a whole series of developments threatening revolution—war and changes in the European power structure inimical to their security. Europe in the 1830s was likened by one American minister to a smoldering volcano. Russia's military adventures in the Near East, Austria's expeditions to suppress revolts in the papal states, Belgium's war for independence, the revolt of the Poles against Russia, Don Pedro's military campaign to replace Don Miguel on the Spanish throne—all these affected the interests of neighboring states and posed the danger of a general war.

Each eruption endangered the interests of one or more states. Revolts in one country awakened sympathy and even admiration among peoples in other countries, thereby creating general unrest. The Polish revolt in 1830 caused the Polish community in Paris to demand that French troops be sent to assist, and Frenchmen at large favored the Poles. The Belgian revolt revived dreams of French annexation, and at the same time the powers of eastern Europe flirted with aiding the Dutch in order to diminish the status of Great Britain and France. The refusal of the Dutch king to accept the fact of Belgian success and Dutch hopes of retaining Antwerp because of its commercial importance generated a crisis. Finally, in 1832, Great Britain and France entered into an alliance that included an agreement to eject the Dutch by naval and military means. The powers of eastern Europe, as the American chargé in Paris observed, looked upon the alliance as a tremendous blow. France, ever since the wars of the French Revolution, viewed as Europe's troublemaker, was an object of distrust. Russian hostility was so great that rather than participate in Louis Philippe's New Year's soiree in the year 1832, the Russian ambassador departed for London.

Don Pedro benefited by quiet support from the French and the British, but Spain saw in his return to Portugal the unleashing of liberal ideals and threats to the monarchy. In the spring of 1832 fear prevailed that the overthrow of Don Miguel would bring general war. Spain declared it would intervene to prevent the change in Portugal. England promptly declared it would send troops to prevent Spanish intervention. Nathaniel Niles, American chargé in Paris, wrote to Secretary of State Livingston that France wanted a constitutional regime in Portugal so that in event of a general European war it would not have to worry about Spain, who would be deterred by uneasiness over hostile moves by Portugal. England, he believed, was motivated solely by hopes of regaining and securing mercantile ascendancy.[2]

Europe's foreign ministries lived amidst continuing crises close to home. The American state department viewed the scene with great interest, for a general European war would expose the United States to all the trials of the years of Napoleon; however, no secretary of state confronted the dangerous instability that commanded the full attention of European ministries.

Repeated crises in domestic politics likewise had a higher priority than relations with the United States. A revolutionary spirit was astir throughout Europe. The shakiness of the structure presided over by Louis Philippe came to the fore in June 1832. The death of the military hero of the Revolution, General Lamarque, aroused memories of heroic days. The funeral procession sparked a tremendous demonstration aimed at discrediting the monarchy. Paris rose in revolt, and the ministry ordered troops to quell the uprising. Four hundred were killed. In the following days the government abolished the Polytechnic School and the Royal Veterinary School because students had participated in the disorders.[3] This was only one of many revolts during the regime of Louis Philippe. The working class in the manufacturing center of Lyons engaged in a number of uprisings, but Paris was the focal point of disturbance.

The revolutionary stirrings made themselves felt throughout Europe after the overthrow of the Bourbons in France in 1830. Revolts took place in Italy and Spain and only to lesser degree in the German states. The long and painful debates over the Reform Bill in 1832 in England caused serious unrest, but final passage postponed the day for more radical measures. However, England did not escape. In 1838 widespread strikes aimed at political goals spread throughout the manufacturing districts. The ministry dispatched sizable detachments of troops to put down the workers, and after the restoration of tranquility deported hundreds of young rebels.

Violence in the United States did not include political turbulence. Only the nullification movement in South Carolina caused serious political disturbance during the 1830s. Party warfare generated heated quarrels, but the efforts to gain office did not portend fundamental economic or social reform. The two major parties differed chiefly on such questions as the tariff, the National Bank, the public land policy, and internal improvements.

Those who governed the United States enjoyed one other luxury denied to their counterparts in Europe. The federal government often faced treasury surpluses, and congressional members did not face the jeopardy that came with the necessity of levying direct taxes. In Europe the French government faced serious financial straits, and taxes were a major political issue. Great Britain fared better, but even there the government in 1839 encountered financial difficulties.

The European nations certainly had interests in the New World that they promoted with vigor, but problems closer to home inhibited bold moves and, more often, caused them to relegate difficulties with the United States to second rank. They did not play down the importance of the new republic; rather they marveled at its growth and prosperity, at the same time fearing that the combination of industry and boldness would some day spell trouble.

At a gathering of the diplomatic corps in Paris in 1832 the Russian ambassador pronounced the United States one of the great powers, and a year later French eyes opened wide when the new American minister, Edward Livingston, arrived on the *Delaware*, a powerful warship for its day. The king and his attendants entertained Captain Bullard, along with his fellow officers, at dinner. The king complimented the captain on his splendid ship and expressed the hope that if the United States should find it necessary to depart from neutrality in some future war it would side with France. Captain Bullard replied that in an emergency "we had the means of putting to sea, at a short period, fifty heavy ships, one half of which would equal that of his own, and the other half would consist of frigates carrying fifty or sixty guns." "This report of our naval capacity," wrote Chargé Levitt Harris, "excited lively attention in the Prince."[4]

Yet the United States suffered weaknesses in the realm of foreign affairs. The federal government, a loose federation of states, could not control local affairs that touched upon relations with Europe. Moreover, the very size of the nation created a variety of interests that came into conflict on questions of foreign affairs. This led to a situation in the late 1830s when European statesmen might well have asked whether the Union had the power to govern. In both Maine and upper New York violence occurred that gave rise to sharp British protests and caused a serious rift. Washington could not police in matters reserved to the states. Even more serious, the South paralyzed the national government's early efforts to curb the slave trade, and thereby a crisis in Anglo-American relations came to the fore.

The successful negotiations of Albert Gallatin as minister to England removed all except one pressing problem—in fact the most pressing problem—in Anglo-American relations, the closing of the British West Indies to American ships. The British adhered to the legacy of the old-established monopoly of trade within the empire.

It was not only British shipping that sought to perpetuate the hold it enjoyed in the trade with the West Indies but the Canadian Maritime Provinces, and those who had invested in them opposed any relaxation of the British policy. These provinces served as an economic hinterland of the all important British colonies in the Caribbean, providing them with the agricultural commodities the islands required.

Gallatin found the British so determined not to give way that, with the consent of the Adams' administration, he gave up trying to bring about a relaxation. At home, Adams' policy irritated American producers of exports to the islands and became a focal point in congressional debates and later a major issue in the election campaign of 1828. The administration of Andrew Jackson determined to change course, and Secretary of State Martin Van Buren sent instructions to Louis McLane, the new minister in London, to open negotiation on the question.

A wall of opposition awaited McLane. In his first dispatch to Secretary of State Van Buren, McLane stated that patience would be required. However, as time elapsed, he concluded the British government would recognize that its policy only served to do injury to the West Indies' plantations, which labored under heavy debts. Moreover, existing restrictions on trade with the United States only added to the costs of imports.[5] Lord Aberdeen admitted that the present state of trade injured both parties but he fended off McLane's statements by citing the new tariff of abominations enacted in 1828, a measure he described as "peculiarly hostile to Great Britain."[6] Feelings in England ran high, and Aberdeen knew there was no possibility of winning the assent of Parliament to a change of course.

After talking to every member of the ministry and to the president of the Board of Trade, McLane advised that existing feelings made it futile to pursue the effort to negotiate. At the same time McLane perceived that if the United States would take the initative by repealing all retaliatory measures enacted since 1822, Aberdeen would be freer to make a conciliatory move. In his dispatches to Washington McLane suggested that the administration take this step.[7] He reported that interests with large investments in shipping and in the northern Maritime Provinces counted on continuance of the present policy to protect them from American competition.[8] These interests argued that the Americans had rejected generous measures in 1825 and were not deserving of any consideration.

As the months passed, McLane continued to appeal to Aberdeen, observing that "ancient prejudices and unworthy animosities" lingered among the people of both countries; these fostered a spirit of commercial jealousy, which he regretted. The interests of both countries called for a change. In a lengthy letter to Aberdeen he wrote:

> It should be the desire as it is the interest of both governments to extinguish these causes of a mutual bitterness, to correct the errors which may have interrupted the harmony of their past intercourse, to discard from their commercial regulations measures of hostile monopoly and to adopt instead a generous system of frank and amicable competition.[9]

In a dispatch to Van Buren, McLane again recommended that the United States rescind "the measures which may be alleged to have contributed to the present evil and repeal the laws which have been matters of complaint." The British, he believed, were now ready to withdraw their restrictions, that they never intended to prohibit direct trade, and that the time had come when they would welcome an agreement consistent with British interests.

He sought to persuade Aberdeen with a statistical analysis, showing that the West Indies would benefit by free trade and even under the existing prohibition American produce found its way there by a circuitous route through the ports of the other islands. He asked Aberdeen: ". . . with this view of the subject, why may not these supplies, which must necessarily be drawn from the United States, be furnished by means of direct trade?" His forty-nine page letter to Aberdeen had all the strength of logic on its side; however, as he wrote to Van Buren, British investors in the Canadian provinces relied on a continuation of the policy of excluding the United States and they were "untiring and importunate in their opposition to any arrangement of this question; insisting pertinaciously that we ought not to be allowed to trade now, at a sacrifice of their advantages, which we heretofore refused to accept."[10]

Then, in the spring of 1830 the Jackson administration recommended, and Congress enacted, a law authorizing the president to suspend the restrictions prohibiting the entry of British ships from the West Indies. Jackson responded promptly. At the same time Congress sweetened the conciliatory gesture by reducing the duties on a number of imports from the West Indies. These actions, as McLane had hoped, caused the British ministry to alter its position. On August 17, 1830, Aberdeen notified McLane that the British government restored to the United States freedom to trade directly with the British colonies. McLane, ebullient with success, observed that the friendship of the two nations was now on a permanent foundation and that it was a great advantage to be on friendly terms with powerful England.[11] Unlike Adams, the practical Jackson did not demand that Great Britain abandon the imperial preference system.

The British yielded because of the injuries suffered by the British plantations and the realization that neither orders-in-council nor legislation could alter the natural course of trade. They were also influenced by the precarious state of affairs on the continent. Revolts in Poland and in Italy, plus the war separating Belgium from the Netherlands, threatened to engulf the entire continent in war. McLane believed that war would have taken place had it not been for the determination of the British to keep the peace.[12] As he also noted, Europe everywhere was astir with revolution. The crises nearer home enhanced the importance of good relations with the United States.

McLane wrote lengthy reports on the early stages of the British struggle for political reform. Aaron Vail, chargé d'affaires, after McLane's departure, provided detailed reports of the final political battles in Parliament. The Tories conjured up visions of disaster in their effort to ward off change. Only the threat that the king would appoint a sufficient number of new peers to the House of Lords served to break the barricades of reaction. "The people," wrote Vail, "have determined to take the management of their affairs in their own hands, and to correct the abuses which paralyze the energies of the country." Vail was no egalitarian nor was he an advocate of the masses taking control. The essentially conservative nature of the Reform Bill accorded with his political point of view. He believed that "power instead of falling into the hands of the numerous degraded and ignorant class which exists in this country, and concerning which doubts exist as to its ability to take part in public affairs, . . . will be deposited in those of that intelligent, useful and industrious class which constitutes the strength of the nation, and has interests hitherto unrepresented in Parliament, . . ."[13]

The opening of trade with the British West Indies did not bring permanent friendship between the two nations but it did bring to a close a controversy of long standing. Friendly relations between the two governments reigned supreme for the next few years in spite of the hostility of British Tories and the prevalence of Anglophobia among Americans.

The settlement of the colonial trade question with Great Britain coincided with the beginning of a new era in relations with France. In July 1830 the Bourbons were overthrown, and Louis Philippe ascended the throne. William C. Rives, the American minister, described the upheaval as "one of the most wonderful revolutions which have ever occurred in the history of the world."[14] Wherever aristocracy fell from power, Americans hailed the dawn of a new day of freedom and government by the people. Quite apart from the cheer evoked by the triumph of liberal ideology, it appeared that national self-interest would be well served by the ascendancy of popular governments free of hostility toward the American republic. Moreover, the new king, who for a time had resided in the United States, admired the American republic and could be expected to initiate a course of friendly relations.

Louis Philippe took each succession of American ministers into his confidence and discussed with them in disarming fashion the problems confronting his government and the forces contributing to turbulence. In turn, Americans admired him, and the flow of hundreds of gifts from the United States to the legation created such a problem of storage space that the minister feared it would be necessary to establish a warehouse.

From the beginning of his reign, Louis Philippe faced uprisings that threatened to bring about his downfall. Admirers of Napoleon, reactionary royalists, and republicans of varying persuasions launched violent outbreaks that necessitated the calling out of the army to restore order. In the Chamber of Deputies opposition groups thwarted the programs of the king's ministers. France prospered and industry advanced. Extensive internal improvements were carried out. None of these assuaged the opposition to Louis Philippe. Early in his reign he confessed to the American minister that he had found it necessary to part ways with the groups who had placed him in power. These groups called for a vigorous foreign policy and the restoration of French dominance. Louis Philippe set aside their plans and committed himself to peace at almost any price, knowing that all Europe feared that the fall of the Bourbons meant the advent of another holocaust like that initiated by the events of 1789. The king sought to quiet these fears by avoiding foreign adventures and by allying his country with Great Britain.

But Louis Philippe's friendliness did not remove the issue of unpaid claims that had long clouded relations between France and the United States. These originated in the seizure or destruction of American ships and the confiscation of cargoes by Napoleon. The government of Louis XVIII acknowledged the validity of the claims, but desperate conditions in France immediately after Napoleon's defeat caused the United States not to press with any vigor. As the years passed and France procrastinated, the American stance changed to one of firmness. The American claimants placed no great pressure on the government, but both the Adams and Jackson administrations held that failure to press the claims would be viewed by France and other nations as a sign of weakness and that it was a primary function of government to defend its citizens, including the claimants who had suffered unjustly. This attitude flowed naturally out of the recent colonial past and the buffetings the republic sustained during the Napoleonic wars.

Albert Gallatin struggled with the question during his tenure as minister to France in the years 1818 to 1823. His successors pursued the same goal with no success. When Andrew Jackson entered the presidency, his secretary of state, Martin Van Buren, instructed the new minister to France, William C. Rives to press the French for a settlement. Rives adhered to the instructions tenaciously, and in the final days of the Bourbon regime it appeared that he was making progress.

The settlement of claims with any country at any time has invariably led to difficult questions. Claimants exploit them to the full and often seek compensation in dubious cases and usually ask for sums in excess of losses. The defending government, on the other hand, seeks to ward off claims. In the controversy with France many questions arose. Was the government so accused responsible for the loss? Had the claimants violated the laws of France, and were those laws consistent with the law of nations? Had the ship sought to violate a legal blockade? Was the present government of France responsible for the wrongdoing of Napoleon?

Skeptics in Congress did not hesitate to criticize the claims. In a congressional debate on the claims in 1834, John Tyler of Virginia said: "A great part of these claims would go to the ensurers." If the government shared the losses of these companies, Tyler held, then the government should also share their profits. Isaac Hill of New Hampshire observed that claims of all sorts were presented again and again and then noted: "The value of perseverance is demonstrated in more successful cases than that of Amy Dardin's horse, which, after having been brought upon the journals year after year, for at least forty years, was finally paid in the generous year of 1832, when there was quite a desire to get rid of as much money as possible from the treasury, in order that high taxes might be continued for the benefit of protecting American manufactures."[15]

Louis Philippe hoped that a settlement could be reached but he could not override the Chamber of Deputies. The opposition rested in part on the belief that the amount claimed was excessive and in part on domestic political considerations.

During the closing months of the Bourbon rule, in early 1830, Foreign Minister Polignac made a few minor concessions. France would pay for vessels burned at sea and for property that had been taken without any official condemnation, but Rives demanded more.[16] Rives ascribed French delinquency to "the national mode of thinking, in relation to all questions of this sort." The French newspapers, he reported, now criticized Polignac for not turning the American claims to the advantage of France.[17]

At this point the French resurrected their interpretation of Article VIII of the Louisiana Treaty, an issue that had come to the fore in 1822. France held that under the Louisiana Treaty the French were entitled to most-favored-nation treatment in all ports of that territory. Indeed, Article VIII did lend considerable credence to the French contention. The United States not only rejected the interpretation, but both John Quincy Adams and Andrew Jackson held that the question was not even open for any further discussion. If the American position on the treaty violated a literal interpretation of Article VIII, this did not matter. Given the Constitution, no administration could have acceded to the French demand, for it would have subsidized one portion of the Union at the expense of the remainder. However, the French unquestionably believed the treaty bestowed upon them a favored position, a belief strengthened by the fact that they found it useful in counteracting American pressure for payment of the long-standing claims.

Rives faced further French procrastination in spite of his persistent nagging of Polignac at every opportunity. In May 1830 he appealed to the commercial motive, holding out a promise that the United States would reduce duties on French wines if the claims were paid. He wrote to Van Buren: "While on this subject, permit me again to speak of the great importance of husbanding our commercial favours, as sources of negotiation with this government." He observed, "I have found no appeal so effectual as that I have made to their commercial interests." He had told the French that there was danger of their losing the advantages "they now possess in that commerce, if they did not very soon do justice to our citizens."[18] The United States, as the American ministers to France never tired of pointing out, was the most important market for French exports.

However, other considerations weighed more heavily than did interest in the American market. In addition to the serious financial straits of the government, Louis Philippe faced determined internal enemies, who seized on every issue. The public could readily be swayed against paying the claims, and politicians used the issue to win popularity. Bourbons and Republicans challenged the regime at every turn. Lafayette advised Rives that the present moment "was not well chosen for pressing this business."[19] To add to the difficulties, a government commission investigating the claims held that they were exaggerated.

In April and early May 1831 Rives' campaign culminated in a heated exchange. On April 23 the French foreign minister made an offer of a settlement, but the United States must first agree to a deduction from the claims of the losses suffered by France because the United States had refused to abide by Article VIII of the Louisiana Treaty. Rives declared this wholly impossible. The foreign minister countered by stating that the king's government had finally decided to make an offer of fifteen million francs. Rives recorded ". . . that I was altogether astonished at such a proposition —that the government of the U. States, instead of seeing in it an evidence of good faith, could regard it in no other light than as a mockery, and equivalent to an absolute refusal of justice—that if it was to be considered as a definite proposition on the part of France, I had only to say that the negotiation was at an end . . ." The foreign minister begged Rives to reflect.[20]

Five days later Rives proudly reported that the firmness of his declaration resulted in success. He had been invited to another interview when Foreign Minister Count Sebastiani raised the figure to twenty million francs. When Rives termed this inadmissible, the foreign minister raised it to twenty-six million francs. Rives refused to accept this but conceded that the United States would accept a sum considerably below the amount claimed. Rives then proposed forty million francs.[21] The foreign minister explained the financial difficulties faced by the government and said it was highly doubtful that the Chamber of Deputies would appropriate so high a figure.[22]

Count Sebastiani observed that the American claimants were not pressuring the American government and that no official in Washington had ever mentioned the problem when he was there. Rives then sought the aid of Lafayette, asking him to seek out the opinion of the various ministers. Lafayette shortly reported that an offer no greater than twenty million francs could be obtained.[23] At this point Sebastiani said France expected a fair and just equivalent for the failure to adhere to Article VIII of the Louisiana Treaty, and suggested that this could be met by a reduction of duties on French imports. In addition, the United States must meet certain French claims, including those of the heirs of Beaumarchais, who had supported the Americans during the War for Independence.[24] A succession of American presidents had recommended payment of these claims, but Congress had failed to act.

Rives, reflecting on the prospects, recalled that Gallatin had once made the statement that the valid claims did not exceed five million francs and that the United States should not expect to receive two million of that figure, Finally, a treaty settling the claims was signed on June 30, 1831. Rives noted that the American claimants would receive five million dollars, and at the same time the United States had rid itself of the embarrassing claims under Article VIII of the Louisiana Treaty. The sum, he said, would be amply sufficient to meet all just claims.[25] He informed Van Buren that there had been two major difficulties. The first of these was the extreme financial difficulties of the French government, and the second that the new government, responsible to the public, was deeply sympathetic to the taxpayers who were sharply opposed to new or additional levies.

Rives resigned as minister a year later, and Levitt Harris served as chargé. In March 1832 the United States presented a draft for the first installment of the payment of the claims only to find that the French would not honor it. France expressed shock that the draft should have been presented without prior notification and in spite of the fact that the American government must have known that no payment could be made until the Chamber of Deputies had appropriated the money. A new stalemate ensued. The United States complained that payment was twenty years overdue. Members of the Chamber of Deputies believed that the amount to which the ministry had agreed was far in excess of what was legitimate.

The failure of the ministry to present the treaty to the Chamber of Deputies for approval and appropriation of the money led to further distrust. The ministry feared that the Chamber would refuse to make the appropriation and this would cause stronger American feelings to erupt. Other considerations of the ministry contributed to delay. In May 1833 Foreign Minister De Broglie was anxious to extend a loan to Greece, and when he granted a higher priority to this than to a settlement with the United States, it led to increased tension.[26] The difficulties in that part of Europe were of more immediate concern to France than relations with the United States.

But of all the factors delaying payment the most important was the feeling of the French that the amount asked for was exorbitant. Chargé Harris attended a levee early in May where he met many of the peers and members of the Chamber of Deputies. "As soon as I appeared in the different groups," he reported, "I became by special reference to some of the gentlemen a necessary speaker on the merits of it." He was asked whether the sum of fifteen million, instead of twenty-five million, would not be sufficient to satisfy all just demands.[27] In June 1833 Harris was the guest of Louis Philippe, who expressed disappointment over the failure of his ministers to submit the treaty to the Chamber, but he also cited the difficulties faced by the ministry—reorganization of the ministry, war on the side of Belgium, financial difficulties. He then pointed to De Broglie, the foreign minister, and said that De Broglie opposed the treaty for internal political reasons.[28]

A week later the treaty was presented to the Chamber of Deputies. However, the ministry faced deep hostility in the Chamber, and Harris had reason to fear the result. Concerned that his government would be tempted to take strong action after these many delays, Harris warned De Broglie that the president might be induced to suspend all orders for French goods. Certainly, he said, the foreign minister could not be indifferent to what this would mean in terms of unemployment in Lyons, a manufacturing center that had already been the scene of violent outbreaks.[29] The warning had no effect, since the ministry was in no position to push the treaty in the Chamber of Deputies.

The new minister to France, Edward Livingston, a distinguished legal scholar, from his arrival in September 1833 labored to persuade the government to push through the necessary appropriation. He viewed the failure to pay a breach of good faith ending in disgrace. At least, he wrote to Secretary of State McLane, ". . . it is impossible they can be blind to the power we have over the trade in their two staples of silk and wine."[30] But even this might not prevent a negative vote in the Chamber of Deputies, for the legitimists of the former Charles X would refuse to vote the appropriation so as to embarrass the ministry, the Republicans would oppose it in hope of extending the powers of the legislative branch, and the president's party would oppose it in hope of making room for themselves in the ministry. Livingston's fears were realized in April 1834 when the Chamber rejected a bill appropriating the money by eight votes. Livingston now concluded that France would never pay unless the United States took strong action. He recommended that the president take a vigorous stand in his message to Congress and that a law be passed prohibiting importation of any article manufactured or produced in France.[31] He also raised the question of his being recalled and diplomatic relations with France being severed. In July he wrote to the secretary of state expressing regret that the measures he had recommended had not been taken.[32] He advised the French that unless action was taken at the meeting of the newly elected Chamber in August the president of the United States would have no choice but to recommend strong measures.

When the Chamber of Deputies met, the question was not presented on the ground that this was merely a preparatory session. Livingston now advised the secretary of state that he believed that a law prohibiting importation of French goods would be better than reprisals.[33] In December when Congress met, President Jackson reported that no progress had been made and that the recent session of the Chamber of Deputies had refused to consider the matter. At an earlier stage Jackson had staved off calls for action.[34] However, in his annual message to Congress he now proposed sequestration of all French property in the United States. No one doubted that this belligerent message presented a real danger of war.

In fact, it was so understood in both Washington and Paris. When the message reached Paris, the public excitement knew no bounds and the government immediately recalled its minister from Washington and invited Edward Livingston to call for his passports. Livingston wisely refrained from doing so, but he did make a trip to England. In the meantime he did his best to convince Foreign

Minister De Broglie that Jackson's message was purely an intra-government communication and was not directed to France.[35] De Broglie gave the same explanation in the Chamber of Deputies when he called on the Chamber to appropriate the funds. However, he also stipulated that no payment would be forthcoming until Jackson had offered an apology.

The reluctance of the French government to permit the crisis to end in hostilities was matched by the same feeling in Congress. Archer, a member of the House from Virginia, denounced Jackson's message and questioned the claims. Was the United States to go to war for a paltry five million dollars?[36] A few took the foolhardy position that if stern measures led to war so be it. The committees on foreign affairs in both the Senate and the House, however, while defending the American side in the controversy, held that the measures called for by the president were inexpedient. Both Henry Clay and John Quincy Adams defended this position, but the intractable nationalist, John Quincy Adams, also found it necessary to affirm that the United States must show its teeth if it were to be respected. The treaty, he said, must be upheld or "every nation in the world will violate its engagements with us." But to this he added that he considered the measure recommended by the president as imprudent.[37]

Neither nation could face war over an issue of this kind, and word soon reached both capitals that the other party sought a peaceful settlement. Jackson, however, was adamant in refusing to render any apology. In his message to Congress on December 7, 1835, Jackson declared that it had never been his intention to menace or insult the government of France. He would not, he said, offer an apology. Early in January 1836 he again stated that he would not offer an apology, but this time he added a mildly conciliatory note stating that he had offered full explanations prior to the French making an apology the condition of payment.[38]

In February Great Britain offered mediation to both nations. The mediation was successful. France now accepted Jackson's latest explanation as honorable and as removing the difficulties concerning national honor. The Chamber of Deputies having appropriated the funds the previous May, the ministry ordered the payment of the first installment on March 19, 1836.

To the French it had appeared that the United States was acting in the spirit of Shylock; to Americans it seemed that the French were acting dishonorably in not paying a just debt. Given the financial burdens faced by the French government and the factionalism in French politics at the time, the delay is understandable. It is even more so given the evidence that lends support to the French charge that the amount claimed was excessive.

American representatives in Paris pointed to the difficulties faced by France, but as appointees of the Jackson administration they could only endanger their own careers by failure to assert that France was obligated to pay the claims in full. Of the several American ministers who represented the United States in Paris, no one was more distinguished than Edward Livingston, who was widely known in Europe as a legal expert and who had achieved distinction in the United States prior to his mission to France. Yet, it was Livingston's advice from Paris, in 1834, that nothing but stern measures would bring France to carry out her obligation. This report, coming from a highly respected and long-term friend must have influenced Jackson in great measure when he flirted with the use of force. No one man nor party nor even one of the contesting nations should be made to bear all the blame, but Livingston miscalculated seriously in advising measures that could only compel France to stand on honor.

NOTES TO CHAPTER V

1. Aaron Vail to Secretary of State Edward Livingston, Feb. 27, 1833. Despatches from London, National Archives Microfilm Copy, Roll 36. Correspondence from National Archives Microfilm will be cited simply by the number of the roll.
2. Nathaniel Niles to Livingston, Dec. 20, 1832. Despatches from Paris, Roll 29.
3. Ibid., Levitt Harris to Livingston, June 16, 1832.
4. Ibid., Levitt Harris to Secretary of State Louis McLane, Sept. 29, 1833, Roll 29.
5. Louis McLane to Secretary of State Martin Van Buren, Oct. 14, 1829. Despatches from London, Roll 33.
6. Ibid., Oct. 17, 1829.
7. Ibid., Nov. 14, 1829. For a detailed discussion of the genesis of McLane's instructions and his mission in London, see John A. Munroe, *Louis McLane Federalist and Jacksonian* (New Brunswick: Rutgers University Press, 1973), pp. 264–65, 272–79.

8. Ibid., Nov. 28, 1829.
9. Ibid., Mar. 15, 1830.
10. Ibid., Apr. 14, 1830.
11. Ibid., Nov. 5, 1830.
12. Ibid., Mar. 14, 1831.
13. Vail to Livington, May 22, 1832, Roll 35.
14. W. C. Rives to Van Buren, July 30, 1830. Despatches from Paris, Roll 27.
15. *Register of Debates in Congress*, 1834, Vol. XI, pp. 18 and 47.
16. Rives to Van Buren, Feb. 16, 1830, Roll 27.
17. Ibid., Feb. 25, 1830.
18. Ibid., June 8, 1830.
19. Ibid., Dec. 18, 1830.
20. Ibid., Apr. 28, 1831.
21. Ibid., May 7, 1831.
22. Ibid., May 29, 1831.
23. Ibid., June 14, 1831.
24. Ibid.
25. Ibid., July 8, 1831.
26. Levitt Harris to Secretary of State Edward Livingston, May 14, 1833. Roll 29.
27. Ibid.
28. Ibid., June 6, 1833.
29. Ibid., June 28, 1833.
30. Livingston to Secretary of State Louis McLane, Sept. 29, 1833. Roll 30.
31. Ibid., Apr. 3, 1834.
32. Ibid., July 26, 1834.
33. Ibid., Aug. 4, 1834.
34. Eugene I. McCormac, *Louis McLane Secretary of State May 29, 1833 to June 30, 1834*, Vol. IV of *The American Secretaries of State and Their Diplomacy*, ed. Samuel Flagg Bemis (New York: Pageant Book Co., 1958), p. 284.
35. Livingston to Secretary of State John Forsyth, Jan. 14, 1835. Roll 30.
36. *Register of Debates*, 23rd Cong., 2nd Sess., 1835, Vol. II, Part 2, p. 1552.
37. Ibid., p. 1534.
38. Eugene I. McCormac, *John Forsyth Secretary of State July 1, 1834 to March 3, 1837*, Vol. IV of *The American Secretaries of State and Their Diplomacy*, pp. 314–15.

Chapter VI

Trouble on the North American Frontier

The final settlement of the claims question with France in 1836 marked the beginning of a period of tranquility in the relations of the two countries. The focus of administrations in Washington now shifted to a series of difficulties threatening an eventual confrontation with London. Four questions emerged, the Northeast boundary, violence on the Canadian frontier connected with the uprising in Upper Canada in 1837, disputes over British efforts to suppress the slave trade off the coast of Africa, and the freeing of slaves on board American ships driven by storms and mishaps into British ports in the West Indies.

Failure to settle the Northeast boundary question left the territory open to dispute by the state of Maine and British provincial authorities, as well as the people residing on both sides of the border. Neither side was restrained by the larger considerations that faced those charged with the conduct of foreign affairs. It was just this that had caused Canning and Gallatin concern when they were negotiating in 1826 and 1827. Unless a settlement of the boundaries could be reached, energetic frontiersmen on both sides would inevitably seek to assure control for themselves.

The early negotiation led to the agreement providing that the unresolved boundary questions should be submitted to the king of the Netherlands for settlement. Surveys of the territory in question and study of the vast array of documents, including the Treaty of

Paris of 1783, did not yield any clear answer and the king, therefore, proposed a compromise line. Authorities in Maine held fixed opinions as to what was rightfully theirs and maintained that under the Constitution the federal government could not deprive them of any territory. The United States, therefore, rejected the proposed compromise. The British government reluctantly agreed to seek a new settlement and in the next several years sounded out the United States on various propositions. Faced with the intransigence of Maine, the United States declined to respond. In the meantime British provincial authorities governed the area in dispute, holding that they did so to assure that the eventual owner would receive the territory with its property intact. The people of Maine saw this as intrusion by the provincial authorities in New Brunswick. By 1838 petty warfare in the area created a brief crisis.

A second source of conflict developed as a result of the insurgent movement in Upper Canada in 1837. The British succeeded in restoring tranquility within a year, but rebellious remnants continued to resist. The Canadian revolt opened the doors to American adventurers and unscrupulous entrepreneurs to ply their trade in fighting and in the sale of arms and munitions. Widespread unemployment in the United States added incentive to American support of the Canadian insurrection. The insurgents across the border exploited the situation by holding out promises of bounties and 160 acres of free land. The border of upper New York, particularly around Buffalo, served as the gateway to excitement and profit. Given the American view that the triumph of republicanism around the world was inevitable, it was only natural that the Canadian insurgents would enjoy wide public sympathy within the United States. In Buffalo and other cities public meetings devoted to denouncing British rule in Canada became everyday occurrences. United States officials opposed the unruly elements, as did the great majority of community leaders who owned property, practiced law, managed newspapers or other business enterprises; but the United States government was unable to exercise control. British monarchical rule struck many as an anachronism, and they could not believe that Canadians enjoyed the same liberties as Americans. Expansionism was at its height, and the annexation of Canada appeared to many as inevitable.

The suppression of the slave trade provided the third source of conflict. After the conclusion of the Napoleonic wars Great Britain undertook to suppress the slave trade. In 1820 the United States declared anyone carrying on the nefarious trade to be guilty of piracy, a crime punishable by death. The British sought to mobilize other nations in the cause, including the United States. This immediately raised the issue of the right of one nation's warships to police the seas and to intercept any vessel carrying slaves or equipped to do so. The other nations of western Europe finally agreed, but sailors had been impressed by the hundreds by the British during the Napoleonic Wars and the United States was paranoic on the right of the British to board American vessels. Given the fact that the British had refused to enter into any treaty binding them to give up impressment, the American reaction was understandable. However, the emergence of the antislavery movement, followed by the rise of a belligerent defense of slavery in the southern states, soon embroiled the issue of the rights of search and impressment in domestic politics. As the American flag became the guarantor against search by British vessels policing the seas in an effort to stop the nefarious slave trade, it also became the chief protection for Portuguese, Spanish, and Brazilian slave traders, who readily flew the American colors. When British naval ships stopped vessels to determine whether their papers offered proof that they were actually American, British sea captains on occasion overreached themselves, and some American ships not engaged in the traffic were subjected to search and to long delays.

A closely related issue concerned American ships carrying slaves from one American port to another that were forced by bad weather or other factors into British ports in the West Indies, where slavery was prohibited. The slaves, according to British rulings, gained their freedom the moment they entered British territory, a view that ardent defenders of slavery considered to be the equivalent of confiscation of private property.

By 1841 these four issues created a crisis of sufficient magnitude to cause talk of war in both Great Britain and the United States. The emergence of these issues and how and why they were finally resolved constitutes the line of inquiry.

On the American side the brunt of the difficulties fell on the Van Buren administration and Secretary of State John Forsyth. The collapse of the economy in 1837 and the enmities bred by the fight over the National Bank and other measures of the Jackson administration made the administration vulnerable to criticism. One consequence was that it could ill afford to leave itself open to accusations of weakness in dealing with foreign powers.

Forsyth had long experience in foreign affairs, having served as minister to Spain and later on the Committee on Foreign Affairs in the Senate. On occasion he had advocated bold steps that indicated a willingness to ride roughly over those who were not powerful enough to cause him difficulty. This was true of his tenure in Spain, where he was indiscreet in seeking to dictate to the Spanish government what it should do on the question of the Florida treaty. On the other hand, Forsyth handled the question of diplomatic recognition of Texas, and also the question of annexation, with the greatest of caution. He could be a "shirt sleeve diplomacy" practitioner, but he could also combine toughness with restraint. However, his hostility toward England made him truculent. He was not a creative man, capable of taking an overall view and giving long-term interests priority over more immediate difficulties. Consequently, in relations with Great Britain he became entrapped in the brush fires of the moment and took rigid stands that protected him from charges of weakness at home. This only served to perpetuate quarrels, without offering any solution to the more general problem of restoring amicable and advantageous friendly relations.

Forsyth's weakness was compounded by Van Buren's choice of Andrew Stevenson as minister to Great Britain. Stevenson, like Forsyth, was a loyal Jackson man, a thoroughgoing nationalist who lacked finesse and the ability to grasp the overall world situation and its implications for American diplomacy.

Forsyth and Stevenson faced the necessity of dealing with Palmerston, a master of diplomacy, self-assured, patient, and also quite capable of callous treatment of adversaries. Throughout 1839 and 1840 Palmerston was deeply immersed in extremely delicate and complex negotiations with Russia, Austria, and France on a Near East question. The balance of power favorable to Great Britain was threatened by Russian and French expansionism. How to bring about a firm agreement that would tie the hands of all parties required Palmerston's mastery. In 1840 France promoted a major crisis by supporting Mehemet Ali, pasha of Egypt, in his campaign against the sultan to the point of war, thereby isolating itself from Great Britain. The crisis did not come to an end until October.

Within the British cabinet some members sided with the French, so Palmerston had to tread with great care.[1]

During the summer and fall of 1840 it was necessary to avoid any conflagration of issues with the United States. Firmness was required in the face of developments on the borders of Upper and Lower Canada so as to bring home to the government in Washington that it could ill afford to close its eyes to its responsibility for putting down the unruly elements engaged in disturbing the peace of the two countries and at the same time dampen belligerent American spirits with evidence that London desired peace and friendly relations. The problem of relations with the United States was distinctly subordinated to the Near East question, and Anglo-American relations can only be understood if viewed in this broader context.

Stevenson, who had been on a visit to Paris, did not learn of the *Caroline* affair until early March 1838, when he read about it in the British press. He discussed it with Palmerston only informally because he had not yet received an official account from Washington. However, he feared that while the ministry was anxious for peace and sought to promote friendly relations it would not grant redress. The British press defended the action taken by the British forces, and Palmerston upheld the move by British troops as legitimate self-defense. Stevenson did not receive instructions until May. He then presented an official demand for redress to the foreign ministry. To the secretary of state he confided that he had found the outrage committed by the British troops "one of such signal atrocity" that he felt it his duty to represent it in that light and to make his note as strong as possible.

By direction of the president, in his note to Palmerston, he asked for redress and submitted a series of documents collected in Washington that provided evidence of the outrage. Stevenson included a summary of the important facts. A steamboat, the *Caroline* of Buffalo, cleared the port to carry passengers and freight to another port in New York. She was fired upon from the Canadian shore but was not damaged and so proceeded down the river and stopped briefly at Navy Island. She then docked at Schlosser at three o'clock in the afternoon on December 29. That evening twenty-three American citizens asked for lodging on the *Caroline* because there was no room at the local inn. At midnight four or five boats approached and shortly afterward a number of men, armed with pistols, swords, and cutlasses, came aboard and launched an attack on the unarmed crew. One crewman was killed, and several were injured. The attackers cut the *Caroline* loose from the dock, set her on fire, and then towed her into the current to drift. Stevenson charged that the outrage was planned by a portion of the British force at Chippewa.[2] The British defended their action on the ground that the vessel was piratical and had been delivering arms and men to the insurgent forces. Stevenson held that the vessel was not piratical, that under the law of nations foreign volunteers were subject to punishment only if they were found participating in the actual fighting, and even then they were to be treated as prisoners of war. In this instance a man had been killed within the boundaries of a friendly nation. A boat had been destroyed by troops of a foreign power. These, he maintained, were actions contrary to the law of nations, and the United States was entitled to redress.

Stevenson's statement, though factually correct, did not place the incident in context. Upper Canada lived in a state of alarm as armed insurgents, some of them Americans, with supplies from the United States, conducted raids, causing loss of life and destruction of property. Given the failure of officials in New York to stop the traffic, the British officer had concluded that he had no choice but to take action and he saw it as self-defense. This was the British point of view and became the official position.

Palmerston waited three weeks before acknowledging Stevenson's note and receipt of the scores of documents that the American government had forwarded. He said no more than that the British government would give them the most careful attention. Stevenson made no protest for the delay, as the months passed and the administration in Washington did not press.

The attack on the *Caroline* sparked fires of revenge, and in the spring of 1838 organizations dedicated to an invasion of Canada mushroomed. The feeling in the towns of upper New York accorded with those expressed by the Rochester *Democrat*: "In recording this horrid tragedy we dare not give utterance to our feelings: but we must say that if this outrage be not speedily avenged—not by simpering diplomacy—BUT BY BLOOD our national honor deserves the indignity it has received."[3] Hundreds of citizens joined the Sons of Liberty and Hunters Lodges. Some estimates of the number enrolled in the Hunters Lodges place the figure as high as two hundred thousand, but Albert Corey, who has written the most reliable account of the movement, accepted the more conservative number of from forty to fifty thousand. Regiments were organized, arms collected, and a series of raids on Canadian cities and towns launched. None of these proved successful, but the Canadian Refuge Relief Association, of Lockport, New York, did succeed in destroying the British steamboat, the *Sir Robert Peel*, on May 28, 1838.[4]

The reckless spirit that burst forth on the Canadian-American frontier alerted responsible statesmen in both London and Washington to the danger that further collisions would embroil the two nations in a war that neither party wanted. Public opinion in both countries decried extremism. Leading newspapers in the United States demanded that the government send armed forces to the frontier to suppress the filibustering. The *New York Courier and Enquirer* wrote of the destruction of the *Sir Robert Peel* that it was "disgraceful to our national character, and pregnant with consequences of the most serious import."[5]

President Van Buren was no less convinced that every effort should be made to dampen the threatened conflagration. The new governor general of Canada, the Earl of Durham, was equally determined to restore peace, and he combined friendly gestures toward Americans with warnings to Van Buren that he was determined to protect the lives and property of British subjects. Van Buren, in his message to Congress on January 5, 1838, called for strengthening the neutrality legislation. The neutrality act of 1818 provided penalties for a series of unneutral actions but did not give the president authority to take measures to prevent the actions before they took place. Congress emasculated much of the bill presented, but the new law did grant the president authority to order the military forces to suppress unneutral activities.[6] Van Buren made good use of the limited power granted to him. He appointed Major General Winfield Scott commander of the forces on the Canadian frontier. Scott was firm in his denunciation of all filibustering expeditions and did much to restore peace. Van Buren held the view that the disputes that arose largely because of the difficulty of effectively governing remote areas and people of an ungovernable disposition should not be allowed to destroy the larger interest that both nations had at stake in friendly relations.

Other incidents occurred on the border of Upper Canada in the wake of the *Caroline*. On April 14, 1839, the steamboat *United States* left the port of Ogdensburg, New York, to sail up the St. Lawrence River to the Great Lakes. Prior to leaving, the captain of the boat, Whitby, was informed by a person to be trusted that if he went into Prescott, on the Canadian side, his boat would in all probability be fired upon. On sailing up the channel, on the American side, he was fired upon as he passed Prescott. During the firing there was loud cheering from persons on the dock. Proceeding further, some twelve miles up the river past Brockville, the *United States* was again subjected to fire, and the American authorities had reason to believe that the firing was done under orders of a British soldier.[7]

One month later, on May 16, the American ship, *G. P. Weeks* of Oswego, cleared from that port and set out for Brockville on the Canadian side. On approaching Brockville the captain saw a large crowd was gathered on the wharf. After pulling alongside the dock, he delivered the bill of lading for the goods to be landed and received in return a permit to land the goods. Still on board was an artillery gun to be delivered to Ogdensburg. The people assembled on the dock attempted to seize the gun but were prevented from doing so. At this point a detachment of troops arrived, took station on the boat, and protected it. However, shortly after the customs collector from Prescott appeared upon the scene and seized the vessel on the ground that it had a gun aboard. The gun was taken on shore, the American flag was lowered, and the British Union Jack raised in its place. In reporting the incident to Palmerston, Stevenson commented on the fine behavior of the British troops and was especially complimentary to the British officers, but he also declared the action of the British custom's official outrageous and illegal. Incidents of this nature, he wrote, delayed the re-establishment "of that neighborly confidence between the inhabitants of the two countries (which the Governments of both are sincerely anxious to promote) . . ."[8]

The British were obviously impatient with Stevenson's frequent badgering protests. In the summer of 1839 the ministry faced far more important difficulties than minor problems with the United States. They were particularly concerned about Russia's advances in Turkey, the civil war in Spain, and the heated debate over the Corn Laws at home. Parliament was in session until September.

Stevenson acknowledged that Palmerston had good reasons for his delay in responding.

When the response came, Palmerston's answer on the question of the actions taken by the customs official at Brockville disturbed Stevenson. He saw in it a sharp reversal of attitude and thought it was intended to serve as a reply to the *Caroline* protest, as well as the more recent episode. Palmerston not only defended the seizure of the American boat but he censured Stevenson for taking upon himself a pronouncement as illegal the act of the British customs official. The American minister, as a foreigner, was out of order in assuming such a knowledge of the law of another country as to take upon himself "arbitrarily to pronounce such a seizure illegal and vexatious." Moreover, the American officer, Colonel Wirth, at Ogdensburg, had actually proceeded with an armed force into British territory to demand the restitution of the vessel and he had made the demand by a letter written in an offensive tone and style. Should American officers in the future conduct themselves in the manner of Colonel Wirth then, Palmerston warned, "those officers will become responsible for the hostile collisions between the two countries to which such proceedings must inevitably lead." He ended his highly charged declaration with a sharp censure of the United States for allowing "offenders of the worst description to congregate in American territory and to sally forth from thence in order to commit within the British borders the most atrocious crimes." He declared that it was the duty of Her Majesty's Government to protect the lives and property of her subjects "at all risks and at whatever consequences."[9] In his reply to this note Stevenson challenged Palmerston's interpretation of the law, stating that the gun present, which had been used as the justification for the seizure of the vessel, was destined for an American port. Stevenson saw nothing in Colonel Wirth's letter that was insulting to Her British Majesty and given the gross insult to the American flag, Stevenson called Wirth's conduct most understandable.[10]

The incidents in western New York followed an outbreak of violence in the disputed territory between Maine and New Brunswick. Late in 1838 Canadian lumberjacks moved into the valley of the Aroostook River and proceeded to cut timber. The governor of Maine dispatched an agent to investigate. The agent was seized and sent to prison. Thereupon, troops from Maine marched into the area with the aim of driving out the Canadians. This frontier fray quickly gained the name of the Aroostook War.

Congress, in turn, authorized the president to call out fifty thousand volunteers and appropriated ten million dollars for defense. Fortunately, the administration sought peace rather than war and instructed General Winfield Scott to arrange a truce. Scott succeeded in having the governor of Maine and the lieutenant governor of New Brunswick enter an agreement providing that Maine should hold the Aroostook valley, with British authorities continuing to retain the valley of the upper reaches of the St. John River. President Van Buren demonstrated firmness in the crisis, announcing that the boundary laid out in the Treaty of 1783 must be upheld unless Maine consented to a new boundary or unless the American construction of that treaty was found to be erroneous.

When Stevenson received a report of these developments, he took the cue from Forsyth that the administration hoped to negotiate and he accordingly appealed to Palmerston. He feared that the Tory leaders, Peel and Wellington, would come to power and their hostility toward the United States might lead to war. To Forsyth, in Washington, Stevenson offered the advice that the United States should be prepared: "that best policy was to be able to do injury to any hostile quarter." "My own opinion," he wrote, "ever has been and now is that the best and only security of our country, is to be found in the firmness of its councils, and its ability to resist and punish injuries come from what quarter they may." The accounts of hostilities in the press, he reported, had caused great excitement in Parliament. He feared that unless negotiations took place shortly the controversy would become even more heated as repeated collisions took place.[11]

Border incidents in upper New York and Maine would have sufficed to nourish public feelings of hostility and tension between London and Washington. In many respects American relations to the slave trade and British policy concerning American vessels carrying slaves from one port to another within the United States and driven by weather or slave revolt into British ports in the West Indies provided even more explosive questions. Just as within the United States, slavery itself was a highly moral issue capable of generating emotional crusades, so it was in foreign affairs. Strong antislavery feelings swept England during the decade, and opposition to slavery in France was only slightly less vibrant. From time to time American diplomats encountered denunciations of slavery as barbarous, and no aspect of American society contributed more to lowering European estimates of the republic. Great Britain led the was in suppressing the slave trade and sought to have the United States and the nations of western Europe join in her efforts.

When the founding fathers drafted the Constitution in 1787, they banned the importation of slaves into the United States after 1808. Strong feelings on the subject continued, and in 1820 Congress declared the slave trade to be piracy. This was the severest measure taken by any country up to that time. In 1824 the United States and Great Britain negotiated a convention for its suppression that included the right of each nation to search the ships of the other. However, after the Senate crippled the agreement with amendments, including a provision exempting the coast of North America from surveillance, the British withdrew approval. By this time southern slavery defenders were determined to prevent any agreement with the British. In the diplomatic exchanges then and later the United States based its opposition on the point of search, a convenient argument sanctified by the old issue of impressment.

In 1831 and again in 1834 American ships forced into the West Indies led to the freeing of the slaves on board. The two ships, the *Comet* and the *Encomium*, engaged in carrying slaves from Virginia to New Orleans, were compelled to put into Nassau, where the slaves were set free. Stevenson, carrying out instructions, demanded payment for the loss of property. Palmerston was no less vigorous in his opposition. In 1838 Stevenson proposed an agreement that would avoid future cases. This project was the work of Secretary of State Forsyth. Stevenson's note began with the fatuously phrased proposal that Great Britain should refrain from "forcing liberty upon such American slaves as hereafter may be forced by stress of weather or unavoidable contingency within British Colonial Ports near the United States." The proposal also called on the British to place stranded Negroes "in a fortification or other place under military command for temporary safe keeping until the owner could provide the means of reshipment without unnecessary delay." Stevenson offered to consider any other proposal by which the colonial authorities would be prevented from interfering "with this species of property belonging to citizens of the United States."[12]

Palmerston could not resist the opportunity to place the minister and the government of the United States in an awkward position. The proposal, he said, to use force to cause slaves to choose bondage was scarcely consistent with the known principles of human nature. To ask the British to pass a law preventing British courts from freeing American slaves was intolerable. "Such a law would be so entirely at variance with every principle of the British Constitution, that no Government could venture to propose it to Parliament and no Parliament would agree to adopt it." British law, said Palmerston, must apply in British colonial ports. Regarding putting slaves under military guard, he said, this would be so repugnant to feelings of British officers and men of the British army "that Her Majesty's Government would be extremely unwilling to call upon Her Majesty's troops to perform it."[13]

In May 1839 the British paid $23,500 for the slaves taken on the *Comet* and the *Encomium*, but otherwise they firmly resisted. They knew that Americans were engaged in the slave trade and that the American government had lost all interest in taking effective measures. The British commissioners charged with enforcing the prohibition of the trade provided a strong indictment of Nicholas P. Trist, the American consul in Havana. Trist was also serving as Portuguese consul, and the Portuguese were among the worst offenders. According to the British commissioners, Trist repeatedly cleared ships equipped to carry slaves and bound for African ports where no other trade was carried on. The commissioners also held that Americans owned slave ships and operated them by employing Spanish and Portuguese crews.[14]

These ships, sailing off the coast of Africa and flying the American flag, undermined British efforts to suppress the slave trade. Late in 1840 four ships flying the American flag were seized by the British. On receiving this information Stevenson assured Secretary of State Forsyth that he had presented the subject in the strongest manner to Her Majesty's Government. The American brig, *Douglas*, of Massachusetts, was seized and detained by a British naval vessel in October 1839. A few days after presenting this case to Palmerston, the American minister reported two more seizures. Deploring the interference with American vessels, Stevenson took the position that Great Britain had no lawful right to search or detain an American ship and that it was wholly immaterial "whether the vessels be equipped for, or actually engaged in, slave traffic or not, . . ."[15] Palmerston delayed replying to Stevenson's complaint.

On April 16 Stevenson expressed dismay over the failure of Palmerston to respond and included in his note four more cases of American ships searched and detained off the coast of Africa. Further delay in bringing an end to British interference with American commerce must, he warned, interrupt the amicable relations of the two countries.[16]

Finally, in the middle of May, Palmerston informed Stevenson that orders had been issued to commanders of ships engaged in suppressing the traffic to avoid any interference with American vessels. Palmerston complained that efforts to suppress the slave trade were rendered ineffective by the practice of some nations of carrying on the trade under the American flag and by the building of ships for this trade in the United States. He expressed the hope that some way could be found to determine the true character of the ships and he held that the right existed to determine this by examination of a ship's papers. The flag a ship flew offered no assurance as to its actual identity.[17] Stevenson immediately denied the right to examine a ship's papers. The United States, he said, could not consent to British naval captains having the authority to decide whether or not a ship flying the American flag was an American ship.

On August 5 Palmerston forwarded a lengthy note giving the findings of the admiralty concerning the seizure and detention of the *Douglas*. The facts that emerged placed the incident in a radically different light than the account Stevenson had presented. The British captain on boarding the *Douglas* found seven Spaniards aboard and discovered that the ship was headed for a point in Africa where only the slave trade was carried on. The ship's papers showed that it was consigned to a well-known slave trader, who was on board. Two of this Spaniard's vessels had recently been condemned for participation in the slave trade. On examination of the hatches, the British captain found she was outfitted for the slave trade. Given these facts, the captain detained the *Douglas* for eight days. Palmerston held that the detention accorded with the agreement reached by an American naval captain and a British commander. Had she been sent to the United States, Palmerston believed, she would have been condemned and if she had been sent to Sierra Leone to be tried by the mixed commission for the suppression of the trade, the evidence was so strong that the *Douglas* was, in fact, a Spanish enterprise that she would have been condemned as a Spanish slaver. The United States attributed the death of three crew members to having been detained in a hot climate, but the British investigation revealed that the ship remained in the African seas for two months after being released. Two other charges were likewise refuted. The American captain, not the British captain, had hauled down the American flag, and the prize crew had brought its own provisions and not taken those of the *Douglas*, as alleged.[18]

In a second note concerning the detention of the *Iago*, Palmerston cited a formal agreement entered into by the commanding officer of British naval forces off the coast of Africa and the commanding officer of the United States vessel sent to suppress the slave trade. They had agreed to detain all vessels under the United States flag found to be fully equipped for and engaged in the slave trade. Stevenson had not been notified of this agreement. Palmerston explained that the British, in detaining two American vessels, had acted in accordance with this agreement. However, he explained, there would be no further detentions because the British had issued positive orders in February not to detain any American ship. In conclusion he delivered a sharp rebuke, stating that Her Majesty's Government could not bring itself to believe "that the Government of Washington can seriously and deliberately intend that the flag and the vessels of the Union shall continue to be, as they now are, the shelter under which the malefactors of all countries perpetuate with impunity crimes which the laws of the Union stigmatize as piracy and punish with death." Unless the United States entered into some agreement similar to that negotiated by the two naval officers the end could only be "that the slave trade will be carried on exclusively under the shelter of the flag and by the special protection of the Executive Government of that nation whose legislative was among the first to pronounce the crime infamous . . ."[19]

The controversy over slave ships reached its climax in 1841, at the very time that the McLeod case threatened to bring about war. McLeod, a Canadian, had boasted, it was alleged, that he had killed one of the crew members of the *Caroline*, and he was consequently arrested and arraigned for trial in the state of New York. His arrest inflamed the British press and public opinion, and there was widespread talk of war should McLeod be found guilty and sentenced to execution. In the midst of this excitement Palmerston sent a note to Stevenson wholly defending the British action in the *Caroline* affair. In the House of Commons one member had denounced McLeod's impressment and warned that even at that moment he might have lost his life. Henry S. Fox, British minister in Washington, received instructions to ask for his passport if McLeod was executed.[20] Secretary of State Daniel Webster did make two efforts to free McLeod. He sent word to Governor Seward of New York that if he would order the case transferred to a federal court the president would issue an order to have the case discontinued. Seward refused. Webster then presented evidence to the New York court that Great Britain had assumed responsibility for the destruction of the *Caroline* and consequently the New York court lacked jurisdiction. Again he failed. The New York court maintained that it had the right to try McLeod.[21] At this time the ministry had discouraged discussion of the case in Parliament and had been relieved of alarm when it received word that the attorney general of the United States had been instructed to release McLeod once the trial was over. This proved to be a false report. As it turned out, McLeod offered the alibi that he was far removed from the scene at the time of the incident, and the court ruled in his favor and released him.

The accumulated tensions of three years of heated controversy found release in the autumn of 1841 with the retirement from office of Palmerston and Stevenson. The new foreign minister, Lord Aberdeen, brought to his office a disposition the very opposite of Palmerston's truculent traits. And the hard-working but churlish Stevenson, always fearful of failing to please his superiors in Washington, was replaced by Edward Everett, a man of cosmopolitan tastes, versed in literature, and an admirer of much that was British. Unlike Stevenson, he had the good fortune of having Daniel Webster as his superior and not Forsyth, a man of very limited views and myopic vision.

A change took place at once. In a letter to Everett on December 23 Aberdeen disclaimed all right to search, detain, or in any manner interfere with American ships whether they were engaged in the slave trade or not.[22] Thereby, Aberdeen closed the door to further incidents such as those that had taken place recently; also it appeared that he was repudiating the old practice of impressment. Time and again since the War of 1812 the United States had sought an agreement renouncing this practice. Everett expressed delight, noting that the foreign minister now restricted former pretensions to boarding only vessels strongly suspected of belonging to other nations and flying the American flag falsely. Some months later the British decided to indemnify the owners of the *Tigris*, which brought to a close a case of long standing.[23]

On the final day of 1841 Aberdeen informed Everett of a decision that proved to be a major turning point in the relations of the two countries. The British government decided to send a special envoy to the United States to seek a settlement of all outstanding issues. It selected Lord Ashburton, the well-known banker with an American wife and long-term connections with the former National Bank and other business enterprises, and known for his cordial feelings toward the United States. The selection of Ashburton offered assurance that the London government strongly desired a settlement.

While Ashburton and Secretary of State Webster were in the midst of their negotiations, another incident took place. An American ship, the *Creole*, owned in Virginia, was carrying 135 slaves to New Orleans. Not far from Cuba a number of slaves revolted, took control of the ship, and sailed to Nassau. There the governor sent some twenty African soldiers aboard. The American consul was called before the governor and his council and was told that there was to be an investigation of the murders that had taken place on board the *Creole*, and if the allegations proved correct, then the American secretary of state would be asked if the United States desired to have these men turned over to them. Once this had taken place, the slaves still aboard the *Creole* would be set free.

Everett, the Massachusetts Whig, had defended slavery on more than one occasion and was a bitter critic of the abolitionists. He took up this case apparently without qualms. The United States launched a vigorous protest, holding that the *Creole* had been forced into port by boats manned by civilians and the British forces should have prevented this from taking place. The *Creole*, Everett maintained, should have been restored to the control of its regular crew and permitted to resume its voyage to New Orleans. Nor did the British authorities have the right to apply British law on board a foreign ship. Everett stressed that the captain of a ship must have the authority over the passengers aboard or all sea-going commerce would be in jeopardy.[24] Aberdeen, however, ruled that slavery was illegal within the British empire, and any slaves setting foot on British soil were immediately free. The impassioned British public would not have tolerated any decision that appeared to condone an institution they viewed as barbarous. In the United States the antislavery people expressed delight, while southern slavery defenders burst forth in denunciation.

The Webster-Ashburton negotiations took four months. Each party to these negotiations entertained specific aims as to boundary questions and each labored under apprehensions as to what the legislative branch would approve. Party rivalry in both countries could undo what sober and prudent judgment dictated, since neither the administration of Sir Robert Peel nor that of John Tyler was free to ignore popular prejudices and strongly held convictions. Tyler and Webster had launched an important propaganda campaign, supported with money from an executive fund authorized by Congress. The man in charge of the campaign, O. J. Smith,

> converted editors of newspapers and local political leaders by private interviews, by confidential correspondence, by articles written under a non de plume in a strategically placed religious journal, and by memorials printed and extensively circulated and signed, addressed to the governor of the state and the legislature, asking that the boundary dispute be brought to an early conclusion by a negotiation for a conventional line.[25]

Webster and Ashburton did not haggle by preferment but out of political prudence, and their negotiations occupied them from early April to early August. Both had to convince their respective publics that they had fought manfully for every advantage and secured the best bargain possible. These considerations did not nullify the fact that both governments prized a settlement more highly than they did any one point in dispute. There were exceptions to this. Great Britain could not have yielded territory that would have barred her from having a free passage from the coast to Quebec, and the United States could not have sacrificed the Aroostook valley. Both Ashburton and Webster covered their tracks by sharp bargaining, but they never lost sight of the importance of an overall settlement.

Because this was so, the two men devoted much of their efforts to preparing the way for acceptance of the final agreement by their respective governments. Ashburton maintained a frequent and regular correspondence with Lord Aberdeen, in London, warning him that not all British aims were attainable, while Webster busied himself overcoming the resistance of the state of Maine, in cultivating public opinion, and in nursing Senate predilections toward a favorable reception of the final outcome. In his letters to Aberdeen, Lord Ashburton gave a careful account of the obstacles he faced, while Webster arranged for the representatives of Maine to meet with Ashburton, overcame their resistance with a map, provided by Professor Jared Sparks, on which Professor Sparks had drawn a boundary on the basis of a map he had seen in Paris that supposedly showed the lines drawn by Benjamin Franklin at the time of the peace negotiations in 1782. The map allotted to Maine much less of the territory in dispute than the state was convinced rightfully belonged to her. Webster also spent secret service funds made available by President Tyler to influence the press in favor of final approval of the treaty.[26] These shrewd calculations served a good cause, one that both men were determined to achieve, namely a settlement that squared with the interests of both countries, that would win general approval and enjoy the confidence of both countries.

The northeastern boundary provided the most severe test. The people of Maine had recently discovered that the Aroostook valley offered the finest agricultural land in the area.[27] Maine's consent was necessary to any settlement, and Ashburton learned early that it would be futile to insist on cession of the Aroostook. He was no less aware that any settlement that deprived the British of the area providing a route from the coast to Quebec would be unacceptable to his government. Aberdeen, prior to drafting his instructions, consulted four military experts, and they laid down the dicta that a route that could be used at all seasons was essential to the defense of Canada and particularly Quebec.[28] The St. Lawrence River, the usual transit route for supplies, was inaccessible during winter months. But the exact location of the line that would be most desirable furnished a subject for long debate in London. The cabinet had been ready to give Ashburton great leeway, but at the last moment the Duke of Wellington submitted a memorandum insisting that Great Britain was entitled to the whole course of the St. John River and that the boundary should not be drawn close to the St. Lawrence River.[29] Considering his prestige, Wellington could not be ignored. However, neither Aberdeen nor Ashburton yielded wholly to his dicta. The debate on Ashburton's instructions continued after his departure from London, and Ashburton received revised instructions after his arrival in the United States. These dealt wholly with the question of the Maine boundary, and Ashburton was informed that it was desirable that Great Britain retain the district between the St. John and St. Lawrence rivers. At all costs American settlements must be kept at a distance from Quebec. Ashburton had his own ideas as to what was necessary and also what was attainable. He was intent on holding the Madawaska settlements, but he yielded when the Maine representatives threatened to walk out when he met with them.[30] It was the one point in the final settlement that Ashburton later looked back upon with regret. The final line in the treaty gave the British control of the military route that they had laid down as a *sine qua non*, and the Americans gained the valuable Aroostook valley. According to Ashburton's view, the Maine delegation had only yielded because of Professor Spark's map that had shown the validity of British claims to much of the area in dispute.[31] Of the total area in controversy, the United States received some seven thousand square miles and Great Britain some five thousand square miles.

The other major boundary question was the line from Lake Superior to the Lake of the Woods. This area was already known to Americans as one rich in minerals. Ashburton appears to have either been uninformed on this or to have belittled the report, for he professed to see the territory as of no great importance. What was important to him was the drawing of a line that would prevent future disputes. The United States gained an immense territory of sixty-five hundred square miles, with one of the most valuable iron ore deposits in the world. The fact that the area was completely unsettled probably swayed Ashburton. At least the absence of any settlement simplified the solution.

Article 10 of the final treaty provided for extradition of those charged with crimes of a nonpolitical nature but excluded fugitive slaves and military deserters. The importance of this article lay in the recent history of border disturbances in the area stretching from Lake Ontario to Detroit. Criminals readily escaped court trials by fleeing across the border to the country where they were assured of not being apprehended with violating the laws. The ease with which they escaped clearly encouraged illegal activity. After the insurrection in Canada in 1837 many who had participated fled to the United States, including William Lyon Mackenzie, the leader of the movement. The lieutenant governor of Upper Canada, Sir Francis Bond Head, requested the governor of New York to return him. The request was denied. The United States deplored the situation quite as much as the officials of Upper Canada, and Secretary of State Forsyth had proposed to the British minister in Washington the opening of negotiations in the hope of reaching an extradition agreement.[32] Palmerston promptly prepared a draft of a treaty on the subject, but no further move was made until Ashburton arrived.

Webster and Ashburton labored to find a satisfactory agreement. The British were adamant on the question of fugitive slaves. Webster did not contest this point. Both agreed to omit deserters from the armed forces, although this had been a matter of importance to the provincial authorities because as many as ten percent of their troops had deserted.[33] They also agreed to omit political offenders from the list of those who could be extradited. On the eve of the final negotiations, Sir Charles Bagot, governor-general of Canada, wrote to Ashburton, stating that if something could be done to facilitate the giving up of each other's delinquents "you will have done more for the peace and quiet of These Provinces than I perhaps shall ever be able to do."[34] The treaty, signed a few days later on August 9, provided what Bagot had hoped for.

The long and heated controversy over the slave trade embraced not only the difficult question of the right of search but southern opposition to suppression of the trade. Strong feelings rendered it less amenable to negotiation. Americans equated British efforts to have the United States accord it the right to search ships flying the American flag with abject demands to police the seas and reduce the oceans to a British lake. Webster made it clear at once that he would not discuss the British proposal, which called for no more than the right to inspect a ship's papers to determine its nationality. The British were prepared to accord Americans the same limited right of search. The South viewed British efforts to suppress the slave trade as an attack on slavery itself and vigorously opposed an agreement. However, opposition was not restricted to the southern states. Lewis Cass, former governor of Michigan, and at the time of the Ashburton-

Webster negotiations United States minister to France, sought to have France reject a treaty with Great Britain providing for the right to search, charged the British with using the suppression of the slave trade as a cover-up for its own insatiable urge to dominate the seas, and eventually attacked the Webster-Ashburton treaty because it did not include a provision explicitly denying to the British the right of search.[35] For this last action Cass was recalled and relieved of his post.

Webster committed the United States to stricter enforcement of its own laws against those who engaged in the slave trade. The treaty itself included a provision obligating the United States to maintain a force of eighty guns off the African coast to seize ships flying the American flag that were engaged in the trade. This provision, as it turned out, did not prove effective, but it did serve to remove the controversial issue from disputes between the two countries.

The almost interminable controversy over the *Caroline* affair was not resolved. Ashburton stood on firm ground. The *Caroline* had supplied the rebels on Navy Island, a British possession, with arms to be used in the overthrow of British rule. Failure of the United States to put an end to this traffic meant that it devolved upon Great Britain to act in its own self-defense. The British envoy would only go so far as to express regret that the British foreign office had so long delayed replying to the American demands for redress. Webster chose to interpret this as an apology and was successful in silencing critics who seized on this point.

The treaty was approved by overwhelming votes in both the United States Senate and in Parliament but it did not lack critics, among them Thomas Hart Benton in the Senate and Palmerston in the House of Commons. Palmerston condemned the treaty on the ground that it yielded too much to the United States and he fully exploited the fact that Webster had withheld Spark's map from Ashburton until the negotiations were completed. Sir Robert Peel then revealed that the government had a copy of Mitchell's map, the authentic map used for marking the boundary by Richard Oswald, the British negotiator in 1782. This map was marked by boundaries that coincided completely with the claims the United States had first put forth. Aberdeen convinced Edward Everett that he had not known of the map until after negotiations were completed, although Palmerston had seen the map long before. Members of the House of Commons promptly lost interest in the debate and then passed a resolution congratulating Ashburton by a vote of 238 to 96. Everett believed that many of the negative votes could be explained as those of personal friends of Palmerston who did not wish to abandon him.

The weakness of the opposition offered testimony to the strong desire in both countries to set aside differences and avoid war. The issues that had separated the two nations were not trivial, but neither were they of a kind that involved security, economic well-being, or shifts in the world power configuration that would reduce the stature or the influence of either. The issues could only have achieved that degree of importance if permitted to drift and set off a chain of endless collisions. Stevenson and then Everett testified repeatedly that Great Britain did not seek war, that the British government was sincere in its expressions of friendliness and hopes for a peaceful resolution of the difficulties. The British minister in Washington repeatedly informed his superiors in the foreign office that the United States wished for peace even though the government sometimes found itself paralyzed in dealing with questions that were reserved to the states. Much has been written concerning Webster's newspaper campaign in favor of the treaty and his careful handling of Congress, and by implication it has appeared that he alone carried the day. His influence on the final approval of the treaty by the Senate cannot, of course, be measured, but it is worth noting that Webster's strongest argument was that an overall peace was of far greater importance than any one point in dispute. Here he was nourishing a sentiment that already widely prevailed.

The negotiations failed to settle two important questions before the two countries. Lord Ashburton had instructions to seek a settlement of the Oregon question, but Webster was unresponsive. Immediately upon the approval of the treaty, Lord Aberdeen proposed a second negotiation on this question. Edward Everett had suggested to Webster that he had good reason to believe that Great Britain would agree to surrendering the right of impressment provided the United States would agree to enter the Quadruple Treaty for the suppression of the slave trade. The Tyler administration had supported Cass in his efforts to have France refuse to ratify this treaty and dismissed Everett's suggestions.

NOTES TO CHAPTER VI

1. Charles Webster, *The Foreign Policy of Palmerston 1830–1841* (London: G. Bell & Sons, Ltd., 1951), Vol. II, pp. 689–94.
2. Andrew Stevenson to Forsyth, Apr. 14, 1838, Despatches from London, Roll 41.
3. Alastair Watt, "The Case of Alexander McLeod," *Canadian Historical Review*, June 1931, p. 112.
4. Albert B. Corey, *The Crisis of 1830-1842 in Canadian-American Relations* (New Haven: Yale University Press, 1941), pp. 37–43, 71.
5. Corey, *The Crisis of 1830–1842*, p. 83, quoting *National Intelligencer*, June 5, 1838.
6. Corey, *The Crisis of 1830–1842*, p. 55.
7. Stevenson to Forsyth, June 26, 1839. Enclosure Stevenson to Palmerston, June 22, 1839. Despatches from London, Roll 42.
8. Ibid., July 2, 1839.
9. Ibid., Sept. 28, 1839, Enclosure Palmerston to Stevenson, Sept. 19, 1839.
10. Ibid., Enclosure Stevenson to Palmerston, Sept. 26, 1839.
11. Ibid., Mar. 21, 1839.
12. Ibid., July 21, 1838, Enclosure Stevenson to Palmerston, July 10, 1838. Despatches from London, Roll 41.
13. Ibid., Nov. 5, 1838, Enclosure Palmerston to Stevenson, Sept. 10, 1838.
14. Stevenson to Forsyth, Roll 42 Jan. 22, 1840, Enclosure Palmerston to Stevenson, Dec. 31, 1839, and I. Kennedy & Campbell I. Dalrymple to Palmerston, Oct. 27, 1839.
15. Stevenson to Secretary of State Daniel Webster, Apr. 7, 1841, Despatches from London, Roll 44.
16. Ibid., Apr. 16, 1840.
17. Ibid., May 18, 1841.
18. Ibid., Aug. 18, 1841, Enclosure Palmerston to Stevenson, Aug. 5, 1841. Everett later detected an error on the part of Palmerston. The detention of the *Douglas* took place in October 1839, and the agreement entered into by the American naval captain was not made until March of 1840. Aberdeen then acknowledged that the British had been in the wrong. Webster did not press for payment because, while the British were in the wrong, the *Douglas* was a slave ship.
19. Ibid.
20. Ibid., p. 150.
21. Watt, "The Case of Alexander McLeod," *Canadian Historical Review*, June 1931, p. 155.
22. Edward Everett to Webster, Dec. 28, 1841. Despatches from London, Roll 45.
23. Ibid., Aberdeen to Everett, Mar. 17, 1842.
24. Ibid., Everett to Aberdeen, Mar. 1, 1842.
25. Frederick Merk in collaboration with Lois Bannister Merk, *Fruits of Propaganda in the Tyler Administration* (Cambridge: Harvard University Press, 1971), p. 9.
26. For a brief but useful discussion of Webster's dealings with the press, see Richard N. Current, *Daniel Webster and the Rise of National Conservatism* (Boston: Little, Brown and Company, 1955), pp. 122–26.

27. For a full and carefully documented analysis of how the Aroostook valley came to be viewed as valuable agricultural land, see Thomas Le Duc, "The Maine Frontier and the Northeastern Boundary Controversy," *American Historical Review*, Oct. 1947, pp. 30–41.

28. Wilbur Devereux Jones, "Lord Ashburton and the Maine Boundary Negotiations," *The Mississippi Valley Historical Review A Journal of American History*, Dec. 1953, pp. 480–81.

29. Ibid., pp. 479–80.
30. Ibid., pp. 486–87.
31. Ibid., p. 488.
32. Corey, *The Crisis of 1830–1842*, p. 171.
33. Ibid., p. 177.
34. Ibid., p. 179.
35. Lewis Cass to Webster, Feb. 15, 1842, Despatches from Paris, Roll 32. Cass, in Paris, campaigned vigorously to have the French government refuse to ratify the treaty. He not only sought to convince Foreign Minister Guizot, he published anonymously a pamphlet entitled "An Examination of the Question now in Discussion Between the American and British Governments concerning the Right of Search." Cass was assisted by Duff Green who was in Paris at the time. Green wrote a series of articles for the French *Journal of Commerce* contending that the purpose of England was "to monopolize and give greater value to her trade with Africa and India." The articles were entitled "England and America, Examination of the Causes and Probable Results of a War between These Two Countries." See St. George L. Sioussat, "Duff Green's 'England and the United States': With An Introductory Study of American Opposition to the Quintuple Treaty of 1841," *Proceedings of the American Antiquarian Society*, October, 1930.

Chapter VII

The Texas Question

The issues creating tension between Great Britain and the United States from 1837 to 1842 did not elicit widespread public excitement. Consequently, the administrations of Van Buren and Tyler enjoyed a considerable degree of latitude in their negotiations with the British. This was not so after the Webster-Ashburton Treaty. At no other time in the nation's history have domestic and foreign affairs become so intertwined and given rise to an international crisis of so great a magnitude. Texas and Oregon evoked powerful forces in domestic politics. Expansionism, proslavery feelings, and the rising tide of antislavery sentiment engulfed questions of foreign affairs. Political leaders could not sidestep the demands of determined protagonists. The presidential aspirants of 1844, Henry Clay and Martin Van Buren, tried to do so to their later grief. Indeed, to a large degree many political leaders sought to capitalize on the popular stirrings abroad in the land. The more conciliatory spirit of the earlier years gave way to fierce determination and deep distrust of foreign antagonists. Compromise was as difficult to achieve in foreign affairs as it was in domestic politics.

The basic cause of the difficulties lay in the absence of strong national power in some of the most promising and desirable strategic locations on the rim of civilization. Texas, California, and Oregon were as yet among the world's waste spaces, largely uninhabited, under the firm control of no one. All three areas attracted the attention of statesmen devoted to the advancement of national interests. The well-established and rich and powerful states lived in the grip of a vision of the future that exalted the growth of commerce and territorial expansion. Mexico's outlying territory in Texas and California, an area larger than western Europe, appeared to provide keys to future economic growth and greatness, and Mexico itself was too paralyzed by internal strife to develop or to control the territory. Oregon, stretching from the 42nd to the 54th parallels, was as yet a wilderness legally under joint occupation by the British and the Americans but in fact unoccupied except for the presence of hunters and trappers of the Hudson's Bay Company and the tiny settlements around the seaports. Beyond lay the Pacific, and in the 1840s the prospects of future trade with the Orient held the attention of enterprising men of commerce. China already attracted the entrepreneurs of London and Liverpool and their counterparts in Boston and Salem The opening of five Chinese ports to trade by the Treaty of Nanking in 1842, at the close of the Opium War, offered the excitement of new opportunities. Statesmen in Great Britain, France, and the United States entertained visions of a new era made opulent by the profitable exchange of the superfluities of mankind. Faced with vast new vistas of development, international rivalry accelerated.

On the edge of this scene lay Mexico, a country buffeted by violent factionalism, torn apart by diverse interests that had their roots in class structure, the Spanish heritage, and the religious establishment. It, too, offered great promises of trade and mineral wealth, and after Mexico achieved independence in 1821, the British and the French anticipated highly profitable economic relations. Trade grew, but the dreams of extracting rich minerals soon gave way to engineering difficulties, transportation barriers, and the internal disorders that made investment hazardous. The country was wracked by uncontrollable robber bands and ambitious military chieftains. In short, Mexico was on the verge of being unable to govern itself and it was more of a headache to Great Britain and France than a useful partner in commercial affairs and in counterbalancing the adventurous, ambitious, and at times swashbuckling American empire.

The prospect of a division of the waste places of the earth came at the time that both Great Britain and France faced internal problems and difficulties in Europe and the Middle East. The British suffered crop failures at home and a famine in Ireland. Relief for Ireland equaled the total budget of the American government. At the same time, England was immersed in a fight over factory legislation, Corn Laws, and the question of financing a Catholic university in Ireland.

Fights over the issue of tollgate charges in Wales and uprisings among the Welch wrenched the unity of the tight little island. The British government, after years of rivalry and conflict, had arranged an entente with France, but in the 1840s Louis Philippe and French Foreign Minister Guizot were under sharp attack for bowing to the British. The belligerence of the French was so great as to provoke exertions for defense of the British Isles, and Palmerston and Wellington charged the ministry of Robert Peel with shamelessly making concessions to both France and the United States. The Tory ministry of Peel was far from secure and teetered uneasily in the face of divisions in the party and attacks from the Whigs.

The situation in France was no better. Louis Philippe, as he faced threats of assassination, complained that he was the fairest game in the kingdom. Guizot, his foreign minister, labored under charges of knuckling under to the British. Red Republicans and Royalist reactionaries launched repeated campaigns to unseat the July republic. As in the case of Great Britain, France lived in constant anxiety over Russian threats of expansion in the Middle East, the instability in Italy, and the turmoil in Spain. Neither Great Britain nor France was free to devote full attention to the rapidly rising American empire that was on the verge of establishing its hegemony in the New World.

Politicians in each country had to take into account sporadic conflagrations of public feelings fixed on the evils of rivals. Yankeephobia in England had its counterpart in Anglophobia in the United States and France. Fortunately, Aberdeen in England and Guizot in France wanted peace and did not give way readily before ugly outbreaks of public feelings. Neither was an avowed expansionist, both dreaded war, and both were cautious statesmen who felt no need to exhibit a strident spirit. Both viewed the United States as a rival but both preferred friendly relations. They were good judges of their respective national interests and therefore preferred an independent Texas and disliked the prospect of American control of California.

Texas and the Oregon question need not have led to war or even a crisis. No leading statesmen wanted war. The Oregon question was within reach of early settlement. The annexation of Texas followed cautious efforts on the part of the British and the French to prevent it. Neither nation encouraged Mexico to take a belligerent stand and offered Mexico no hope of support in the event of war with the United States. And Mexico posed no real threat to either Texas or the

United States. Yet war with Mexico ensued, and relations with England hovered close to war over the Oregon question.

What brought about the crisis? Fears of British ambition were all the more real because so many Americans entertained the same ambitions themselves. Below the surface of diplomatic exchanges, public pronouncements, and newspaper editorializing was land hunger. Americans faced no foreseeable shortage of land; yet they were avaricious in their desire for more territory, since more territory would give them ports and push back the threat of powerful neighbors. The more immediate and more visible element in the high-level serious diplomatic exchanges was the drive for seaports, an objective that Americans knew was equally prized by the commercial-minded British.

These underlying forces complicated the lives of statesmen from Aberdeen to Tyler. James K. Polk, destined to play a major role, can hardly be said to have found the problems facing him complex. His own simple self-image owed much to his admiration for Andrew Jackson and to his placing decisiveness and unbending conduct highest in the demands he made upon himself. His able biographer, Charles Sellers, found him devious, and contemporaries learned that his silence in a conversation and his statements often had a double meaning. Yet, he was not inclined to conspiracy, and what others saw as deviousness undoubtedly appeared to Polk as discreetness. These qualities do not explain his diplomacy or his belief that the best way to win a controversy was to take advanced ground, give no appearance of compromise since compromise indicated weakness, and to appear immovable. This gave him a sense of rectitude; and if this should lead to war he was prepared to accept it, although he preferred peace. But Polk was little more than an accident viewed from a larger perspective. His singlemindedness did not accord with the nation as a whole and his was a troubled presidency.

In 1821 Stephen Austin led a group of three hundred families to Texas, where his father, by then deceased, had secured a grant to establish a colony. The decentralized federal regime of Mexico permitted the new inhabitants a large degree of autonomy. The prohibition against slavery and the requirement that settlers conform to the Roman Catholic Church posed no obstacle. Contract labor offered a substitute for Negro slavery and the secular-minded frontiersmen thought Texas worth a Catholic mass. In 1830, scenting future trouble, Mexico placed restrictions on American colonization and began to infringe on local autonomy. Its sins of omission were equally unsatisfactory, since Mexico failed to provide what Americans were accustomed to, namely public schools and local courts. Equally serious, the government in Mexico City paid no attention to the Texans' need for a market for their produce and failed to open channels of trade to Mexico itself, and at the same time imposed higher duties on imports.

The transformation of the Mexican political regime from its original decentralized structure to centralized control under the new leader, General Santa Anna, ran counter to the immigrants' expectations of home rule. Nor was this an idle threat, for troops made up of former convicts were dispatched to Texas to assure control from Mexico City. In 1832 the Texans drafted a memorial asking for repeal of immigration restrictions, reduction of the tariff, local government for the purpose of protecting land titles and courts, for its own militia to provide protection against Indians, and for the separation of Texas from the state of Coahuila. A year later Stephen Austin went to Mexico City to explain local grievances, only to be arrested. He became convinced that Santa Anna was bent on centralization. A Texas war party came into being. Hopes of reconciliation faded when intercepted letters showed clearly that Mexico had plans for military occupation.

In 1836 a war for independence ensued. The Mexican army triumphed in the famous battle of the Alamo, but later in that same year General Sam Houston surprised the Mexicans while they were enjoying a siesta at San Jacinto, and Santa Anna was captured. Faced with the threat of death, Santa Anna signed a treaty according Texas its independence. During the course of the war the United States took a position of neutrality, but the Texan cause enjoyed widespread popularity. Americans rallied to serve in the Texan army, funds were raised to aid the Texans, and finally an American general, E. P. Gaines, led a foray into Texas ostensibly to prevent Indians from siding with the Mexicans. The American neutrality law of 1818 was simply inadequate. American juries would not convict transgressors, and the popularity of the Texan cause, especially in the southern states, reduced neutrality to a near nullity. Yet, it was the Texans who won the war rather than American assistance.

In 1837 Texas applied for admission to the United States. President Martin Van Buren, mindful that annexation would erupt in a dangerous sectional clash over the slavery question, rejected the offer. Thereby time was allotted for the gradual emergence of Texas as an international issue.

The new republic began rich in territory, rich in ambition to expand, and rich in opportunities for land speculators and a few merchants. It had a population of 30,000, which grew to 164,000, including 24,000 slaves, by 1845. It had no past, little in the present, but as all believed, an important future. The government faced bankruptcy in the years ahead, and its currency declined in value to the point of near worthlessness. The capital shifted from Houston to Washington, a village with only a few houses; then to Austin, and finally back to Washington. Austin at the time was a clearing, whose only differentiation from its uninhabited surroundings was the presence of a few log cabins. Only the seaport of Galveston offered any of the amenities of a settled community. Yet foreign visitors, though depressed by the crudities of life, uniformily applauded the energy, enterprise, and determination of the hardy frontiersmen.

From the beginning, the population largely viewed itself as an adjunct of the United States; but, once embarked on independence, leaders such as Houston and Anson Jones were far from adverse to perpetuating the Texan republic. Mexico was too occupied at home to launch a major campaign of reconquest. A rebellion in Yucatan, the French blockade of 1838, frequent uprisings aimed at seizure of control of Mexico's government, and serious financial difficulties limited Mexican efforts to predatory raids. Three major ones occurred in 1842. War between Mexico and Texas did not cease—it merely languished. The Texans lived in expectation of a large-scale Mexican campaign, and this prospect plus the raids created a sense of insecurity that led to consideration of gaining the support of an outside power, if not the United States, then Great Britain and France.

Shortly after his arrival in Texas in 1837, the agent of France, Dubois de Saligny, reported that the new republic had "a fertile soil, a delightful climate, a geographical position most favorable to commerce." The Americans, he wrote, were "pitilessly pushing the Indian hordes before them" and "creating a civilization from a desert." The United States, he added, "for many years have considered Texas simply as a future addition to their already immense territory." He then raised the question whether it would be wise for France to negotiate a treaty with Texas. Would Texas "be likely long to remain separate from the United States?" Will not Texas, he asked, "whose lands adjoin the United States and whose inhabitants are Anglo-Americans, be in fact in a position of dependence?" "Will it not merely wait until the natural course of events makes it an acknowledged member and integral part of their federation?"[1]

Prospects of commerce, strategic interests in the Gulf of Mexico, and a desire to curb the further expansion of the United States led both Great Britain and France to take an interest in Texas. Early in 1839 the British foreign minister, Palmerston, instructed the British minister in Mexico, Pakenham, to make every effort to persuade the Mexican government to recognize the independence of Texas. To do otherwise would push Texas into the arms of the United States.[2] Respectively, the British appointed Captain Charles Elliot and the French appointed Alphonse Dubois de Saligny to represent them in Texas. Both worked energetically to promote commerce and to ward off annexation to the United States, but their home governments moved with caution, with Palmerston and Guizot avoiding commitments to either Mexico or Texas. Both statesmen faced internal problems that imposed a restraining influence.

Not until the autumn of 1843 did the Texas question become one of pressing importance. Several developments contributed to the crisis. Texas itself was in an almost desperate condition. In December 1842 the United States chargé d'affaires, Joseph Eve, wrote to Secretary of State Daniel Webster, "No man possessing the common feelings of humanity could hear them speak of their deporable condition without sympathizing with them." They believed, Eve reported, "that if they could have peace with Mexico, they would have but little difficulty in driving the Indians or compelling them to make peace, but that they cannot sustain themselves longer against the mode of war waged against them by Mexicans and Indians, unaided by men or money from this government, and that they will be compelled to abandon their homes and move to some place of more security."[3] In January 1843 the Texan chargé d'affaires in Washington sought to have the United States negotiate treaties with the various Indian tribes.[4] The Indians, he charged, were hostile to Texas. Present appearances, he noted, indicated the renewal of active hostilities between Texas and Mexico. These difficulties caused Texas to propose a triple mediation of difficulties with Mexico by Great Britain, France, and the United States.[5] The problems faced caused Texas to become more aggressive in seeking to have other powers protect her.

In spite of the instability Texas experienced growth and became ever more attractive to land speculators. By 1842 her exports had increased to $1,667,086. Americans, many of them men of political influence, invested in Texas lands. Among them were Thomas Gilmer, former governor of Virginia, Duff Green, a close associate of John C. Calhoun, Nicholas Biddle of the United States Bank, and Robert J. Walker, senator from Mississippi.[6] All were early advocates of the annexation of Texas.

Probably more important in pushing the Texas question to first place on President Tyler's agenda were reports from highly biased parties of British plans for Texas. Great Britain, and to a lesser extent France, favored a buffer state cutting off further American expansion, thereby avoiding having one powerful nation able to dictate to a large degree their relations with the New World. Both were dependent on imports of American cotton and saw an advantage in having a supplementary or alternative source in an independent Texas. Also, given the increasing dedication of the United States to a protective tariff, Texas as a low tariff market loomed important.

American proannexationists expanded these legitimate British concerns into a vast and diabolic conspiracy to rule the world. The British, having abolished slavery in the West Indies, it was charged, found that their colonies could not compete with areas where slavery existed. Sir Robert Peel had acknowledged the same before the House of Commons. The antislavery movement in England aimed at nothing less than the abolition of slavery everywhere. This provided a philanthropic shield for practical and zealous British imperialists who had plans for world domination. So ran the rhetoric of American annexationists.

This was the state of mind of proannexationists in the United States in the autumn of 1843, and their views were shared by President Tyler and Secretary of State Abel P. Upshur. Fear of British commercial rivalry could not rival the fears deliberately aroused of a Texas where the blacks were free, a place of refuge for fugitive slaves, a black republic akin to that of Haiti stirring up slave revolts in the United States.[7]

The obsession with British designs to bring about abolition in

Texas came to the fore in late 1843; proannexationist sentiment was strong well before then. Tyler favored annexation when he entered the presidency in 1841.[8] Andrew Jackson not only supported annexation but was so certain it would take place that before leaving the White House he tendered the governorship of Texas to Governor K. G. Burton of North Carolina.[9] Interest in annexation had languished in the intervening years but was not dead. With the resignation of Daniel Webster as secretary of state in 1843, Tyler was free to reopen the question and he hoped to strengthen his chances of re-election by carrying through the project. His appointment of Legaré, and upon Legaré's death, Abel P. Upshur, as secretary of state, committed him firmly to a cause he already cherished.

There could not have been a more opportune time for promoting annexation. Duff Green, Tyler's special agent in London, wrote to John C. Calhoun and then sent a copy to Upshur, warning them of an alarming development.[10] He had already written to Tyler telling him that Ashbel Smith, the Texan representative in London, was told in an interview with Aberdeen that Great Britain desired to prevent the annexation of Texas to the United States and that to accomplish that would recommend a loan for the abolition of slavery.[11] One month later the United States chargé d'affaires in Texas, William S. Murphy, wrote to Upshur informing him of further supposed evidence of British intrigue. His close friend, Anson Jones, Texas secretary of state, had shown to Murphy his correspondence with Captain Charles Elliot, the British chargé. He enclosed copies. These told of the successful negotiation of an armistice between Mexico and Texas promoted by Captain Elliot. Santa Anna, again in power in Mexico, had laid down the condition that Texas must recognize Mexican sovereignty, but the Britisher also contended that this was a face-saving move and that if a cessation of hostilities took place Mexico was now prepared to recognize Texan independence.[12]

Chargé Murphy interpreted this British move as a sinister effort on the part of the British to abolish slavery in Texas, an aim they could not publicly avow in the face of Texan opinion, but an aim that had the support of Texan President Houston. Murphy cited the letter he had received some weeks before from Upshur, quoting a report from Duff Green that a Texan abolitionist had submitted a plan to Aberdeen whereby a loan would be extended to Texas for the purpose of compensating slaveholders in return for freeing their slaves. The British financiers extending the loan would be paid in grants of land. According to this report, Aberdeen had agreed to guarantee the payment of interest on the loan.[13] An additional reason for fearing British intrigue was that Houston and his cabinet were constantly seeking to bring about a breach with the United States.[14] The British, with the connivance of Houston, were prepared to reestablish Mexican sovereignty and abolish slavery in Texas.

Charges of British interference were highly useful to the annexationists. They believed that the opposition of antislavery people in the North would be overruled by business interests enjoying profitable relations with the southern states who placed the profits from cotton sales and the southern market above conscience. The annexationists set out to exploit distrust and fear of Great Britain. Certainly both Great Britain and France desired an independent Texas, but the annexationists greatly exaggerated both British and French willingness to pay a high price in order to achieve their goal.

Aberdeen did take steps in the hope that British and French influences could bring about the permanent independence of Texas but he was cautious and clearly did not give this aim a high priority. The question came before Aberdeen in the summer of 1841. James Hamilton, Texas agent in London, wrote a series of letters to Aberdeen presenting all the arguments as to why Great Britain should assist Texas and oppose American annexation.[15] Aberdeen was sufficiently interested that he presented the question to his cabinet. Henry Gaulburn, chancellor of the exchequer, raised objections to Hamilton's plea for a loan. He asked if a loan would not arouse the hostility of Americans who, he noted, were Great Britain's best customers.[16] Hamilton's proposal received a cool reception.

Aberdeen appears to have kept the Texas question at a distance. His instructions to Pakenham simply advised Mexico to accept Texas as an independent nation, and accompanied this with the firm warning that Great Britain would remain strictly neutral if Mexico became involved in war with Texas or the United States.[17]

In the summer of 1843 Duff Green wrote his famous letter to Upshur, reporting what he had supposedly learned from the Texan representative in London, Ashbel Smith. There is no record of what Smith said to Green, but Smith's letters to Aberdeen and to the secretary of State in Texas are revealing. In the first letter Ashbel

Smith affirmed that Aberdeen had never shown any disposition to interfere with slavery in Texas. The report Smith sent to Texas of his conversation with Aberdeen differed. When he had asked Abereden if it were true "that Great Britain was preparing to secure the abolition of slavery in Texas by making a money compensation to the slaveholders," Aberdeen spoke of the "well known policy and wish of the British Government to abolish slavery everywhere," including Texas. He added "that there was no disposition on the part of the British Government to interfere improperly" and would give Texas no cause to complain. Whether he would consent "to make such compensation to Texas as would enable the slaveholders to abolish slavery," Aberdeen reserved for the future.[18]

Aberdeen did not hide the fact that Great Britain preferred the abolition of slavery. Given the passionate antislavery views that prevailed in England at the time, a fact well known to the American government, Aberdeen's observation was a statement of fact and not a declaration of intention. Duff Green chose to see in it the latter and informed both Upshur and Calhoun that the British were ready to interfere and extend a loan to bring about abolition.

Edward Everett, American minister in London, saw Ashbel Smith frequently but he had heard nothing that was worthy of reporting on the subject. Late in October 1843 he received instructions from Secretary of State Upshur to make a direct inquiry. Aberdeen professed to be glad to discuss the question and he cited reports in American newspapers alleging that annexation of Texas was necessary to counteract the designs of England. He told Everett that if annexation "were undertaken on any such grounds, it would be wholly without provocation." England, said Aberdeen, "had long been pledged to encourage the abolition of the Slave trade and of Slavery as far as her influence extended and in every proper way; but had no wish to interfere in the internal concerns of foreign governments." Aberdeen went out of his way to discuss Hamilton's appeal for a loan, acknowledged that he at first favored it, explained that his colleagues deemed the loan "wholly inexpedient," and he stated that the loan had no connection with the abolition of slavery. Aberdeen likewise told of his meeting during the previous summer with a group of American abolitionists.[19]

Everett, aware of the excitement aroused in the United States and the importance of his inquiry, took notes during the interview and after writing his dispatch asked Aberdeen to check it for accuracy, which Aberdeen did. On this occasion Aberdeen affirmed in even more vigorous terms that the British government had never made any proposition to Texas on the slavery question and had no intention of so doing.

In a private letter to Upshur, Everett sought to throw further light on the attitude of the ministry. It was true that the public favored abolition, but there were great variations in how far they were willing to go to achieve the goal. No British government could avoid subscribing to the general sentiment, but this did not mean that the government was prepared to act. He noted: "The action of the present government has, in this respect, been frequently of a restraining rather than of a stimulating character." If the secretary of state would examine the record, Everett believed he, too, would conclude "that they are disposed in this, as in all other questions to resist sudden change and are disinclined to endanger the public peace, for the promotion of ends recommended by their opponents on liberal principles."[20]

Aberdeen had repudiated Duff Green's charges and firmly committed his government to a hands-off policy regarding slavery in Texas. He had not obligated himself or the British government to refrain from seeking to avoid annexation by the United States.

Then came President Tyler's message to Congress in December 1843 deploring the continuation of hostilities by Mexico, and warning that Mexico's threat to declare war should the United States annex Texas would not stand in the way of deliberations. He also served notice that the resulting weakness of Mexico and Texas rendered them, and particularly Texas, "the subjects of interference on the part of stronger and more powerful nations" in a manner "detrimental to the interests of the United States." "We could not be expected quietly to permit any such interference to our disadvantage," the president maintained.[21]

Tyler's message prompted Aberdeen, on January 12, 1844, to take steps to counter the American annexation move. He instructed his minister in Paris, Lord Cowley, to present Guizot a proposal that Great Britain and France inform their representatives in Washington and Texas that they deprecated any interference by the United States in Texas on "the adoption of any measure leading to the destruction of the separate existence of that State; . . ."[22] The proposal, extended to the logical limits, would have committed Great Britain and France to the use of force to prevent American annexation. However, it is doubtful that Aberdeen foresaw any danger of developments reaching the extremity of a final test. His information indicated that Sam Houston, in Texas, opposed annexation and that an armistice had been arranged between Mexico and Texas. What Aberdeen did not know was that annexationist sentiments in the United States were mounting, and his unawareness of this also blinded him to the fact that an emergency might soon cause him deep regret. He had failed to foresee certain dangers. However, the proposal to Guizot was not followed up by instructions to the representatives in Washington and Texas apparently because there appeared to be no need for haste; consequently Aberdeen's proposal remained just that and not a commitment.

During these same weeks another important development was in the making, namely the well-known Calhoun-Pakenham correspondence. On December 26 Aberdeen sent a dispatch to Pakenham instructing him to inform Secretary of State Upshur of the British position. Aberdeen again acknowledged that Great Britain favored the abolition of slavery everywhere but had no secret design for interfering with slavery in the United States and had "no thought or intention of seeking to act directly or indirectly in a political sense on the United States through Texas."[23] A second note from Aberdeen, dated February 26, repeated what he had stated in his earlier dispatch. Aberdeen's note was pacific in tone and in no way captious, although Calhoun's biographer views Aberdeen's letter as devious and threatening.[24]

Calhoun seized upon this dispatch as an opportunity to respond. He read Aberdeen's message in the light of what he believed to be true, finding in it not a disavowal of intentions to intervene but a devious cover up. Behind Aberdeen's wording, he saw British efforts to capture markets around the world, and the British antislavery movement aiming at bringing about abolition in both Cuba and Texas and eliminating the slave trade. In short, he read between the lines. Calhoun's finest biographer concluded that if he had done less he would not have been fit to be secretary of state.[25] The eight long pages of Calhoun's letter ignored Aberdeen's disavowal of intentions to interfere and focused on Aberdeen's opposition to slavery. The letter had the tone of an insulting reprimand. Calhoun launched out upon an essay to prove statistically that the slaves in the South were better off than the free blacks in the North. In addition, Calhoun held that an independent Texas, unable to resist indirect control by Great Britain, "would endanger both the safety and prosperity of the Union." He wrote: "That, from the geographcal position of Texas, the weakest and most vulnerable portion of our frontier to inroads, and place, in the power of Great Britain, the most efficient means of effecting in the neighboring States of the Union, what she avows it to be her desire to do in all countries, where slavery exists."

Pakenham replied on the following day. He took sharp issue with Calhoun on the ground that the secretary of state made the annexation of Texas a project necessitated by Aberdeen's dispatches. The note, wrote Pakenham, was "assigning to the British Government some share in the responsibility of a transaction which can hardly fail to be viewed in many quarters with the most serious objections." He then quoted Aberdeen's note, pointing out that Aberdeen had stated "we shall not interfere unduly, or with an improper assumption of authority with either Party (either Mexico or Texas) in order to ensure the adoption of such a course." He quoted further: "We shall counsel, but we shall not seek to compel, or unduly controul either Party, so far as Great Britain is concerned, provided other States act with equal forbearance . . ."

It is true that British antislavery leaders saw the question of slavery in Texas and in Cuba as the decisive turning point, that the further growth of slavery in both places would signify the extension of slavery, that it was the obligation of the British government to use its influence to prevent this extension. Texas was, in their eyes, the fulcrum on which hung the growth or the decline of the barbarous institution of slavery. This was also the view of American antislavery leaders, who had made their views known to the British government.[26]

Not only antislavery people but southern proannexationists professed to see that slavery within the Union hung in the balance. Calhoun has been charged with making the annexation of Texas a slavery issue. Calhoun did so in an official diplomatic note but certainly he did not invent the argument. Tyler, Upshur, Gilmore, and Duff Green made this the question long before. However, antiannexationists seized on Calhoun's letter and used it effectively.

The more significant question is why Calhoun chose to send what amounted to a defiant dispatch to Aberdeen.[27] Calhoun, obsessed with protecting the South and its "peculiar institution," acted in response to the antislavery movement in England quite as much or perhaps more than to Aberdeen's note. Aberdeen's dispatch offered complete assurance of noninterference subject to one condition that no other nation including the United States would interfere. At the same time the British foreign minister had acknowledged that the British government favored the abolition of slavery everywhere, a statement offensive to Calhoun. As Calhoun saw it, the United States possessed the right to interfere in Texas because the abolition of slavery there posed a danger affecting the nation's existence. The British, Calhoun held, had no such right.

Calhoun released his letter to Aberdeen to the Senate, and Senator Tappan of Ohio released it to the New York *Evening Post*. Once made public, Calhoun's undiplomatic letter served to confirm the charges of the antislavery leaders that Texas was to be annexed to protect slavery. This contributed to the defeat of Tyler's treaty of annexation in the Senate by a vote of 16 to 35 on June 8, 1844.

At this point Texas was up for bargaining. Neither President Sam Houston nor Anson Jones, Texas' secretary of state, were averse to accepting an alternative to annexation to the United States providing they received assurance of protection against Mexico.

In late May 1844 Aberdeen took up the cause of Texas independence once again. The Gulf of Mexico was of major importance to British commerce, and Texas in the hands of the United States would create a situation dangerous to British shipping. Texas itself offered prospects of a free market and an independent source of cotton. Given the importance of British interests, the British had every reason to try to preserve Texas independence. Aberdeen consulted Tomás Murphy, Mexico's minister in London, and proposed that Mexico immediately recognize Texas as independent. In turn, Great Britain and France would seek to guarantee the independence of Texas and the boundaries of both Texas and Mexico. Should Mexico refuse, Great Britain could not oppose annexation. Two days later Aberdeen consulted Ashbel Smith seeking assurance that Texas, if supported by Great Britain and France, would not consent to annexation. Smith gave him a cautious but reassuring answer.[28]

At the same time Aberdeen initiated discussions with France conveying to Guizot the proposal he had made to Murphy. He proposed that Great Britain and France commit themselves to defending Texas against any attempt by the United States to use force. This he undoubtedly viewed as only a very remote contingency. A firm stand by England and France, he assumed, would be sufficient to restrain the United States.[29] Both Louis Philippe and Guizot approved, but the final answer revealed a lukewarmness clothed in suggestions for greater specificity. On June 24 Aberdeen amending his earlier proposal, presented Ashbel Smith with what was to become known as the "Diplomatic Act." Mexico was now to be required to become a party to the guarantee.

Reports from the United States aborted the move. News that the Senate had refused to approve the treaty of annexation was accompanied by reports that the Tyler administration was ready to pursue a new approach. Pakenham advised that any step by England would strengthen the hands of American annexationists. Letters from Pakenham and from William Kennedy, British consul in Galveston, warned that Americans were determined to annex Texas and would do so at any cost. Pakenham held that any overt moves by the British would only serve to strengthen the position of Polk in the coming election. These reports brought about an abrupt change in Aberdeen's estimates, and Aberdeen promptly withdrew the "Diplomatic Act" proposal.[30]

However, the proposal was already on its way to Texas and Mexico. In Texas Anson Jones, the president-elect, rejected the proposal.[31] This made little difference, since Aberdeen had already withdrawn it. A revised version reached Mexico, where Santa Anna had recently announced that Texas was to be reconquered. He was not about to grant Texas the recognition proposed by London. Additional difficulties came to the fore in September. The Mexican foreign minister, Bocanegra, resigned, and Santa Anna appointed Manuel Crescencio Rejon to take his place. Rejon, an ultraliberal and friendly to the British, was, however, determined not to grant recognition to Texas. He was convinced that any yielding on Texas would only lead to the United States trying to acquire California. Rejon's distrust of the United States soon increased as a result of another move by Secretary of State Calhoun.

In the summer of 1844 Calhoun instructed William R. King,

minister to France, to determine French intentions concerning Texas. Louis Philippe and then Guizot assured him that France would not join hands with the British to preserve Texan independence. However, Guizot did explain that his country preferred an independent Texas and he closely questioned King on various aspects of the question. King replied that it was not the desire for more territory that caused Americans to favor annexation but fear of the dangers should Great Britain control Texas. In his letter of July 31, reporting on the interviews, King offered the conclusion that French policy presented no danger "nor will that of England proceed to the extremities which have been so fearfully paraded in certain quarters." Great Britain, he wrote, would not hazard "the employment of any arms, besides those of diplomacy, a cheap instrument if it proved successful." In a second letter to Calhoun on August 1, King wrote of the tensions between Great Britain and France promoted by the Morocco question; but he was also certain that, while the old entente was dead, peace would be preserved by both countries because of their great commercial interests.

Upon learning of Santa Anna's pronouncements about reconquering Texas, Calhoun sent Duff Green to Mexico to instruct Wilson Shannon, the United States minister, to inform Mexico in blunt language that the United States could not look upon a Mexican war against Texas with indifference. Green was scarcely a reliable instrument for conveying diplomatic messages, and Shannon, a wholly inexperienced man in foreign affairs and whose experience in politics was limited to Ohio, was no more suited to the task. Shannon antagonized Rejon, entered into a useless argument, and finally threatened breaking off relations unless Rejon apologized. In this way he destroyed his usefulness at a critical time.

During the interregnum the drift continued toward annexation. The ambiguous positions taken by Houston and Jones in Texas could not cover up the fact that Texas public opinion favored annexation. In the United States the Tyler administration, and especially Calhoun, nurtured proannexationist sentiment in Texas, while the public took alarm at Santa Anna's avowal that he would reconquer Texas and execute any Texan who opposed Mexico. Under the Constitution, the president was limited in the commitments he could make, but Calhoun stretched this power beyond the limit. Van Zandt, Texas minister in Washington, had questioned Calhoun on this point at a meeting on January 17, 1844. In responding Calhoun gave the assurance "that should the exigency arise *during the pendency of the treaty of annexation,* the president would deem it his duty to use all the means placed within his power by the constitution to protect Texas from invasion."[32] Calhoun renewed this assurance in April. On the basis of these statements Anson Jones, in August, called on General Tilghman A. Howard of the United States "to take the necessary steps to cause to be carried into effect these assurances, and to extend to Texas the aid which the present emergency requires."[33]

The new American chargé d'affaires in Texas, Andrew J. Donelson, worked energetically to convince Texan leaders of the dangers of falling under the sway of Great Britain and France.[34] He was no less vigorous in urging upon Calhoun prompt action. The merchants in Galveston, Donelson wrote, were tempted by the advantages they would derive in free trade with Great Britain.[35] On December 5 Donelson again sounded the alarm. "Texas," he wrote, "can avail herself of the mediation of England and obtain the recognition of her independence by Mexico whenever she chooses." And Texas, he reported, could obtain this without being restrained by any stipulation on the subject of slavery, *even*, without an agreement to reject another overture for annexation from the United States."[36]

The Tyler administration needed no urging to make haste. When Congress met in January 1845, a joint annexation resolution had been drafted and was presented to Congress. Texas had now become the test case of southern annexationists and proslavery defenders. On all sides, as the southerners saw it—in Great Britain, in France, and in the northern states—a frightening new world was emerging that viewed slavery as a moral stain bequeathed to the present by a past now dead. Southern defenders felt under siege and encircled by hostility on all sides. Neither strictly rational considerations nor cool calculations could penetrate the beleaguered mentality that exalted southern values, the hierarchical society, and slavery as a labor system and as a social system for maintaining white supremacy. Southern fears for the future spawned distrust of the new world that impinged, and Texas became the lodestar guiding them into a port secure from the surrounding storms.

The resolution to annex Texas came before Congress in January 1845. The question occupied the attention of both houses. Advocates and opponents latched on to a great variety of arguments to bolster their respective sides, and in the manner of propagandists spread wide nets in the hope that one or another consideration would lure the undecided. Some clearly sought to assure home constituencies that the senator or representative was carrying out their wishes. Party discipline, especially among the Democrats, played a part, and the president-elect used his position and the patronage at his command. The campaign of 1844 blazoned with a hurrah spirit and banners calling for Texas and Oregon. Annexationists interpreted Polk's victory as a mandate.

It was a claim open to serious questions in part because the Whigs might well have won had not many Whigs voted for the Liberty Party candidate, James G. Birney. Which of the several arguments in favor of annexation carried the greatest weight is a question yielding at best only an approximate answer. The considerations weighed differently among annexationists, but among southern advocates the protection of slavery stood forth as the most important.

James Belser of Alabama maintained in the House of Representatives that annexation was a matter of self-preservation for the South and for the Union.[37] The South could not survive unless the cotton-growing areas of Texas became a part of the United States where slavery would be free to grow. Isaac Morse of Louisiana declared that slavery was not an evil. "It was, on the contrary, one of the greatest blessings of God Almighty, for the protection and proper keeping of a large portion of his creatures who had not the capacity to care for themselves."[38] Now, he declared, antislavery men at home and abroad were seeking to crash that institution by closing the door to Texas. R. Barnwell Rhett of South Carolina, future secessionist, argued that northern abolitionists had destroyed the tranquility of the South to which southerners were entitled and tranquility could only be restored by approving the annexation of Texas.[39] Many did not exhibit as belligerent a spirit as Rhett, but southern members of Congress clearly believed that the South was under attack, that those opposed to the annexation of Texas saw defeat of annexation as the first battle of a long campaign to eradicate slavery, and that only the extension of slavery into Texas could turn the campaign around and provide assurance that slavery was invulnerable to attack.

Isaac E. Holmes of South Carolina, long-time admirer of Calhoun, best revealed the beleaguered feelings. There was, he said, "a tremendous maelstrom, a whirlpool, that was gathering in blackness and fury to drink up and absorb all that was estimable in our southern institutions, all that imparted vitality and vigor to them, and all that they held sacred connected with their hearth-stones and their homes."[40]

Holmes, as did many others, believed that the Union itself could not survive unless southern rights were protected. Southerners were not sectionalists simply because they defended what they held most dear. He asked: "Was it sectional in them to defend those rights and interests which had been assailed by the ruthless band of abolitionism?"

But annexation, even for ardent defenders of slavery, was also an economic matter. This side of the question, referred to frequently, received greatest attention from George A. Caldwell of Kentucky, a member of the House of Representatives. An independent Texas, favored by England, in the matter of commerce, would soon become the sole dispenser of cotton. The southern states "must then raise grain and stock in lieu of the cotton which they now raise, and this grain and stock will supersede those articles now supplied by the West." The West would then become a rival of the North in manufacturing. What, then, would a protective tariff avail the North?[41]

The alleged British threat did not occupy the center of the stage in Congress, but it did receive considerable attention. Senator William Allen, Democrat of Ohio, dwelt on the British ruthless campaign for commercial supremacy and saw in the British opposition to annexation British determination to cut down the United States, her major rival. Allen taunted New Englanders with the questions as to why they were ready to reject the opportunity to assure themselves of a market in Texas and to turn over to their British rivals the extensive carrying trade from Texas to Europe.[42] At least one New Englander, Senator Levi Woodbury, a New Hampshire Democrat, sided with Allen and denounced the abolitionists.[43] Woodbury, who aspired to the presidency, had received some support in the Democratic convention of 1844, and could ill afford to alienate the South.

Constitutional questions inevitably gained much attention. Did Congress have the authority to legislate a foreign nation as a state into the Union? Was this not reserved to the Senate and the chief executive as part of the treaty-making power? In speeches of two hours and longer each side on the question of annexation contended that it was correct in its interpretation. The Senate Committee on Foreign Affairs, by a vote of 4 to 1, reported that Texas could only be annexed under the treaty-making power. Only Buchanan held otherwise. Senator Morehead of Kentucky, member of the Committee on Foreign Affairs, warned that if Congress could annex Texas it could annex any other foreign territory, including Cuba, if "she came demanding admission with the assent of the Spanish Government." Buchanan interjected: "I wish she would."[44]

Certainly, Tyler's resort to annexation by a joint resolution of both houses of Congress was at the very least of dubious constitutionality, but this aspect did not worry the annexationists. Appeals to the Constitution were not wholly a matter of bending that documen to fit individual preferences as to annexation. Three notable leaders among southerners—Alexander Stephens of Georgia, and William S. Archer and William Rives of Virginia—opposed the resolution on constitutional grounds. All three favored annexation but feared that if Congress by a simple majority vote annexed Texas this would serve as a precedent for a majority to take steps ruinous to the South. Northern opponents of annexation, aside from arguing against the extension of slavery, stressed the constitutional question.

In New York, following the election and during the congressional debate, President Tyler's brother-in-law, Alexander Gardiner, member of Tammany Hall and an aspiring politician, organized a campaign promoting annexation. Gardiner enlisted the support of the Democratic Empire Club, led by Isaiah Rynders. Robert Seager, biographer of Tyler, describes Rynders as a "duelist, gambler, traveler, patriot, Democrat, expansionist, and soldier of fortune in the Texas Revolution." A contemporary newspaper reported that "women and wine, fighting, sporting, dancing, and free living, all receive his due attention." The club opposed Van Buren and abolition and prior to the election gave vent to the physical prowess of its members by breaking up Henry Clay rallies and demonstrated its party loyalty by pushing the naturalization of recently arrived immigrants. Gardiner, with the lusty help of Rynders' boys at a large assembly of Democrats on January 24, committed the local organzation to annexation. He believed that his efforts "had a material effect upon the action of Congress."⁴⁵ The efforts in New York, notes Tyler's biographer, paralleled those of Tyler's family in Washington, where "the Gardiner and Tyler ladies cajoled, wheedled, flirted, danced, entertained, and otherwise stalked and buttonholed every walking vote that came within polka distance."⁴⁶

The fight for annexation centered in the Senate. The resolution passed the House on January 25 with votes to spare. In the Senate there was strong opposition, based on antislavery views and fear of a war with Mexico. Thomas Hart Benton, who originally sought a treaty with Mexico, introduced a proposal calling for negotiations with Texas. His object was to lay down conditions concerning not only slavery but, more important, to limit the western boundary of Texas to the Nueces River.

In the final weeks the resolution passed by the House still lacked majority support. Benton and Dix of New York made clear they could not vote for it. It was not until the last few days that the resolution was amended, giving the president the option of either adopting the House formula for presenting Texas the terms of annexation or Benton's formula whereby the president would appoint commissioners to negotiate with Texas. Only then did the resolution pass the Senate by a 27 to 25 vote. Benton and Dix believed that Polk had assured them he would follow their option. Polk did not.⁴⁷

While Congress debated the joint resolution, Aberdeen made one final move in London to commit Mexico to a recognition of Texas independence and to commit Texas to preserving her independence. In his instructions to Elliott in Texas, Bankhead in Mexico, and Cawley in Paris, Aberdeen was specific in declaring that Great Britain would not accept any obligation to preserve Texan independence.⁴⁸ Risks of war with the United States were to be avoided. The British representative in Texas was instructed to avoid any interference in the internal affairs of Texas. This final move by Aberdeen rested on the reports he had received which indicated that the leaders in Texas might reject annexation and that Mexico was finally ready to concede Texan independence. Guizot of France agreed to go along with Aberdeen, who now opened the door to Texas to postpone all action on annexation for a limited period of time, and to Mexican authorities to promise Texas recognition.⁴⁹

Elliott and Saligny succeeded in gaining the assent of Anson Jones, now president of Texas, and Ashbel Smith, the secretary of state. The Texas capital had been moved from Austin to Washington on the Brazos, and the negotiations took place in a room over Hatfield's grocery store. Elliott then journeyed to Mexico where he, Bankhead, and Saligny promptly secured an agreement from Mexico on May 19.[50]

This last effort of Great Britain and France collapsed as it became clear that the people of Texas were determined to accept annexation to the United States. Elliott and Saligny, on their return to Texas in June, recognized the futility of their cause and promptly departed.

The expression of interest by Great Britain in maintaining Texas independence played, at most, a minor part in annexation. It had hastened the action of Tyler and Calhoun in promoting annexation, but Anglophobia appears not to have done more than to serve as one of many arguments in its favor.

Probably no final answer can be given as to why the annexationists triumphed. Southerners were deeply influenced by the proslavery "safety-valve" theory. Some northern Democrats were undoubtedly moved to support annexation because they wished to preserve support of the party in the South. Both Levi Woodbury of New Hampshire and Lewis Cass of Michigan supported annexation in considerable part because they recognized that their own personal ambitions could only be realized if they had southern support. Senators Dickinson and Dix were not aspiring to become president, but both had occupied political offices for a long time, and their careers depended upon the success of their party in national elections.

Another, less visible factor was the popular notion that the United States was not guilty of aggrandizement; it was doing no more than giving its consent to another country uniting "with us in government—and that country formed of one hundred thousand of our brethren, our kith and kin, . . ."[51] Senator Dickinson, of New York, made a highly rhetorical appeal to this sentiment. Texas, he said, "now appeals to the common parent; and shall her voice be unheeded?" He did not, he said, "advocate the annexation of Texas merely because it was desirable as a military position, nor for its vast commercial advantages; but upon broad principles of national faith and justice." The people of Texas were entitled to rejoin their American brethren.[52]

The narrow victory of the annexationists was due in part to opposition to war with Mexico. As a result from the first days of his presidency, Polk knew that he could not lightly call for a declaration of war against Mexico because Congress might well repudiate him.

Of greater interest to the student of foreign relations is the haste in which annexation was carried out. The British and French were shunted to one side in a blunt and wholly unnecessary fashion, and no effort was made to assuage the feelings of Mexico. In Europe, where nation-states were compelled to give consideration to the legitimate interests of their next-door neighbors, such brusqueness would have engendered a complete lack of confidence in the offending government. The United States was free from this restraint, and bold action was confused with strength of masculinity. The way in which annexation was achieved sowed seeds of distrust in Europe and opened the door to war with Mexico.

NOTES TO CHAPTER VII

1. *The French Legation in Texas*, ed. Nancy Nichols Parker, Vol. I: *Recognition, Rupture, and Reconciliation* (Austin: Texas State Historical Association, 1971), pp. 39–40, 45.
2. Norman A. Graebner made a most significant contribution in examining the importance of seaports in the expansionism. His findings enriched understanding of the forces at work. See Graebner, *Empire on the Pacific; A Study in American Continental Expansion* (New York: Ronald Press Co., 1955).
3. *Diplomatic Correspondence of the United States Inter-American Affairs 1831–1860*, ed. William R. Manning, Vol. XII *Texas and Venezuela* (Washington: Carnegie Endowment for International Peace, 1939), p. 261.
4. Ibid., p. 264.
5. Ibid., p. 266.
6. David M. Pletcher, *The Diplomacy of Annexation Texas, Oregon, and the Mexican War* (Columbia, Mo.: University of Missouri Press, 1973), p. 86.
7. Ibid., p. 122.
8. Ibid., p. 114.
9. Manning, *Diplomatic Correspondence of the United States*, Vol. XII, p. 141.
10. Duff Green is described by Merk "as above all a restless manipulator and propagandist," who in this case unscrupulously distorted the facts. For an interesting and revealing account of Duff Green's activities, see Merk, *Fruits of Propaganda in the Tyler Administration*, pp. 17–23.

11. Ibid., pp. 296–97.
12. Ibid., pp. 299–309.
13. Ibid., p. 44.
14. Ibid., pp. 305–307.
15. Ephraim Douglas Adams, *British Interests and Activities in Texas 1838–1846* (Baltimore: The Johns Hopkins Press, 1910), p. 70; Pletcher *The Diplomacy of Annexation*, p. 83.
16. Gaulburn to Aberdeen, Oct. 1, 1841, Foreign Office, Texas, 2, quoted by E. D. Adams, *British Interests and Activities in Texas 1838–1846*, pp. 71–72.
17. Ibid., p. 104.
18. Ibid., pp. 140–41.
19. Everett to Upshur, Nov. 3, 1843, Despatches from London, Roll 47.
20. Everett to Upshur, Nov. 3, 1843. Despatches from London, Roll 47.
21. *Messages and Papers of the Presidents*, ed. James D. Richardson, Vol. III, pp. 2113–15.
22. E. D. Adams, *British Interests and Activities in Texas 1838–1846*, pp. 158–59.
23. Ibid., p. 162.
24. Ibid., pp. 162–63; Pletcher, *The Diplomacy of Annexation*, p. 143.
25. Charles M. Wiltse, *John C. Calhoun Sectionalist* (New York: The Bobbs-Merrill Co., 1951), p. 169.
26. For the fullest exposition of these views and the close relations between the British and American antislavery movements, see *A Side-Light on Anglo-American Relations, 1839–1858 Furnished by the Correspondence of Lewis Tappan and Others with the British and Foreign Anti-Slavery Society*, ed. Annie Heloise Abel and Frank J. Klingbert (Lancaster, Pa.: The Association for the Study of Negro Life and History, Inc., 1927).
27. Pletcher, in *The Diplomacy of Annexation*, offers several speculations as to why Calhoun chose to write what he calls a "reckless" letter (see p. 144).
28. E. D. Adams, *British Interests and Activities in Texas 1838–1846*, pp. 167–70.
29. Ibid., p. 172.
30. Pletcher, *The Diplomacy of Annexation*, p. 160.
31. For a discussion of the conflicting evidence as to Jones' motives see Pletcher, *The Diplomacy of Annexation*, pp. 164–65.
32. Manning, *Diplomatic Correspondence of the United States*, Vol. XII, pp. 362–63.
33. Ibid., pp. 360–61.
34. Ibid., pp. 371–72, 378–81.
35. Ibid., pp. 371–72.
36. Ibid., pp. 378–81.
37. *Congressional Globe*, 28th Cong., 2nd Sess., Special Sess., 1844–45, Appendix, p. 88.
38. Ibid., p. 126.
39. Ibid., p. 167.
40. Ibid., p. 136.
41. Ibid., p. 169.
42. Ibid., p. 342.
43. Ibid., pp. 298–300.
44. Ibid., p. 281.
45. Robert Seager, *and Tyler too A Biography of John and Julia Gardiner Tyler* (New York: McGraw-Hill Book Company, 1963), pp. 280–81.
46. Ibid., p. 279.
47. Charles Sellers, *James K. Polk Continentalist 1843–1846* (Princeton, N.J.: Princeton University Press, 1966), pp. 189, 205–207.

48. E. D. Adams, *British Interests and Activities in Texas 1838–1846*, pp. 204–205.

49. Ibid., pp. 205–206, 209.

50. Ibid., p. 214.

51. Speech by Senator Woodbury, *Congressional Globe*, 28th Cong., 2nd Sess., p. 297.

52. Ibid., pp. 321–26.

Chapter VIII

Oregon: An Unnecessary Controversy

The Democrats, who gathered at Baltimore in 1844 to nominate a presidential candidate and adopt a platform, had victory in the forthcoming election as their highest goal. This did not distinguish them from preceding political gatherings, but in making the annexation of Texas and all of Oregon their campaign slogan they reduced what had been a question of diplomacy to a vote-getting maneuver. The strategy proposed to exploit the popularity of expansion and also widespread bias and distrust of Great Britain. In harmony with their choice of strategy, the Democrats named James K. Polk to be their candidate, a man who had long advocated expansion and who had won their confidence during twenty years in Congress by adhering firmly to the policies of Andrew Jackson. Expansionism, clothed in colors of contempt for European monarchical tyrants and a dislike of the haughty and all grasping British, it was thought, would conceal serious and widespread party division; it was especially calculated to combine the South, with its interest in Texas, and the Northwest, with its interest in Oregon, into a winning tandem. The summer of 1844 rang with cries for Texas and Oregon. Fires of expansionism fed by a spirit of defiance swept the land. However, Polk emerged victor by only a narrow margin and might well have lost to Henry Clay, the Whig candidate, had not large numbers of Whigs deserted to James G. Birney and his Liberal Party.

Yet, the Oregon question cannot be viewed as simply a contrived politically motivated issue. Since 1839 the agricultural potential of the Willamette valley had become a magnet for settlers, and by 1845 there were 5,000 Americans in the area and hundreds of others on the way. These migrant farmers were petitioning Congress for the establishment of a territory. British trappers and traders lived under the government provided by the Hudson's Bay Company, but Americans had no equivalent. The day when a government must be established was approaching. Joint occupancy no longer jibed with the existing situation.

The British recognized this at least as early as 1842, and Ashburton received instructions to seek an agreement dividing the territory. Daniel Webster chose not to negotiate on this problem. The secretary of state faced a difficult situation within the Whig party. Hopeful that he could recapture the leadership and win the party's nomination for president, he planned to become minister to Great Britain and win glory as the negotiator of a settlement of the Oregon question. Therefore, as secretary of state, Webster postponed negotiating.[1] Webster's plan went awry when Edward Everett refused transfer to another post. Secretaries of state Upshur and Calhoun did enter into negotiations, but these were still at an early stage when Polk took over the presidency.

The Polk administration did not create the Oregon problem; it had existed before the election of 1844 and in all probability would have been easier to settle prior to then. This situation was to lead United States Minister Louis McLane in London to comment at the height of the diplomatic controversy in February 1846 that he became indignant whenever he thought of Webster evading the problem.

In 1845 Polk, who only two years before had lost the Tennessee governor's race, faced the fact that he had committed himself to acquiring all of Oregon, a commitment that ignored the well-established claims of Great Britain to large parts of the area, that pushed to one side positions taken by previous diplomats representing the United States, and challenged the British sense of national honor.

Above all, Polk faced a divided party. Sharp rifts soon paralyzed the Democratic majority in the state legislature of his home state. In New York so-called radicals, the Barnburners, did battle with the conservative Hunkers. In Pennsylvania the Democrats were split between Vice President Dallas, the leader in Philadelphia, and Buchanan, spokesman for the western part of the state. In both states these factional fights erupted into bitter struggles. And between Calhoun and McDuffie of South Carolina, on the one hand, and Allen of Ohio and Hannegan of Indiana, on the other, there was more contempt or distrust than harmony.

Polk, an experienced and pragmatic politician, was neither a crusader nor was he conspiratorial. No evidence exists to show that he drafted a long-term plan to achieve his political goals. However, given the situation he faced within his party, given his long experience in political hustings and debates in the House of Representatives, and considering his oft-repeated faith in "firmness and boldness," a euphemistic synonym for quiet blustering, Polk had few options. The options were limited by the commitments made regarding Oregon and Texas, by the importance of maintaining party unity, and by his firm conviction that the British would not come to a reasonable settlement unless faced in a determined fashion.

The orchestration of party harmony would be difficult, as Polk well knew. However, he was a dedicated party man, saw the Democratic party as the ark of the covenant of traditional Jeffersonian and Jacksonian principles, found all Whigs untrustworthy, and considered any Democrat siding with the Whigs on an issue as guilty of treason or an indecently ambitious aspirant for the presidency.

Polk had few interests outside of politics and his plantation. He attended the Presbyterian Church every Sunday and on occasion pondered how he would fare on Judgment Day. His horizons at the moment were as vertical as they were horizontal.

The exciting intellectual currents of his age were far outside his orbit. He possessed neither broad interests nor intellectual vigor. In the early days of his presidency Dabney S. Carr, minister to Constantinople, and the witty and garrulous Christopher Hughes, long-time friends while representing the United States in Europe, chanced to call on Polk at the same time. They promptly engaged in a discussion of European art, and Polk was left a silent bystander. He resented being left out and noted in his *Diary* that they had been too long in Europe. He entertained a distrust of all European monarchies but reserved his strongest dislike for the British, whom he found haughty, grasping, and treacherous.

Nevertheless, the country never had a more conscientious president. He worked endless hours, left his office for an entire day only once during his first year in office, pursued relentlessly his goals of a low tariff and an independent treasury, spent endless hours listening to callers from Congress, although the Sabbath Day was sacred and no business was transacted. He was a man of integrity, led a virtuous life, and was devoted to the public interest as he understood it. At the same time he was distrustful of almost everyone except his old college friend in the Senate, William Haywood of North Carolina. He quickly jumped to conclusions, assessing low motivations to fellow politicians, a characteristic that led him to be secretive in his dealings, giving the appearance of frankness but often hiding behind declarations that revealed nothing to his inquirers. For instance, prior to cabinet meetings he did not discuss nor reveal his thinking about questions of foreign relations to Secretary of State Buchanan, with the result that Buchanan could only take issue before the entire cabinet, leaving him in the position of a challenger rather than a discussant. It must also be said that Polk's experience late in 1845 and early 1846 gave him ample reason to be distrustful.

Polk, the party politician, confronted the presidency with a determination that his administration would be one of glorious accomplishments, and he lived with the knowledge that he had become president on a platform calling for the annexation of Texas and Oregon. He was in part a willing prisoner of the expansionists but not as extreme as Allen of Ohio, Hannegan of Indiana, or Cass of Michigan. Expansionism, too, must be subordinated to unification of the party and the carrying through of the overall program including domestic reform. He announced early that he would not be a candidate for a second term and thereby allowed himself four years to build the party into a cohesive organization and one that could take credit for territorial gains, a lower tariff, and an independent treasury. He was aware that skillful political maneuvering would be required and that he could not rely on charismatic qualities, such as those possessed by his hero, Andrew Jackson, to carry him through.

Foreign affairs became his first and almost all-consuming concern. The proposed termination of the 1827 Convention with Great Britain providing for joint occupancy of Oregon placed this question highest on Polk's agenda. Polk soon elected a course that almost closed the door to any genuine negotiations. Oregon posed as much of a domestic political question as it did a question of negotiations with Great Britain. How to achieve gains on both fronts without losing the support of major party factions presented difficulties.

Polk repeatedly expressed in his *Diary*, letters, and conversations that his course was pacific, but he also told his listeners that if war came, let it come. As an admirer of Jackson's brusqueness, he held that firmness and boldness offered the only assurance of success. During the critical months from September 1845 to June 1846 he repeatedly affirmed his faith in firmness. The way to deal with John Bull, he told James A. Black, member of the House of Representatives from South Carolina, was to look him straight in the eye. "A bold and firm course on our part," he noted, was "the pacific one." Any indication of hesitation, he assured Black, and "John Bull would immediately become arrogant and more grasping in his demands & that such had been the history of the British Nation in all their contests with other Powers for the last two hundred years."[2] Behind the facade of firmness, however, there was a willingness to compromise. The firmness Polk chose to display was dictated quite as much by circumstances as it was by his own drive to appear as the strong man. To exhibit publicly a spirit of compromise would alienate the fire-eaters in his party and, as Polk saw it, lead the British to offer only unacceptable concessions.

The bravado of the election campaign gave way to sober negotiations conducted in a spirit of compromise once Polk took office and learned that Everett, American minister in London, and British Foreign Minister Aberdeen had been engaged in conversations on the Oregon question. Late in 1843 Everett had taken the initiative in seeking a settlement. He sought to convince Aberdeen of the reasonableness of dividing the territory at the 49th parallel. Everett reported that it "produced an obvious effect upon Lord Aberdeen who observed that if the legislative bodies of the two countries refrained from precipitous action he did not think we shall have much difficulty." He repeated this remark. Aberdeen spoke of one difficulty; his predecessors had twice rejected the 49th parallel as a boundary. It would be difficult to accept it now unless the Peel ministry could cite some concessions from the United States as justifying the change. Everett, in reporting this conversation to the secretary of state, proposed that to meet this difficulty "it may deserve the President's consideration, whether he would not agree to give up the Southern extremity of Quadra & Vancouver Island, (which the 49° would leave within our boundary) on condition that the entrance of the Strait of Juan de Fuca should at all times be left open & free to the United States with a free navigation between the islands and the mainland, and a free outlet to the North."[3]

Everett became convinced that a settlement on this basis was within reach and so informed William Sturgis, a leading Boston merchant, who promptly became a public advocate of the Aberdeen-Everett formula. In January 1845 Sturgis delivered a public address outlining the proposal, stating that the United States could not settle for less. The printed version soon reached London, where it was used with good effect, and before long the proposal gained the support of several leading British Whigs and Tories.

When Polk entered office, he readily fell in line with the search for a peaceful settlement. The administration newspaper, the *Union*, began to prepare the public for a settlement of compromise.[4] Secretary of State James Buchanan went out of his way to assure Pakenham, British minister to the United States, that the administration sought a settlement by negotiation. In June, still in pursuit of a diplomatic solution, the new minister to Great Britain, Louis McLane, received detailed instructions that called for him to find a settlement along the lines of the Everett-Aberdeen formula.

During these months neither side could afford to state openly that this formula was wholly acceptable for the reason that their political rivals at home would in all probability insist on emendations in harmony with their own party interests and would charge those in power with weakness. Aberdeen had reason to fear a truculent assault from the Whig opposition and from Palmerston, who had attacked him bitterly after the Webster-Ashburton Treaty.[5] Polk could defend a settlement along the 49th parallel as necessary due to precedent but he, too, had reason to protect himself against political enemies; more important, he believed that only insistence on what he considered a reasonable settlement would cause the British to retreat from their long-time insistence on dividing the territory at the Columbia River.

This cautious treading in the waters of diplomacy came to an abrupt halt. On July 16, 1845 Secretary of State Buchanan called Pakenham to his office. After a lengthy justification of American claims to all of Oregon, he proposed a division of the territory at the 49th parallel. In a private letter to McLane, Buchanan explained the reasons for this move. He began with a history of the negotiations of 1818, 1824, and 1827. Three times the United States had offered to divide the territory at the 49th parallel and to yield to the British free navigation of the Columbia River. Buchanan wrote that "it is not to be supposed that the British Government will now consent by negotiation to yield to us the whole territory up to 54° 40′ after our Gov't had thrice offered to divide it by the parallel of 49°—they had thrice refused this offer even when accompanied by a grant of the free navigation of the Columbia." The Jackson administration had looked forward to a compromise and had not claimed all the territory. The Tyler administration had likewise proposed a compromise. When Polk entered office, Buchanan explained, he found negotiations in progress based on compromise and he had adhered to this course.

Buchanan shared with McLane what had taken place in the inner councils and Polk's views. What was important was access to the fine harbors of Puget Sound. "We know but little of the country north of that parallel; but from all the information we have obtained," Buchanan noted, "it is with the exception of a few slots wholly unfit for agriculture & incapable of sustaining any considerable population." To demand exclusive jurisdiction over the whole territory could only mean war and this was inconsistent with the spirit of "the present enlightened and Christian age." Buchanan's next observations had a jarring note that was contrary to his previous pacific tone. Should Great Britain decline the offer now made, the United States would stand justified before world opinion in resorting to war. The president would then "feel himself perfectly free to insist upon our rights to their full extent up to the Russian line."

Buchanan thought the one serious obstacle to British acceptance of the offer would be the fact that it did not include free navigation of the Columbia. The president, he reported, would not include this because it would lead to collisions between the citizens and subjects of the two nations. To offset this the president would be willing to make the ports on the southern tip of Vancouver Island free ports or to agree to British retention of the southern part of that island that was below the 49th parallel.

Again Buchanan introduced a note that did not bode well for the future. "Should it be rejected," he wrote, "the President will be relieved from the embarrassment in which he has been involved by the actions, offers & declarations of his predecessors."[6]

Pakenham the British minister in Washington rejected outright Buchanan's offer. In London Aberdeen deplored Pakenham's action. He invited the American minister, Louis McLane, to an interview on September 30. Aberdeen, McLane reported to Buchanan, "not only lamented, but censured the rejection by Mr. Pakenham." He assured McLane that if the proposal had been forwarded he "would have taken it up as the basis of his action, and entertained little doubt that he would have been able to propose modifications which might ultimately have resulted in an adjustment mutually satisfactory to both Governments." Indeed, McLane stated, if Polk had not withdrawn his proposal, Aberdeen would have pursued this course and would do so even now "if he could be certain that in withdrawing the proposition the President did not intend to terminate the negotiation." Since McLane had no instructions he chose not to respond. Moreover, he sensed Polk might wish to take advantage of Pakenham's error, and therefore did not wish to open the door for Aberdeen to advance a proposition.

Pakenham's rejection of the offer of the 49° line in July 1845 extricated Polk from a situation not to his liking. In spite of Buchanan's contrary advice, Polk insisted on delivering his reply to Pakenham promptly. After delivering it at a cabinet meeting on August 30, Buchanan sadly observed: "Well the deed is done, but he did not think it was the part of wise statesmanship to deliver such a paper in the existing state of our relations with Mexico." Polk said he was glad it was delivered, "that it was right in itself, and he saw no reason for delaying it because of our relations with Mexico."[7]

Polk was relieved that Pakenham had rejected the proposal, took great satisfaction in having withdrawn the offer to compromise at 49°, and said that now he was free to return to a stronger demand. The president's self-assurance burst forth in a cabinet meeting on October 21 when McLane's dispatch, telling of Aberdeen's lamenting Pakenham's rejection, was under discussion. Buchanan wished to know what he was to tell Pakenham, since he expected the British minister to call in a day or two. Pakenham would inquire as to whether the president would receive and consider any proposition. Polk did not hesitate. All that could be said was that if Pakenham had any further proposition to make it would be received and considered. Pakenham was to be left in the dark as to what Polk's attitude would be. Buchanan said "if we stopped the negotiation, where it was, it would inevitably lead to war." The president said he was well pleased with the situation and that if the British now offered to settle at the 49° line he would reject it. Buchanan asked if he could say to Pakenham that the president would submit a British proposition to the Senate for advice. Polk retorted that the British had no right to know what he would do.[8]

Polk, keenly aware of the situation confronting him at home, had reason to be pleased. He had now assumed that bold and firm position that accorded with his own high estimate of masculinity. He had avoided losing the support of the extremists in the party who demanded all of Oregon, and had not revealed his hand to southern Democrats who favored a conciliatory course. And he did not see his actions as brinksmanship leading to war. The British had demonstrated a conciliatory spirit—a sign of weakness to be exploited. On October 24 he revealed his own thinking but only slightly to Senator Thomas Hart Benton. Polk explained that he would conform with the provisions of the treaty of 1827, and he outlined how notice of termination would be given, blockhouses and stockaded forts erected on the route to Oregon, and civil and criminal jurisdiction extended to Americans living in Oregon. None of these, he said, would violate the treaty or give just cause of offense to Great Britain.[9]

His course was now set. He would focus on putting through notification of termination of the treaty within the year provided, "a glorious measure." All attention could be directed to this, and the more controversial aspects of a final settlement postponed. This would free Polk from exposing himself to the British and, more important, protect him from attack by the diverse elements in his own party. It would also enable him to maintain the firm and bold stance so necessary to his own composure.

Polk experienced no anxiety over the Oregon question during October and November 1845. He repeatedly expressed the view that

Great Britain would not offer a proposition that would be acceptable, but this did not worry him. In a personal letter, written on November 27, he repeated once again that he did not expect a proposition the United States ought to accept and that he would shortly "lay the whole subject before Congress." He said, "This is the only course left unless we abandon our clear territorial rights which is not for a moment to be thought of." As he prepared his message to Congress, he reported to a correspondent that it "is likely to create anxiety on both sides of the Atlantic lest peace be disturbed." Then, giving expression to his feelings of the moment, he stated: "It is however right in itself and I am fully satisfied with it. I have no doubt I shall be sustained in it by a large majority of the country. I do not believe there is any real danger of its leading to war, but if it is war I act upon Gen'l Jackson's maxim in conducting our Foreign affairs—to 'ask nothing that is not right and to submit to nothing that is wrong.' "[10]

Polk did not employ emotional language in his message to Congress, but he set forth in bold terms the claim to all of Oregon and called on Congress to pass a resolution giving the required one-year notice of termination, recommended that Congress pass legislation for the establishment of American jurisdiction, and provide for the establishment of blockhouses on the route to protect prospective settlers. Again he warned Europe against interference in the New World, a note directed against any British interest in California.

In a cabinet discussion of the message prior to its delivery Buchanan advised that his own talks with members of Congress showed they favored a settlement at 49° and would object to the warlike tone. But, as recorded in his diary, Polk

> told him that my greatest danger was that I would be attacked for having yielded to what had been done my predecessors ... I told him that if my proposition had been accepted by the British Minister my course would have met with great difficulties, and in my opinion would have gone far to overthrow the administration had it been accepted.[11]

The popular response indicated that Polk was correct. Buchanan reported to McLane, "The message has been better received throughout the country than any similar communication in my day."[12] Polk wrote exultantly to his brother in Naples that his message won wide acclaim and "Upon the Oregon question the opposition has been taken all aback and know not what to say."[13] Alexander Everett, former Whig turned Democrat, hailed it as one that would be viewed with delight and admiration by the friends of liberty throughout the world."[14] The president had stood up to Europe, had warned that those powers had no right to interfere, and had refused to bow to the British. The message was as irresistible to the national ego as the reading of the preamble to the Constitution.

The publication of the message was accompanied by Buchanan's letter to Pakenham the previous summer setting forth the validity of the claim to Oregon. Buchanan, who had been a "nervous Nellie" throughout the fall, expressing fear of war, now took on the appearance of the stalwart and courageous defender of national honor. His political agents reported how he had acquired new stature. Caleb Cushing of Massachusetts told how the letter had convinced everyone of the justice of American claims.[15] More important, Buchanan received a glowing report from James Forney, his chief promoter for the presidency, influential newspaper editor, and chief adviser to Buchanan on patronage questions. Forney spoke before Tammany Hall in New York in mid-December and while there consulted with a score of politicos. He reported: "Your letter has been a perfect big gun among the politicians, and has made you thousands of new friends."[16] Buchanan soon became a hard liner on the Oregon question. Polk noted the change and correctly ascribed it to Buchanan's presidential aspirations.

The self-assurance of Polk in mid-December was to be shortlived. Seemingly, he had preserved party unity. Congress would vote for his program, including the "glorious measure" of notification, and he had acted within the terms of the treaty. He had ample reason to believe that once notice had been given the British would offer more generous concessions. McLane had advised him more than once during the fall that the British were ready to settle.[17] There had been a change in British opinion. Now, McLane reported, on December 1, all seemed willing to accept a division along the 49th parallel. The commercial and banking classes favored compromise. The problem facing Polk by late December was not the British, but how to reach a settlement without splitting his party.

Polk expected opposition from Calhoun. This towering figure had long since made clear to Buchanan where he stood. He had warned that war with England over the Oregon question would be a disaster. With their naval superiority, the British would take Oregon and hold it until the United States achieved equal power on the seas.[18] The president could expect the Whigs to give him trouble, for they spoke for the commercial interests who insisted on peace. A combination of Whigs and southern Democrats led by Calhoun could delay, if not wholly block, Polk's program.

Other signs of disarray appeared among the Democrats in December, and the trouble extended up to cabinet level. Polk spent hours almost every day seeing applicants for office and reading letters recommending candidates. He deplored the time spent on office seekers and complained that all offices had been filled. To meet the demand he would now have to replace competent people with men who were largely a sad lot. However, the patronage game determined who among party leaders and local chieftains would support him. Mistakes could be costly.

In mid-December trouble struck. Polk made two appointments from Pennsylvania. He named Henry Horn as collector of customs duties at Philadelphia and George C. Woodward to the Supreme Court. Forney, Buchanan's political henchman in Pennsylvania, protested angrily that the administration was filling offices with Buchanan's enemies. Buchanan's followers were utterly disgusted; unless some explanation could be offered, all was lost.[19] The appointment of Woodward created a noisy uproar. This alarming news ignited Buchanan's deepest feelings, and he promptly drafted a letter to Polk that bristled with hostility. He protested that Polk slighted him seriously in "withholding [from him] all knowledge of the nomination of a Judge of the Supreme Court of the United States from my own circuit" and termed the occurrence unprecedented. He pointed to the appointment of Horn as another slight and the filling of the customhouse in Philadelphia with his enemies.[20]

The fight over patronage came to a climax in January, when the Senate refused to confirm six of Polk's nominations, including that of Woodward. The six Democrats who voted against confirmation were Buchanan's friends. The difficulty, Polk noted, was the factionalism in Pennsylvania.[21] As he looked on helplessly while his party split, he attributed it to the presidential aspirations of Allen, Buchanan, Cass, and Calhoun. On March 8 he noted in his diary that he feared "that these factions . . . will so divide and weaken the Democratic party by their feuding as to defeat my measures and render my administration unsuccessful and useless."

Part of the difficulty lay in Polk's determination to reduce the tariff. Manufacturing districts of the country saw themselves being sacrificed to the demands of the South. Polk did not view this as a sectional question, but as a matter of traditional party principle. A protective tariff, he thought, was an unconstitutional use of the federal power for the benefit of special interests. Again, it was Buchanan who appeared as the enemy. Senator Spright of Mississippi confided to Polk that Buchanan was using his influence to prevent a reduction of the tariff and that many persons from manufacturing districts in Pennsylvania had visited Buchanan and urged "that sooner than suffer a modification of the tariff, the country had better have war by insisting on 54° 40′, and make no compromise on the Oregon question."[22]

Party patronage squabbles, the maneuvering for advantage by aspirants for the presidency, and the tariff question undoubtedly explain to some degree the opposition Polk encountered in the Senate on the question of giving notice of the termination of the treaty providing for joint occupancy. However, the primary reason why the Senate delayed action on the notice was that Polk had provided evidence that he would insist on acquiring all of Oregon. This, in fact, was not his position; however, his secrecy, in fact dogmatic refusal to give the slightest clue as to what he would do after notice had been given, promoted fear and distrust. Polk refused to confide in the leaders who repeatedly came to him. They warned that a majority in the Senate favored a reasonable compromise and sought for some word that Polk would compromise. In remaining silent, he not only offended the pride of senators, but temporarily appeared prepared to by-pass them. This was a dangerous course to pursue, and more than any other one factor it split his party.

Polk took account of the situation in late December and gradually came to terms with political realities. The day before Christmas two senators called, Allen of Ohio, an extremist, and Hopkins Turney of Tennessee, a moderate. To Allen, chairman of the Senate Foreign Relations Committee, Polk put the question as to whether the president should submit to the Senate the anticipated compromise if it were offered by Great Britain. The question, given Allen's position in the Senate, was no more than rhetorical and of course he could only answer in the affirmative. Turney warned Polk that he faced opposition in the Senate. Polk acknowledged the danger of war and assured Turney that if Great Britain offered a proposition, "I would take the advice of the Senate confidentially before I acted on it."[23] The key word "confidentially" meant that he might do no more than consult a few, without submitting it to the Senate for approval.

Two days later at a cabinet meeting Buchanan put the question in more specific terms. If Pakenham proposed a settlement along the 49th parallel, giving Great Britain the southern half of Vancouver, would Polk submit it to the Senate, and could Buchanan say so to Pakenham. Polk recorded in his diary: "I told him he was not authorized to say so, that the British Minister should not know anything of any consultation with the Senate,—even if I had determined to act on the advice of that body, which I had not."[24]

Yet, two days earlier the president had polled the cabinet. If Great Britain made the proposal anticipated, should he refer it to the Senate previous to acting upon it. The cabinet agreed unanimously that Polk should do so.[25] Having put the question and received a unanimous answer, it would appear that Polk had committed himself to this course, but he had no intention of revealing this to the British or to Congress. In a conversation with James G. Black, South Carolina member of the House of Representatives, he adhered to his earlier strategy and simply referred to his message to Congress and then lectured him on the wisdom of a bold and firm course, including his famous remark, "the only way to treat John Bull was to look him straight in the eye."[26]

On January 10 he gave the same answer to the troubled John C. Calhoun, who advised Polk that the British title to the valley of the Fraser River was as good as the United States' title to the Columbia River. Polk was as secretive as ever. Privately, his position had moved toward compromise, but he chose not to share his views. Calhoun and his supporters had no way of knowing that as early as December 29 Polk had written to McLane, "Peace is our policy and I most anxiously desire to pursue it, but it must be an honorable peace, and one consistent with our national rights and interests."[27] He would consult with the Senate confidentially. Any proposition acceptable to us, Polk wrote, "must be as favorable as the one that was withdrawn with perhaps slight modifications." Given McLane's repeated statements in his letters to both Buchanan and Polk that such a settlement was within reach, Polk could have opened the door but he choose not to do so.

Why? Polk conceived of himself as the true representative of all the people as opposed to members of Congress, who spoke for sectional interests. He repeatedly asked himself what the people would accept. His stance in his annual message had been popular, and he had no wish to destroy the image of firmness and boldness he had created.

At this time Polk expressed conflicting views from day to day. Upon some occasions he probably felt real danger that any sign of compromise would cause the British ministry to present a proposal he could not accept. The divisions at home already increased this danger. George Bancroft wrote to a friend protesting that Polk was a man of peace and that he was confident Great Britain would do justice. "I fear nothing," he wrote, "but division at home, which may impel England to unreasonable and impossible demands." Bancroft was probably not alone in holding this opinion.[28] Given the pressures at work on the British government, the fear was not unreasonable.

The president fully confided his thoughts to his trusted and able friend, Louis McLane. In a revealing letter to McLane in London, he described a proposal he had already set before the cabinet. In both countries there was a strong movement to reduce import duties, and Polk raised the possibility of tying the Oregon question to a reduction of tariffs on each other's exports. He was convinced that the British had no great interest in the territory in dispute but that it was the matter of national honor that prevented them from conceding all of Oregon. A general reduction of duties on British imports would enable Great Britain to escape from this point of honor. He believed that a treaty incorporating concession of all Oregon and at the same time lowering duties would be approved by all three groups in the Senate—the extreme expansionists, the low tariff advocates, and the champions of peace.[29] Nothing came of this proposal, but it is significant in revealing Polk's thinking.

In his letter to McLane, Polk also dwelt on other major points. The first was the rapidly growing conviction among the public that the United States must have all of Oregon. His second point was that the British were determined to avoid war with the United States because they would probably lose their colonies in addition to suffering all the other burdens of war. He thought the interests of Great Britain in preserving peace were so great "that she would submit to almost any honorable terms to avoid war."[30]

George Bancroft, secretary of navy, was convinced that Polk followed the right course. In a letter to McLane in London, Bancroft maintained that the country would never accept a settlement permitting the British free navigation of the Columbia. He attributed the opposition to the resolution to terminate the treaty to unworthy political motives and predicted that the resolution would pass by a large majority, Bancroft defended the president and blamed the British. In Bancroft's estimation, the British, by failing to make an offer after Pakenham rejected Polk's offer, were the guilty party.[31]

In his letter Bancroft stated that he had not changed his views during the negotiations. He was convinced that public opinion would be satisfied with a settlement at the 49th parallel, a cession of Vancouver and Quadra islands, and a granting to the British of free navigation of the Columbia River for from seven to ten years, "but that is the limit." "On the question of permanent navigation of the Columbia some of the Whigs would give way, but the country never." Bancroft strongly supported the opposition to granting free navigation. He referred to public opinion as "intemperate and unwavering." He likewise described the president as extremely sensitive and therefore preserving his dignity was "a high object."

Bancroft was as mindful of the difficulties facing Polk as he appears to have been unaware of the difficulties facing the British government. He wrote to his friend and former professor at Harvard, Edward Everett, that he had no apprehension of war, "if we are but resolute and prepared."[32] Everett thought otherwise. He replied that the British ministry of Sir Robert Peel was desirous of peace, even to the point of generous concessions but "they are as unable as the President, to fall much below the public opinion, which there as here is very apt to take an *ex parte* view." Human nature, he wrote, is the same on both sides of the water. "What could the President and his cabinet do to preserve peace, if every arrival from England brought from Parliament the counterpart of the Resolutions, Reports, and speeches which are daily appearing in the two houses of Congress,

from the known friends and representatives of the Administration."
He warned against the illusion that England could not be kicked into
a war. The reverse was true.

> The army and navy of course pant for service; no small
> portion of the People of England have got to think that a war
> with the U. States affords the best hope of putting an end to
> Slavery, an object paramount with them to all others; the
> Whig party, who ought to be our friends, are led by political
> position to taunt the Ministers for their alleged want of spirit
> in their relations with America; and many of all parties think
> that after a generation of peace a foreign war would be no
> bad purge for the domestic maladies of the body politic.[33]

Should the British ministry call for war, Everett predicted that it would be the most popular war England had ever participated in.

In the meantime, the British exasperated with what Prime Minister Peel termed Polk's blustering, let McLane know there were limits to their patience. Early in January McLane questioned Foreign Minister Aberdeen concerning the military and naval preparations that were taking place. Aberdeen explained that they were not originally intended for defense against the United States but they could be so used should war come. Again on January 9, Aberdeen, while still encouraging hopes for peace explained that he could no longer oppose war measures. McLane relayed this to Buchanan. In Washington the report was taken as a threat. McLane held that Buchanan misinterpreted the report. "You," he wrote to Buchanan, "have made a sad mistake in your interpretation of my Despatch of 3 Feb."[34]

In February the action took place on two stages. The first featured relations between Polk and the Senate, and the second the correspondence between Polk and Buchanan on the one side and McLane in London. Buchanan informed the American minister in London that he doubted that the Senate would ratify a treaty that did not secure the ports on Puget Sound. If the United States were to surrender those ports, Buchanan thought the United States might as well surrender the whole territory. There must be, he thought, a prompt settlement before the swelling tide of migration into Oregon led to a collision. As for Aberdeen's thinking that Polk may have determined to cut off negotiation, he was wrong. Polk not only favored negotiation, he believed "no two nations on earth were more closely bound together by the ties of commerce, so there are none who ought to be more able or willing to do each other justice, without the interposition of any arbitrator." The president, Buchanan wrote, would, if the much-discussed offer were made, submit it to the Senate. This was provided for by the Constitution and, moreover, should it develop that negotiations failed, the president must turn to Congress for measures of defense. The evidence, he wrote, indicates that the Senate would approve of the compromise proposition. The only obstacle would be if the British insisted on free navigation of the Columbia, a facet of the overall settlement that could only lead to trouble in the future.[35]

On February 6 Buchanan wrote another private letter to McLane, seeking to clarify the position of the president. Time, he said, was running out. The president would not agree to free navigation of the Columbia, and he hoped for specific agreements on the border in Puget Sound so as to avoid future difficulties, but he was ready to receive and approve of a compromise. He went on to warn of the importance of time. If Congress adjourned and returned home without a settlement, they were likely to take a tougher stand in the fall, for public opinion was becoming more demanding. He thought the British were too much influenced by newspapers in the eastern coastal cities. These, he stated, were controlled by commercial interests who desired peace. Buchanan thought the British should know that these newspapers were not representative. He wrote: "The strong & irresistible public opinion throughout the vast interior of our country, which controls the action of the Government, is but little, if at all affected by the considerations which influence the mercantile community."[36]

The notification resolution readily passed the House. On February 10 debate began in the Senate and promptly erupted into a battle between fire-eater expansionists and peace advocates. While the Senate debated, the secretary of state sought to indicate, through McLane, the reasonableness of the president.

In the Senate the opposition to the notice of termination enjoyed the advantage of the skilled orators, Webster and Calhoun. On February 26 Webster, in a powerful speech, asked what Polk intended to do. "Compromise," he said, "I can understand, arbitration I can comprehend; but negotiation, with a resolution not to settle unless we obtain the whole, is what I do not comprehend in diplomacy or matters of government."[37] Fear that Polk would pursue an extreme course increased because Senator Allen of Ohio, chairman of the Foreign Relations Committee, in warlike tones demanded all of Oregon and senators assumed that he spoke for the president.

The violent debates led Polk's long-time and esteemed friend, Senator William Haywood of North Carolina, to call on the president. Polk noted that Haywood was excited. Haywood deplored the course taken by Calhoun and then explained his own position. He favored acceptance of the 49th parallel with modifications and, like Polk, opposed conceding free navigation of the Columbia to the British.[38] In his diary, Polk did not reveal whether he gave Haywood reason to believe that he concurred, but Haywood acted on the premise that he did. On March 4 and again the following day Haywood spoke at length in the Senate, contending that the president's intentions were pacific. He did not refer to his conversation with Polk. Instead, he established his case on an interpretation of Polk's annual message.

The result was pandemonium. Haywood's friendship with Polk was well known, and the extremists, Senators Allen and Hannegan, leaped to the floor to castigate Haywood and to question the trustworthiness of Polk. If the president actually held the views attributed to him by Haywood, then, said Hannegan, Polk was "an infamous man—ay, an infamous man." If, as Haywood had argued, Polk had merely inserted some extreme phrases in his message to quiet the "ultras," then the president's conduct was "most vile and infamous."[39] After this outburst the Senate adjourned.

The fight in the Senate transferred itself to the president's mansion. Senators Cass and McDuffie called to talk about the violent debate. Regarding Haywood's speech, Polk declared no one was authorized to speak for him, that he had made his own position clear in his message to Congress, and he urged passage of the notice of termination. Cass and McDuffie were followed by Hannegan of Indiana and Atchison of Missouri. Again Polk said no one was authorized to speak for him and his position was made clear in the message. Then the volatile Hannegan asked him directly if he would settle for the 49th parallel. Polk retorted that he would tell him no more, for what he might do he would be responsible to God and his country. He added that he had been charged with the foreign relations of the country, "and it was unheard of that the President should declare in advance to any one out of his Cabinet, his intentions in reference to them."

Hannegan and Atchison were followed by Allen, who asked the same questions and received the same answers. Polk told Allen that if the Democrats in the Senate became divided on the question it was certain that the Whigs would take advantage, "and that my administration and its usefulness to the country would be destroyed at the first Session of the Congress."[40] After a visit with Allen the next day —he broke his rule about not transacting business on Sunday—he again expressed dismay. And by now he felt as threatened by the extreme expansionists, such as Allen and Hannegan, as by Calhoun and his following. Allen and Hannegan had staked their careers on the slogan "all of Oregon"; they had reason to believe that Polk agreed, for prior to his nomination he had taken this position and had campaigned with the same slogan in 1844.

The debate continued for weeks. Dickinson and Dix of New York contended for passage of the resolution authorizing the president to give notice of termination. Calhoun, who had consulted with Polk a number of times, had advocated compromise, and had asked Polk to make clear what he would do. On March 16 Calhoun made a moving speech on the evils of war. Calhoun's speech, probably one of the finest in the long annals of Congress, won acclaim from friend and foe alike.

On April 10 the able Louis McLane wrote a memorable letter to Buchanan from London. He had been ill and confined to his room for weeks. He was desperately troubled by the course followed by Polk and felt that his mission had been rendered useless. From the beginning he had expressed the view that the British were willing to come to a reasonable settlement, but as winter turned to spring, in 1846, he feared that the British in exasperation were taking a harder line. However, Aberdeen had kindly sent word that he would call on him in his room at any time he wished to confer. McLane wrote:

> Looking to the actual position and vastly increasing progress of our country in all that constitute the power and greatness and prosperity of a great people, and to the similarity of their language, institutions and religion and habit it cannot have failed to occur to you that under peaceful relations and an intimate intercourse in trade the U.S. and Great Britain should now become the two most powerful nations in the world.

He did not think the day far distant "when their example, if not their power," would be called upon "for the protection of freedom, or the limitation of tyranny in many parts of Europe."[41]

This long-term view of relations between the two countries appeared to be more in harmony with the peace advocates in the Senate than with the stance of Polk, but McLane did not see it this way. He regretted the delay in passing the resolution giving notice of termination.[42] Unlike the senators opposing the measure, McLane was certain the president was committed to compromise and peace, a fact due to his instructions prior to leaving for London, and to the tone of the letters he had received from Polk and Buchanan. He was strongly opposed to extremists such as Allen and Hannegan, and he assumed that Polk was of the same view.

The Senate passed the resolution to give notice on April 17. The resolution of the House was amended to remove notes of belligerence, and the preamble expressed the hope that the two countries would enter upon negotiations leading to a mutually satisfactory solution. Polk had advised that the House accept the Senate version for fear the Senate would delay further or fail to pass the resolution. If this should happen, Polk told the cabinet, "the great leading measure of my administration would then be defeated."[43]

Polk lost no time in sending the notice of termination to McLane in London, who presented it to Aberdeen on May 15. It was accompanied by words of assurance that the United States would consider any suitable proposal. Aberdeen's proposal, sent to Washington only four days after he received notice of the termination, arrived in Washington on June 6, and on June 12 the Senate approved it by a vote of 38 to 12. The British might well have withheld their offer had they known that the United States and Mexico were at war. This they did not learn of until weeks later.

The new treaty was identical with what Everett had advised the British would accept. The boundary along the 49th parallel was extended to Puget Sound. Vancouver Island, including that part south of the 49th parallel, was reserved to Great Britain, and the Columbia River was to remain open to the British Hudson's Bay Company. Polk expressed concern over this provision and the lack of specificity as to exactly where the boundary was to be drawn on some of the offshore islands in the Juan de Fuca Strait, but only because he

Oregon: An Unnecessary Controversy 165

feared future controversies. The United States was already at war with Mexico, and these niceties were set aside.

War with Great Britain probably would have resulted had the Polk administration not compromised. Great Britain placed a higher value on the territory north of the 49th parallel than Polk believed, and simply the matter of national honor stood in the way of a concession of the whole territory.

Compromise enjoyed the support of the British and a majority of the United States Senate. It was so for a number of reasons, the importance of the commercial ties between the two countries and an underlying sense of common cultural and political ties. In late January several members of Parliament had pleaded for peace and friendship with the United States. Lord Brougham expressed the same sentiments and added:

> But most especially do I regret the possibility that any differences or difficulty should exist between ourselves, and those with whom a community of blood and language forms a union not less binding than those strong ties of mutual requirements and friendly intercourse which have grown up between us to the advantage of both and which the results of human skill and invention have so largely in late years facilitated and matured.[44]

Brougham received lusty cheers.

Much of the opposition and distrust of Polk had its source in the recognition of the importance of the ties with the British and in the acknowledgment that the United States did not have exclusive rights to all of Oregon. To pursue a course that could lead to war on the basis of blatantly false claims did not accord with the thinking of the well informed who took a mature view of foreign relations. Among the critics of Polk was Albert Gallatin, who perhaps knew better than anyone else the nature of both American and British claims and their limitations.

The settlement reached in June 1846 might well have been within reach ten months earlier. Polk was severely criticized by a host of contemporaries, and later by historians. Two of Polk's basic assumptions explain the course he followed. First, his distrust of the British was not ameliorated by any large view of international affairs nor by an understanding of contemporary British politics. Secondly, he was possessed of an almost pathological personal necessity of appearing "firm and bold," as opposed to firm but conciliatory. The serious divisions of his political party appear to have challenged his sensitivity and to have accentuated this personal trait. It was not inordinate ambition or unwillingness to compromise, but a deep aversion to giving the appearance of a compromiser that moved him. Yet, he is also deserving of understanding, for the difficulties he faced were certainly not entirely of his own making.

Senator Willie Mangum, a Whig from North Carolina, said he had never known a case that had been so "botched."[45] Mangum's indictment did not stop with this censure of Polk. The error, he said, began at the Baltimore convention, when the party made the annexation of all of Oregon an election issue. Polk persisted in that error in his first inaugural address and in the public course he pursued in the autumn of 1845. It was, said Mangum, a popular stance, for the American people had "a strong disposition to war." The politicians, Mangum continued, had recklessly thrown the Oregon issue—he called it a firebrand—out among the people, and by the time the Senate discussed the issue it was unfortunately found that the firebrand had been flung in all directions, defying any calculations, *a priori*, as to the result. Ignorance, emotion, and the aspirations of politicians, not only in the great interior, but especially in New York and Philadelphia, had temporarily dethroned reason and responsibility, and Polk was too weak a man to deal with the situation forthrightly.

NOTES TO CHAPTER VIII

1. Robert F. Dalzell, Jr., *Daniel Webster and the Trial of American Nationalism 1843–1852* (Boston: Houghton Mifflin Co., 1973), pp. 44–45.
2. James K. Polk, *The Diary of James K. Polk during His Presidency, 1845–1849* (Hanover, N. H.: Dartmouth College of the University Press of New England), Jan. 4, 1846.
3. Despatches from London to the secretary of state, Microfilm Copy, Roll 47.
4. Sellers, *James K. Polk*, p. 245.
5. For a detailed and useful analysis of the instructions to McLane, see Sellers, *James K. Polk*, pp. 248–49.

6. Microfilm copies of papers of James Buchanan, Pennsylvania Historical Society, draft of a private letter to McLane, July 12, 1845, Roll 47.
7. Polk, *Diary*, microfilm copy of Polk's papers, Aug. 30, 1845.
8. Polk, *Diary*, Oct. 21, 1845.
9. Ibid., Oct. 24, 1845.
10. Polk Papers, microfilm copy, Series 4, Letter Press Books.
11. Polk, *Diary*, Nov. 29, 1845.
12. Buchanan Papers, Reel 47.
13. Polk to William Polk, Dec. 13, 1845, Polk Papers, Series 4, Letter Press Books.
14. Alexander Everett to Buchanan, Dec. 31, 1845, Buchanan Papers, Reel 9.
15. Ibid., Cushing to Buchanan, Dec. 18, 1845.
16. Ibid., James Forney to Buchanan, Dec. 22, 1845.
17. Despatches from McLane in London. See those for Oct. 3 and Dec. 1, 1845; also private letter of McLane to Polk, Dec. 1, 1845, Polk Papers. See also letters from McLane to Buchanan of Sept. 18 and Nov. 3 in Buchanan Papers.
18. Calhoun to Buchanan, Aug. 20, 1845, Buchanan Papers.
19. John W. Forney to James Buchanan, Dec. 28, 1845, Buchanan Papers, Reel 9.
20. Buchanan to Polk, Dec. 24, 1845, a draft, Buchanan Papers, Reel 9. He also discussed this matter with the president, Polk, *Diary*.
21. Polk, *Diary*, Jan. 25, 1846.
22. Polk, *Diary*, Mar. 4, 1846.
23. Polk, *Diary*, Dec. 24, 1845.
24. Ibid., Dec. 29, 1845.
25. Cushing to Buchanan, Dec. 18, 1845, Buchanan Papers.
26. Ibid., Jan. 4, 1846.
27. Polk to McLane, Dec. 29, 1845, Polk Papers, Letter Press Books.
28. Bancroft to Charles Sumner, Jan. 13, 1846. Papers of George Bancroft, Massachusetts Historical Society.
29. Polk to McLane, Jan. 29, 1846. Polk Papers, Letter Press Books.
30. Ibid.
31. Bancroft to McLane, Mar. 29, 1846, Papers of George Bancroft.
32. Bancroft to Everett, Jan. 30, 1846. Papers of George Bancroft.
33. Everett to Bancroft, Feb. 2, 1846, Bancroft Papers.
34. McLane to Buchanan, Mar. 17, 1846. Buchanan Papers, Reel 10.
35. Buchanan to McLane, Feb. 7, 1846, Buchanan Papers, Reel 47.
36. Ibid., Feb.. 26, 1846.
37. *Congressional Globe*, 29th Cong., 1st Sess., p. 432.
38. Polk, *Diary*, Feb. 26, 1846.
39. *Congressional Globe*, 29th Cong., 1st Sess., Mar. 5, 1846, p. 460.
40. Polk, *Diary*, Mar. 7, 1846.
41. McLane to Buchanan, Apr. 10, 1846, Buchanan Papers.
42. McLane to Buchanan, Apr. 17, 1846, Roll 52, Despatches from London. McLane believed that giving the notice would not at any time have been viewed as a hostile measure. Ibid., McLane to Buchanan, May 3, 1846.
43. Polk, *Diary*, Apr. 20, 1846.
44. McLane to Buchanan, Feb. 3, 1846, Despatches from London, Roll 53.
45. *Congressional Globe*, 29th Cong., 1st Sess., Apr. 4, 1846, p. 635.

Chapter IX

War With Mexico

Two factors played a major role in bringing about war with Mexico. First, interest in the acquisition of the excellent ports in California and a convenient route for a railroad to the Pacific gripped the imagination of commerce, agents who believed that the greatest future for trade lay in the exchange of goods in Asia. Second, the weakness of Mexico and American denigration of that country invited bold measures.

The magnitude of constructing a transcontinental railroad posed no problem to a brash and enterprising generation, convinced that commerce served as the key to greatness. California would be the terminus of steamship lines to China, with interoceanic canals and railroads linking the Mississippi valley, the Great Lakes, and the rising cities of Memphis and New Orleans to the markets of the Orient. Asa Whitney alerted the nation to the opportunities at hand. A fifteen-month stay in the Orient netted Whitney a fortune sufficient to keep him for life. Dazzled by the thought of future trade, he gathered statistics on commerce with China and demonstrated that future trade would depend on a railroad to the Pacific. In 1844 Whitney returned to New York, where he drafted a memorial to Congress.[1] Other leaders were discussing the building of such a railroad, and in November 1845 six hundred men of politics and business from fifteen states and three territories met at Memphis. John C. Calhoun, who presided, called for a railroad moving beyond the Mississippi, toward the Rockies and then to the Pacific. Stephen Douglas of Illinois who campaigned for all of Oregon, had spoken earlier of a Pacific railroad that would tie the great Northwest to Chicago, also attended the sessions in Memphis, as did J.D.B. DeBow, who wrote in a spirit of ecstacy of a route from the cities of the lower Mississippi to southern California. De Bow's route enjoyed three advantages: it would be slightly shorter, it had the lowest gradient and therefore the lowest cost of construction, and it circumvented the snowbound passes to the north.[2]

Determination to capture the Pacific trade made the question of the Texan boundary a matter of prime importance. If the boundary were set at the Nueces River, the way would still not be open for a Pacific railroad; if it were set at the Rio Grande the way would be open, and the final stretch could be cleared by securing a change in Mexico's northern boundary.

Achievement would demand political adroitness. Polk faced a strong Whig minority in the Senate, ready to make political capital out of any injudicious move by the president. In addition, Polk knew well the danger of the Democrats splintering throughout the northeastern states and the problem posed by the possible revolt of some prominent Democrats, led by Calhoun. Relations with Mexico were, therefore, a dangerous political reef in domestic politics that would have to be skirted with careful calculation. The appearance of plotting war would have to be avoided. The olive branch of peaceful negotiation must be extended.

Polk avoided the reef with skill during his first year in office. He seized upon opportunities to negotiate, but did so in a way as to never compromise on the Rio Grande boundary. In fact, the bankrupt condition of Mexico and the political disarray that prevailed offered some slight hope that it would yield to American demands rather than fight a war it could not win. Polk did no more than offer Mexico the opportunity to yield in negotiations or to yield as a result of military defeat.

With the annexation of Texas in February 1845, immediately prior to Polk's taking office, four issues brought about a direct confrontation between the two countries: the Texas question, the western boundaries of Texas, Mexican failure to abide by an agreement calling for payment of more than two million dollars in claims, and California. Equally important in their relations was the fact that these issues existed in an atmosphere of distrust, contempt, racial hostility, and a difference in terms of political stability and economic development. The United States was the wonder of the western world, while Mexico was the scene of despair, poverty, political and financial bankruptcy. Waddy Thompson, American minister to Mexico during the Tyler administration, summed up the American attitude when he wrote to Secretary of State Upshur: "The truth is that I have never been able to elevate Mexico as to regard her as an adversary."[3] Mexican ministers in Washington met with so much arrogance and condescension that at least two became lifelong enemies of the United States.[4]

Contempt on the part of Americans had as its corollary Mexican fear and disdain of the Yankees. In the 1820s, thanks to early diplomatic recognition by the United States, friendly feelings prevailed and the United States was pointed to as a republic to be emulated. By 1830 the drift of Mexican opinion moved in the opposite direction. It developed into a rush of hostility when Poinsett, the American minister, interfered in internal affairs, when efforts to purchase Texas came to the fore and when Americans heaped both praise and assistance on the Texans as they fought for independence. From then on Mexican newspapers saw the United States as a ruthless expansionist.

Manifest Destiny inspired Mexican fear for the future, while in the United States cultural differences engendered scorn and a feeling of superiority. Americans were viewed as crude money grabbers, devoid of good taste, and racist. Mexicans could point with pride to the absence of slavery in their country and dwell on the barbarism of slavery in the United States. The hostile attitude of Americans toward the Indians differed sharply from the friendly attitude of the Mexicans. Mexicans resented Americans lumping Indians, Blacks, and Mexicans into one bag of inferiors.

The gaining of independence by the Texans, in Mexican eyes, was an American enterprise. The Texans were Americans and they had the help of Americans in the United States. Mexicans did not accept the loss of Texas as final, and from time to time Mexican troops carried on small campaigns in western Texas; in 1842 alone there were three. Only internal weakness stood in the way of reconquest. The Texas question never ceased festering in Mexico. Political rivalry between the Centrists and the Federalists, each party blaming the other for the loss, served to keep the question before the public. Feelings reached new heights when the United States annexed Texas.

The Mexico of 1845 had yet to achieve the real unity expected of a nation. Various provinces practiced such a degree of autonomy that they were reduced to loose appendages of the central government. The struggle between Federalists and Centrists related to this problem of trying to weld the many isolated regions into a whole, but none of the many governments that took power succeeded. Texas revolted, and in 1841 Yucatan followed and temporarily achieved independence. Although California did not revolt, to a great degree it ignored Mexican laws and orders that did not jibe with local interests.

Overwhelming political difficulties bequeathed to Mexico by its Spanish heritage, class divisions, and the clash of clericals and anti-clericals contributed to a political paralysis. The absence of a sound fiscal system, the almost complete absence of roads, large-scale brigandage, and the nature of the Mexican economy permitted an almost free play of centrifugal forces. The accompanying political instability—in the short span 1837 to 1851 sixteen different men served as president—conveyed an image of anarchy.[5]

These conditions caused Mexico to lose the respect of foreign powers. Both the British and French were interested in trade and investment, but the returns were small and capriciously forced loans and the setting of prohibitively high duties on imports contributed to a loss of faith. American attitudes were partly a product of the disarray they saw in Mexico.

Mexico's weakness may well explain the violent Mexican hostility toward the United States and Mexico's clinging to illusions which would have been better discarded. Incapable of effective action the tendency was to compensate by the use of extravagant rhetoric. After Texas had maintained its independence for ten years and achieved diplomatic recognition in the late 1830s, the Mexican minister in Washington, immediately following the annexation of Texas, severed diplomatic relations. The move would obviously accomplish nothing as far as restoring Texas to Mexico.

The effect of this quite irrational Mexican response to an accomplished fact was merely to confirm the prejudices of Polk and his administration, further decreasing their respect for Mexico. The angry denunciation of the United States in the Mexican press and bravado pronouncements about making war satisfied the thirst for showing resentment but contributed nothing to the solution of the problem. Consequently, Polk and his cabinet took Mexico only half seriously and resorted cavalierly to tactics of duress. Mexico had indirectly, and quite contrary to intent, brought on this treatment and, therefore, it contributed to some degree, to the coming of the war of conquest that Mexican leaders saw as catastrophic.

However, the Texan question, the major facet of difficulties, was not the only matter of concern, for Mexicans feared that this was only the first intrusion. The Texans, in 1843, launched a military expedition against Santa Fe, and the presence of American merchants and sailors in California aroused fears for that area. Mexican distrust increased in intensity when Commodore Jones of the American navy, on the basis of false rumors of war, occupied Monterey in 1842. Jones was recalled by the United States, and Monterey was restored to Mexico, but Mexican authorities demanded that Jones be punished or otherwise other American naval officers would feel free to repeat his performance. Mexican sensitivity on the California question increased as the Spanish-speaking population in that area drove out representatives from Mexico City, disregarded orders from the capital, and practiced autonomy while professing loyalty. Consequently, when the crisis of Texas annexation came in 1845, Mexican officials believed that any concessions on the Texas question would only serve to jeopardize other outlying territories.

After 1840 American interest in California increased rapidly, thanks to glowing accounts of its natural beauty and riches and the excellence of its harbors. No one contributed more to the growing interest than Thomas Larkin, a successful merchant whose reports sent back to the East coast sparked public attention. These reports were later supplemented by John Charles Fremont, who, in 1843 and again in 1844, led an exploration party into California. His enthusiastic published account changed the status of California from that of remoteness to that of candidacy for acquisition.

Fremont, a skilled topographer and daring adventurer, led an expedition to Oregon in 1843. It appears almost certain that his father-in-law, Senator Thomas Hart Benton, and Senator Linn of Missouri had encouraged him to go into California, although his government-sponsored expedition did not have that as its mission. Fremont reached California on his second trip in 1844. Already some 900 American settlers lived in the area near Monterey. On his return to Washington in the autumn of 1844 he became immersed in discussions with political leaders visiting in his father-in-law's home who looked forward to expansion and who exhibited great interest in California. Fremont satisfied their curiosity with descriptions of the favorable climate, the fertile soil, and, in all probability, the loose control exercised by Mexico. At the same time he worked feverishly on writing his report. His eye for the glamorous, the beauties of nature, and the graphic language he employed so impressed Buchanan that he moved an amendment to the Senate resolution increasing the number of copies of the report to be printed from 5,000 to 10,000. Before long the report was taken up by book publishers and newspapers.[6]

California made its way into discussions of relations with Mexico. In April 1844 the American chargé d'affaires in Mexico City informed the secretary of state that there was not a cent in the Mexican treasury and that in spite of a convention providing for payment of American claims it was unlikely they would be paid. He observed that "we have nothing to gain by quarrelling with her unless indeed we should end by gaining possession of California, and thereby secure a harbourage for our shipping on the Pacific and one of the finest countries on the Globe . . ."[7] Given the acclamations of California as the finest portion of the earth and the inability of Mexico to meet the payments due on claims, inevitably the creditor saw the possibility of canceling claims in turn for a cession of territory. Polk, who admired Andrew Jackson's blunt and inept dealings with American claims against France, entertained this possibility. Jackson's method was to have an influence on how Polk handled difficulties with Mexico.

Polk exemplified the new expansionism, combining the desire for land and the acquisition of ports important to the development of commerce, and the determination to build a railroad to the Pacific. Ports on the Pacific ran as a central thread throughout his dealing with the Oregon question, and he was even more impressed with the possibilities of the San Francisco Bay area.

The other propellant to expansion—the readiness of Americans to assume that it was the destiny of the republic to extend from coast to coast and to serve as the haven of free republican institutions, safe from the intrusions of European imperialism and French and British designs for a New World balance of power—jibed wholly with Polk's parochialism and his almost morbid distrust of Europe. He rang the bell on European intrusion in his inaugural message and again in his message to Congress in December 1845. As he confided to Thomas Hart Benton, in reaffirming the Monroe Doctrine, "I had California & the fine bay of San Francisco as much in view as Oregon." Great Britain, said Polk, "intended to possess it if she could."[8] Benton agreed, and the senator from Missouri, a strong opponent of war with Mexico, believed at least as firmly as did Polk that British plans for taking California were already underway.

Polk confided to George Bancroft, his secretary of navy, that he aimed at the acquisition of California.[9] In all probability, Polk had not at the time determined how this was to be accomplished but, given the situation in Mexico and the fact that he must have been familiar with the stirrings of discontent in California, he need not have considered that war would be necessary.

Polk chose not to dodge questions relating to Mexico at the time he took office. Would Texas accept annexation or would it prefer independence? The British were now seeking to have Mexico grant Texas recognition, and both Sam Houston and Anson Jones cast furtive glances toward continued independence and a working relationship with the British. Before long Mexico did offer to recognize Texas if Texas would remain independent. These developments explain to some extent Polk's haste. In addition, the Texans feared that, on receiving information that the United States offered annexation, Mexico might launch military operations. The danger was exaggerated both in Texas and by Polk, but Polk took steps to be ready for such an eventuality. Accordingly, he ordered General Zachary Taylor to move his troops to the Gulf coast and to be ready to embark for the Rio Grande, and an additional naval force was dispatched to the Gulf of Mexico and to the Pacific coast.[10]

A group of Texans and a small number of Americans, including Charles A. Wickliffe, an agent of Polk, and Commodore Robert F. Stockton of the navy sought to provoke war with Mexico. They circulated rumors of a Mexican attack and urged prompt measures of defense. In cooperation with General Sidney Sherman, commander of the Texas militia, they promoted a project calling for a volunteer force to drive out the Mexicans. The emissaries of Polk went well beyond their instructions. In a conversation with Anson

Jones, the newly elected president of Texas, Stockton's secretary claimed that Polk had given his approval "so that, when Texas was finally brought into the Union, she might bring a war with her."[11]

The zeal of this small group of Texan imperialists should not lead to the conclusion that they were spokesmen for Polk. Andrew J. Donelson, American chargé d'affaires in Texas, pursued quite a different strategy. He centered his attention on having the Texans approve annexation. It would be embarrassing and create Mexican hostility should fighting break out in western Texas between Mexican troops and the Texan militia. This was to be avoided because of expectations that Mexicans in the disputed territory would quietly accept annexation. Likewise, should hostilities commence the United States would appear to be annexing Texas by conquest. Donelson was particularly opposed to Texas sending Texan troops, for he believed they would be brutal toward the Mexicans and would stir up hatred. Therefore, he encouraged "no aggressive movement on the part of Texas to take forcible possession of the Rio Grande."[12] Polk, too, was not ready to go to war.

However, Polk assured the Texans that the United States would defend Texas' claims to the Rio Grande boundary. This bold decision set aside the fact that the United States had long looked upon the Nueces River, one hundred miles to the east as the boundary of Texas. The only basis for the Texas claim to the Rio Grande boundary was the unilateral action of the Texas legislature. The Joint Resolution of annexation did not commit the United States to uphold the Texas claim. Indeed, the reason why the resolution provided Polk with the option of negotiating a treaty with Texas, aside from the necessity of including this option so as to muster the necessary votes, was the widespread opinion that the territory between the Nueces and the Rio Grande was in dispute and should be settled by negotiation. Both Mexicans and Americans had settlements in this area, which Texas had never exercised jurisdiction over.

In December 1844, when Donelson consulted with President Houston and other leaders, he explained to them that the United States would be willing to alter the terms of the treaty negotiated early that year, if necessary, to secure passage in Texas. The Texans made no mention of the boundary question. Donelson informed Calhoun "that you might recognize Texas as including all the Ter-

Republic of Texas

ritory East of the Nueces to its source, and thence North to the Red River—leaving the remainder of the Territory as claimed by her to be adjusted by future negotiation with Mexico."[13] He added that the territory west of the Nueces was not represented in the Texan Congress. However, by early April President Houston insisted that Texas "never would come into the Union without recognition of her claim as far west as the Rio Grande." Donelson assured him that the United States would support the claim; however, if the claim to the Rio Grande boundary was found to be untenable, then the United States would negotiate with Mexico.[14] As late as October 1845, while still at Corpus Christi, General Zachary Taylor anticipated that the boundary question probably would be decided by negotiation.[15]

Did Polk have reason to expect that Mexico would go to war after breaking off diplomatic relations? The answer is almost wholly in the negative. Every American minister since 1836 had sent graphic reports of the hostility to the United States. Wilson Shannon, in a report to the secretary of state in March 1845 told of the warlike spirit that prevailed and that the new administration in Mexico had been compelled to adopt the same attitude with a view to conciliating the army and the people, but hostility did not mean that Mexican leaders were ready to declare war.[16] From late May through August in 1845 Buchanan received almost weekly letters from William Parrott, Polk's confidential agent in Mexico, and from John Black, consul in Mexico City. These letters spoke of the public enmity toward the United States, described the paralysis suffered by the government, dwelt on the empty treasury and complete failure of the effort to negotiate a loan, and repeatedly and without exception predicted that Mexico would not declare war.[17] Recent scholarship analyzing public pronouncements of Mexican officials during this same period and for the months ahead concludes that, to conciliate the public, many demonstrated hostility, but on the question of actually going to war with the United States the pronouncements were deliberately ambiguous and that there was no prospect of Mexico going to war.[18]

However, Polk did receive at least one jarring warning that Mexico was ready to make war. Bancroft had been in conversation with Baron von Gerolt, Russian minister in Washington, who claimed to have private information. Polk asked Bancroft to see him. Bancroft appeared to be convinced that the information Gerolt had was authoritative. On the basis of letters received from Mexico, Gerolt told of large-scale preparations and held that war was inevitable. Polk read Bancroft's letter and Secretary of War Marcy, with Polk's approval, sent reinforcements to Taylor.[19]

During August Polk also received advice that certainly influenced his thinking, at least to the degree that he gave more thought to options suggested to him. In August Richard S. Coxe, eminent Washington jurist, who is reported to have participated in more cases before the Supreme Court than any other man of his time, wrote a lengthy letter to Buchanan. He represented the claimants against Mexico and therefore had a direct interest in American-Mexican relations. Coxe recommended war. He wrote:

> You may rely upon it Sir, that the claims of our citizens upon Mexico furnish the government with a most potent lever with which to operate upon that nation. The annexation of Texas leaves open a most important question of boundary, which must be adjusted sooner or later. If this powerful lever is adroitly managed you may move this question as you will and adjust the boundary as you will. With a view to a satisfactory arrangement it would perhaps be desirable that Mexico should declare war. If she should not resort to that measure under the present feeling of excitement which exists in that country is it practicable to avoid hostilities long when you come to take possession of Texas, and to extend your authority to the lines upon which you mean to insist.[20]

Coxe held out no hope that the boundary could be extended to the Pacific by negotiations. Since Mexico had severed diplomatic relations, the United States was absolved from making any offer and it "almost imposed upon her the duty, certainly to invest her with the right herself to fix the amount and character of the indemnity to be paid and promptly and effectively to demand and enforce such payment." Mexico should be faced with a demand for payment; if she refused, the United States should take the desired territory and then pay the claims.

Similar ideas were stirring elsewhere. On July 26 Parrott wrote Buchanan stating "that nothing but a severe chastisement would secure our people, in future, from such vexatious annoyances and insults as those to which they have hitherto been exposed, . . ." Parrott thought it would be better if Mexico declared war than propose negotiations because then the United States could secure the desired boundaries, which could not be achieved by negotiation.[21]

On August 29 the cabinet unanimously approved a new set of instructions to General Taylor, who had now set up camp at Corpus Christi, on the south bank of the Nueces River. If Mexico attacked, Taylor was to drive the Mexican army back to the Rio Grande. Any crossing of the Rio Grande by Mexican troops was to be considered an act of war, and Taylor was to be free to attack, if he so chose. The commander of the naval squadron, on learning of war, was to blockade all Mexican ports. Even as early as June 24 Bancroft had instructed Commodore Sloat, in the Pacific, to seize all ports in California if Mexico declared war.[22]

On the morning of September 5 Richard Coxe called on Buchanan and warned that Mexico would not declare war, but simply let matters drift. Coxe observed that the acquisition of California was as important as the acquisition of Texas. Buchanan was sufficiently impressed to ask Coxe to draft a memorandum.[23]

Then in mid-September developments took a new turn as dispatches from Parrott and Black in Mexico stated that Mexico was willing to negotiate. As Polk recorded it in his diary, Mexico wished to re-establish diplomatic relations and would receive a minister.[24] What Parrott actually said was quite different; Mexico would welcome a commissioner. Parrott spoke of negotiations and not of the restoration of diplomatic relations.[25] The cabinet unanimously agreed that it was expedient to reopen relations and that John Slidell, who spoke Spanish, should be sent. Polk promptly broadened the nature of the prospective negotiations, noting in his diary that the "one great object of the Mission . . . would be to adjust the permanent boundary between Mexico and the United States." He considered the amount of pecuniary consideration to be paid as of small importance. He was ready to pay forty millions for a boundary along the Rio Grande and west to the Pacific along the 32nd parallel, the line that would permit the building of a Pacific railroad along the advantageous southern route.

Alarming news of a readiness of Mexico to go to war appeared in a New Orleans newspaper and caused Polk and his cabinet, on the following day, to delay sending the mission and to agree that the American consul in Mexico City should ascertain if the Mexican government would negotiate.[26]

Black saw the minister of foreign affairs, Peña y Peña on October 13, and two days later Peña y Peña sent him a note stating "my Government is disposed to receive the commissioner of the United States subject to the withdrawal of the American naval force off Vera Cruz." Three days later Black again called on Peña y Peña. As Black reported the conversation to Buchanan, the Mexican foreign minister expressed the hope "that your Government, will not think of sending Mr. Parrott out as commissioner."[27]

Mexican confirmation that it would be willing to receive a commissioner reached Washington on November 8, but the previous day Polk had already discussed the nature of the instructions and the appointment of Slidell. A few days later Parrott called on the president; Polk informed him that he wished him to serve as secretary of legation in Mexico, and Parrott accepted.

Instructions were sent to Slidell at Pensacola on November 10. At this point it appears that Polk was optimistic that the whole question of Texas and its boundaries could be settled. Parrott had conveyed this view, and Polk noted in his diary that he was of the same opinion.[28]

The instructions to Slidell, drafted by Buchanan, raised the question of a complete revision of the boundary between the two countries. There could be no settlement that did not offer the United States a boundary on the Rio Grande. In turn, the United States would assume the claims of Americans.

The remainder of the instructions referred to three possible boundary lines beyond the Rio Grande. The first would have given New Mexico and California to the United States. The second would have given the United States northern California, including San Francisco but not Montèrey. The third option would have extended the boundary of Texas to the Rio Grande and would have transferred New Mexico to the United States. Mexico was to be offered $25 million for accepting the first, $20 million for the second, and $5 million if it agreed to no more than the third. Mexico was not required to meet any of the last three options but it could not obtain a settlement unless it accepted the Rio Grande boundary.

During the summer and fall General Taylor reported that his forces were adequate to meet any crisis.[29] Reinforcements, however, arrived, including seven new infantry companies and two artillery companies on August 30. Taylor anticipated no crisis. A confidential agent, who had been in Matamoros, informed Taylor early in September that no extraordinary military preparations were underway and that the people did not want war with the United States.[30] Taylor was confident that he would not need more troops and asked that no volunteers be sent. Yet, in the first days of October five companies of the 5th infantry, two companies of the 8th infantry, and one company of the 7th infantry arrived.[31] By October 15 Taylor had 3,733 troops.[32] Whether this movement of troops was precautionary or in anticipation that war was inevitable cannot be determined, but as late as February 1846 Taylor did not foresee any hostilities and he continued to believe that there would be negotiation of the question of the disputed territory.

Negotiation would determine whether it was to be peace or war. Slidell rushed off to Mexico, in accordance with instructions, arriving at Veracruz November 30. Peña y Peña asked that Slidell delay his approach to Mexico City. The government of Herrera now faced an overthrow by General Paredes, who denounced Herrera for failure to take a firm stand vis-à-vis the United States. The political crisis in Mexico would probably have sufficed to kill negotiations, but Polk had already placed obstacles, intentionally or not, in the way of success. Slidell came as minister plenipotentiary, and to receive him meant the restoration of diplomatic relations prior to a settlement. Also, whereas Peña y Peña had consented to negotiate on the Texas question, Slidell's instructions aimed at a much broader problem, the disposition of more Mexican territory. Further, Polk had appointed Parrott as secretary of legation in spite of Peña y Peña's expressed aversion to Parrott. Even if Mexico had been a stable and secure government, it could not have agreed to begin negotiations, given these considerations.

When the Herrera government fell before Paredes' forces on December 29 Polk decided Slidell should remain and seek to negotiate with the new government. During his stay, Slidell engaged in an exchange of correspondence with Peña y Peña that exhibited a strident spirit that could only further alienate the party with whom he was seeking to establish friendly relations. In their correspondence with Slidell, Polk and Buchanan approved of Slidell's style of diplomacy, and Buchanan dismissed the Mexican objections as "ridiculous pretenses." Slidell's efforts to negotiate with the new Paredes government gave hope that a settlement could still be reached, and the Mexican question was not discussed in the cabinet again until mid-February.

The first reports from Slidell, telling of his difficulties with the Herrera government, reached Polk and Buchanan during the second week of the new year. The decision was then reached to order General Taylor to proceed to the Rio Grande and Commodore Connor to proceed to Veracruz. Both officers were to avoid aggressive actions and not to disturb Mexican settlements. These orders were essentially the same as those given the previous July. At that time

Taylor, having been granted freedom of discretion, moved only as far as Corpus Christi, south of the Nueces River. Commodore Connor had been in the waters of Veracruz until recalled in October, at the time the Herrera government stipulated that it would only negotiate if Commodore Connor withdrew his squadron. These movements were to lead the new Paredes government to protest that it was being asked to negotiate under duress. It was precisely so. Polk had concluded that Mexico would only give way if the United States staged a bold confrontation.

On January 20 Buchanan followed with a set of instructions to Slidell, which demonstrated growing impatience. Should the Mexican government refuse to receive Slidell, "nothing would then remain for this Government but to take redress into its own hands." Slidell was informed that Taylor had been ordered to the Rio Grande and a strong fleet had been assembled in the Gulf of Mexico so the president will "be prepared to act with vigor and promptitude the moment that Congress shall give him the authority."[33] Buchanan sent Slidell a dispatch similar in tone on January 28. Again, the notice was given that refusal to receive Slidell would mean that forbearance had been exhausted. However, Slidell was to "wait patiently for a final decision." No time limit was placed on how long he was to wait, but once he had been rejected then the president would submit the whole case to Congress.[34]

On February 13 Colonel Alexander J. Atocha, an American citizen of Spanish birth, who had served with Santa Anna and had been expelled from Mexico, called on Polk. He conveyed a message from his former chief, who was now in Havana, stating that if he were restored to office in Mexico he would sell upper California to the United States. Polk did not take this seriously but he was impressed by Atocha's contention that the only way to deal with the Paredes government was to present a threat of such overwhelming force that Paredes could explain that he had no choice but to yield. Polk saw Atocha again two days later and heard the same line of argument, and this corresponded with his own way of thinking.[35]

The situation regarding Mexico did not change during February and the first four weeks of March. On occasion Polk showed impatience but not alarm. Reports from Mexico continued to suggest that the country would not go to war. On February 16 General Taylor warned against exaggerated accounts of Mexican preparations for war. "From the best information I am able to obtain," he wrote, "and which I deem as authentic as any, I do not believe that our advance to the banks of the Rio Grande will be resisted."[36] The dispatches from Slidell spoke of Mexico's financial stringency. Bancroft, too, received reports from Mexico via his Boston merchant friend, W. Kemble, that Mexico did not want war.[37] Bancroft wrote to Minister McLane in London that affairs with Mexico appeared to be going well. If Mexico were to venture on war "every port from San Francisco to Acapulco lies open to our ships. In the Gulf of Mexico we have a still larger force; and the army of occupation is advancing to the Del Norte." No war, he wrote, is apprehended. In Mexico itself, Bancroft explained, a better feeling was prevailing. Mexicans disliked the United States "but they dislike monarchy even more; and the open suggestion of placing a prince on the throne to be erected there, has created a party in favor of [peace with?] the United States."[38] Mexico received little attention because the administration, in late February and early March, was absorbed with the feverish debates in the Senate on the Oregon question.

In Mexico, Slidell, braced by Polk's and Buchanan's approval of the course he had pursued and inspired by the bold tone of Buchanan's dispatches of late January, wrote to Joaquin M. de Castillo y Lanzas, Paredes' foreign minister. The note sounded a peremptory call for a decision on whether he was to be received. Slidell, after explaining that Polk was wholly conciliatory and desired to preserve peace, gave notice that the United States could no longer tolerate "the state of quasi hostility," and it was up to Mexico to decide "whether it shall give place to friendly negotiation or lead to an open rupture."[39] Slidell instructed Black, consul at Mexico City, who was to deliver the note, "that if a definite and favorable reply were not received . . . on the 15th instant, I should then apply for my passports." The ensuing correspondence between Slidell and Castillo y Lanzas merely reiterated all the arguments exchanged in the past. On March 15 Slidell received word that Mexico would not receive him, and he promptly asked for his passports.

During those two crucial weeks of March, General Taylor undertook to march his troops from Corpus Christi to the Rio Grande. At Corpus Christi he encountered no Mexican hostility but as he moved southwestward Mexican friendliness changed to sharp enmity. Taylor expected Mexicans to be conciliatory, and he issued orders that there must be no interference with their civil or religious rights. However, when Taylor reached the Colorado arroya, the Mexicans demonstrated complete hostility. A small force of Mexicans distributed leaflets denouncing the United States. The leaflets had been issued by General Francisco Mejia, who was at Matamoros. These leaflets made it clear the Mexicans felt much more strongly about American troops west of the Nueces than they did about the loss of Texas itself.[40] On March 23 the prefect of the department of Tamaulipas warned Taylor that the people of the district were startled by invasion of a territory that had never belonged to Texas. The prefect held that the United States had never mentioned this territory as belonging to Texas and the people wished to remain part of Mexico.[41] By the time Taylor reached the Rio Grande and set up camp across the river from Matamoros he found the people very hostile. Taylor took comfort in the fact that his artillery could destroy the heart of the Mexican town at a moment's notice.

The report of the failure of the Slidell mission did not reach Washington until April 8. In the meantime Polk, still holding out some hope of Slidell being received, discussed with his cabinet and the leading members of the Senate the possibility of the Senate appropriating one million dollars to be used as a down payment. If this could be paid to Paredes immediately, then possibly Paredes might agree to a treaty drawing new boundaries. The cabinet and several senators approved, but the proposal was dropped after Calhoun withdrew his support, and Allen of Ohio concluded the Senate would not approve.[42]

Polk's final effort testifies to his desire for peace, but his desire was inextricably linked to his conviction that new boundaries must be drawn giving California to the United States. He had months earlier, and on several occasions thereafter, committed himself to asking for a declaration of war if Slidell were refused recognition. The cabinet had not raised a dissenting voice with the exception of one occasion; at a cabinet meeting, on February 17, Buchanan objected to setting any kind of deadline for Mexico's receiving Slidell, preferring that Slidell return to the United States and await developments. In late March, when Polk consulted Senators Allen, Benton, Cass, and Calhoun on the possibility of a special appropriation, each declared in favor of the acquisition of California.

Polk should have been, and apparently was, deeply concerned when told that a special appropriation could not pass the Senate. Given this situation, he could expect difficulties when he turned to Congress to grant him the authority to handle Mexican affairs as he saw fit. He did not bring the question before the cabinet until April 25. On May 3 he consulted with Thomas Hart Benton and told him he planned to send a communication to Congress on Mexican relations and explained that he had only delayed because he awaited the arrival of Slidell. Benton expressed great reluctance to go to war.[43] On the evening of May 11, the day his call went to Congress for a declaration of war, Polk expressed fear that a combination of Whigs and dissident Democrats might well defeat the measure. Significantly, he took comfort in the view that fear of the people would deter them from doing so.[44]

Polk's quandary, if he really experienced one, was relieved in part by what he knew about California. Fremont, on another expedition, and his party entered California in January. The Mexican authorities described him as leading a band of "Bandoleros," and ordered that he be driven out. Larkin, Polk's confidential agent, reported that the Mexican order was nothing more than a ruse and that Fremont was annoyed rather than fearful. If Fremont wished, wrote Larkin, he could easily raise a force at least as great as the Mexicans could raise. Larkin expressed the view that "if a New Flag was respectfully planted, it would receive the good will of much of the wealth and respectability of the Country, those who live by office and the absence of Law, would faintly struggle against a change. Many Natives and foreigners of Wealth and pursuits are already calculating on the hopes, fears and expectations from the apparent coming change now before them, from the great influx of Strangers."[45] It is not known when Buchanan received this letter; probably it arrived after the commencement of hostilities.

The letter is significant because it reveals how easy it would be for the United States to take California and also because, at a time of great tension when Polk presumably sought peace, an American of prominence and under government orders to explore Oregon marched into Mexican territory. It appears that Fremont did so with the approval of Polk, although this cannot be documented. The administration sent a messenger, A. H. Gillespie, to California with instructions for Fremont. What those instructions were is not known.[46]

That California could be taken readily was well known, and Commodore Sloat with his Pacific squadron received orders dated June 24, 1845, to seize as many ports as possible if he ascertained that Mexico had declared war. The order included this significant sentence: "The Mexican ports on the Pacific are said to be open and defenceless."[47] The same view of the ease with which California would fall into American hands prevailed in the spring of 1846; shortly after the declaration of war Bancroft observed: "A connexion between California, and even Sonora, and the present government of Mexico, is supposed scarcely to exist."[48]

So at the time that Slidell returned to Washington it was clear to Polk and his cabinet that highly prized California could easily be taken and then transferred to the United States in a peace treaty incorporating the principle of *uti possidetus*. This delightful prospect counterbalanced at least in some degree, possibly wholly, Polk's concerns as to how the troublesome Senate would respond to a call for a declaration of war.

Polk's frustration led to the decision to go to war. Mexico would not negotiate and did not go to war. She preferred to drift. No solution acceptable to Polk was in sight. Polk, who in frontier style prided himself on being firm and bold, had only two paths open to him, military action or patiently to await further developments. For several reasons the latter course did not suit Polk. First, Polk's conception of the presidency was that of national leader, and he firmly believed he represented all people of the country whereas members of Congress represented only their own constituencies. Secondly, given the vast diversity of the United States, it was next to impossible to achieve a national consensus on foreign policy, and therefore the president must act even in the face of a lack of unity. Thirdly, military and naval forces had been in place for a vigorous prosecution of war for months. Finally, he believed that the war would be of short duration and that the people at large would rally once war was declared.

By May 6, with the concurrence of his cabinet, he had decided to send a special message to Congress. That evening dispatches arrived reporting that a party of Taylor's dragoons sent out on April 24 became engaged with an enemy force. Sixteen were killed or wounded, and the remainder taken prisoner. Polk could now say American blood had been shed on American soil. His message to Congress called for appropriations, authority to recruit volunteers in support of Taylor's troops, and a declaration of war. The message gave rise to heated debate. All were willing to vote support, but many were opposed to a declaration of war. Calhoun sought delay and pleaded for "high, full, and dispassionate consideration."[49] War did not exist, Calhoun maintained, simply because of an invasion. Only Congress could declare war. Clayton of Delaware held "that the whole conduct of the Executive in this case has been utterly unjustifiable."[50] Polk, Clayton charged, had "sent an army to take up a position, where, as it must have been foreseen, the inevitable consequence would be war." Several sought to separate the vote on supplies from the vote on the declaration of war, but the chair overruled them.

Prior to the vote on the declaration of war, supplies, and recruiting of volunteers, the opposition introduced motions aimed at delay and rejection of the war declaration. These included a motion to send the bill to the Committee on Military Affairs, a motion to strike out the preamble, and a motion to strike out the declaration of war from the preamble. On each of these motions the opposition to Polk garnered twenty votes, with Polk's supporters casting twenty-five.[51] This suggests that a vote limited to approval or disapproval of war would have resulted in a bare majority in favor. Had this taken place the faith of the country at large in the necessity of war would have been shaken from the beginning, whereas the violent opposition did not develop until late in 1846.

Had, then, Polk placed the country in the position of a man about to go over Niagara Falls, who had to be rescued? This may not have been his intention but this was nevertheless, to a considerable degree, the effect, which created distrust then and later. Several of Polk's actions provoked Mexico into a confrontation. The first, laying claim to the Rio Grande at the very outset, when it was generally recognized that Texas' claims to the territory were at least dubious, was an act bordering on aggression. Secondly, ignoring the Mexican specification that the envoy should be a commissioner and not a minister, together with the appointment of Parrott as secretary of legation, plus tying to the negotiation the question of territory all the way to the Pacific, distorted the mission from settlement of the Texas question to a question of aggrandizement. Thirdly, encircling Mexico with military and naval forces, including the stationing of Taylor's troops on the extreme western edge of the disputed territory, did not accomplish what Polk hoped, namely deterence; instead it injured

Mexican pride. If Polk had wanted war, these three steps practically assured it.

However, the evidence also supports the hypothesis that he wanted peace. Therefore, consideration must be given as to why he initiated these aggressive moves. The major explanation lies in the contempt and bias he and the cabinet entertained toward Mexico. That country's political instability, financial bankruptcy, inability to command the loyalty of outlying provinces such as Yucatan and California, and its defenseless condition, plus a feeling that the population was socially inferior, excluded it from consideration as a sovereign state. This attitude came to the fore, for instance, in the cavalier dismissal of the able notes wrtten by Peña y Peña and Castillo y Lanzas. Their arguments had been dismissed as mere pretenses. Buchanan termed them evasions and subterfuges. Polk's view that Mexico, considering its empty treasury, would be willing to dispose of a large part of its territory in return for payment in money reflected a low opinion of Mexican national feeling. He was wrong. At the depths of the humiliation the Mexican people reached out to restore their pride. It was not only Polk that misjudged the situation, but his cabinet and the Democratic majority in Congress.

Polk's arbitrary proceedings were exhibted in the fact that, from the first days of the crisis in July 1845, the Polk administration decided that any crossing of the Rio Grande by Mexican forces would be considered a cause for war. At the same time he ordered Taylor to occupy the same disputed territory. If Mexican entry into this territory constituted aggression, then the entry of American troops into the area likewise constituted aggression. It was Polk and the United States who transgressed, not the Mexicans.

Polk's zig-zag course did not pertain to his objectives. He was a boldly determined man who discounted both domestic and Mexican opposition. He had one major objective, the acquisition of California, and he never once swerved from that objective.

Once war was underway, the United States promptly took over California, New Mexico, and occupied the northern states of Mexico. On June 22 Bancroft wrote to his friend Samuel Hooper, who was a leading figure in Bryant and Sturgis, the leading shipping concern in the Pacific trade, stating that he had ordered the seizure of San Francisco, Monterery, Magellan, and Guaymas but had not included San Diego. He asked Hooper, who was thoroughly familiar with southern

California, for his views, adding "If Mexico makes peace this month the Rio del Norte and the parallel of 35° may do as a boundary; after that 32° which will include San Diego."[52] Hooper responded immediately and recommended that the boundary be drawn at the 32° parallel. He offered three reasons for so doing. The population in the area would be in constant revolt against Mexican rule, the people of Los Angeles favored annexation to the United States, and it would be important "to the mercantile interests to have these two places taken as well as Monterey and San Francisco as it would ensure a peaceful state of things through the whole country and enable them to continue their trade as before along the whole coast and to collect their debts as they expected from the crops of this year."[53]

The Americans in command in California and New Mexico promptly issued orders establishing new governments and new codes of law. The minutest details from election procedures, form of government, and police enforcing agencies were spelled out. In both territories the victors announced that the conquered territories were now a part of the United States.

Neither Polk nor any other expansionist could foresee the tremendous difficulties of making peace. At the outbreak of war Polk assumed that the war would be a brief encounter, with American military forces promptly taking control of the territory required, and the Mexicans overawed by American superiority. Mexican resistance proved to be more tenacious, and Mexican public opinion more determined to resist the inevitable than anyone could prophesy. The American army was frequently outnumbered, and the Mexican forces provided more than one severe test; however, superiority in arms and supplies proved decisive.

Polk began his search for peace shortly after the military victories of the first two months of fighting. When these brought no response, it was decided in November 1846 that General Winfield Scott should launch a campaign against Veracruz. That city fell before Scott's forces, but the approaching season would bring with it yellow fever and decimation of the troops. Scott had little choice but to march inland. At the outset the aim was not to occupy Mexico City, for there was reason to believe that continued military victories would convince the Mexicans of the necessity to make peace. Scott delayed his march to the capital but finally occupied it in August 1847.

Politics in Mexico twisted and turned with various factions succeeding each other in control. A cloud of financial bankruptcy encouraged drastic measures. At the outset, the Paredes government levied a forced loan on the clergy and suspended payment of foreign debts, thereby alienating both the clergy and foreigners. In August 1846 Paredes was overthrown, and General José Mariano Salas assumed power as provisional president. He promptly invited Santa Anna, who was in Havana, to return. That colorful but opportunistic leader of earlier years had already been approached by a representative of Polk and asked if he would negotiate peace on Polk's terms. Santa Anna gave an evasive answer but encouraged the representative to believe that he would. Consequently, Santa Anna was permitted to get through the cordon of American warships. Once in Mexico he shrewdly waited for the right moment to assume leadership of the army. He succeeded in raising an army and late in 1846 he was elected president by the Mexican Congress. Fully aware of the distrust that he might sell out to the United States, he moved with caution as to American peace feelers and at the same time engaged Taylor and then Scott in large-scale battles. His army fought well but was defeated. Finally, Santa Anna retreated to the capital, but his army remained intact.

Polk's repeated efforts to make peace proved futile, and failure served to encourage his political enemies at home and the critics of the war to seize every opportunity to embarrass him. Congress in December 1846 reduced his proposals to a quasi-trial of Polk's good faith in the prewar negotiations. When it became apparent that the president was ready to adopt ever sterner measures and invade central Mexico, some newspapers, organizations of business interests, and church groups called for restraint and, not without sufficient grounds, denounced the aggressiveness as a blot on the country's morals.

On the political front the majority of the Whigs, the more conservative wing, denounced Polk for unconstitutional and devious machinations in bringing about the war. They also attacked him for making the war an instrument for expansion. Finally, the Whigs in the House of Representatives managed to amend a bill expressing thanks to General Taylor so that the resolution included "in a war unnecessarily and unconstitutionally begun by the President of the United States."[54]

The majority of Whigs never ceased to protest that they acted out of patriotism, and they continued to vote for war appropriations. However, they eagerly seized on any Polk measure that allowed them to be critical without opening themselves to charges of betraying the nation. The Whigs defeated Polk's proposed creation of a position of lieutenant general to command all forces, took a stand against all territorial acquisition, and delayed passage of certain revenue bills. While sincere in their opposition to the war, the Whigs were also anxious to turn the war to their own political advantage.

The antislavery wing among the Whigs, who enjoyed their greatest strength in New England, not only condemned Polk but labeled the war a conspiracy of the slavocracy. The heart of their opposition lay in the belief that the war was immoral, and they damned fellow Whigs who voted for appropriations. James Russell Lowell contributed his famous satirical *Bigelow Papers*, portraying the war as a greedy, ignorant slavery plot.

The Concord group of literati, represented by Emerson and Thoreau, expressed despair for the republic, as they saw a departure from high principle. Theodore Parker, brilliant intellectual, admirer of Immanuel Kant, the advance representative of the social gospel, spoke at an emotion-packed assemblage at Faneuil Hall and condemned the war and the Whigs who voted funds to support it. Parker, stronger on ethical pronouncements than political realities, saw in the war a conspiracy of slavocracy.

The Democrats, too, had serious doubts about the war. Van Buren's followers at first hesitated to condemn Polk, fearing that they would weaken their position in the party, for they hoped to capture control of the party in 1848. However, when it became clear that Polk's aim was the acquisition of territory, thereby raising the question of the extension of slavery, they became increasingly critical. Senator John Dix, who had supported Polk on the Texas annexation question and voted for the declaration of war, was among the first to express disillusion. In a letter to a fellow New Yorker on May 15, he stated that the war "begun in fraud last winter" would end in disgrace.[55]

In the late winter of 1847 Polk proposed to his cabinet the sending of a peace commissioner. Nicholas P. Trist was selected for the mission. He was not lacking in qualifications, for he held the position of chief clerk in the state department and he was fluent in Spanish; however, once in Mexico, Trist displayed both arrogance and a proclivity for reckless and undiplomatic statements. His instructions regarding peace terms included the Rio Grande as a boundary and the cession of upper California and New Mexico as *sine qua nons*. Lower California was included as a desirable goal. Should Mexico agree to these terms, the United States would cancel all claims and pay Mexico $15 million; however, Polk and Buchanan allowed Trist some leeway on the amount to be paid.

The irrepressible diplomat no sooner arrived in Mexico than he insulted General Winfield Scott, whose own pride matched that of Trist. When Trist gave Scott a sealed envelope to be delivered to the Mexican foreign minister and refused to reveal its contents, Scott, already irritated by the sending of this emissary, took offense. A heated written exchange followed, and for weeks the two men were not on speaking terms. Fortunately, a reconciliation took place when Scott bestowed friendly attention during an illness suffered by Trist.

Scott and Trist received peace proposals from the three Mexican peace commissioners appointed by Santa Anna. The terms proposed by Mexico indicated a determination to ignore Mexican military failures. The United States was asked to give up all occupied territory, lift the blockade, accept the Nueces River as a boundary, and pay the costs of the war. These demands were in large part adhered to throughout the remainder of 1847. In September Trist sent back to Washington the Mexican proposals for peace, including a settlement of the boundary at the Nueces River. Polk, who had lost confidence in Trist because of his earlier behavior, ordered Trist's recall. At the same time, Polk ordered Scott to take firm measures that would compel the Mexicans to negotiate on the basis of American terms. Trist was prepared to leave Mexico; but, under pressure to remain from both British and some Mexican peace advocates, he resolved to extend his stay and finally negotiated the peace.

Peace prospects improved in October after Santa Anna resigned, and his place was taken by Peña y Peña, who earnestly desired peace. However, no real progress was made until the new year. Finally, on February 2, 1848, the peace treaty was signed at Guadalupe Hidalgo. The treaty provided for the cession of upper California as far south as San Diego and New Mexico and set the boundary of Texaxs at the Rio Grande. The treaty canceled American claims set at $3,250,000 and provided that the United States pay Mexico $15 million.

NOTES TO CHAPTER IX

1. House Executive Documents, 28th Cong., 2nd Sess., No. 72.
2. For the Memphis Convention, see St. George L. Sioussat, "Memphis, the Gateway of the West," *Tennessee Historical Magazine*, Vol. III, 1932; *The Commercial Review of the South and West*, ed. J.D.B. De Bow, Jan., 1846; Robert W. Johannsen, *Stephen Douglas* (New York: Oxford University Press, 1973), p. 171 and Wiltse, *John C. Calhoun Sectionalist, 1840–1850*, p. 238.
3. Waddy Thompson to Upshur, Aug. 25, 1843, Manning, *Diplomatic Correspondence of the United States*, Vol. VIII, p. 558.
  On his return to the United States Waddy Thompson wrote a book entitled *Recollections of Mexico*. He had a few kind words to say about Mexican friends and the general cordiality that prevailed, but the book abounds in unfavorable comparisons of Mexico with the United States. Even in his Preface he professed to find disgusting "the mummeries and impostures which degrade the Christian religion into an absurd, ridiculous, and venal superstition." He compared Mexico and Massachusetts and in all that made a people great. Massachusetts represented the finest. The general population in Mexico was "lazy, ignorant, and, of course, vicious and dishonest." Throughout the book, Thompson exhibited a sense of superiority and made facile judgments of condemnation.
4. Gene M. Brack, *Mexico Views Manifest Destiny An Essay on the Origins of the Mexican War* (Albuquerque: University of New Mexico Press, 1975), p. 63.
5. Charles C. Cumberland, *Mexico The Struggle for Modernity* (New York: Oxford University Press, 1968); see Chapter VII "Marking Time" for an excellent account of these years.
6. Allan Nevins, *Fremont The West's Greatest Adventurer* (New York: Harper & Brothers, 1928), pp. 228–29.
7. Benjamin E. Green to the secretary of state, Apr. 8, 1844, Manning, *Diplomatic Correspondence of the United States*, Vol. VIII, pp. 583–84.
8. Polk, *Diary*, Oct. 24, 1845.
9. Bancroft recorded this view no less than five times, but not until years later; thus, it is open to question, even though the various versions are essentially in agreement. See Sellers, *James K. Polk*, p. 213.
10. Sellers, *James K. Polk*, p. 227.
11. Anson Jones, *Memoranda and Official Correspondence Relating to the Republic of Texas, Its History and Annexation. With a Brief Autobiography of the Author*, pp. 46–51, quoted by Sellers, *James K. Polk*, pp. 224–25. Sellers concluded that these agents of Polk exceeded instructions and that Jones may have exaggerated what was said.
12. Donelson to Buchanan, July 11, 1845, Manning, *Diplomatic Correspondence of the United States*, Vol. XII, pp. 448–52.
13. Donelson to Calhoun, Dec. 24, 1844, Manning, *Diplomatic Correspondence of the United States*, Vol. XII, pp. 389–91.
14. Ibid., Donelson to Buchanan, Apr. 12, 1845.
15. Taylor to adjutant general, Oct. 4, 1845, House Executive Documents, Document 60, 30th Cong., 1st Sess. Taylor thought it would be useful to occupy one or two points on the Rio Grande so as to strengthen the American claim in the event of negotiations.
16. Wilson Shannon to secretary of state, Mar. 27, 1845, Manning, *Diplomatic Correspondence of the United States*, Vol. VIII, p. 704.
17. These letters are to be found in Manning, Vol. VIII, pp. 714–55.

18. Brack, *Mexico Views Manifest Destiny, 1821–1846*, pp. 147–49, 155–56, 158, 172–73.
19. George Bancroft to James Buchanan, Aug. 7, 1845, and Polk to Buchanan, Aug. 7, 1845, Buchanan Papers.
20. Richard S. Coxe to Buchanan, Aug. 4, 1845, Buchanan Papers.
21. Parrott to Buchanan, July 26, 1845, Manning, *Diplomatic Correspondence of the United States*, Vol. VIII, p. 472.
22. *House Executive Documents*, Document 60, 30th Cong., 1st Sess.
23. Coxe to Buchanan, Sept. 5, 1845, Buchanan Papers.
24. Polk, *Diary*, Sept. 16, 1845.
25. Parrott to Buchanan, Aug. 26, 1845, Manning, *Diplomatic Correspondence of the United States*, Vol. VIII, pp. 746–47.
26. Polk, *Diary*, Sept. 17, 1845.
27. Black to Buchanan, Oct. 18, 1845, Buchanan Papers.
28. Polk, *Diary*, Nov. 10, 1845.
29. Taylor to adjutant general, House Executive Documents, Document 60.
30. Ibid., Taylor to adjutant general, Sept. 6, 1845.
31. Ibid., Oct. 11, 1845.
32. Ibid., Oct. 15, 1845.
33. Buchanan to Slidell, Jan. 20, 1846, Manning, *Diplomatic Correspondence of the United States*, Vol. VIII, pp. 185–87.
34. Ibid., Jan. 28, 1846.
35. Polk, *Diary*, Feb. 13 and 16, 1846.
36. Taylor to adjutant general, Feb. 16, 1846, House Executive Documents, Document 60.
37. Pletcher, *Diplomacy of Annexation*, p. 368.
38. Bancroft to McLane, Mar. 29, 1846, Papers of George Bancroft.
39. Slidell to Castillo y Lanzas, Mar. 1, 1846, Manning, *Diplomatic Correspondence of the United States*, Vol. VIII, pp. 814–15.
40. Taylor to adjutant general, Mar. 21, 1846, House Executive Documents, Document 60.
41. Ibid.
42. Polk, *Diary*, Mar. 28, 29, 30 and Apr. 3, 1846.
43. Polk, *Diary*, May 3, 1846.
44. Ibid., May 11, 1846.
45. Larkin to Buchanan, Apr. 2, 1846, Manning, *Diplomatic Correspondence of the United States*, Vol. VIII, pp. 839–41.
46. Ibid., Larkin to Buchanan, June 1, 1846, p. 856.
See Pletcher, *Diplomacy of Annexation*, pp. 284–85.
47. Bancroft to Sloat, June 24, 1845. House Executive Documents, Document 60.
48. Ibid., May 15, 1846.
49. *Congressional Globe*, 29th Cong., 1st Sess., p. 783.
50. Ibid., p. 786.
51. Ibid., pp. 797, 803.
52. Bancroft to Hooper, June 22, 1846. Papers of George Bancroft.
53. Hooper to Bancroft, June 25, 1846. Papers of George Bancroft.
54. John H. Schroeder, *Mr. Polk's War American Opposition and Dissent, 1846–1848* (Madison: University of Wisconsin Press, 1973), p. 154.
Schroeder's account of the domestic political conflict during the war is by far the most complete and useful.
55. Dix to Azariah Flagg, May 15, 1846, quoted in Schroeder, *Mr. Polk's War*, pp. 20–21.

Chapter X

First Glimpses of World Power Status

The close of the Mexican War and the coming of the 1850s marked a significant turning point in the nation's history. The last of the founding fathers' generation were gone, and with them the proclivity to look back and give adulation to republican principles. The nation was no longer a daring experiment; it was a power in its own right, fantastically successful economically, equally successful in having gathered unto itself a territory larger than western Europe, and bursting with more economic opportunities by far than any other nation. As early as 1838 Abraham Lincoln had observed that earlier in the century America had been felt "to be an undecided experiment; now, it is understood to be a successful one."

The age of the large-scale enterprise had arrived. Railroads, steamships, mining, and industry came to the fore, while the rich soil of the Middle West, tilled by immgirants who came in ever-increasing numbers, furnished wheat, flour, meat, and hides for export. The nation was also a society torn by division over the slavery question and threatened with disunion. The irony of robust economic health threatened by crippling political division had its effect in the confusion surrounding the proper conduct of foreign affairs.

Abbott Lawrence, wealthy Massachusetts textile manufacturer and minister to Great Britain from 1849 to 1852, in a letter to Secretary of State John M. Clayton, depicting the land of good fortune, wrote:

With a country ranging in its climate and productions almost from the torrid to the frigid zone—with a soil outstripping in fertility the industry of man—with boundless mineral wealth —with a people stimulated into activity by the productiveness of nature and the unconscious possession of freedom, . . ., with large rivers permeating the surface of the land, bearing on their waters the wealth of commerce, with hundreds of thousands of immigrants annually coming to our shores, to settle new states, to create new wealth, and to establish new branches of industry—acknowledged now as one of the great nations of the world, and with elements of power such as no other one has—who can say what may not be the destiny of United America?[1]

But, as Lawrence gloomily observed, a dark cloud of domestic dissension almost obscured these bright prospects from view.

Bustling America had its eye on foreign markets around the world. The business community affirmed its faith in commerce as the great agency spreading civilization and creating an interdependence among nations that would stand as a barrier to war. Commerce unleashed the energies of man, enriched the parties to it, broke down barriers of isolation, and carried with it the seeds of revolution that would break down ancient tyrannies. In both Great Britain and the United States, where commerce made people rich and powerful, bright hopes flourished. In other parts of the world commerce appeared as an unsettling threat, creating unfavorable balances of trade and leading to the breakdown of traditional societies.

In the United States, in spite of its near self-sufficiency, exports made the difference between economic recession and prosperity. In 1850 the country produced 100,479,150 bushels of wheat, 14,188,457 bushels of rye, 592,141,230 bushels of corn, and 2,468,625 bales of cotton. The value of exports the following year totaled $178,546,555. By 1854 all exports reached $252,047,806. Cotton continued to be the major export, mounting to $131,386,661 in 1858 and $161,434,-923 in the fiscal year ending June 30, 1860.[2]

Economic growth extended to the industrial sector. By 1850 manufacturing establishments represented an investment of more than $500,000,000, and the products they poured forth were valued at $1 billion. Almost one million persons were employed in manufacturing. The expansion of manufacturing promoted the mining industry.

The Pennsylvania anthracite mines produced 3,358,899 tons of coal in 1850. Ten years later the figure reached 8,513,123 tons. Copper production jumped from 650 tons in 1850 to 7,200 tons in the same ten years.[3] From 1850 to 1855 the value of pig iron produced in the United States increased from $12,675,926 to $31,187,500. The textile industry was in the midst of rapid growth; by 1855 the value of cotton cloth exports reached $5,857,181.

The zeal for markets carried Americans to the far corners of the globe, to China, Japan, Siberia, Africa. In 1848 Captain Roys, of the whale ship *Superior*, penetrated the Arctic Ocean through the Bering Strait. This opened the way for large-scale whaling. In 1851 some 299 ships were employed, 8,970 seamen, and the value of ships and cargoes was estimated at seventeen and one-half million dollars.[4]

Whaling in the north Pacific created an interest in Japan and Siberia. Perry McD. Collins received an appointment as commercial agent for the Amur region. In a tour that lasted more than two years Collins traveled 30,000 miles, exploring the most remote regions of Siberia and studying the possibility of developing trade. The area had rich grazing lands, but most inhabitants, estimated to number four million, lived at a bare subsistence level. The capabilities of the country, Collins concluded, was much greater than the wants of its inhabitants, and if the foreign market was opened to them it would lead to great increases in production. The United States, on the opposite shore of the Pacific, could have easy access to the Amur River and Siberia. He wrote: "I have no hesitation in saying, from my observations of trade while in that country, that, should it become known to American enterprise, it will be but a very few years before our trade will be counted in millions."

Whaling provided the immediate impetus to the effort to open Japan. In 1851 Commander Glynn took his ship to Japan for the purpose of picking up sixteen American seamen. The sailors had been on the whaler *Pagoda* from New Bedford. He rescued the sailors after negotiations lasting two days. Glynn concluded that Japan could be opened and converted into a liberal republic in a short time. He was no less convinced of the desirability of opening a steamship line from San Francisco to Shanghai. On his return Glynn wrote to President Fillmore presenting the case for an expedition, a recommendation that led two years later to Matthew C. Perry's historic voyage.

In 1857 the commissioner of patents appointed John Claiborne to make a firsthand study of the consumption of cotton in Europe. Claiborne prepared detailed studies of the textile industry in France, Switzerland, the German states, Russia, and Austria. He gathered statistics on imports of cotton, barriers to imports such as high duties, technology, and prospects for increased consumption of cotton. The highly informative report on the state of the industry concluded with the observation that no greater blessing had been allotted to mankind than the rise in the production of cotton and the textile industry. The influence of raw cotton "among the nations who are our chief customers contributed to social well being by furnishing labor, sustenance, and cheap and comfortable clothing to many thousands of their subjects or citizens, . . . to capital it offers the means of profitable investment and returns, and aids greatly in its accumulation." Finally "by opening and extending commercial relations, between different nations, it has created sympathies and ties of common interest, which makes the policy of peace and its attendant blessings far more easy to maintain than was once the case; that it adds to the national wealth and resources, and by furnishing employment and support to many thousands who might otherwise be without either, it makes contented those who would, through illness or suffering, become burdens to the state."[5] Claiborne, prominent southern newspaper editor and publicist, reflected something more than statistics—namely, the general exuberance of the age of capital.

Individual entrepreneurs and small aggregates of men with access to capital focused on personal rewards. Throughout the eastern states and the Middle West were new smaller enterprises. But it was the rapid rise of two new major industries, railroading and steamboat transportation, that attracted the more venturesome capitalists. In 1850 railroads were still in their infancy, with only 9,026 miles constructed. Ten years later the mileage was 30,626, an increase of nearly 300 percent.[6] Transcontinental lines were widely discussed, but these still remained to be built at the close of the Civil War.

More important, by far, in terms of transportation of both goods and passengers, was the new steamboat industry. In 1852 Thomas Corwin, secretary of the treasury, provided the Senate with a detailed survey of steamboat navigation. Steam-driven ships numbered 1,390, with a total tonnage of 417,226 tons; the number of seamen employed was 29,377. Steamboats were not new, but in the years 1843 to 1851 the tonnage almost doubled. Coastwise shipping and transocean navigation now came into its own. The invention of the screw propeller revolutionized transportation. The new steam-driven propeller vessels made the trip from New York to Liverpool in ten days.

The first regular steamship line to Europe was established in 1840, but not until 1848 did rapid expansion take place. In June 1851 there were 26 American ocean steamers, with another 26 under construction. Among the latter was the *City of Pittsburg*, a three-decked ship, with a saloon, staterooms, and cabins. Corwin noted that she had berths for 420 passengers and "ample room for stores, ice, water, and every convenience and security which can be devised for the comfort and confidence of voyages on the Atlantic."[7] The industry opened a new field for entrepreneurs and investors and ended in some degree the isolation from Europe. In 1851 large numbers of Americans made the trip to London to see the first international exposition in the Crystal Palace.

The steamboat industry continued its phenomenal growth throughout the 1850s. An average of 280 ships were built each year. American ministers to Great Britain complained increasingly of the time consumed in seeing tourists who often had letters of introduction, who sought information, or who asked for visas. In 1850 the American legation in London approved 1,167 passports.[8] On the first of July 1851 more than 1,100 Americans were visiting in London.

Government became more, rather than less, important as these economic developments took place. Overseas trade created a demand for navy protection of sea lanes and merchants residing abroad. Every prospector in the building of railroads looked to the federal government and the states for subsidies in the form of land grants. From September 1850 to March 1857 various states granted 33,192,473 acres of land to railroads, but it was the national government that proved to be the most generous handmaiden of industry. In May 1850 Congress passed a bill to aid in the construction of the Illinois Central Railroad. The federal government granted the states of Illinois, Mississippi, and Alabama the right of way plus alternate sections on either side to a distance of six miles.[9] The law set the precedent for the granting of a huge largess to transcontinental railroads after the Civil War. Men of capital in the eastern states benefited directly. Stephen Douglas, senator from Illinois and the political dynamo in back of the bill, had the support of the northeastern states. This support was forthcoming, it appears, partly as a result of a deal in which the northeastern members of Congress won support for a high tariff bill. There is also evidence that some votes were induced by promises of financial reward. Finally, easterners had invested heavily in Illinois state bonds, and these had declined in value. The generous land grant to Illinois would, as Douglas maintained, enable Illinois to fulfil its obligations and pay off its debt. Land companies in the East with investments in Illinois likewise saw in the proposed railroad the prospect of a rise in land values.[10]

Steamboat navigation also enjoyed subsidies from the national government. The British owed commercial success to its merchant marine; and, therefore, argued members of Congress and capitalists interested in shipping lines, the United States must also encourage oceanic steam navigation. Subsidies in the form of the payment of large sums for carrying the mail became the policy. Companies likewise profited under the act of 1847 authorizing the secretary of navy to contract with companies to construct ocean-going steamships that could be quickly converted into ships of war. Immediately the secretary of navy authorized construction of five steamships by shipbuilder Albert G. Sloo, of New York, to transport mail from New York to Havana and New Orleans, another contract for three steamers by Howland and Aspinwall, and five by E. K. Collins. The contractors built and paid for the ships and, in return, received contracts for carrying the mail. Navy officers captained many of these ships; among them Matthew C. Perry.

The mail contracts provided remuneration in excess of the service rendered. The United States Mail Steamship Company received $290,000 annually for carrying mail twice a month from New York to Havana and New Orleans. An auditor's report in February 1852 reported that the navy had paid this company $941,925 from September 20, 1848, to February 12, 1852, and $1,039,500 to E. K. Collins for carrying mail between New York and Liverpool.[11] In his report for 1852 the secretary of navy, citing the increase in the number of ocean steamships, observed: "It is not necessary to add that these great and important results could not have been effected, or even attempted, without the liberal and undoubted aid and cooperation of Congress."[12]

Postmaster General James Campbell, who served under President Pierce, protested against the excessive charges for carrying mail. In his report of December 1854 Campbell cited the fact that the British government paid the Cunard line $867,700 and received weekly service. The United States government paid E. K. Collins $858,000 for biweekly service, or $33,000 a trip.[13] One year later Campbell again pointed to the excessive cost.[14]

The law of 1847 providing for the construction of ocean-going vessels that could be converted into ships of war did not strengthen the navy. By the mid-1850s the secretary of navy stated that these ships could only be converted with difficulty and even then would not be suitable as warships. At most they could be used to carry troops or as privateers.[15]

The opening of great vistas of new economic opportunities when aggregates of capital played a major role in national development sharply affected not only the nature of domestic politics but foreign relations, for in this sphere government support and protection were essential. This was true in regard to the negotiation of favorable commercial treaties, an adequate consular service, and support and promotion of a merchant marine. In Central America, Asia, and the Pacific, navy squadrons were stationed to protect commerce and American merchants trading in those areas. The enterprising spirit of the entrepreneur had its corollary in an assertive posture on foreign relations.

Historians have long been of the view that the decade of the 1850s represented a significant change. The "goody-goody" age of the 1840s, with its emphasis on reform, gave way to a concentration on the slavery issue. The passion to create a distinctly national literature gave way to a renewed interest in European literature.[16] The ideal of the self-made man replaced more limited goals of achievement. John Higham, distinguished intellectual historian, wrestled with this question in his essay, *From Boundlessness to Consolidation: The Transformation of American Culture 1849–1860*, outlining the character of the change that took place in intellectual and social thought.

There was, of course, both change and continuity. Except for a brief flurry of excitement over the prospect of the triumph of republican principles in Europe, leaders remained convinced of the wisdom of noninvolvement in European affairs. They carried over from the past and now gave a new emphasis to the importance of commerce, a view directly related to improved means of transportation and surplus domestic production. Territorial expansionism receded after the acquisition of Oregon and California, and some observers, forty years prior to Frederick Jackson Turner's famous essay, spoke of the end of the frontier and implied that expansion had come to an end. An underground feeling persisted that the British North American colonies were intended by nature to join the great republic, but no political leader of stature in the 1850s made annexation a cause.

Leaving the realm of intellectual history and concern with abstractions for further analysis elsewhere, there remain three quite clear and readily discernible characteristics of the 1850s that had an impact on foreign relations. Unprecedented economic growth, and more particularly the alluring vision of grand-scale economic projects in industry and transportation, awakened an aggressive spirit of enterprise uninhibited by timidity. At the same time the vision of the future changed from that of a nation achieving inherited republican principles to a vision of a nation of wealth, advanced technology, and production. Confidence in this future had its parallel in the conviction that America was already ahead of the nations of the European continent and rivaling Great Britain. The United States as the greatest of world powers came into sight.

Paradoxically, this decade of confidence was also the decade of fear. The conquests of the Mexican War transformed the antislavery movement from a reform into a political battle over the question of slavery in the territories. The fight over the compromise of 1850, the Kansas-Nebraska struggle, the Dred Scott case, and the ominous split of the old political parties along sectional lines gave rise to apprehension for the survival of the Union. The very success of the nation—it had never appeared more so than after the Mexican War—caused leaders to see in the antislavery agitation an absurd readiness to throw overboard what had been achieved, just as the door was opening to even greater triumphs. Abbott Lawrence, at the beginning of the great Congressional debates of 1850, wrote of the threat of disunion and attributed the danger to "the schemes of agitators and the hopes of traitors." A breakup of the Union "would be a treason not only to America and the present generation, but to the world and all time."[17] Politicians like Stephen Douglas and James Buchanan perceived early in the decade that their own careers were in danger and so did successful northern business leaders. William Henry Seward pleaded for concentration on the development of the West, thereby "leaving all our contentions behind us."

Fear of the future proved at least as powerful as avarice. To conciliate the South, northern Democrats gave their support, and at other times tolerance, to filibustering and to the annexation of Cuba. The chief argument used for the "necessity" of acquiring Cuba was that it was about to become a second Haiti, a black republic and therefore, in the words of Buchanan, as well as extremists such as Pierre Soulé, a threat to national survival. This wild conjecture, reasonable only to men dominated by fear, threatened for a time to become a basis for action.

A second fear pervading the years after 1848 manifested itself in a popular belief that Great Britain and France shared the common aim of a balance of power in the New World. Foreign Minister Guizot had indeed advocated the promotion of an equilibrium among the powers in the Western Hemisphere, and certainly various British statesmen subscribed to the ideal in theory but did not embody their views in any single public declaration. The rise of Louis Napoleon to emperor of France exacerbated the American feeling of distrust. Much was said of British and French efforts to encourage Texas to maintain her independence and of alleged British plans to acquire California. The myth took on new dimensions in the first half of the decade due to British-American rivalry in Central America. Members of the Pierce administration subscribed to the belief that Great Britain and France had entered into an agreement to prevent the separation of Cuba from Spain, a belief that was without foundation. The Crimean War led to renewed allegations in the press that Great Britain and France made war on Russia with the aim of dominating all Europe. When they were victorious in that war, many newspapers warned that having achieved the goal in Europe, Great Britain would turn attention to the New World.

Both fears injected asperity into the conduct of foreign relations. At the same time these fears became exaggerated because the alleged plans of the two European allies ran counter to American plans for hegemony in the Caribbean.

The greater the fear of disunion became the more vigorous became the desire to demonstrate that the success of the Union was so great as to subordinate all other political questions, including slavery, to its preservation. Many of those ready to compromise with slavery— Lewis Cass, Stephen Douglas, James Buchanan, George Dallas, and others—were, ironically, among those most inclined to denounce the rule of aristocracy in Europe, to speak of the depressed laboring classes on the continent, and to deplore the suppression of liberty in the monarchical states. Buchanan and Dallas, while serving in the legation in London, refused to issue visas to black people, declared their passports fraudulent, and later self-righteously seized on the Dred Scott ruling that Negroes were not citizens. Cass, one of the most evangelical of the Young America group, while not defending the slave trade, took every opportunity to undermine British efforts to suppress it. These firm exponents of American republicanism, entertained, as Pierce said in his inaugural, no timid forebodings of expansionism. The South wanted Cuba for reasons of protection; these leaders wanted the presidency and required southern support. In a special message to the Senate, President Buchanan declared that "it is the destiny of the race to spread themselves over the continent of North America" and the tide of emigrants would flow to the South. "Central America," he wrote, "will soon contain an American population which will confer blessings and benefits as well upon the natives as their respective Governments."[18]

American convictions that the republic set a model of universal validity that would eventually become the pattern for all Europe took on new meaning with the revolutions of 1848. On March 4 of that year Richard Rush, American minister in Paris, wrote of the momentous events that had occurred in recent days. Barricades rose up in the streets, the masses captured the palace of the Tuileries, the king abdicated and the royal family fled, the monarchy was overthrown, and the people were victorious.[19]

A few days later Rush received word that his personal presence would be welcome at the Hôtel de Ville on February 28 "to cheer and felicitate the Provisional Government." Rush not only appeared, he delivered an address of support. He acknowledged that the course he had pursued departed from diplomatic usage. No other diplomat attended. His action received the prompt approval of President Zachary Taylor, who immediately offered diplomatic recognition. On April 5 Congress passed joint resolutions tendering the congratulations of the American people to the French people.[20] In forwarding the resolution Buchanan remarked that "it was but an echo of the voice of the American people in favor of the French Republic."

The glorious days of February and March, when Rush found so much to praise in the moderation of the new government, gave way to a second uprising by more radical elements on May 15. Rush described it as "a criminal enterprise," applauded the efficiency of the National Guard in suppressing it, but confessed the event "awakens anxious thoughts for the future."[21]

The uprising in France sparked revolutions in the German states, Austria, and Italy. Americans in Europe appealed to the commander of the American squadron in the Mediterranean for protection. He, in turn, pleaded with Rush that his small force could not possibly provide security. Rush immediately recommended a doubling of the squadron, noting that it had not been increased for thirty years, during which commerce had doubled. But Rush was concerned about a larger question than the protection of Americans. He wrote:

> I believe that at this most extraordinary epoch in European affairs, when the republican principle is facing the monarchical principle more closely than ever before, the presence of the United States in that sea, by a powerful, highly equipped, and highly disciplined squadron, would carry a moral weight for the Republican principle; thus attesting to the world's eye its amazing advance in the Western hemisphere in throwing, in the midst of convulsions, a precautionary shield over American interests and citizens abroad, after raising both to an enviable prosperity by equal laws and equal rights at home.[22]

It would be, Rush maintained, an "encouraging exhibition" of the strength of republicanism and the rights of nationalities.

The upheavals of 1848 ended in the use of force by the absolute monarchs to suppress the liberal sentiments of the populace. Russia provided the clearest case of the use of arbitrary power in intervening in Austria to put down the Hungarian revolt led by Louis Kossuth. No one of the many European developments so caught the eye of Americans, and it gave rise to popular discussion of the question first raised by Rush. Could the United States any longer sit by when absolute monarchs put down with force those liberal groups who emulated the United States and sought to establish republics on the American model?

The Young America movement of the early 1850s in the words of a recent study, "was nothing more than an emotional reaffirmation of America's system of society and government, and an unthinking willingness to allow that feeling to interfere with the conduct of the nation's foreign policy. It did not challenge the vital interests of either major party; it raised no question of the extension of slavery, no prospect of a Wilmot Proviso."[23] Merle Curti described it as a slogan expressing a set of ideals and emotions.[24] In most respects it represented the same ephemeral feelings that had found vent in Congress during the Greek Revolution of the 1820s. This time the movement found its home in the Democratic party and its strongest support in the Midwest, where Stephen Douglas of Illinois, Lewis Cass of Michigan, I. P. Walker of Wisconsin, Edward Hannegan of Indiana, and William Allen of Ohio expounded on the duty of republican America to support the revolutionary movements in Europe. It had support from brash young leaders such as George Sanders of New York, and Pierre Soulé of Louisiana. Sanders, who became editor of the *Democratic Review* in January 1852, campaigned for Douglas for the presidency, and succeeded in making violent enemies in the party and seriously hurting his candidate. Sanders was a reckless and unprincipled character. His support of Young America rested in part on his hope that it would divert attention from sectional controversies. Soulé was no less reckless and hopelessly lacking in balanced judgment. Both men received diplomatic appointments from Pierce.

The Young America movement had a short life, but the assertive spirit it embodied lived on through the 1850s. Congressional committees and American diplomats soon lost interest in promoting republicanism in Europe, but their adventurous policies and readiness to serve private interests permeated foreign relations. The cautious biographer of Franklin Pierce, Roy F. Nichols, wrote with good reason that Pierce and his secretary of state, William L. Marcy, "may have wondered sometimes whether they were managers of foreign policy or errand boys of business."[25]

No study of the 1850s can omit the story of Louis Kossuth's visit to the United States, not because his tour influenced foreign policy but because it illuminates the readiness of Americans to kneel at the altar before some symbol of a cause that at the moment they feel impelled to support. The Hungarian revolt against the Hapsburg monarchy ruling in Vienna signified an heroic thrust against absolutism and an heroic effort of a nationality to achieve self-government. Across the country, in 1849, citizens, prominent and obscure, rallied to the banner of the colorful Kossuth.[26] President Zachary Taylor, discarding all precedents, instructed A. Dudley Mann, a lesser official in the American legation at Paris, to go to Hungary and gave him the freedom to decide if Kossuth's government deserved recognition. Mann, elated at this sudden ascent into the rarefied atmosphere of high statesmanship, wrote: "I shall desire no joy of a more boundless nature during my pilgrimage through life than to be enrolled to report to you that 'Hungary has established her independence on a permanent foundation; that I saw the infant Hercules strangle the mighty serpent.' "[27] Mann's pilgrimage coincided with Russia's intervention and Kossuth's fleeing to Turkey. Russia and Austria both sought his extradition, but Turkey refused. When Taylor made the instructions to Mann public in June 1849, Austria's foreign minister, who had already seen the instructions, chose to launch a vigorous protest against American intervention. Harsh, undiplomatic language invited a sharp rebuke, and in 1850 Daniel Webster, Clayton's successor as secretary of state, launched a sensational reply that included the much-quoted phrase that "the possessions of the house of Hapsburg are but a patch of the earth's surface."[28] Webster employed the opportunity to promote unionist sentiment.

In a temporary burst of enthusiasm, the Fillmore administration invited Louis Kossuth to visit the United States and provided transportation from Turkey to Great Britain aboard the naval ship *Mississippi*. The irascible and arrogant Hungarian had already earned the enmity of the American minister in Turkey, George Perkins Marsh, who had befriended Hungarian refugees and their leader. Rather than showing appreciation of the generous provision of transportation on the navy warship, Kossuth described the *Mississippi* as a slave ship because the captain, guided by the advice of Marsh, kept close watch for fear that Kossuth would jump ship or employ stops at various ports to deliver inflammable speeches that would compromise American neutrality.

Kossuth's arrival in New York led to an outpouring of hero worship in the form of parades, banquets, and financial donations. The Hungarian made clear his mission. As much as he loved adulation and contributions, he asked for something more, American intervention. In New York only the abolitionists rejected him because he shrewdly avoided the hazards of tying his cause to antislavery. Washington society feted him, but President Fillmore, who looked upon the exuberance of the public as dangerous romanticism, kept his distance although he consented to grant an interview. Throughout the southern states Kossuth was greeted with coolness, for southern leaders had no faith in a crusading foreign policy.[29]

The confidence in future national greatness and the many imperialist machinations relating to Cuba and Central America did not culminate in acquisitions of territory nor, apart from Cuba, was there any solid bloc of political strength for territorial expansion. The American objective in Central America was to prevent British domination of the prospective canal routes, not territorial acquisition. Cuba, judged a "necessity" by Buchanan, could not be purchased, and its acquisition by force gained only scattered regional support. Nor did the United States depart from the tradition of noninvolvement in European affairs.

Three factors were in operation that militated against further acquisition of territory. The slavery question dominated all other public issues and made its influence felt in foreign relations. The increasing strength of antislavery views stood as a barrier to Cuban annexation and other projects in the Caribbean that had southern support. The absence of a navy of any strength gave a hollow ring to talk about playing a larger role in world affairs. Every secretary of navy warned that the existing squadrons could not protect the home shores from attack, and each pleaded for more ships every year without any significant success. Finally, the largely empty territories west of the Missouri River called for development and offered more promise of rewards than more distant areas.

When Americans spoke of empire and national greatness, they more often meant commercial development. In this respect, William

Henry Seward was infinitely more in harmony with the times than the expansionists. A recent study of Seward's views on foreign relations concludes that he was not an aggressive advocate of territorial expansion, although when expansion was necessary to promote trade he on occasion favored it.[30] Seward's views on expansion were clearly stated before the Senate on two occasions. In December 1858 in the debate on a Pacific railroad bill he spoke of the "advance of civilization" as governed by nature's laws, by which Seward meant the great historical forces that were at work. Every nation had obeyed these laws dictating expansion. The activity of people pressing outward could not be suppressed. American territorial expansion conformed to this law, but now the United States "have received enough for present uses, and for improvement for a considerable period in the future." Seward decried wars of conquest. Expansion should come only by pacific means: "Peaceful activity is safer, it is cheaper; it is surer; it saves all the elements of national strength and national power, and increases them."[31] In his persistent support of a Pacific railroad, he argued that the recent controversies with Great Britain over Central America were unnecessary and foolish. Seward pronounced similar views in 1859 when President Buchanan asked for a $30 million appropriation for the purchase of Cuba. The time was wholly inappropriate; perhaps in some future day developments would create a situation in which Cuba would be attracted to the Union by magnetic forces.[32] Seward's major interest was in developing the Middle West by means of a generous land policy and a Pacific railroad so as to create a strong base for commercial empire.[33]

Throughout the decade Seward dismissed the blustering of southern senators and Lewis Cass of Michigan to the effect that Great Britain and France sought to acquire Cuba and domination of Central America as based on imaginary fears and misdirected concern for the national interest. Responding to a speech filled with a tone of alarm in January 1853, Seward advised his adversary to look "for those great rivals where they are to be found" on the seas in the East. The commerce of the world, said Seward, "is the empire of the world."[34] It was in the Pacific "where the prize which you are contending with them for is to be found." To make ready for that contest it was necessary to build a railroad to San Francisco.

The coming of the Crimean War coincided with one of the most heated political battles in the nation's history. In January 1854 President Pierce gave his support to the Kansas-Nebraska bill, introduced by Stephen Douglas, and Congress debated it in a spirit of hatred and bitterness until the end of May. This eruption in domestic affairs lowered the interest in the Crimean War, but American newspapers provided a variety of interpretations and judgments on the causes of the war and on the belligerents. The *New York Times* ran almost daily editorials throughout the winter months denouncing Russian despotism. The editor criticized both Great Britain and France for their slowness in coming to Turkey's rescue. Horace Greeley, in the *Tribune*, called for a curse on both sides, attributing Turkey's poverty to Great Britain having imposed free trade, thereby ruining Turkey's traditional domestic industry. No consistent editorial position emerged. Before the year was out, the *Times* dismissed the war as carried on solely because of selfish ambition, holding that neither party deserved sympathy.

The old question of neutral rights remained in the background. At the outbreak of the war Great Britain and France announced a very liberal policy toward neutrals for the duration of the war, and the United States had no cause to protest but sought to have Great Britain enter into an agreement binding itself to a permanent recognition of neutral rights. The British, in return, asked the United States to abolish privateering. The Pierce administration rejected this on the ground that privateering would be a major weapon in the event of war. The British entertained fears of the United States selling privateers to Russia, and in October 1855 sent a strong fleet to North America. Buchanan promptly asked the British foreign minister for an explanation. Lord Clarendon spoke of having information that one large ship in New York was about to be transferred to Russia for privateering and three more were under construction. Doubting the accuracy of the report, Buchanan soon provided full information showing that the ship in question was going to China, that it had four missionaries aboard, and that the guns in the hold of the ship were going to American merchants in China, who would use them to protect themselves against pirates.[35] Lord Clarendon withdrew his protest. A more explosive issue arose when the Pierce administration held the British minister and three consuls guilty of violating the laws of the United States by recruiting soldiers for the British army. Pierce delivered to all four their passports.

The British foreign office questioned their guilt but resigned itself to swallowing its pride and accepting the American action, although it is doubtful that the British representatives were guilty of any serious infractions.

For a brief time Pierce saw in the Crimean War an opportunity to play a greater role on the world stage. In the summer of 1854 he and the cabinet prepared a plan of mediation and communicated with the British minister in Washington on this proposal. Determined to carry on the war to a successful conclusion Great Britain rejected that proposal.

However, while the Crimean War came to a close without any serious controversy between the United States and the belligerents, it did provide occasion for Americans to voice strong opinions as to what foreign policy ought to be. Richard Rush, former minister to France, warned that Great Britain and France, having defeated Russia, would now turn their efforts toward interfering in American affairs. The editor of the *New York Times* observed that American commercial interests were "getting more and more complicated with European affairs" and the nation could no longer remain a silent bystander. He argued that the United States should have a voice in the peace settlement.[36] In terms of the full press coverage given the war in American newspapers, lengthy almost daily reports on battles and peace negotiations, it is clear that what happened in Europe was now a matter of public concern.

Views on foreign policy emanating from the press, from Congress, and, on occasion, presidential messages alternated between swashbuckling and serious pronouncements that complicated the day-to-day conduct of foreign relations. Allegations against Great Britain in congressional speeches were often directed at home constituencies and domestic political opponents. The impulse to have the United States play a larger role, denunciation of selfishness and despotism in Europe, and appeals for a moral system of international relations could not be repressed.

The first issue of *Putnam's Monthly* in October 1853 asked the rhetorical question of what policy abroad should be. Involvement, the editor contended, was inevitable. Policy should be "based on our convictions of right and duty" and should be concerned "with something greater than petty selfish interests." There should be "prompt and full protection for every citizen, guiltless or wrong, wherever he may be." There must be insistence on the very letter of treaty obligation. Europe must be excluded from the Western Hemisphere. There must be a willingness "to receive into the Union new nations." There should be a readiness to enlarge commerce. Finally, there must be an "unreserved sympathy with people struggling for their emancipation" from despotism.[37]

This array of objectives offered a wide choice but took little account of the world's power structure, the resistance to change, or the limits of American influence. The peculiar combination of gestures in favor of altruism and of national interest reflected how the amiable public viewed the nation's role. It bore little relationship to the actual conduct of American foreign relations, where self-interest, real or imagined, and advantages to be gained in the rough and tumble of party politics ruled. However, the editor, as so many others, envisioned the day when the United States would be a world power.

NOTES TO CHAPTER X

1. Abbott Lawrence to Secretary of State John May Clayton, Apr. 5, 1850. Despatches from London, Roll 56.
2. Statistics on exports and manufactures are taken from the annual reports of the secretary of treasury published in Senate Executive Documents.
3. *Mineral Resources of the United States*, ed. Albert Williams (Washington: Government Printing Office, 1883), pp. 13 and 215.
4. Senate Executive Documents, 32nd Cong., 1st Sess., Report of Seward, p. 42.
5. House Executive Documents, No. 85, 35th Cong., 1st Sess., Vol. X, Doc. 85, p. 94.
6. *Statistics of the United States in 1860; Compiled from the Original Returns and Being the Final Exhibit of the Eighth Census* (Washington: Government Printing Office, 1866), p. 323.
7. Senate Executive Documents, 32nd Cong., 1st Sess., Vol. VIII.
8. Abbott Lawrence to Secretary of State Webster, June 13, 1851, Despatches from London, Reel 58.
9. Ray Billington, *Westward Expansion A History of the American Frontier* (New York: The Macmillan Co., 1960), p. 394.
10. Johannsen, *Stephen A. Douglas*, pp. 313–14.
11. Senate Executive Documents, 32nd Cong., 1st Sess., Vol. VIII, Report of the Secretary of Navy.
12. Ibid., p. 107.
13. Senate Executive Documents, 33rd Cong., 2nd Sess., Vol. 2, Report of the Postmaster General, p. 630.
14. Ibid., 34th Cong., 1st Sess., Vol. III, Report of the Postmaster General, pp. 332–33.

15. House Executive Documents, 33rd Cong., 1st Sess., Document 75.
16. John Higham, *From Boundlessness to Consolidation The Transformation of American Culture, 1848–1860* (Ann Arbor: William L. Clements Library, 1969), p. 20.
17. Abbott Lawrence to Secretary of State John Clayton, Apr. 5, 1850. Despatches from London, Roll 56.
18. *Messages and Papers of the Presidents*, ed. J. D. Richardson, Vol. IV, p. 3000.
19. Rush to Secretary of State James Buchanan, Mar. 4, 1848, Despatches from Paris, Roll 34.
20. Ibid., Apr. 27, 1848.
21. Ibid., May 20, 1848.
22. Ibid., June 3, 1848.
23. Donald S. Spencer, *Louis Kossuth and Young America A Study of Sectionalism and Foreign Policy 1848–1852* (Columbia, Mo.: University of Missouri Press, 1977), pp. 21–22.
24. Merle Curti, "Young America," *American Historical Review*, Oct. 1926, p. 34.
25. Roy F. Nichols, *Franklin Pierce Young Hickory of the Granite Hills* (Philadelphia: University of Pennsylvania Press, 1958), p. 330.
26. Spencer, *Louis Kossuth and Young America*, p. 24.
27. Mann to Secretary of State Clayton, July 13, 1849, Senate Document 276, 61st Cong., 2d Sess., quoted by Spencer, *Louis Kossuth and Young America*, p. 26.
28. For more detailed discussion of American response to the revolution of 1848 and this particular incident, see Arthur James May, "Contemporary American Opinion of the Mid-Century Revolutions in Central Europe" (Philadelphia: University of Pennsylvania Ph.D. thesis, 1927); Spencer, *Louis Kossuth and Young America*, pp. 38–40. For a most useful account of the preparation of Webster's reply and Webster's motivation, see Kenneth E. Shewmaker, "Daniel Webster and the Politics of Foreign Policy," *The Journal of American History*, Sept. 1976, pp. 303–15. The author argues convincingly that Webster used the incident to promote Union sentiment. Congress printed 5,000 copies, and Abbott Lawrence, minister to Great Britain, had it published at his own expense.
29. Spencer's account of Kossuth's receptions is both sprightly and illuminating, and his analysis of the sectional differences in approach to foreign relations as seen in the response to Kossuth in different sections of the country is particularly useful. See Spencer, *Louis Kossuth and Young America*. The thesis, upon closer analysis, may be subject to challenge but it does constitute a most interesting contribution. There is room to question Spencer's view that Southerners were realists and Northerners romantics. There were also realists who were swept up in Kossuth frenzy, none more prominent than William Henry Seward.
30. See Ernest N. Paolina, *The Foundations of the American Empire William Henry Seward and U.S. Foreign Policy* (Ithaca: Cornell University Press, 1973).
31. *The Congressional Globe*, 35th Cong., 2nd Sess., p. 159.
32. Ibid., pp. 540–42.
33. Walter G. Sharrow, "William Henry Seward and the Basis for American Empire, 1850–1860," *Pacific Historical Review*, Aug. 1967, pp. 325–42.
34. *Congressional Globe*, 32nd Cong., 2nd Sess., Appendix, p. 127.
35. Buchanan to Secretary of State Marcy, Nov. 9, 1855. Despatches from London, Reel 64.
36. *New York Times*, Apr. 4, 1854.
37. "What Impression Do We, And Should We Make Abroad!," ed., *Putnam's Monthly*, Oct. 1853, pp. 345–54.

Chapter XI

Anglo-American Rivalry in Central America

Aside from the important commercial connections, the noninvolvement in European affairs owed much to the fact that in Europe the United States confronted powerful states and an alliance system that discouraged an adventurous policy. In sharp contrast, the small republics of Central America and the countries of East Asia, in terms of power, constituted a near vacuum. In the 1850s the greater portion of diplomatic negotiations related to the latter rather than to Europe. However, the motivations, political considerations, and basic assumptions of relations with the Latin American republics of the Caribbean differed as much from those operating in relations with Asia as the geographical distance separating the two regions. Domestic politics go far to explain the policies of Pierce and Buchanan in the Caribbean; these had no influence on the course pursued in Asia. The display of assertiveness in the far reaches of the Pacific was almost wholly commercial in motive. In Central America, and particularly Mexico, the actions taken were bolder.

This difference, in turn, reflected the sharp divisions internally. The North and the West, linked closer by the rapidly developing system of railroad transportation, represented the emerging capitalism with its attention focused on future economic development. The South, in contrast, was on the defense not only regarding the preservation of the slave labor system but also low tariffs and a decentralized political order which accorded it a large measure of autonomy. The gulf between sections might not have been so wide or the contentions so sharp had not slavery injected a moral dimension, and on moral issues compromise is always difficult. Yet, the abolitionists in the North were few in number. The issue in the North, except for the extreme abolitionists, was not the stamping out of slavery but the preservation of free land for the next generation and the blocking of the extension of slavery so that some time in the future slavery would die out. This is precisely what many southerners apprehended. In turn the South, frantically fearful of the emancipation of blacks, demanded assurances; one assurance, as southerners saw it, was the annexation of Cuba, and another the opportunity to exploit and to dominate undeveloped Mexico and Central America. Texas, a few years before seen as the safety valve that would allow for the perpetuation of slavery, was no longer deemed sufficient, given the ever-increasing antislavery sentiment in the North. The South needed a new victory if it was to be assured that the Union was to be useful to it in the future.

George Dallas, minister to London while Buchanan was president, took an uncompromising position on the Central American and Cuban questions. Former vice-president under Polk, Dallas was obsessed with a deep distrust of the British. In a revealing letter from London in 1856 he wrote that the British had secret arrangements with the governments of Central America and desired control of the area. He added that the British hoped to get rid of the Clayton-Bulwer Treaty "so as to disjoint our Union, and monopolize the commercial avenue."[1] The evidence to support these suspicions was in short supply, but Dallas did clearly believe that unless the South received benefits promptly, reinvigorating its faith in the Union, secessionist sentiments would increase in strength.

In depicting the differences between the North and the South it is, of course, necessary to avoid exaggerating these differences, for the South itself was a series of regions, of variations in climate, of an almost equal division between Democrats and Whigs prior to 1850. In some areas unionist sentiment continued strong until war began. Only slavery served to tie the disparate elements of the South together. Entrepreneurs in the South were as eager for profits as the most ambitious merchant of New York. These men played a prominent role in the buccaneering activities in Mexico and Central America; they served as the spearhead of southern expansion. New

Orleans cheered the filibusterers and was the home city of companies organized to exploit opportunities in Mexico and southward; that port city had the most to gain from the removal of Spain's restrictive trade policy in Cuba. The city was on the defensive. Transcontinental railroads threatened to isolate it from the mainstream of commerce.

New Orleans, leading city in the export of cotton, illustrated the complexity of motives nurturing expansionist dreams. In a significant article on the question of why New Orleans supported the many filibustering expeditions launched from that city with such marked public enthusiasm, a writer for the *Louisiana Historical Quarterly* has observed that while it was "the natural outcome of a sectional inferiority complex," the South "needed more attractive ones to rationalize its imperialistic behavior."[2] The acquisition of new slave states enabling the South to maintain the sectional balance in the Senate received much attention.[3]

A more attractive rationalization, and one long hallowed throughout the country, was that expansion extended the blessings of the American political system. The optimism and idealism embodied in this view gave to expansion a savory flavor far more attractive than mere avarice. And now that in the South slavery had come to be viewed as a "divine trust," the annexation of Cuba was readily justified as rescuing the island from British abolitionists but likewise protecting the sacred institution in the South. Walker's filibustering in Nicaragua and his restoration of slavery there awakened again aspirations for expansion.[4] When an officer of the Nicaraguan army spoke in New Orleans in November 1856, the *Louisiana Courier* reported that at no time was there more cheering "than when he spoke of Southern institutions being planted in Nicaragua."[5] Lopez and his expeditions to liberate Cuba earned him the reputation for gallantry in New Orleans.

However, some northern interests also supported southern expansionism. Prominent Democrats with presidential aspirations— men like Buchanan, Cass, Dallas, and Douglas—had sufficient reason in the fact that they could not receive southern support for the Democratic nomination for president without standing forth as strong advocates of the annexation of Cuba. Caleb Cushing, attorney general under Pierce, was no less belligerent than the presidential aspirants. These northerners were free to pursue this course because there was considerable interest in expansion among their home constituencies. The annexation of Cuba would lead to an increase in trade. Spanish trade policy placed high duties on many agricultural commodities coming from the United States. Reduce these duties, noted the Pittsburgh *Post*, and the Cubans would probably purchase a million barrels of flour each year, and they would make equally large purchases of meat, butter, lard, olive oil, and whiskey.[6]

More important than the prospect of commercial gains was the simple and readily understood argument that now that California had become a part of the Union the isthmian territory was essentially a part of the American coastline. The East and California must be tied together by a canal or railroads crossing from the Atlantic to the Pacific in Mexico, Nicaragua, or New Granada. The prolonged controversy with Great Britain over the Clayton-Bulwer Treaty, which extended from 1852 to the close of the decade, centered on the question of control of a canal route. Buchanan, minister to Great Britain from 1853 to the spring of 1856, devoted almost all his time to the question, and his successor, George Dallas, did the same. The diplomat antagonists labored hard and long on the precise legal meaning of the provisions of the Clayton-Bulwer Treaty, but it was never essentially a legal question but one of who was to control the transit routes. In fact, it was more than that; it was also a question of domestic politics exaggerated by the Pierce and Buchanan administrations for domestic political advantages. Great Britain, in that stage of its history, was no less aggressive in promoting commercial interests but it often did so without establishing colonies. Faced with formidable opposition in the United States to British political control in Central America, the British were prepared to compromise but were not willing to yield full control of a canal to the United States, for this would have posed dangers to their trade.[7] The limits of British aims might have deprived the Pierce and Buchanan administrations of a domestic political asset had not the extremist allegations in Congress and the messages of the presidents, plus the challenge to the age-old possession of Belize, elevated the question in British eyes to a matter of national honor.

Politicians persisted in exploiting the issue of Cuban annexation after it became clear that this was not to take place. In 1859 President Buchanan asked for an appropriation of $30 million for the purpose of negotiating with Spain to sell Cuba. All of the old arguments were brought out—danger of Cuba becoming a black republic, danger of Great Britain and France employing their influence to gain control, Spain's need for funds. Given Buchanan's experiences as minister to Great Britain, he must have known that Great Britain was not ready to intervene and that there was not even a remote possibility of Spain selling the island. In the debate in the Senate Seward pulled back the curtain for all to see the futility of the proposed negotiation and correctly concluded:

> These considerations satisfy my mind that it is not expected, that it is not intended, that Cuba shall be acquired in consequence of this proceeding, but that it is supposed some domestic and local benefit will be secured to the President of the United States by provoking a debate on this subject in Congress.[8]

But Seward's opposition to territorial expansion in the 1850s was in some considerable degree a matter of political expediency. As a northern Whig, and later Republican, he could not advocate expansion as long as expansion meant the extension of slavery.[9]

Turning from the Caribbean to the Pacific and the exertions of the United States in that area, the issue from the point of view of Americans was simply the right to trade on the basis of the most-favored-nation clause. No question of territorial annexation was involved; no sectional interests at home came into conflict. No political advantage was to be gained by opposition to the advancement of commerce.

The Mexican War stimulated great interest in the Caribbean and the republics south of the border. Fear prevailed that Great Britain had employed the war period to gain control over Central America and, given the steps taken by the British, the fear appeared to be warranted. Great Britain had long claimed a protectorate over the Mosquito Indians, who inhabited a territory along the Atlantic coast claimed by Nicaragua. On January 1, 1848, the British government declared that the territory extended southward to the mouth of the San Juan River, and the British occupied San Juan.[10] Considering the fact that San Juan was the key to the trans-isthmian route, the move could only be interpreted as evidence of British determination to control the eastern terminus of the proposed canal. Nicaragua, convinced that San Juan and the Mosquito territory were rightfully hers, looked to the United States for assistance.

Reports from American consuls in Central America kept the Polk administration well informed concerning the aggressive British moves, and in 1848 Polk appointed Elijah Hise to investigate. Hise soon reported that the British had almost a monopoly of the commerce and British warships constantly hovered on both coasts. "It is clear to my mind," he wrote, "that Great Britain designs to become the owner and occupant by force or stratagem of the ports on the Atlantic and Pacific coasts of Nicaragua which will be the points of termination of the canal communication between the two oceans . . ."[11]

At the same time that Hise was courting Nicaragua, Frederick Chatfield, British consul general, lectured that government as if it were an errant schoolboy. Both representatives eyed each other's activities in the jealous spirit of rival suitors.

Hise concluded that the British would soon seize all the ports of Nicaragua. Convinced that haste was necessary, although he had no instructions, he negotiated a treaty with Nicaragua granting Americans exclusive rights to build a canal; in return, the United States was "to protect the sovereignty, liberty and independence of Nicaragua."[12]

This treaty was wholly unsatisfactory to the new administration of Zachary Taylor, and Nicaragua was so informed. It was contrary to American policy to guarantee the territory of another independent state. More important, it conflicted with the hopes of Secretary of State Clayton to work out an arrangement with Great Britain. Clayton appointed George Squier to enter into negotiations. Squier promptly secured a treaty which did not commit the United States to protect Nicaragua in its territorial claims. The commitment in the Squier Treaty was limited to protecting the neutrality of the canal. It too, however, challenged the British takeover of San Juan, but Clayton hoped to modify it, on that point.

Squier's British counterpart in the area, Frederick Chatfield, countered with a reckless move. Using debts owed by Honduras as a lever, he demanded their prompt payment; when this did not take place, he ordered the seizure of Tigre Island on the Pacific side of the proposed canal route. Two months later the British repudiated Chatfield's action; however, American suspicions had been further increased. Chatfield denounced the machinations of the United States, and Hise and then Squier made bitter accusations against Chatfield and other British agents. These petty maneuvers were not repudiated by either London or Washington, but neither did they cancel out the larger and more important considerations of a canal open to all nations and whose neutrality was to be guaranteed by the two powers. Clayton and Palmerston both subscribed to this objective and gave it first priority.

The difficulties lay in undoing what had been done or, given the reluctance to retreat from positions taken, to try and find a circuitous route around them that would not give to domestic opposition parties in Congress and in Parliament the opportunity to make political gains. Word of the Hise Treaty received wide publicity in London. In Washington, Clayton faced the danger of denunciation in Congress when he decided not to submit that treaty to the Senate. Congressional members were already angry over what they perceived as British pretensions in the Mosquitos. Further, preliminary soundings in London by Bancroft, who served as minister to Great Britain from 1846 to 1849, provided ample evidence that Palmerston, while disclaiming any intention of taking possession, was averse to a prompt withdrawal from San Juan and the British claims of a protectorate over the Mosquito kingdom.

The British soon learned that the United States was adamant on the Mosquito question. Abbott Lawrence, Bancroft's successor as minister in London, although friendly to the British and dedicated to the promotion of friendly relations, firmly opposed the British on the Mosquito question. Lawrence, in a note to Palmerston during the closing days of 1849, made a point of the fact that both American and British capitalists were involved in the recently organized canal company. Although each group might do it alone, Lawrence thought neither would probably desire to do so. The chief obstacle, wrote Lawrence, was in the boundary disputes between the Central American republics. The two powers could bring about a settlement, but the United States, Lawrence observed, was convinced that the British claims to a Mosquito Protectorate stood in the way. Unless the views of Great Britain and the United States on this subject

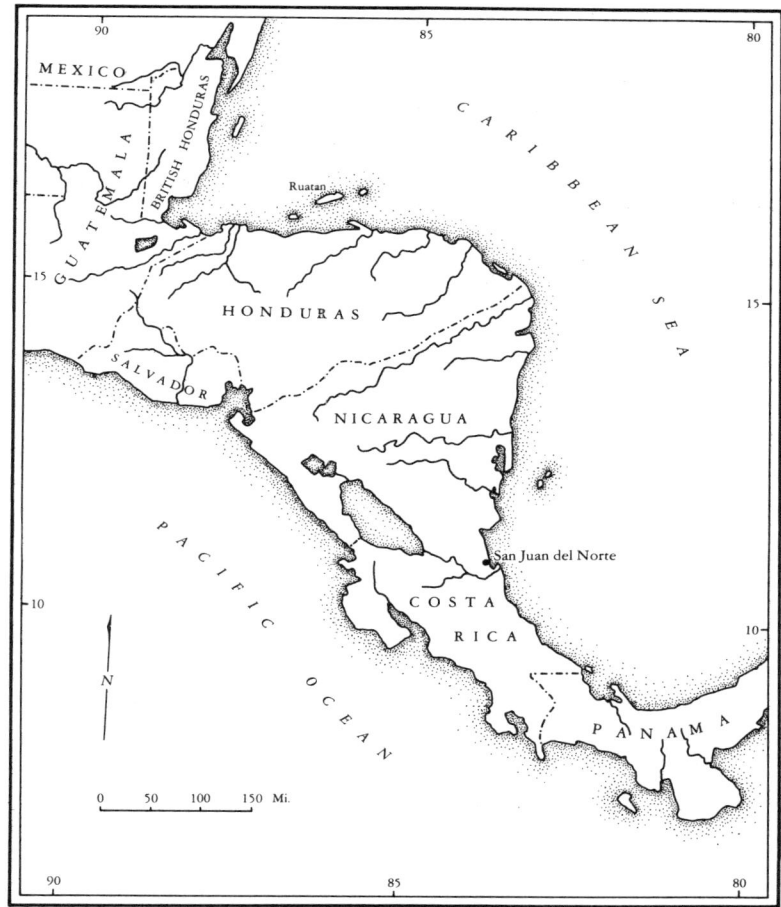

Central America

could be harmonized, their cooperation in this great project would be prevented.[13] Palmerston responded with a twenty-five page memorandum from Chatfield on the history of the Mosquito Protectorate. Lawrence found nothing in it to change his views.

Palmerston renewed discussions in January 1850. Since Lawrence was confined to his residence by illness, Palmerston called on him there. Palmerston announced the abandonment of Tigre Island, which the British had recently occupied, and told Lawrence that Great Britain had no intention of "annexing, settling, colonizing, or fortifying any part of Central America." In turn, Lawrence stressed the importance of an early settlement because political parties in both countries could create difficulties by exploiting current distrust. He had learned that "there was a body of men [in Great Britain] inclined to secure the canal in the hands of British subjects." Palmerston acknowledged that this was so but he had discouraged this; he believed that if a canal was to be built "it must be done by Great Britain and the United States and dedicated to the world at large."[14]

Yet, distrust continued. Palmerston aroused Lawrence's suspicion by stating that in giving up Tigre Island the British did not give up their claims against Honduras and remained free to take appropriate action. Palmerston, too, renewed his distrust of the United States when he learned of the Squier Treaty with Nicaragua, a treaty that challenged British control of San Juan.

In April 1850 negotiations were transferred to Washington. The energetic Lawrence, however, prepared a memorandum of 128 pages for Palmerston on the Mosquito question, maintaining that British claims rested on false assumptions.[15] Palmerston sharply disputed Lawrence's conclusion. The negotiations in Washington took place with each side anxious to reach agreement on the canal, but at the same time the American and British leaders were equally anxious to protect their flanks from attack by their opponents in Congress and Parliament. No agreement had been reached on related issues, the Mosquito territory and the dependencies of British Belize.

No treaty in the history of American foreign relations was to give rise to so prolonged a controversy as to its meaning as the Clayton-Bulwer Treaty. The difficulty arose not because of any lack of skill on the part of Clayton and Bulwer. Both men were, in fact, able and honest negotiators.

Two points of dispute emerged in the course of the negotiations. Both of these points were subordinate to the chief aim of each party, the construction of a canal that would be controlled by both nations and that would be equally open to all nations. This overriding purpose fell afoul of two questions, the British claim to a protectorate over Mosquito and what was rightfully included in the term "dependencies" of Belize. The only importance of both these bits of minor territory lay in their proximity to the proposed canal. The United States held that the claimed British protectorate over the small stretch of coastal territory inhabited by the Mosquito Indians was not only an ill-concealed device to control a strategic position, but it was an unprecedented arrangement; nowhere else did a native Indian population have the status of a protectorate. The question of the Bay Islands centered on which islands were included under that term. Were the Bay Islands only those tiny pieces of real estate immediately next to the coast of British Belize, or did the Bay Islands include the somewhat larger islands farther out to sea such as Ruatan, which was sufficiently large and comprised bays making it a prospective site for an important naval base?

The negotiations of the British minister in Washington, Sir Henry Lytton Bulwer, and Secretary of State Clayton were conducted privately and without consultation with the president and his cabinet. To facilitate agreement, Clayton agreed not to make an issue of the Mosquito Protectorate, believing that the United States and Great Britain could arrange a settlement later. By February 3 the proposed treaty appeared to be in final form. It provided for joint control of the canal and committed both powers not to occupy, fortify, or colonize any part of Central America. This draft was forwarded to Palmerston, and Clayton presented it to the president and his cabinet.

Difficulties now came to the fore. The cabinet called for a specific pledge from Great Britain to give up the Mosquito Protectorate. Bulwer and the British foreign office were equally adamant in refusing to yield on the protectorate. The cabinet reflected strong American convictions, which gained even greater strength when word arrived from Lawrence that Palmerston, in informing him of British withdrawal from Tigre Island, held that this withdrawal in no way committed Great Britain to refrain from taking whatever action would be necessary to settle claims against Honduras. A stalemate was temporarily avoided when Palmerston explained, in an instruction to Bulwer, that the British would not use the Mosquito Protectorate to occupy, fortify, or colonize the territory.

Then President Zachary Taylor again, in bold language, demanded that nothing in the treaty should be interpreted as an admission by the United States of any British right or title to the Mosquito coast. At this point Bulwer took offense at the president's indirect reference to the Squier Treaty which, as then worded, challenged the British position on the Mosquito question. The difficulty was removed when Taylor agreed to withdraw his offensive letter, and Bulwer agreed to include in the treaty a clause stating that neither party would on the basis of "protection" or an alliance with a Central American country commit any act in violation of the prohibition of occupation, fortification, or colonization. This, it was thought, disposed of the Mosquito question.

Another disagreement arose when Bulwer protested that it was rumored that a group of Americans were about to occupy Ruatan. The rumor was false, but it served to raise the issue of the Bay Islands. Palmerston held that Ruatan was under British jurisdiction, and Bulwer asserted that the treaty did not apply to Belize or its dependencies. Clayton, on the other hand, believed that the British claim to the "dependencies" lacked foundation. In a desperate effort to get free of this snag in the negotiations, Clayton and Bulwer finally agreed on a statement that the treaty did not apply to British Honduras nor the small islands in the vicinity. Bulwer then introduced an additional note excluding "whatever are the dependencies of that Settlement." Clayton later denied that he accepted this revision, but this is not certain.[16]

The final treaty left open questions that were to trouble Anglo-American relations throughout the decade. From the American side it appeared that the Mosquito Protectorate was a naked piece of aggrandizement and that the British claim to the more distant islands off Honduras was simply further evidence of insidious British imperialism. The British countered American contentions with arguments asserting that the positions in Central America antedated the treaty, that the protectorate was no more than an age-long commitment to protect the Indians from attack, that Great Britain had exercised jurisdiction in the Bay Islands long before the treaty, and that there were no plans for long-term occupation of San Juan. The British government in London, in contrast to its agents in Central America, was probably prepared to enter into an amicable settlement, but it was also determined to govern the pace of withdrawal and not do so under duress.

Americans, as we have seen, were divided on the question of what long-term aims the British entertained. The South in large part and Democratic leaders found in alleged British imperial designs a rewarding political issue. They could focus attention on the aggressiveness of local British agents, on the questionable bases of British claims, and the thinly disguised British control of affairs in San Juan and the Mosquitos, which went well beyond mere protection of the Indians. British activity on the Central American scene contradicted the disavowals of the British foreign office. The Clayton-Bulwer Treaty did not end American distrust; in fact the distrust gained momentum and reached crescendo proportions early in 1853.

In the two months preceding the inauguration of Franklin Pierce the Senate engaged in a heated debate on relations with Great Britain. Central America, the question of Mexico's cancellation of a grant to build a road across Tehuantepec, and the Clayton-Bulwer Treaty were used as political ammunition by the Democratic party. The aim was to discredit the outgoing Whig administration and to prepare the way for Pierce to take a firm stand against the British in all matters relating to the Gulf of Mexico. Lewis Cass led the charge with the introduction of a series of resolutions calling for a declaration opposing further European colonization, stating that the United States would view "all efforts on the part of any other Power to procure possession" of Cuba as constituting a danger that must be resisted by all means in the power of the United States.[17] Cass spoke of an immediate emergency which the United States must resist or forever hold its peace. Cass was no less determined to annex Cuba. "The Gulf of Mexico, sir," Cass declared, "must be practically an American lake, for the great purpose of security, not to exclude other nations from its enjoyment, but to prevent any dominant Power, with foreign or remote interests, from controlling its navigation."[18] The editor of the New Orleans *Daily Picayune* espoused the same view in declaring that the Monroe Doctrine should be asserted or abandoned.

Stephen Douglas, at this time convinced that Cass was engaged in undermining Douglas' position in the South by identifying him with Young America, attacked Cass because his resolutions excluded "existing possessions," those under British control before the Clayton-Bulwer Treaty, as a cause for protest. Douglas proceeded to outdo Cass by denouncing the Clayton-Bulwer Treaty as a negation and repudiation of the Monroe Doctrine. The Illinois senator went further. He defended the Hise Treaty, attacked Clayton for not submitting it to the Senate, charged that the Squier Treaty was a device for opening the door to an alliance with Great Britain, and contended that the Clayton-Bulwer Treaty was an entangling alliance. Douglas, in this instance, fell to low depths of distortion of facts and clearly deliberate misrepresentations.

In the same session the senator from Louisiana, S. W. Downs, denounced the Fillmore administration for being soft in its dealings with Mexico. That country had refused to approve a treaty giving Americans exclusive rights to build a road over the Tehuantepec route. Downs' resolution stated that if Mexico refused to reconsider "it will then become the duty of this Government to review all existing relations with that Republic, and to adopt such measures as will preserve the honor of the country and the rights of its citizens."[19]

Seward of New York and William Dawson of Georgia, a prominent Whig and strong supporter of the Union, professed to see no cause for alarm and argued that there was time enough for declarations of abstract principles after the facts had been ascertained.[20] Seward declared he would "seek no factious case of controversy." Dawson saw "no disposition in foreign countries to interfere with any great American principle."

The new Pierce administration could not have put out the fires had it wished without splitting the Democratic party from the very outset. The party was firmly committed to challenging British claims. Pierce and the new secretary of state, William Marcy, moreover, undoubtedly did believe that British moves in Central America posed a danger. Not only had the British continued to hold San Juan and to administer the city and port, they had also reorganized the government of Belize, setting up a separate colony of the Bay Islands, maintaining that Ruatan was a dependency of Belize.

Pierce appointed James Buchanan as minister to Great Britain. Buchanan's instructions called on him to protest the British position on the Mosquito Protectorate and its extension to include San Juan, to seek a British withdrawal from the Bay Islands not in the immediate proximity of Belize, and to promote complete British withdrawal from the area.[21] Buchanan not only shared the views of the administration, he held to these views more firmly and had held them earlier than Pierce and Marcy. In addition to what was spelled out in Buchanan's instructions, there was the understanding that he was to prepare the way for Great Britain to accept American annexation of Cuba. Buchanan had hoped to handle the question of reciprocal trade with Canada and to use this as a lever for bringing about a British retreat in the Gulf of Mexico, but he lost this bargaining power when Pierce transferred the negotiation of the fisheries question and the negotiation of a reciprocal trade treaty to Washington.[22]

The appointment of Buchanan was a wise move. He had extensive experience in foreign affairs both as Minister to France and as secretary of state under Polk. He also occupied a strong position in the Democratic party. As a negotiator, he was able, hard-working, well-informed, and both gracious and affable. He made an excellent impression in London society and won the respect of the British foreign office.

Buchanan's Whig predecessors, Everett and Lawrence, both New Englanders, learned to admire the British, wrote lengthy letters of praise of the British, and at the same time ably upheld American interests, They recognized that Great Britain was a zealous supporter of national interests, but they did not distrust the foreign office and firmly believed that Great Britain prized good relations with the United States. Buchanan's experience proved equally pleasant, but Buchanan bore a considerably heavier burden, for he was expected to bring about British acceptance of the claim to American hegemony in the Gulf of Mexico. Buchanan enjoyed two strong advantages in his negotiations. By this time the United States constituted almost as great a market for British manufactures as the entire continent of Europe, and consequently the British commercial and manufacturing classes placed a high premium on good relations with the United States. Also the outbreak of the Crimean War made peace with the United States doubly important.

Buchanan's immediate predecessor, Joseph R. Ingersoll, reported that the British did not deem their interests in Central America essentially important or that there was "anything in the whole subject which ought to occasion controversy between the two nations . . . Nevertheless," he wrote, there were "symptoms of uneasiness, lest, in the manner in which the whole affair may be treated by the United States, there may be incidental cause of irritation."[23] These prophetic words provided an accurate description of coming developments.

Buchanan arrived in London in September 1853 at the time the Turkish question was reaching a crisis. He fully understood Foreign Minister Clarendon's being absorbed in that question and made allowances for it. At their first meeting they discussed the danger of war with Russia, and Clarendon was disarming in his candor and friendly tone. Only at the close of this exchange did Buchanan explain that the purpose of his mission was to promote a settlement of the Central American question. Neither spoke in a belligerent tone. Clarendon said their Mosquito Protectorate "was of no advantage to them, but that for a period of two or three hundred years they had exercised the Protectorate and that the honor of Great Britain required they should not abandon the Mosquitos without proper attention to their interests." Buchanan responded with a frank statement of the American view. He then turned to the question of the Belize and the newly established colony of the Bay Islands. Clarendon professed to know nothing about the establishment of the colony and shifted to "the offensive remarks" concerning Great Britain in Congress. Buchanan replied that his Lordship must know well that free speech could not be restricted in a legislative body.

At this point Buchanan chose to focus full attention on the disturbing effect of British antislavery agitation and implied that this was the chief barrier to good relations between the two countries. These "fanatics" had "exasperated the feelings of the citizens of the slaveholding states." Had it not been for the agitation of British and American abolitionists emancipation might have been achieved. In reporting this conversation, Buchanan observed that Clarendon was "an experienced and able statesman whose manners are frank, courteous and agreeable." In the next two years these friendly feelings matured into a relationship marked by mutual respect and a measure of good humor on both sides, which took some of the sting out of the inflammatory speeches in Congress and Anglophobic newspaper editorials.

In spite of his cordial meeting with Clarendon, Buchanan was disturbed because the British did not appear to take the Central American question seriously.[24] There could be no prospect of a settlement unless the British recognized that the United States was in earnest. Clarendon, busy with the Turkish question, procrastinated, but he invited Buchanan to suggest a manner of proceeding. Buchanan proposed they talk the matter through in a friendly manner. Clarendon said he agreed "with his whole heart."[25] Little did either know that they were to talk for two years. Clarendon gaily professed he did not understand the subject. Buchanan protested that he must not "play diplomat." Clarendon replied earnestly that he was not. Buchanan, well armed with historical facts on every issue, faced unperturbed Clarendon, who listened carefully but warded off agreement with good-natured replies. When the British consented to an agreeable treaty on fisheries and reciprocal trade in 1854, in negotiations conducted in Washington, any danger of conflict receded, and Clarendon had no reason to be alarmed.[26]

The phantom of a conniving, interfering Great Britain was also laid to rest by a clear and fortright disclaimer by Clarendon of promoting the importation of blacks into Cuba, of plans to promote a black republic, and he stated flatly that Great Britain did not have the remotest idea of ever acquiring Cuba. It was difficult to argue with Clarendon, who agreed that Spain had so misgoverned Cuba that if Spain lost it this would be her own fault.[27]

In a conference in early November Buchanan asked Clarendon to state the British position on Central American questions. Clarendon referred to a statement by Webster in 1852 that the Mosquito Protectorate was not covered by the Clayton-Bulwer Treaty. Buchanan took sharp issue; the United States held quite a contrary view. The protectorate, argued Buchanan, was an excuse by which Great Britain exercised exclusive dominion, and the United States would never have ratified the treaty if it had been believed that the British would not carry out an immediate withdrawal. The British shadow rule over the Mosquito Indians served no purpose other than to deprive the Central American states of their rightful possession and thereby it perpetuated confusion. The so-called king of the Mosquitos, Buchanan charged, was a drunken and worthless wretch, and the Indians had been brought into contact with the worst species of white population. They had learned all the vices of civilization and none of its virtues.[28] Clarendon did not dispute these charges; he merely replied that Great Britain wished to get out but it could only do so with honor if some way were found to assure the Indians of fair treatment.

Buchanan returned once again to the question of the Bay Islands. Clarendon replied that those islands "were of small importance & we need not make a mountain out of a mole hill." Ruatan had, Clarendon contended, always been a British possession, and in creating the colony of the Bay Islands Great Britain had done no more than give British subjects settled there a more perfect government. Buchanan maintained that it had not been a British possession until recently, that the establishment of the colony was a violation of the Clayton-Bulwer Treaty, and given the several British violations the treaty had netted the United States nothing.

The issue eventually came into sharper focus. The British contended that the treaty barred new possessions; the United States held that the treaty required Great Britain to withdraw from territory taken prior to 1850.[29] Buchanan came to the conclusion that Great Britain would eventually hold fast only to Belize. In the midst of one interview Buchanan told Clarendon "that whilst our good mother had been all the time engaged, for one hundred and fifty years, in annexing one possession after the other to her dominions, until the sun now never set upon her empire, she raised her hands with holy horror, if the daughter annexed territories adjacent to herself, which came to her in the natural course of events." Clarendon replied: "Well, you must admit, that in this respect, you are a chip off the old block."[30]

No agreement had emerged as late as December 1854, but it had become reasonably clear that Great Britain was in a compromising mood. Clarendon repeatedly minimized the importance of the Mosquito Protectorate and the Bay Islands; Buchanan, in turn, expressed regret that such minor questions should stand in the way of a settlement. When Clarendon fell back on the argument that Great Britain could not sacrifice her honor, Buchanan responded with the observation that considerations of honor were not worthy of standing in the way of achieving so great an object.

At the close of 1854 Buchanan called on Lord Aberdeen, the prime minister, a man well known for having contributed to the settlement of earlier difficulties. He assured Aberdeen of the warm and friendly manner of Clarendon. The conversation moved quickly to a discussion of the Central American question. Aberdeen had read a 100-page memorandum Buchanan had given to Clarendon and bestowed high praise on it. He expressed regret over the recent destruction of San Juan, the important port city in Nicaragua, by American bombardment. Regarding the Mosquito question, Aberdeen was certain it presented no serious difficulties. In reporting the conversation Buchanan offered the conclusion: "I feel satisfied they are nearly as anxious to relieve themselves from the Mosquito Protectorate as we are that they should withdraw from it." Aberdeen said he was not prepared to discuss the question of the Bay Islands, but again he assured Buchanan this question could present no insurmountable difficulty. He doubted that Great Britain could build a strong case for holding the islands except those close to the coast of Belize. Buchanan left the interview believing there had never been a better prospect of settling the questions providing nothing occurred "on the other side of the Atlantic further to complicate the Greytown difficulty, on which they are extremely sensitive."[31]

Buchanan was probably not fully aware that Aberdeen as prime minister did not dominate his cabinet but he did fear the influence of Palmerston. He also feared public opinion, which he concluded had forced the ministry into the Crimean War. Given the hostility of the British press to the United States and the general ignorance of the public about the United States, there was always the danger of the public being swept up into a war fever against America.

The exchanges suffered a setback in November 1854 due to a serious incident at San Juan. Across the river from San Juan, at Punta Arenas, Vanderbilt's Accessory Transit Company had its headquarters. The captain of one of the American ships shot a resident of San Juan who tried to board his ship. A group from Greytown sought to arrest the captain, and a melee ensued in which the American minister, Solon E. Borland, was slashed. After this happening President Pierce ordered Captain G. N. Hollins to take a firm stand in protecting the Americans. Hollins went beyond his instructions and bombarded San Juan, completely destroying the town. The British, quite naturally, deplored the incident.

Clarendon also found it more difficult to yield because of the repeated vicious attacks on Great Britain in the American press and Congress. Buchanan found it necessary to urge that the administration newspaper, the *Union*, refrain from extreme outbursts against the British.[32] Clarendon was particularly disturbed by Caleb Cushing's frequent denunciations of the British. Because Cushing was a member of the president's cabinet, his statements carried great weight.[33]

A crisis in the late summer of 1855 further delayed a settlement. Two developments endangered the negotiations, the dispatch of a British squadron when a British intelligence report, quite incorrectly, told that American-built ships in New York were under construction for use as Russian privateers, and American charges that the British minister in Washington, J.F.T.C. Crampton, and three British consuls were recruiting soldiers for the British army. When the report of the privateers proved false, the squadron was reduced in size. The other difficulty, alleged recruiting for the British army, led to the accused being given their passports. Buchanan expected that, in turn, he would receive his passport, but the British did not choose to retaliate. The crisis reached a serious magnitude, and Buchanan delayed his retiring from September 1855 to March 1856.

The deterioration in relations caused alarm in Great Britain. Buchanan discussed the situation with several British leaders. The commercial and manufacturing classes, Buchanan noted, were unhappy about the deterioration in relations with the United States and their leaders were making "strong representations" to members of the British cabinet.[34]

In January 1856 Buchanan and Clarendon once again took up the Central American question, and the conversations were friendly. Buchanan was not to see a breakthrough while he was minister. In March he returned to the United States to enter the presidential race. His place in London was taken by George Dallas, a fellow Pennsylvanian and Democrat, a man less experienced in diplomacy and given to suspicion and a considerable measure of Anglophobia.

In the summer of 1856 a treaty was concluded in Washington providing for a settlement. The Bay Islands were recognized as belonging to Honduras, and the Mosquito Protectorate was given up. The Senate offered several amendments, only one of which was unsatisfactory to Clarendon. The Senate refused to approve Article II, Section 2, concerning a guarantee of certain rights of British subjects in the Bay Islands. Clarendon objected on the ground that Costa Rica had not yet ratified a convention protecting British inhabitants, and that the Senate amendment would cause Costa Rica not to ratify a treaty which included a guarantee of protection for British subjects. Thus Great Britain would be handing over a large number of British subjects to a wretched government without any assurance of protection.[35] The treaty was not finally approved until 1860. Before this took place Great Britain returned the Bay Islands to Honduras and conceded the Mosquito coast to Nicaragua.

Fear of British designs in the Gulf of Mexico had undoubtedly been exaggerated. Her refusal to retreat earlier was based on grounds of national honor and not on firmly held plans to dominate the area. In fact, she chose to pursue a nonaggressive policy, while at the same time avoiding signs of weakness by giving in to American demands. The end of the Crimean War made retreat easier. By April 1858 Lord Malmesbury told Dallas that Great Britain had no objection to the United States taking control of all of the southern part of North America. Dallas, an ardent expansionist, reported:

> His Lordship said that he [Malmesbury] was one of that class of statesmen who believed that all the Southern part of North America must ultimately come under this Government of the United States: that he had no objection to what seemed the inevitable course of things: that on the contrary, he thought it would be beneficial as well to the populations occupying the countries referred to as to the United States, and the rest of the world.

Malmesbury added that Great Britain did not offer to abrogate the Clayton-Bulwer Treaty, "but if such be the disposition of the President, we shall make no difficulty whatsoever."[36]

American sensitivity and the presence of Anglophobia, especially in the Pierce administration, had led to an exaggeration of supposed British designs for control of an isthmian canal. Both British and American government representatives in Central America added to the mutual distrust by rash actions. What Great Britain sought was not control but joint Anglo-American control of the future canal. Given the extreme and deep fear of British and French interference and possible hopes of establishing a balance of power in the New World, even the more modest British desire of joint control of a canal, the Clayton-Bulwer Treaty was inevitably unpopular. It was in this decade that the Monroe Doctrine, reiterated repeatedly in both Congress and the press, became enshrined in the national credo.

NOTES TO CHAPTER XI

1. Dallas to Marcy, May 27, 1856. Despatches from London, Reel 65.
2. C. Stanley Urban, "The Ideology of Southern Imperialism: New Orleans and the Caribbean, 1845–1860," *The Louisiana Historical Quarterly*, Jan. 1956, p. 48.

3. Ibid., p. 57.
4. Ibid., p. 65.
5. Ibid., p. 69.
6. Pittsburgh *Post*, Jan. 24, 1859, quoted in Robert E. May, "A 'Southern Strategy' for the 1850s: Northern Democrats, the Tropics, and the Expansion of the National Domain," *Louisiana Studies An Interdisciplinary Journal of the South*, Winter 1975, p. 345.
7. For a persuasive argument that Great Britain in the Victorian era continued a policy of imperialism often relying on informal empire rather than direct political control, see John Gallagher and Ronald Robinson "The Imperialism of Free Trade" in George Nadel and Perry Curtis, *Imperialism and Colonialism* (London: The Macmillan Company, 1964), pp. 97–111.
8. *Congressional Globe*, 35th Cong., 2d Sess., Jan. 24, 1859, p. 540.
9. In a speech before the Senate on Jan. 26, 1853, Seward opposed the annexation of Cuba and gave a series of arguments in support of his stand, but it was the "immediate and early annexation" he opposed. He was specific: "nor see how I could vote for it at all until slavery have ceased to counteract the workings of nature in that beautiful island." Ibid., 32d Cong., 2d Sess., Appendix, p. 126.
10. Manning, *Diplomatic Correspondence of the United States*, Vol. VIII, p. 296.
11. Ibid., p. 323.
12. Ibid., p. 325.
13. Lawrence to Clayton, Dec. 28, 1849, Despatches from London, Reel 56.
14. Memorandum of an interview between Lawrence and Palmerston on the 27th January, 1850, Despatches from London, Reel 56.
15. Lawrence to Clayton, Apr. 19, 1850, Despatches from London, Reel 56.
16. This explanation of the Clayton-Bulwer negotiations is based on the account by Mary Wilhelmine Williams, *John Middleton Clayton Secretary of State March 7, 1849 to July 21, 1850*, in the *American Secretaries of State and Their Diplomacy* series.
17. *Congressional Globe*, Appendix, 32d Cong., 2d Sess., p. 90.
18. Ibid., p. 93.
19. Ibid., p. 138.
20. Ibid., pp. 127 and 134.
21. Nichols, *Franklin Pierce*, p. 264.
22. Ibid.
23. Ingersoll to Marcy, Apr. 22, 1853. Despatches from London, Reel 60.
24. Buchanan to Marcy, Oct. 7, 1853. Despatches from London, Reel 61.
25. Ibid., Nov. 1, 1853.
26. Sharp rivalry developed in the late 1840s between Montreal and the Erie Canal for control of overseas trade. Montreal hoped to become a great port city and vied for shipments of wheat. At the same time the Maritime Provinces launched bitter protests against American fishermen using the inshore fisheries and engaging in smuggling. Canadians took the initiative in launching a campaign for reciprocal trade. In 1852 the British government sent out a small squadron to protect the fisheries, and there was imminent danger of a clash. The treaty of 1854 provided for reciprocal free access to Atlantic coastal fisheries north of 36°, for free trade in natural products, the opening of Canadian waterways to Americans, and the free navigation of Lake Michigan by Canadians. See John Bartlet Brebner, *North Atlantic Triangle The Interplay of Canada, the United States and Great Britain* (New Haven: Yale University Press, 1945), pp. 154–58.
27. Ibid.
28. Ibid., Nov. 12, 1853.
29. Ibid., Apr. 7, 1855, Reel 63.
30. Ibid., Nov. 12, 1853, Reel 61.

31. Buchanan to Marcy, Dec. 30, 1854, Despatches from London, Reel 62.
32. Buchanan to Marcy, Apr. 7, 1854, Despatches from London, Reel 61.
33. Buchanan to Marcy, Feb. 8, 1856, Despatches from London, Reel 64.
34. Ibid., Nov. 23, 1855, Reel 66.
35. George Dallas to Secretary of State Cass, Apr. 16, 1857, Despatches from London, Reel 66.
36. Ibid., Apr. 13, 1858, Reel 67.

Chapter XII

Reaching for Forbidden Fruit

The acquisition of California created a national interest in the development of communications between the Atlantic and the Pacific. How this was to be done opened up a sharp conflict of sectional interests. The East and Northwest supported transcontinental railroad projects linking the Pacific to St. Louis or to points north of there. Southerners in general and some New York-based shipping companies concentrated on railroad and canal projects through Nicaragua and New Granada. New Orleans and the entire state of Louisiana opposed transcontinental railroads and vigorously asserted that the most practical line of communication lay across Mexico, the Tehuantepec route.

To build the line of communication through Central America or Mexico raised questions of foreign relations. Complex issues with Great Britain, with the Central American republics, and with Mexico ran parallel to sectional rivalry in domestic politics. The alignments followed no broad base among the general public, but rather of private interests in a particular city and small groups of speculators who saw an opportunity to make a profit.

These special interests had the advantage of enlisting political parties or factions. Small groups elevated themselves to national influence and gained a voice in the national government. This was so because the margin between victory and defeat of the major political parties was narrow. Both the Democrats and the Whigs were national parties; both were dependent on gaining support in all sections and this, in turn, hinged on catering to local interests. In 1852 Pierce, the Democratic candidate for president, won by only 1,392 votes in Louisiana. What appears to have mattered to voters in that state, and more particularly in New Orleans, was support of the Tehuantepec route, of Cuban annexation, and of appropriations for removing barriers at the mouth of the Mississippi which hindered the entry of the new and much larger steam-driven ships.

New Orleans in the early 1850s lived in fear of her decline as a major port. The *Daily Picayune* denounced transcontinental railroad proposals launched by Thomas Hart Benton and Asa Whitney. A railroad connecting St. Louis with the Pacific, wrote the editor, financed by large grants of the national domain, would "carry all the commercial and political advantages, the wealth and the power, which are anticipated from them to the Atlantic ports of the free states—leaving the Southern States, and particularly the Southwestern States, entirely isolated, while all the benefits of the great work, made out of the common property, in which they are joint owners, are drawn to the North."[1] Benton appeared even more of an ogre in the summer of 1852, when he contended that the Tehuantepec project should be set aside and all effort concentrated on a Pacific railroad with St. Louis as a terminus.

The Mexican grant of the right to build a road or railroad suffered a long and dubious history. The original grant in 1842 to a Mexican was extended by General José Mariano Salas in 1846. At the time of the negotiations of the Treaty of Guadalupe Hidalgo in 1847, the United States sought a grant, but Mexico turned down the request, explaining it had already been given to two Englishmen, merchants in Mexico City. By 1850 P. A. Hargous of New York took over the contract. He, in turn, negotiated with a committee in New Orleans, which soon organized the New Orleans Tehuantepec Company. The grant, known as the Garay grant, was transferred to the company, and Hargous was to receive one-third of the profits and retain one-third of the stock. The company, soon headed by Judah P. Benjamin, a prominent political leader, secured the support of Secretary of State Clayton. What was necessary was a treaty with Mexico so that the company would be assured of diplomatic support in the event of difficulties with Mexico.

The route across Mexico, some 200 miles, offered the advantage of the Coatzacoalos River, supposedly navigable by ocean vessels for 25 miles and by river boats another 85 miles. The company expected great profits from five million acres of land, alleged to be rich in minerals, that was part of the grant.

The treaty, negotiated with Mexico's President Mariano Arista in June 1850, met opposition in Mexico. Strong suspicions of Americans persisted since the war, and the prospect of a colonization scheme aroused memories of Texas. When word of this opposition reached Hargous in New York and the promoters in New Orleans, they appealed to Secretary of State Webster. Webster not only assured them of support but, according to the *Daily Picayune*, met with the entire Louisiana congressional delegation.

The promoters protested to Webster that the treaty was unsatisfactory because it did not provide firm assurance of protection if Mexicans or Mexican provincial officials interfered with the work of construction or with American employees living in the area. The treaty provided that American force could only be called in by order of Mexico, and this was restricted to the zone specified in the Garay grant. Hargous acknowledged that such protection was not ordinarily provided for in treaties but, given conditions in Mexico, capitalists would not invest without full assurance.[2] Webster complied with the request, withheld the first treaty, and instructed the United States minister in Mexico, Robert P. Letcher, to ask for several amendments, more particularly the right of the United States to intervene without Mexican approval. If Mexico refused, Webster instructed Letcher to inform the Mexican government that the United States would, in the event of Mexican violations of engagements, "be compelled to view that as a national grievance justifying and requiring it to demand amends for such a violation, and for the future to take upon itself the protection of its citizens who are the holders of the grant."[3]

Mexico vigorously opposed Webster's proposed amendments and the restriction of the grant to citizens of the United States.[4] After conferring with the interested American capitalists, Webster agreed to drop the demands.[5] In spite of this concession, Letcher reported early in 1851 that "the opposition is violent from every quarter."[6] A revised convention was signed on January 25, 1852, but there was little prospect of approval by the Mexican Congress. In April Mexico rejected it by a vote of 34 to 7. To complicate matters further, the Mexican government notified the United States that it did not recognize the Garay grant, which had been made by two revolutionary chieftains who did not have proper authority and that Garay had also forfeited his rights by failing to start construction in the time specified. The grant was formally annulled in May.

Webster held Mexico's action a violation of good faith. A survey party was exploring the area, and Americans had already spent thousands of dollars believing Mexico had given its approval.[7] Webster employed language that Mexico interpreted as a threat of war.

Refusing to accept the rulings of Mexico, the New Orleans Tehuantepec Company made every effort to push the government in Washington into a belligerent stand. A company publication late in 1851 contended that Mexico had no right to annul the Garay grant, that the company would file claims for damages and proceed with the work no matter what Mexico might do.[8] As the company and members of Congress became more demanding, Mexican opposition likewise rose to fever pitch. Finally, on April 7, 1851, the Mexican Chamber of Deputies, by a vote of 71 to 1, rejected the treaty.[9] Letcher reported: "It is altogether impossible to make a treaty having the least connection with the Garay grant. The government, the Congress, in short the whole nation, are deadly hostile to the grant . . ."

Hargous promptly put in a claim against Mexico for $5,283,000. The Fillmore administration reacted cautiously. In a note to Webster, the president cited Mexican objections to the large territory granted on each side of the proposed road and then observed that the Mexican apprehensions "that it might turn out to be another Texas colony which would involve their nation in war, and might result in another annexation; and considering what has passed, these apprehensions were not unreasonable."[10] Fillmore, anxious to keep the door open to some future agreement, wrote a friendly letter to President Arista of Mexico.

Throughout 1850 and 1851 the New Orleans *Daily Picayune* strongly supported the Tehuantepec project, scarcely mentioning the opposition in Mexico and repeatedly affirming that Secretary of State Webster gave the company his full support. When the first report of Mexican rejection of the treaty arrived in July 1851, the

New Orleans editor called on the national government to support the rights of the company.[11] The editor first suspected that the British were responsible, but some weeks later he placed the blame on northern interests, closing with a warning as "to just expectations of the South."[12] Upon final word of rejection of the treaty, the editor called Mexico's action "an outrage . . . It ought to be signified at once to Mexico that in no case will this Government permit the fraud upon the rights of the Tehuantepec Company to be consummated; in no case will the privileges vested in them by the most sacred rites, conceded by so many sanctions and confirmations, and acquired, and thus far improved at such expense, be allowed to be transferred to any other parties."[13] Two months later the *Daily Picayune* contended concerning the company's rights: "It is absolutely their property as a house and lot would be, purchased and duly conveyed, according to all the forms of the law in the city of New Orleans; . . ."[14]

The company stockholders and the editor contended that not only were the private investments at stake but the future of New Orleans. The proposed Tehuantepec road would place New Orleans closer to the Pacific coast than any other city. It would become the terminus of commerce with the Pacific coast and Asia.

Mexico's repudiation of the Garay grant and the treaty aroused hostility in Congress; spurred on by Senator James Mason of Virginia, the Senate Committee on Foreign Relations approved a resolution stating that the United States should not, as a matter of honor, take the initiative in renewing negotiations with Mexico, and if Mexico proposed negotiations they should be on the basis of the Garay grant. The United States was to insist on its rights and if Mexico refused, the United States should "adopt such measures as will preserve the honor of the country and the rights of its citizens."[15] Brooke of Mississippi proposed an amendment stating that if Mexico did not accede to the Garay grant by March 1, the United States would protect the New Orleans company in their occupation of the territory.

The question came to the fore again in April 1853, when A. G. Sloo, a New York shipbuilder, and a group of Mexicans secured a contract. Sloo lost his grant when he was unable to pay $500,000 as provided in the contract, and the contract went to a British subject, who had no interest in carrying out construction. Sloo and his associates, however, became active supporters of their claim, competing with the company holding the Garay grant.

Later in 1853 the Pierce administration appointed James Gadsden minister to Mexico. Gadsden, a railroad promoter from South Carolina, was instructed to offer to purchase Lower California and a considerable portion of northern Mexico. The minimum he was to agree to was the purchase of a strip of land between the Rio Grande and Colorado rivers so as to permit the building of a southern transcontinental railroad. He succeeded in purchasing the latter. The treaty, however, went further and included a provision granting the United States the right to construct a railroad across the Tehuantepec route. This provision affirmed the rights of the Sloo associates, as opposed to the New Orleans company with the Garay grant, a point that led to President Pierce getting caught between the senators who supported the Garay group and the Sloo group.[16]

The negotiations with Mexico, continued through 1859, ended in failure, although Buchanan and Secretary of State Cass pushed with vigor. In view of the revolutionary war going on in Mexico and many assaults on American citizens, they insisted on a treaty provision giving the United States the right to intervene to protect its citizens in the zone allotted to the company.[17] Quite understandably, Mexico feared American intrusion and refused to grant the right to intervene.[18] The campaign to have Mexico agree to the right of intervention paralleled repeated efforts by both Pierce and Buchanan to purchase large parts of Mexico.

In March 1857 Judah P. Benjamin, longtime leader in the New Orleans company and now a member of the United States Senate, went to Mexico and negotiated a private contract. This did not meet the demands of President Buchanan and Secretary of State Cass, both of whom insisted on a treaty provision granting the United States the right to intervene militarily to protect American citizens. As the United States minister to Mexico, John Forsyth, stated in a note to Cass on September 15, 1857, if Mexico agreed to the demands, it would mean the establishment of a protectorate. Mexico flatly rejected this, not only in 1857, but again and again in the ensuing negotiations.

In the 1850s Cuba became the most controversial issue in American foreign affairs. In the public mind it became the symbol of despotic oppression on the one hand and of fear for the future on the other.

From 1848 into the first years of the next decade revolutionary movements against Spanish rule in Cuba made it possible for American advocates of Cuban annexation to employ an emotional appeal for aid to the desperate victims of Spanish oppression. Cuban exiles in New York and New Orleans promoted the campaign with skill, and Cuban filibusterers achieved the status of heroes in several American cities. The blood of executed martyr-filibusterers helped arouse public feelings.

The arguments employed for annexation do not necessarily explain the real motivation of the advocates. The variety of these arguments employed by propagandists testify to skill in appealing to a wide range of interests aimed at building popular support. In the South the most frequent appeal was to the fear that Cuba was on the way to becoming a black republic. British influence in Madrid and the antislavery movement in Great Britain, it was asserted, aimed at emancipation in Cuba. Slaves were still being smuggled into Cuba in considerable numbers, and blacks constituted approximately 30 percent of the population. Speakers and journalists set forth conjectures that at any moment Spain would emancipate the slaves. This appears to have been the most frequently used appeal.

A second prominent note in the campaign concerned alleged British interference and possible plans for annexation. British activities in Central America were, it was charged, part of a larger plan, to control the entire Caribbean, including Cuba. This view took on fresh vigor in 1852 when the British proposed that the United States enter into an agreement with Great Britain and France to guarantee Spain's possession of the island.

A third argument stressed economic advantages. Spanish duties on American agricultural products ranged from 50 to 175 percent, and the duty on flour was $8.50 a barrel. New York shipping interests, and particularly George Law, president of the United States Mail Steamship Company, saw a great expansion of commerce taking place if Cuba was freed from Spanish rule. Others, particularly the business boosters in New Orleans, led by De Bow, argued that Cuba was "but a part of our own South," that it might be the key that would unlock the door to markets in Brazil. Whoever held Cuba would control the commerce of the entire New World.[19]

The economic argument for annexation gained strength due to southern concern over the exhaustion of lands suitable for the raising of cotton. Planters recklessly used up their lands and then moved on to new areas. Cotton culture by 1850 had, it seemed, gone about as far westward as it could go. A considerable number of planters in Louisiana would be wiped out. Cuba appeared to offer a solution. On the other hand, sugar plantation owners in Louisiana feared the competition of Cuban sugar. The publicists for annexation took up the challenge, and although they may not have banished the concern of sugar growers, they neutralized it by appeals to patriotism and national interest and predictions that once Cuba was annexed the cost of producing sugar on the mainland and on the island would be equalized.[20] Each of these arguments gained a ready hearing among the myriad of interest groups in the boom years after the Mexican War.

Prosperity leavened ambition, inspired dreams of empire, and quickened the impulse to extend freedom and republican principles. The war demonstrated the strength of American arms; the huge acquisition of territory created lust for ever more territory, rather than satisfying the urge. The war propelled the interest southward, and the interest rode aloft on the reasonable conclusion, particularly of New Orleans entrepreneurs and New York shipping interests, that nature ordained that the most feasible and cheapest route between East and West lay through the Gulf of Mexico. Cuba, port of call for all ships going to or from New York to New Orleans or to Central America, took on new importance to those who would profit directly, as well as to aspiring politicians such as Lewis Cass, who on May 10, 1848 proposed the purchase of the island and asserted that the Gulf of Mexico "must be practically an American lake."[21]

The founding fathers viewed Cuba wholly as a question of security and limited their interest to preventing its transfer to some nation more powerful than Spain, but by 1848 Cuba looked like the bright red apple on the neighbor's tree ready for picking. Polk, amenable to such exploits, was urged on by John L. O'Sullivan, famous for coining the phrase "manifest destiny." This energetic journalist had intimate connections with Cuba. His sister was married to a leading Cuban planter, Cristobol Madan y Madan, the leader of the Cuban

Creole annexationists. O'Sullivan flattered Polk with the argument that the annexation of Cuba would be a fitting climax to his glorious achievements. Polk discussed the project with his cabinet and then laid plans for the purchase of the island. Spain was to be offered as much as $100 million. The public interest in Cuba had already been richly stimulated by Moses Yale Beach through the columns of his New York *Sun* and by a paper in New York, run by Cuban exiles, that was published in both Spanish and English translations.[22] Romulus M. Saunders, minister to Spain, received instructions to seek to make the purchase. Spain made short shrift of the offer, which served as a warning to Spain that she could anticipate difficulties.

In 1849 the new administration of Zachary Taylor closed the door to the Cuban annexationists. Millard Fillmore, successor upon Taylor's death in 1850, firmly opposed meddling in Cuban affairs. While the administration maintained a quiescent policy, the Cuban exile, General Narcissa Lopez, launched a series of filibustering expeditions. Lopez, born in Venezuela, migrated to Cuba, where he had risen to become president of the Military Commission. Like other Creoles, he saw annexation as a guarantee against the emancipation of the Negroes.[23] He was planning a revolt at the time Polk sought to purchase the island, and his plan was well known to Robert Blair Campbell, American consul in Havana, who reported it to Washington. The Spanish authorities learned of the plan through American authorities, and Lopez fled to the United States.[24] He promptly organized an expedition to free the island.

In the course of 1849–1851 Lopez led four expeditions. The men he recruited for the first expedition, according to Secretary of State Clayton's agent, were "the most desperate looking creatures as ever were seen would murder a man for ten dollars."[25] In his next three ventures Lopez had the full support of Governor Quitman of Mississippi, and several of the men, veterans of the Mexican War, came from well-established families, including William L. Crittenden, a nephew of the attorney general. Lopez' plans were widely known and had the support of many southern leaders. In spite of genuine efforts by President Fillmore to prevent the sailing of the four expeditions, each one eluded surveillance in part because the enthusiasm of the public in New Orleans and Mobile intimidated federal officials charged with enforcing the law.

On the final expedition, in August 1851, Lopez and many of his men, including Crittenden, were captured by the Spanish authorities and shot. The Lopez expeditions were planned to coincide with uprisings in Cuba. American sympathizers fully expected a Cuban full-scale revolution and saw the filibustering expeditions in terms of friendly assistance rather than hostile intrusions.

The Cuban cause enjoyed public support. Lopez was received as a hero at Key West, Florida, after the third of his ventures. In New Orleans the public excitement approached mass hysteria, reaching its peak in the summer of 1851 when the first meager reports arrived of a general Cuban uprising. The news was "received with signs of general joy . . . All faces seem to glow with happy anticipations of the struggle commenced in the right way," observed one editor who saw success now that the Lopez force would be fighting side by side with the Cubans.[26] At a public meeting addressed by leading citizens, resolutions were passed by acclamation calling on all Americans to express their sympathy with the Cubans, who were fighting "to achieve their liberties and rid themselves of intolerable oppression."[27] The enthusiasm mounted when reports, clearly false, told of the great success of the insurgents. "It would be impossible," wrote the editor of the *Daily Picayune*, "as it would be unnatural, to repress, in America, feelings of exultation at the spirit which is exhibiting itself in Cuba, of rejoicing at the success of the Patriots, and of zeal to join with them in their struggle and aid them to achieve their independence."[28] In Farmersville, Louisiana, the local festivities included a public meeting, the firing of guns, "an eloquent prayer by the Rev. Mr. Lewis in behalf of the struggling Patriots," and the reading of the Cuban declaration of independence.[29]

Then the sad news arrived of the capture and execution of Lopez and his men. To Spanish authorities the executions were consistent with law and necessary to national survival; to American sympathizers the executions were murders in cold blood. "A thrill of horror ran through this whole community yesterday on the receipt of the bloody news from Havana," read one report. In early September there were riots in New Orleans protesting the executions.

The Cuban junta in New York began to plan another expedition in 1853. Southerners were now doubly alarmed because the new captain-general in Cuba, Marques de la Pezuela, who was known to favor the abolition of slavery, took steps in preparation for emancipation. This enabled the junta to secure the services of the former governor of Mississippi, John A. Quitman. The proposed expedition had the support of several members of Pierce's cabinet, and Quitman carried on a lengthy correspondence with leaders in Cuba; but the expedition was never launched because Pierce persuaded Quitman to withdraw.

Faith in a Cuban uprising taking place and in the effectiveness of American expeditions declined after 1851, but interest in Cuban annexation increased. Enthusiasm was kindled by incidents involving American ships entering Havana. The most important of these concerned the refusal of the Cuban authorities to admit the *Crescent City* on September 3, 1852. The ship belonged to the United States Mail Steamship Company, which was headed by George Law, of New York, an entrepreneur with a highly unsavory reputation, active in the Democratic party in New York.[30] Law, a strong annexationist, not only welcomed the incident but sought to promote further ones by defying Cuban authorities. The authorities in Havana denied the ship entry as long as the Purser, M. Smith, was aboard, charging that Smith was responsible for scurrilous attacks in the New York press on the Cuban government.

The ship captain, Navy Lieutenant David D. Porter, went on to New Orleans, where the news aroused indignation. Two thousand persons attended a meeting at Banks Arcade to protest "the recent insult to our flag." The insult, shouted a speaker, must be atoned for. Three evenings later a second mass meeting was held at Lafayette Square. Judge Larue, in tune with his audience, commented: "It is said that we have been endeavoring to raise an issue with Spain in order that we might take possession of Cuba. Well, suppose we had, Cuba naturally belongs to us geographically." The possession of Cuba, he said, was "absolutely necessary to the safety of the United States." The bare threat of Spain freeing the slaves justified taking possession of Cuba at once. The judge was followed by Judah P. Benjamin, who bemoaned the fact that "our government had looked on the expeditions with almost a hostile eye . . . Had it not done so, had it given the slightest encouragement to expeditions," Benjamin held, "the Island would have been wrested from the power that rules it." The presence of several bands and a fireworks display contributed to the spirit of the festivity.[31]

The excitement over the *Crescent City* was not limited to New Orleans. Annexationist Democrats, in the midst of the presidential election campaign, blasted the Whigs for their failure to take bold action.

The election of Pierce gave promise of action on the Cuban question. Pierce made a series of appointments that held out hope for the annexationists: Caleb Cushing as attorney general, Jefferson Davis as secretary of war, James Buchanan as minister to Great Britain, John Y. Mason as minister to France, Pierre Soulé as minister to Spain, August Belmont as minister to the Netherlands. Each of these agreed with Buchanan that the annexation of Cuba was an absolute necessity. Buchanan, on his appointment as minister to London, received instructions to prepare the British to accept the inevitability of Cuban annexation.

In his second interview with Clarendon, Buchanan raised the question of Cuba. His presentation tells more about the motivation of the annexationists than do the arguments fed to the public in the campaign.

> Your Lordship must be fully aware of the deep and vital interest which we feel in regard to the condition of the colored population of Cuba. The island is within sight of our shores and should a black Government like that of Hayti be established there, it would endanger the peace and the domestic security of a large and important portion of our people.[32]

Buchanan wanted to know if Great Britain advised Spain to emancipate the blacks in Cuba. Clarendon denied this, saying that Great Britain did not have "the most remote idea in any event of ever attempting to acquire Cuba for ourselves." Buchanan then added that Cuba was wretchedly misruled, that Spain had placed severe restrictions on trade, and that Cuba was a constant annoyance, contributing to internal dissension. But again Buchanan returned to the heart of the matter, the question of the blacks, and he stated that if an uprising took place in Cuba and if other governments interfered "no human power could prevent us from interfering in favor of the Creoles."[33]

Throughout 1853 the Pierce administration moved with some

degree of caution. In his instructions to Soulé in Madrid, Secretary of State Marcy stated: "Nothing will be done, on our part, to disturb the present connexion with Spain, unless the character of that connexion should be so changed as to affect our present or prospective security."[34] But should Spain "resort to aid of another power then US will act." Marcy told Soulé he did not think Spain would be willing to sell Cuba and he was not authorized by the president to make any proposition to Spain. Soulé was not to arouse Spanish suspicions but, on the other hand, if an opportunity presented itself, he could say that the United States would favor a voluntary separation, "and, if necessary to effect it, would be willing to contribute something more substantial than their good will towards an object so desirable to them."[35]

Soulé was not one to carry out instructions with finesse, and he made enemies in Madrid shortly after arriving. He acquired further disrepute when he challenged the minister of France to a duel and then wounded that dignitary. At the same time he rushed into discussions with the Spanish minister of foreign affairs and proposed a commercial treaty. For good measure he stressed the benefits to the United States of a separation of Cuba.[36] By December Soulé reported that "we are cordially hated in the Foreign Office," a development he attributed to British and French machinations.[37]

Then during the first days of March 1854 occurred another of those incidents that could be interpreted as an insult to the flag. The American ship *Black Warrior*, on its way from New Orleans to New York, stopped in Havana. On entering, the captain failed to report there were bales of cotton aboard that were to be delivered in New York. Learning of the cotton, the Cuban port authority pronounced the ship in violation of the law and promptly seized it and arrested the captain. The captain of the *Black Warrior* held that it had long been the practice not to report cargo bound for another port.

The incident caused an unwarranted uproar, and Secretary of State Marcy termed it an outrage. He instructed Soulé to demand satisfaction, including an indemnity of $300,000. This time, wrote Marcy, the delay experienced in previous cases could not be tolerated. The impetuous Soulé then delivered a forty-eight hour ultimatum. Soulé demanded not only the indemnity but the dismissal of all Cuban officials who had participated.[38] Calderon, Spain's foreign minister, responded: "Permit me in conclusion, to impress upon the mind of your excellency, that the government of Her Majesty, jealous also of its decorum, is not accustomed to the harsh and imperious manner with which it has been pressed which, furthermore, is not the most adequate for attaining to the amicable settlement which is wished for."[39]

Spain paid the owners of the ship an amount greater than the indemnity demanded. Marcy accepted the private settlement but maintained that an apology was due from Spain for the insult to the United States.[40] In his note to Soulé, however, Marcy stated that the president was unwilling to resort to extreme measures and that the president did not expect Soulé "to take any further steps in relation to the outrage in the case of the *Black Warrior*." Caleb Cushing and Jefferson Davis had argued for bold action but had been overruled.[41]

On April 3 Marcy instructed Soulé that the president authorized him to enter into negotiations to purchase Cuba. Events in Spain, Marcy added, may have diminished the barriers to purchase.[42] But was purchase the only solution Pierce and his cabinet had in mind? On June 24 Marcy reported that the president was deliberating; he wanted "to exhaust all peaceful means before resorting to extreme measures." And at this same moment Soulé was notified that the president planned to appoint a commission to go to Madrid to settle outstanding questions. Pierce then withdrew this proposal. Finally, on August 22 Marcy instructed Soulé, Buchanan, and Mason to meet and confer on the Spanish problem. Marcy stated that past injuries were far less important than the future and that separation of Cuba from Spain was required for the tranquility and prosperity of the United States.[43]

With Great Britain and France immersed in the Crimean War and with the Spanish government beset with a revolution, the chances of reaching a settlement appeared brighter. The three American diplomats in Europe who were to meet and discuss the Cuban question were well known for their proannexation views. They were instructed to draw a plan for coordinating their negotiations in the three capitals where they were stationed.[44]

Buchanan, distressed by the instructions, wrote to Marcy stating that his views were well known and he did not see how he could be helpful. He wished to proceed quietly with an alternative strategy originally proposed by August Belmont, minister at The Hague.

Belmont and Buchanan saw as the best move an approach to Europeans who held Spanish bonds, pointing out to these men that the sale of Cuba would enrich the Spanish treasury and also increase the value of their holdings. These bonds were selling at half their purchase price, and the Spanish government was no longer paying interest on them. Buchanan and Belmont believed the bondholders could be induced to use their influence quietly to persuade the Spanish government to sell so as to replenish the government treasury. Buchanan saw that, with Soulé as a participant and with Daniel E. Sickles, a reckless and garrulous man, present as a special messenger of Pierce, the approach to the bondholders was most likely to give way to a bolder move.[45] Sickles was not one to keep a secret, and he had recently caused a stir when, as a guest in a British home on the Fourth of July in celebration of American independence, he refused to stand when a toast was offered to the queen. Once in Europe, Sickles talked freely.

The commission met at Ostend on October 9 and after three days adjourned to Aix-la-Chapelle in the hope of eluding news reporters and intelligence agents. News of the meetings had already set off speculation. This placed the project in jeopardy.

Buchanan, Mason, and Soulé did not issue a manifesto, but their report acquired that epithet. It did not specifically recommend the use of force. It was left to the administration to decide if the existing situation justified extreme measures. If Cuba "endangers our internal peace and the existence of our cherished Union," then the United States would be justified in using force. The question for the administration to decide was whether the situation threatened national survival. If the United States permitted Cuba to be Africanized "with all its attendant horror to the white race, we should be recreant to our duty . . . unworthy of our gallant forefathers" not to act.[46]

In forwarding the report, Soulé expressed the hope that the question could be settled peacefully, but if it should be war "let it be now" while the great powers were engaged in war with Russia.[47] Buchanan forwarded the report by special messenger, making no comments.

These recommendations arrived in Washington in November 1854 just as the first election returns came in to dampen the spirits of Pierce and his cabinet. The Democrats had lost every northern state. Many factors brought about the defeat, especially the Kansas-Nebraska Act. Obviously, Cuban annexation, viewed by many northerners as a move to appease the South and to give added life to slavery, could become a serious political liability. The Pierce administration rejected the recommendations. Yet, the annexation of Cuba remained a live issue.

James Buchanan, in the presidential campaign of 1856, profited from his stand on Cuba. Influential southerners, such as Senator John Slidell of Louisiana, supported Buchanan for the Democratic nomination in considerable part because of Buchanan's stand on Cuba. Buchanan's friends and other participants in Democratic politics affirmed that his connection with the Ostend Manifesto added greatly to the strength of Buchanan's candidacy.[48]

The cry for Cuba continued in large part because of southern demands, but it also enjoyed support from many northern Democrats. A political swap whereby the South would retreat from Kansas in return for support of Cuban annexation appealed to those who sought desperately to keep the party united. The cause likewise gained support from northerners who saw in the annexation of Cuba a boon to commerce.[49]

President Buchanan continued to seek the annexation of Cuba, and in 1859 asked Congress to appropriate $30 million to facilitate acquisition. The bill, introduced by Senator John Slidell on January 10, aroused a heated debate that continued for many weeks. The opponents denounced the proposal as motivated by a desire to make political capital of this issue in the next campaign for the presidency and contended that there was not the remotest possibility of Spain selling the island. Seward held there was "not the least earthly prospect" of Spain considering the proposal. Supporters of the measure contended that Cuba was an object of great interest to Great Britain and France, who had interfered earlier by seeking to bind the United States to renounce any ambition to acquire the island.

President Buchanan, who had already lost credibility, was now the target of ridicule. The *New York Times* denounced the scheme as futile and deeply offensive to Spain. Buchanan, wrote the editor, could "scarcely be expected to have any scruples as to the morality of the proceeding—but he seems equally insensible to its absurdity."[50]

News of Buchanan's proposal led to debate in the Spanish Cortes, where the proposal was not only rejected but denounced as insulting.

The Cuban question, a useful issue in domestic politics, was kept alive in spite of Spain's adamant refusal to sell and the failure of the Cuban Creoles to overthrow Spanish rule. Any hopes of acquisition had died except with Buchanan and a few senators such as John Slidell and Judah P. Benjamin.

Buchanan's obsession with the necessity of acquiring Cuba, his repeated efforts to buy large parts of northern Mexico and to win from Mexico a treaty right to intervene to protect the prospective canal route paralleled his zeal to negotiate a similar treaty with Nicaragua. Without such a guarantee of security, Buchanan contended, capitalists would not venture to underwrite the canal project. In 1857 Secretary of State Cass and Nicaragua's minister to the United States, A. J. de Yrisarri, negotiated a treaty conforming to Buchanan's specifications. Nicaragua refused to ratify the treaty. Buchanan then turned to Congress for authority to employ force if Nicaragua failed to protect Americans traveling over the route. Congress refused to grant his request in 1857 and again in 1859, when Buchanan once again urged such action.

As in the case of Mexico, Buchanan placed equal emphasis on the importance of a transit route and the danger of interference by Great Britain and France. The anarchy prevailing in Mexico, the repeated assaults on Americans and other foreigners, and the inability of Mexico to pay foreign claims provided a degree of justification for the president's concern that the European nations might employ force and this, in turn, might lead to a permanent foothold. There was considerably less reason to fear such a development in Nicaragua, although a French citizen, Felix Belly succeeded in negotiating a contract to build a canal. Buchanan rightly dismissed this as of no consequence, for Belly had no capital; but Buchanan believed that Belly had used his influence to sidetrack the Cass-Yrisarri Treaty.

As Buchanan readily acknowledged, the filibustering expeditions of William Walker stood as the major barrier to successful negotiations with Nicaragua.[51] Wholly opportunistic, contemptuous of the law, and at the same time able to ingratiate himself with some leading statesmen, including Cass, Buchanan's secretary of state, this will-o-the-wisp adventurer had worked as a journalist in New Orleans, moved to San Francisco, led two expeditions into Mexico, and achieved prominence in the Democratic party in California prior to plotting the take-over of Nicaragua. In 1855 he succeeded in taking over the country, set up his one-man rule, gathered around him an army of 1,200 men, and became a scourge for the peasants and foreign residents. He was expelled after some months by the armed forces of neighboring states.

The Nicaragua adventure made Walker a hero in the eyes of a considerable number of Americans, including Cass, who said: "I am free to confess that the heroic effort of our countrymen in Nicaragua excites my admiration, while it engages all my solicitude . . . The difficulties which General Walker has encountered and overcome will place his name high on the roll of the distinguished men of his age."[52] In both New Orleans and New York Walker received a rousing welcome. A second expedition was halted by his arrest, but he escaped and set off for Nicaragua with another collection of "immigrants."

The expedition Walker organized was advertised in the New Orleans newspapers, noted in the New York newspapers, and freely discussed in the streets of the southern port cities of New Orleans and Mobile. Lieutenant John J. Olney, USN, in New Orleans with orders for the federal district attorney to arrest Walker, thought the public was influenced by the recent refusal to recognize the new government in Nicaragua and by the report that Cass had on one occasion most explicitly said, "American citizens when they emigrate have a right, at all times, to take their arms with them."[53]

Walker and 150 men landed at Punta Arenas, near San Juan, on November 24, 1857. On learning that Walker had sailed for Nicaragua, President Buchanan ordered the navy to watch for him. The commander of the Home Squadron, H. Paulding, was eager to take action, but the question confronting navy Captain Engle was whether he had the authority to act after Walker had landed in Nicaragua. If Walker attacked American property or endangered American lives, the answer appeared to be in the affirmative. Walker, when he occupied the property of a Mr. Scott at Punta Arenas, was promptly warned to evacuate it.[54] On December 8 Captain Engle of the Home Squadron led the men of his ship on shore and ordered Walker to surrender his arms and then placed 150 of Walker's men on board the *Saratoga* to be transported to Key West. At one point in these proceedings Walker threatened to shoot some naval officers. He was arrested on charges of having violated the neutrality laws of the United States and transported to New York.[55]

On his arrival in New York, Walker was dismissed by officers of the federal government. Paulding was commended by Buchanan for his "pure and patriotic motives," but Buchanan also ruled that Paulding had exceeded his instructions.[56] At the same time Buchanan asserted that he was determined to enforce the neutrality laws, and condemned Walker for his criminal acts. In words less comforting to Nicaraguans than to American expansionists, the president stated that Walker's actions retarded American progress. It was, he said, "the destiny of our race to spread themselves over the continent of North America . . . If permitted to go there peacefully, Central America will soon contain an American population which will confer blessings and benefits as well upon the natives as their respective governments."

The Senate response to Buchanan's message suggested that more of the members were interested in discrediting the president than in the serious problem posed by an armed invasion of a friendly state. The Committee on Foreign Relations approved of Buchanan's stand, but Jefferson Davis and Albert Brown of Mississippi, and Robert Toombs of Georgia denounced the arrest of Walker as unconstitutional and upheld the right of Walker, as a voluntary expatriot, to return to his adopted country and extend the blessings of liberty.[57]

Walker launched a third well-publicized expedition in the fall of 1858. This time he was taken into custody by the British navy, turned over to the government of Honduras, and shot.

Tehuantepec, Cuba, and Nicaragua, each suffering from instability, served as the focal points of American interest. Had it not been for the restraints imposed by the slavery question, the Spanish-American War might well have occurred fifty years earlier. The canal question in Tehuantepec and Nicaragua likewise foreboded bold policy in the future.

NOTES TO CHAPTER XII

1. New Orleans *Daily Picayune*, Jan. 15, 1851.
2. P. A. Hargous to Secretary of State Webster, Aug. 12, 1850. Senate Executive Documents, 32d Cong., 1st Sess., Vol. X, Doc. No. 97, pp. 24–26.
3. Ibid., Webster to Letcher, Aug. 24, 1850, pp. 29–32.
4. Ibid., Letcher to Webster, Oct. 12, 1850, pp. 36–38; José M. Lacunza to Letcher, Oct. 23, 1850, pp. 38–40.
5. Ibid., Webster to Letcher, Dec. 4, 1850, p. 41.
6. Ibid., Webster to Letcher, Jan. 17, 1851, pp. 41–42.
7. Ibid., Webster to De La Rosa, Apr. 30, 1851, pp. 60–66.
8. Ibid., José F. Ramirez to Letcher, Dec. 13, 1851, pp. 107–108.
9. Ibid., Letcher to Webster, Apr. 8, 1851, pp. 128–29.
10. Fillmore to Webster, May 20, 1852, *Millard Fillmore Papers*, ed. Frank H. Severance (Buffalo: Buffalo Historical Society, 1907), p. 366.
11. New Orleans *Daily Picayune*, "Our Relations with Mexico," July 6, 1851.
12. Ibid., Aug. 1, 1851.
13. Ibid., May 15, 1852.
14. Ibid., July 14, 1852.
15. *Congressional Globe*, 32d Cong., 2nd Sess., Feb. 1, 1853, p. 458.
16. Nichols, *Franklin Pierce*, p. 339.
17. *Congressional Globe*, 32d Cong., 2nd Sess., Feb. 1, 1853, p. 458.
18. Cass to Forsyth, July 17, 1857, Senate Executive Documents, 35th Cong., 1st Sess., Vol. 13, Doc. No. 72, pp. 39–48.
19. "Destiny of the Slave States," *De Bow's Review*, Sept., 1854, p. 281.
20. For a highly useful account of the economic arguments, see Basil Rauch, *American Interest in Cuba: 1848–1855* (New York: Columbia University Press, 1948), Chapter VII "Economic Considerations."
21. *Congressional Globe*, 30th Cong., 1st Sess., pp. 614–17, quoted by Rauch, *American Interest in Cuba*, p. 71.
22. Rauch, *American Interest in Cuba*, pp. 54–55.
23. Hugh Thomas, *Cuba The Pursuit of Freedom* (New York: Harper & Row, 1971), p. 213.
24. Rauch, *American Interest in Cuba*, p. 77.
25. M. W. Mears to Clayton, Sept. 1849, Department of State Archives, Special Agents, XVIII, quoted by Rauch, *American Interest in Cuba*, p. 114.
26. New Orleans *Daily Picayune*, July 23, 1851.
27. Ibid., July 24, 1851.
28. Ibid., Aug. 1, 1851.
29. Ibid., Aug. 20, 1851.
30. Rauch, *American Interest in Cuba*, p. 192.
31. New Orleans *Daily Picayune*, Oct. 12, 1852.
32. Buchanan to Marcy, Nov. 1, 1853, Despatches from London, Roll 61.
33. Ibid.
34. House Executive Documents, 33d Cong., 2nd Sess., Vol. 10, Doc. No. 93.
35. Ibid.
36. Ibid., Soulé to Marcy, Nov. 10, 1853.
37. Ibid., Dec. 23, 1853.
38. Soulé's antics in Madrid are narrated in detail by Amos Aschback Ettinger, in his book, *The Mission to Spain of Pierre Soulé A Study in the Cuban Diplomacy of the United States* (New Haven: Yale University Press,

beginnings of the American missionary movement. The American Board of Commissioners for Foreign Missions, a joint endeavor of Congregationalists and Presbyterians, sent the first two missionaries, Hiram Bingham and Asa Thurston, to the islands in 1819. These two forerunners of a large missionary effort encountered a society ready for change. Missionaries brought with them the Christian gospel as well as an array of western ideas as to a proper legal system, form of government, education, and efficient systems of agriculture and business, plus a surplus of fixed rules regarding sexual morality, temperance, and Sabbath observance. Unlike the foreign business community in Honolulu, the missionaries identified with the native ruling class and the people of the islands and rose to major political positions. Their success in making converts, in establishing schools, and in injecting western ideas into the body politic in a few short years and their role as trusted counselors of the monarchy earned them both the laurels and the condemnation that are inevitably associated with cultural imperialism. On the one hand, they imposed an extremely strict code of behavior wholly foreign to the natives; and, on the other hand, they showed genuine concern for the natives and sought to protect the Hawaiian kingdom from being taken over economically and politically by a foreign power. They sought to steer the old society into the modern world, but are better remembered as foolish instigators of puritanical taboos.

The extreme feebleness of the Hawaiian kingdom rendered it an easy prey to conquest, and only conflicting rivalries among the foreign powers offered protection. Engrossed in fear of its vulnerability, the native monarchy and its missionary counselors sought treaties recognizing the kingdom's independence and the protection of a powerful state. In reality, Great Britain, France, and the United States, the three nations with interests in the islands, entertained no strong desire to take them over. Their only aims were the protection of their own nationals from discrimination and the prevention of annexation by a rival power. In the case of the Tyler administration, Secretary of State Webster was at first wholly indifferent to the islands, and throughout the 1840s American commissioners at Honolulu were frustrated by the failure of the American government to respond to their dispatches.[1]

In 1841 Hawaii sent a mission abroad seeking diplomatic recognition. At this point Webster did indicate an interest and he supplemented the granting of recognition with a statement that "the United States, . . . , are more interested in the fate of the islands, and of their government, than any other nation can be" and "that no power ought to take possession of the islands as a conquest, or for the purpose of colonization, and that no power ought to seek for any undue control over the existing Government, or any exclusive privileges or preferences in matters of commerce."[2]

Two years later, in November 1843, Great Britain and France jointly recognized the island kingdom's independence. Both sought to have the United States join them in a tripartite agreement, denying themselves the right of future acquisition; but the Tyler administration rejected this on the ground that political commitments of this order with foreign powers were contrary to American tradition.[3]

Bold actions of French and British naval commanders overshadowed the fact that neither government contemplated acquisition of the islands. On two occasions French naval forces occupied Honolulu, Captain Laplace in 1839 and Admiral Tramelin in 1849. Laplace forced a convention on the Hawaiian government that infringed on the sovereignty of the country by setting a low duty on imports of French wines and prescribing that no Frenchman accused of crime be judged otherwise than by a jury composed of foreigners proposed by the French consul. Tramelin occupied a fort, seized the king's yacht, and declared void a treaty negotiated in 1846 that was favorable to Hawaiian interests. The French government upheld the Laplace convention of 1839, but it restored the treaty of 1846. The boldest action taken by the British occurred in February 1843, when Lord George Paulet, commander of the *Carysfort*, took over the government of Hawaii, but with the explanation that his action was subject to approval by the government in London. He ruled Hawaii until July, when the British Admiral Richard Thomas arrived and returned control to the Hawaiians. In each of these instances action was taken on the ground of discrimination against and unfair treatment of French and British residents.

The French actions and especially the stridency of the French commissioner, Louis Emile Perrin, in 1851, together with sharp political cleavages in Hawaii, led King Kamehameha III, to seek treaties from the three concerned foreign powers providing for the establishment of a joint protectorate, or if this were not attainable, annexation by the United States. When the milder solution was rejected, the United States was approached as to annexation. Considerable sentiment in the United States, particularly in California, favored annexation, and with the election of Franklin Pierce to the presidency it appeared that this would take place. However, considering the prospective opposition of Great Britain and France, annexation must first be proposed by Hawaii. The proposal became fact in February 1854. By May the American commissioner in Hawaii, David L. Gregg, received authorization to negotiate an annexation treaty. Sharp disagreement arose in Hawaii, with Prince Liholiho, nephew of King Kamehameha III, opposing annexation. While the available evidence has not permitted historians to conclude that the king's cabinet rejected the proposed annexation treaty at a meeting on December 8, there are some indications that this may have occurred. The death of the king a week later and Prince Liholiho's rise to the throne terminated further negotiation. It is doubtful that a treaty of annexation would have been approved by the Senate, where strong opposition had already made itself heard. The treaty provided for immediate statehood, a feature certain to be objectionable.[4]

The significance of American entry into China and Japan lies less in the story of formal diplomatic relations and the beginnings of a Far Eastern policy than it does in the conflict of cultures. A wider gulf than that between Confucian China and nineteenth-century United States can scarcely be imagined. China was not a nation; it was a civilization.

The United States rested upon the political principles of a nation state, acclaimed the sanctity of the individual, prized representative government, placed its faith in law and sophisticated legal procedures, and held innovation and display of individual assertiveness in great respect. On the other hand, ancient China was a highly decentralized political order, held together not by the power of Peking but by common allegiance to Confucian teaching, family ties, and merchant and craft guilds. Chinese genius lay in the exaltation of learning, the mastery of Confucian principles and the many commentaries on Confucius. Tens of thousands took civil service examinations after long years of intense study. The examinations bore no relationship to the skills useful once in office and offered little or no assurance of an efficient bureaucracy, but the study of China's classics provided a common body of knowledge, moral principles, and rules for personal behavior.

The unity thus engendered was further buttressed by the inviolable bonds of family that nurtured reverence for ancestors, governed behavior, provided security for the aged, and subordinated individual aspirations to the complete dominance of the family elders. The guilds, controlling what was produced, how much, and of what quality, at what price, and the choice of market squeezed out individual enterprise. The system elevated complaisance and forbearance in the face of adversity and injustice. Passivity ruled except in times of famine when the hard-pressed lower classes and beggars often rose up in violence.

Law was limited almost entirely to criminal law. The group, whether family, clan, or village, was held responsible for the wrongdoing of any of its members. Determination of guilt was of a roughhewn character, with guilt often determined by confession after brutal torture. Peking and the ruling dynasty could be arbitrary and cruel in disciplining officials, but custom and long tradition created a barrier to interfering with local problems and local miscreants. By the mid-nineteenth century, the power of the authorities at the capital was severely limited by the decadence of its armed forces.

Neglect characterized the administration of the army. Some 130,000 bannermen in Peking and the immediate neighborhood and 600,000 soldiers in the provinces constituted a kind of constabulary, but they were hopelessly ineffective against foreign armed forces and scarcely able to police canals and highways or to put down border uprisings. Soldiers often went without pay. They were neither well trained nor properly equipped; this was so because China engaged in fewer wars throughout its history than any other country of similar importance, a blessing bestowed by its geographical isolation from any powerful national state. Chinese literature praised peace and denigrated a warlike spirit. Reason was prized more highly than force, forbearance over retaliation. Consequently, soldiers were held in low esteem.

The celestial flowery kingdom had no foreign office. Its relations with border states were that of father and son, not that of equals. Korea, Mongolia, the Loo Chuu islands, and the countries of South and Southeast Asia were tributary states. Treaties, diplomats, and the normative standards of behavior among the sovereign states of the West were unknown. The Chinese viewed this outer world of the West as a form of lower civilization. Their picture of themselves as the center of both ancient wisdom and culture bred a sense of superiority that ruled out any suggestion of equal status among nations.

The realities of China—frequent famines, the violence of the secret societies, the gap between rich and poor, and the beggars of the cities—contrasted sharply with the idealized picture of China held by the landed gentry and the mandarins, although they were well aware of the crevices in the social structure. Rebellion was a frequent threat and must be dealt with firmly. On the other hand, in times of famine the wealthier classes and officialdom contributed to the temporary relief of the unfortunate, partly out of sympathy and partly out of fear of violence. The villages were closely knit communities, where all shared in some measure tragedy and good fortune. The cities posed more of a problem; there a portion of the population was often unruly and threatened the order and harmony that the society at large idealized.

Westerners varied sharply in their response to China, but all were overwhelmed by cultural shock and all were convinced of the superiority of western institutions. Merchants generally accepted the situation in good grace, took comfort in their profits, stayed for a few years, respected their Chinese counterparts, and generally entertained no desire to promote change. Missionaries, and in 1854 there were forty-four American missionaries in China, varied in their response, although they uniformly believed that Christianity alone could save individuals from damnation and pull China out of its decadence. Some achieved a real understanding of Chinese ways, respected much of Chinese tradition, and a few affirmed that Confucian society constituted a remarkable civilization. In addition to the merchants and missionaries, transient seamen and vagrants infested the treaty ports, often engaging in brawls and treating the Chinese with contempt. Finally, there were the officials of western governments. The first American officials carried the title of commissioner. Not until 1857 was the first minister appointed. Commissioners made their entrances and exits with only a year or so between. American consuls, generally merchants, were miserably paid and dependent on the fees they collected. These official representatives usually concluded that force alone could overcome Chinese obstinacy and that China must be brought into a new and modern era.

The only more or less permanent American legation staff in the early years were the missionaries, Samuel Wells Williams and Peter Parker. They gained a fair mastery of the language, understood Chinese customs and mores, were often less critical of the Chinese than they were of westerners engaged in the opium trade and the buying of coolies and of the hooligans who infested the treaty ports. At the same time that they were convinced that China must change its ways, they were firm believers in China's future importance and hoped that the United States would play a leading role. In part they were driven by a feeling that Americans appeared as poor second cousins of the British, whose predominance suggested the United States was present only at British sufferance. The missionaries showed greater determination to open China than did the merchants, who had more limited aims confined to the carrying on of trade, and who feared that too vigorous a push would upset existing arrangements.

American policy was for the government in Washington to determine, but diplomatic representatives enjoyed a considerable degree of discretion due to the time required for letters to make their way between the two nations. The scope for decision making on the spot was also enlarged because only those on the scene could know the prevailing conditions.

The major interest in China was commerce. The increase in trade, thanks to the coming of the clipper ship, whetted the appetite for more. Daniel Webster, as secretary of state, consulted the many merchant firms in Boston, New York, and Salem who were engaged in the China trade prior to drafting instructions for Caleb Cushing, who had been appointed to carry on negotiations with China. Ten firms in Boston, nine in New York, and five in Salem were on Webster's list. Webster's instructions to Cushing called for the most-favored-nation policy, the opening of five treaty ports, the same five opened by the British Treaty of Nanking, and proposed but did not insist on diplomatic relations with Peking. Webster stated that force was not to be used; rather China was to be persuaded by pointing out the benefits it would gain. Webster reflected the contemporary rivalry with Great Britain in his suggestion that Cushing make clear that, unlike the British, the Americans opposed the establishment of colonies and rejected the use of force. The instructions were commercial in aim and not political. In view of the complexities of carrying on trade with China, the innocent tone of Webster's instructions would soon be put to the test.

No set policy emerged in 1844 nor in the next decade, but decisions made in response to the difficulties confronted and the changing scene in China gradually established a pattern of response. American trade ranked second to that of Great Britain in terms of value. In the year ending September 30, 1853, sixty-two American ships entered Shanghai. And when the United States acquired California the interest in China, hitherto confined to merchants along the Atlantic coast, mushroomed into a Pacific mindedness throughout the country. Dreams of a commercial empire flourished.

Paradoxically, rivalry with Great Britain, France, and Russia provided a major stimulant, while at the same time the steadfast resistance of the Chinese promoted an alignment with those same powers. Reduced to its simplest terms, observed an editorial in the *New York Times*, in April 1858, the issue was whether "the Christion Powers" should compel China "to recognize the obligations of the Public Law." The Chinese wall of isolation must be broken down, and the task was a job requiring the cooperation of the western powers. As contemporaries saw it, this was a struggle of civilization versus barbarism, and in this struggle the United States must replace its traditional distrust of Europe with cooperation. A new era was emerging, dimly foreshadowing later global conflicts.

Public policy toward China in these early formative years was not simply arrangements between American shopkeepers and Chinese tea growers and silk producers. A wide range of forces was at work—a bristling new spirit of confidence intertwined with nationalism, the overriding conviction shared with Europeans that the world was entering a new era of progress, the bumptious evangelical spirit penetrating Christianity, and the visions of a new wave of commerce propelled by the wonders of a new system of steamboat transportation. The western world was on the march, and the United States must not be left in the lurch.

The spirit of the times exhibited itself in the daring speculative enterprise of merchants, in the launching of new steamship lines, in the zeal of missionaries bent on Christianizing the world, and in the occasional pronouncements of newspaper editors that the old horror of "entangling alliances" must give way to participation in world affairs. Nevertheless, these propelling forces, powerful as they were, competed with equally powerful forces on the domestic scene, making for restraint—an overriding concern with domestic questions such as slavery, public land policy, the tariff, and the problems of banking and currency. In the feverishness of political struggles the party out of power seized on every possible issue in its efforts to discredit the administration, and would array the forces of parochialism against a bold new foreign policy.

Consequently, restraint characterized the United States in its China policy. Peter Parker, medical missionary and diplomat, and Commodore Matthew C. Perry called for seizure of some of the Bonin Islands and Formosa. Their proposals were promptly repudiated in Washington by political leaders sensitive to the fact that public feeling held the acquisition of colonies unconstitutional. Opposition to the use of force in faraway places, except in self defense, was deeply engrained and provided a restraint on aggressive action. Presidents and secretaries of state repeatedly warned diplomats and naval officers that only Congress could declare war. At the same time there was no hesitation in profiting by British and French use of force, even though there was criticism of their making war. There were also Americans, particularly among those residing in the Far East, who charged that to sit by and then pick up the fruits of war was hypocritical.

Kaleidoscopic changes in China triggered American actions. The Opium War was followed by the British Treaty of Nanking, which provided for the opening of five treaty ports, a treaty tariff, and a measure of extraterritoriality. This set the stage for the Cushing mission. The Taiping rebellion of the 1850s, with the consequent breakdown of Peking's rule in Shanghai, led to the establishment of the Imperial Maritime Customs Service. The hostility of the Chinese to foreigners and the determined efforts of the Manchu-Chinese dynasty to circumvent the early treaties and keep the foreigner at a distance stiffened the determination of westerners, including Americans, to establish full diplomatic relations. Only then, it seemed, would the nations of the West be able to get at the source of their grievances, undermine the Chinese assumption of superiority, and achieve equal status.

Westerners explained Chinese hostility as blind prejudice and arrogance. The never-ending series of riots and mob scenes encountered by missionaries and the severe restrictions limiting the freedom of movement of merchants gained more attention than the cordial relations among western and Chinese merchants and the invariably polite rhetoric of communications. Underlying the total scene of hostility and affability, of crudity and refinement, lay the Chinese view of foreigners as dangerous interlopers. Herein lay the crux of the problem.

Westerners believed that China had no right to cut herself off from the outside world, while Chinese held that westerners had no right to intrude. Americans contended that they had no wish to interfere in the internal affairs of China and other nations, but at the same time they held that there was an overarching system of law among nations providing for both rights and duties from which no nation should hold itself apart.

For China, considering the nature of its society and the highly decentralized nature of its government and the fact that its unity rested wholly on the commonality of Confucian ideals and mores, the meeting of East and West was traumatic. The western intrusion raised the horrifying specter of disharmony in place of highly prized harmony, of the uprooting of an ancient system of closely knit mutual obligations, and of the symbol of the warship taking the place of friendly discourse. Efforts to understand the strange Chinese often ended in frustration and the conclusion that "the barbarian nature cannot be fathomed."[5] Quite naturally, the Chinese found the westerner equally inscrutable.

Given this disparity in viewpoints, relations were beset with misunderstanding, confrontations clouded over with bitter accusations and razor-edged exhibitions of arrogance. The irritability and tension depended in part on the personality of those delegated the task of working out a settlement. The parade of American commissioners began with Caleb Cushing, a former member of Congress from Massachusetts, a lawyer, an impetuous man of strong convictions and few doubts, prone to loud and militant pronouncements. From an American perspective, he was an ideal man for the assignment; for if China was to be brought to an agreement satisfactory to the United States, the appointee would need the redoubtable qualities of a warship.

Cushing met his match in Acting Governor Teiyeng of the two southern provinces of Kwangsi and Kwangtung. Teiyeng carried himself with an aloofness befitting his title "Of the Imperial House, Governor of Kwantung Kwangsi, Director of the Board of War of the First Class, Vice Guardian of the Heir Apparent, Minister and Commissioner Extraordinary of the Ta Tsing Empire." Canton, in Kwangtung, was the bridgehead of the western intrusion. Given the absence of Ch'i-ying, the imperial commissioner who was assigned the responsibility of handling affairs with the barbarians, Governor Teiyeng became the official with whom Cushing must treat. This august personage, spokesman for the emperor, possessed all the imperturbability that a 2500-year-old civilization could bestow, plus the knowledge that the emperor and his councilors would not deal kindly with a servant incapable of fending off intruders.

Cushing arrived at Macao, the sleepy Portuguese village on the mainland south of Canton, in February 1844. He promptly addressed a letter to the governor, inquiring as to the health of the emperor and announced his intentions to go to Peking. He explained that before proceeding it was necessary to collect provisions for the warship *Brandywine*, on which he was to sail. Three weeks later he received a reply stating that if he were to proceed without first memorializing the emperor there would be difficulty and if he should go on a warship "this will put an end to all civility, and to rule without harmony." Moreover, there would be no high officials nor interpreters at Tientsin to transact business. Teiyeng added that a treaty was unnecessary. The only reason for a treaty with Great Britain was that the recent war had aroused suspicions among the people. China and the United States enjoyed peaceful relations, so there was no need for a treaty. Cushing replied that he had no choice for his instructions directed him to go to Peking.[6]

In April the warship *Brandywine* went to Whampoa. Teiyeng protested:

> When your excellency first arrived in the Central Flowery Land, you were unacquainted with her laws and prohibitions —that it was against the laws for men-of-war to enter the river. But now you know and then send the ship to Blenheim reach and fire a 21 gun salute. China cannot return the salute. And you ask for an interview and this is against the law. In short the laws of China and other nations are unlike, and as our countries are now at peace, still more incumbent is it for each to maintain the laws.[7]

In regard to the salute, Cushing sent a curt reply that it was his duty "to tender to China the friendship of the greatest of the powers of America" and "if these demonstrations are not met in a correspondent manner, it will be the misfortune of China." This, he warned, would not be the fault of the United States.

Teiyeng had explained that negotiations could only begin when a commissioner arrived. Cushing, exasperated by the long delay, advised that similar tactics of procrastination had caused England to go to war. If China persisted in delaying, it could only mean that it desired war. Two weeks later, on May 9, Cushing sent another letter, ringing with bold threat.

On May 27 Cushing wrote to the secretary of state noting that he was awaiting the arrival of two men-of-war and that it would be futile to go to Peking. His experience during his first four months may well have led him to conclude that nothing was to be gained, but Tyler Dennett, eminent author of the classic *Americans in Eastern Asia*, concluded that Cushing had never intended the proposal to go to Peking to be more than a threat.[8]

Finally, in mid-June Imperial Commissioner Ch'i-ying arrived at Canton. Negotiations now began. A new tone, contrasting sharply with Cushing's demeanor in his previous correspondence, now prevailed. He entertained Ch'i-ying in a gracious manner and was, in turn, entertained by Ch'i-ying at Whanghia, just outside of Macao. Almost immediately Ch'i-ying informed Cushing that if he insisted on going to Peking the negotiations could not continue, and the idea was then dropped. In a surprisingly brief time a treaty was completed. Throughout the proceedings Cushing wore the uniform of a major general and spurs, but at the same time he struck an attitude of peaceful intent. He assured Ch'i-yeng that the United States sought neither territory nor tribute.

Cushing benefited by the assistance rendered him by Peter Parker and Elijah Bridgman. Both were fervent advocates of widening the gates into China. Parker jumped at the opportunity to participate and professed to see an opportunity of doing more in a few months than in all the rest of his life.[9] While waiting for Ch'i-ying's arrival, Parker became increasingly impatient. When Ch'i-ying stopped to visit the British minister, Sir Henry Pottinger, before seeing Cushing, Parker complained and warned a local Chinese official that the United States had three warships in Chinese waters and would soon have three more. During the negotiations Parker served as more than an interpreter. He helped draft some of the most important articles and was responsible for Article XVII, granting Americans the right of residence and the right to maintain hospitals, cemeteries, and churches. Thus, it was Parker at this very first negotiation who wove the religious thread into American China policy.[10]

The Cushing Treaty by virtue of being the first between the United States and China acquired unique prominence, but before Cushing ever left the United States Americans enjoyed the rights granted to the British in the Treaty of Nanking, namely access to the treaty ports and extraterritoriality. The Cushing Treaty provided a more precise definition of extraterritoriality. It also included extended privileges to merchants. A ship could now enter a port and remain for two days without paying duties; and, if it paid duties, the ship was free to take the cargo to other ports without paying additional duties. The agreement proved to be the entering wedge for foreign merchant ships to large-scale participation in coastwise shipping.

Cushing's stay in Macao coincided with a mob scene in Canton. The American consulate flew the American flag. A weather vane atop the flagstaff was held responsible by the Chinese for an outbreak of illness in the city. The sight of four Americans carrying muskets added to Chinese concern. After protests the American consul removed the weather vane; but this failed to quiet the aroused populace, and a mob approached the consulate. In the ensuing disturbance a Chinese was killed. Governor Teiyeng demanded custody of the accused murderer. The consul refused to surrender him and, instead, conducted a trial in which a jury of six Americans ruled that the accused had acted in self-defense. The case was then turned over to Cushing and Ch'i-ying. Cushing defended the decision, and Ch'i-ying agreed to accept it.

The significance of the incident, aside from setting the precedent for extraterritoriality, lay in the difficulty of the Chinese government in providing the protection to the foreigner required by the treaties. The deep-rooted antagonism toward foreigners, not infrequently encouraged by the literati, was beyond the power of the government to control. Indeed, an important reason why the authorities in Peking disliked entering into treaties was their fear of the consequences of treaty violations they were powerless to prevent.

Ch'i-ying foresaw the difficulties. In a settlement apart from the treaty it was agreed that Americans living in Canton should be permitted to erect walls forty cubits high and that peddlers, fortune-tellers, barbers, beggars, and showmen should be excluded by sentries. Ch'i-ying, in his discussions with Cushing, referred to the "rabble" and "wretches" in Canton.

The Cushing Treaty, unlike the Treaty of Nanking, held the opium trade illegal. The British government in India was directly responsible for the growth of opium and was as much a partner in that noxious trade as the merchants who engaged in it. It chose to close its eyes to the evils connected with the opium trade and to pass off responsibility to the Chinese, who failed to effectively enforce their laws against it. In spite of the Cushing Treaty provision, Americans continued to engage in the opium trade. Because the Cushing Treaty did not place the responsibility for upholding the treaty on the American government, the government did nothing to enforce this treaty provision.

The treaty included the most-favored-nation clause. This was not a concession extracted from the Chinese, but simply Ch'i-ying's application of a long-standing principle that all barbarians should be treated equally. Granting the same privilege as had been granted to the British, moreover, would cause the Americans to feel a sense of gratitude.[11]

Actually, treaties, as it turned out, were readily circumvented by the Chinese in the years ahead. The treaty was, from an American viewpoint, reasonable and recognized Chinese interests, but it could not have been achieved had not China faced overwhelming western force in the hands of the British in the preceding war.

The 1850s saw the opening of China's interior and the establishment of full diplomatic relations. The earlier treaties of Great Britain, France, and the United States provided no more than a bare crack in the door in the form of limited opportunities to trade on the rim of the great empire. Foreigners had yet to gain access to the interior, and foreign governments were restricted to negotiating with the high commissioner in Canton. Trade increased in the years ahead, but access remained truncated. The obstacles to the promotion of trade, to the residence of foreigners, and to missionary enterprise testified to Chinese ingenuity in circumventing the treaties and to a zealous determination to oust the foreigner.

As western impatience with Chinese obstinacy mounted, the Taiping rebellion threatened to bring the Manchu-Chinese dynasty to an end. The rebels marched from the south to the Yangtze River and captured Nanking. The revolt also led to local uprisings, and the central authorities lost control of Shanghai and Foochow. Coming at the very time when the western powers resolved to demand an extension of commercial privileges, security for their merchants and missionaries, and full diplomatic representation in Peking, the dynasty could do little more than engage in bravado and then give way. Palmerston decided to take action for Great Britain as early as 1851, but difficulties in Europe and the outbreak of the Crimean War delayed the day of reckoning until 1857. What took place in the next two years led to a dramatic undermining of China and to eventual subcolonial status.

The cooperation of Great Britain, France, Russia, and the United States in the late 1850s, a remarkable phenomenon in itself, was a response to the unwise intransigence of Chinese officials like Viceroy Yeh. At a time when the western powers were prepared to negotiate and accept more reasonable terms, Yeh engaged in insult and evasiveness.[12]

Peter Parker informed his fellow Americans: "My course with this government will be *friendly* but firm. The time for nonsense is past, and trifling will be endured no longer." The French chargé d'affaires, Count de Courcy, expressed the common feelings of the day that China could only be dealt with by putting forth a grand display of force; it was, he advised, necessary "to inspire the Chinese government with salutary terror."[13]

The spirit in Washington harmonized only in small part with the bellicosity of Parker. The Pierce administration, and even more that of Buchanan, took a lively interest in Asia, called for treaty revision, and worked in close cooperation with Great Britain and France in seeking reform, but the instructions they sent to their representatives ruled out the use of force and seizure of territory. Naval commanders were reminded that only Congress could declare war and were reprimanded when their actions endangered peace. Pierce and Buchanan, besieged by problems closer to home and mindful of congressional opposition, steered a cautious course.

Serious efforts to revise the treaties did not get underway until 1856, but in 1853 and again in 1854 changes of importance took place that were the result of developments in Shanghai. A new vice consul in Shanghai, Edward Cunningham, who had been employed by two firms engaged in trade and had become a partner in Russell and Company in 1850, demonstrated a brusqueness bordering on chauvinism. In 1852 when the local taotai refused to approve a sale of land, Cunningham presented him with the equivalent of an ultimatum. When the taotai again refused to give his approval, Cunningham announced that he considered the treaty suspended at Shanghai. The treaty provided for residence rights, but at Shanghai Great Britain and France had acquired rights to all of the suitable locations. The issue arose as to whether Americans could buy land in the British area and at the same time not be subject to British jurisdiction. The British consul, Sir Rutherford Alcock, conceded to Americans what they asked, and Alcock's decision was upheld in London in 1853. That summer a charter for a municipal government was agreed to by the British, French, and American representatives in Shanghai. Thereby came into being the famous international settlement. The action taken did not deny Chinese sovereignty in the area, but the small community of a few hundred in 1853 eventually became one of the world's great cities and essentially a separate western republic within China.

The second issue, and this was of equal importance, concerned the collection of customs duties. Chinese collection of duties suffered from numerous irregularities, including large-scale smuggling, misrepresentation of both the value and amount of cargo, and corruption. Of the five treaty ports, Amoy most quickly established a reputation for leniency toward smugglers, but all five ports witnessed a highly inefficient collection of duties. Both local officials and merchants of trading nations circumvented the treaty stipulations. The British sought to uphold the treaty and took what measures they could to bring about effective compliance, believing that their own merchants would be disadvantaged if the system of duties was not upheld and made binding on traders from all nations. American government officials did not condone violations; however, American consulates were hopelessly understaffed, and the practice of appointing merchants as consuls also proved ineffective.

The problem reached a peak in September 1853 when local banditti took control of Shanghai and forced the taotai to flee. This local crisis coincided with the victories of the Taipings and their capture of Nanking. The British chose to employ the weakening of the dynasty to seek treaty revision, and France joined hands with the British without reservation. The United States limited cooperation to a promise of cordial relations and consultation. Humphrey Marshall, American commissioner to China, distrustful of the British, viewed his instructions with skepticism, but he cooperated with his British colleague and won his confidence.

With the overthrow of the taotai in Shanghai, the question immediately arose as to who should collect the customs duties. Alcock took the lead in establishing a provisional system under which British merchants would give the consul promissory notes in lieu of cash payments, the arrangement being subject to approval of the government in London. Marshall promptly applied the same rules to American merchants.

Eventually, this arrangement led to the creation of the foreign controlled customs service. The provisional system proved efficient in collecting duties and in less than six months collected the unprecedented amount of 840,000 taels. This amount was to be held in trust until the Chinese imperial government could regain control of Shanghai. When that time arrived, the British superintendent of trade along with the American commissioner, Robert McLane, stipulated that the revenue collected would only be turned over to the Peking government if they could be assured of competent and honest administration. The Shanghai taotai then stated that he could not secure competent customs officers among the Chinese. An agreement was then reached with the governor general at Nanking providing for the establishment of the foreign administered inspectorate of customs. The Imperial Maritime Customs Service, as it became known, was to render honest and useful service in the years ahead.

The larger question was that of treaty revision. Commissioner McLane received instructions to seek revision, and in 1854 entered into discussion with I-liang, the viceroy of the two provinces in the lower Yangtze area. McLane proposed that, in return for an extension of commercial privileges, the United States would assume responsibility for Americans in China abiding by the treaty. The British had already assumed this obligation under the Treaty of Nanking. McLane called for the opening of the Yangtze to trade, an aim his successors were to seek. This far-reaching proposal went far beyond McLane's instructions. The Chinese rejected it without further discussion.

In the autumn of 1854 McLane accompanied Sir John Bowring, the British minister, and a representative of the French legation to the mouth of the Pei-ho, the river leading to Tientsin, in the hope of establishing relations with the emperor in Peking. They were told to return to Canton and to conduct their business there with High Commissioner Yeh. McLane soon returned to the United States. Peter Parker took his place. Parker had already spent twenty years in China, had a command of Chinese, an understanding of the country, and as secretary of legation had a firsthand knowledge of current problems. He received instructions to seek the establishment of formal diplomatic relations with Peking and an extension of commercial privileges, and he supported these aims with iron determination. Like other foreign residents, he was convinced that China would never yield unless confronted with overwhelming force. He was also a firm proponent of close cooperation with other treaty powers.

In view of American naval action in November 1856, it appeared that the United States was prepared to join other powers in the use of force. In reprisal for the Lorcha Arrow affair, a minor incident involving the lowering of the British flag by the Chinese, the British attacked Canton. Commissioner Yeh, unable to protect Americans there, asked that they withdraw. When the American naval ship sent to transport them was fired upon by the Barrier Forts, the American naval squadron destroyed the forts.

Parker apologized to Secretary of State Marcy for the failure to get to the Pei-ho in 1856, but thought the delay propitious. An adequate British naval force arrived late in the year and would be ready to escort the diplomats to Peking in the spring. At the same time he stated the necessity of increasing the size of the American squadron and urged that the United States adopt a firm, friendly, and determined policy. Parker was ready for bold action. Should the Chinese refuse to receive the western diplomats in Peking, the three powers should each occupy a portion of Chinese territory, according to Parker. France, he advised, should occupy Korea, the British should take Chusan, and the United States should take Formosa. This would cause China to yield, and once a satisfactory treaty was negotiated these territories should instantly be restored. This move, Parker advised, would be "far preferable to the destruction of forts, the bombardment of cities, and the destruction of life and property."[14] A few months later, in March 1857, Parker set aside all thoughts of restoration and urged permanent acquisition of Formosa. His rash recommendations caused Pierce and Marcy to recall him.

During the first weeks of the Buchanan administration Lord Napier, the British minister in Washington, proposed that the United States join Great Britain and France in bringing about treaty revision. The proposal would have committed the United States not only to treaty terms jointly agreed upon but also to the joint use of force. While heartily in favor of a good working relationship, Buchanan and Secretary of State Cass knew that any agreement that smacked of an alliance with Great Britain would expose them to the attacks of domestic critics. They rejected Napier's proposal, although they affirmed that the United States would consult with them.

Buchanan appointed William B. Reed of Pennsylvania, who had supported him in the recent election, as minister to China, the first to achieve that rank. Contemporaries and later historians charged Reed with weakness, but no American representative during the nineteenth century other than Samuel Wells Williams displayed greater sympathy and understanding of the Chinese. Reed's instructions directed him to communicate freely with the British and French ministers, to be firm but not sanction the use of force, and to make clear to the Chinese that the United States sought neither territory nor tribute.

Reed, on his arrival in Hong Kong in November 1857, faced harsh realities. The British and French were ready to use force; China persisted in arctic aloofness. Reed observed that the British and French had determined to inflict chastisement on the recalcitrant Cantonese. At the same time the Chinese persisted in putting themselves in the wrong. An anonymous letter from the Chinese to Reed bristled with bravado, asserting that the British could do nothing against the Chinese forts and would "soon see the dead bodies of the English everywhere."[15]

On December 28, 1857, the British, having had no success in their efforts to negotiate with Commissioner Yeh, attacked Canton and burned the city to the ground. On the same day Reed wrote to Secretary of State Cass, stating that he had received two letters from Yeh. They are, he wrote, "curious, among other things in this, that they illustrate the formal punctiliousness of the Chinese officials in answering communications made to them, even at a time when, as now, more pressing exigencies might excuse them. There is, in these letters, all the characteristic artifice of Chinese rhetoric."[16] Yeh acclaimed the friendship of the two countries and described the existing treaty as wholly satisfactory. Moreover, the treaty stated it should not be changed without grave cause. Yeh held that no grave cause existed.

Certain sights appalled Reed. The coolie trade shocked him, and he learned of two American ships involved in the traffic. Most of the coolies were either kidnapped or lured on board by an offer of wages to work on the ship. They had no knowledge of their destination. Many, held in camps before embarking, committed suicide. In 1857 alone, 25,449 victims of the traffic had left China. He concluded that the traffic was contrary to American law and ordered American consuls to so notify masters of American ships.[17] Reed was equally horrified by American smuggling of opium and the bad behavior of seamen and vagrants from California.

During the early part of his stay Reed took the hard line on treaty revision and he concluded that the British treaty demands were wholly moderate.[18] Following his instructions, he worked closely with the British and the French, but he feared that Parker had encouraged them to expect collaboration in the use of force. If the Chinese rejected all overtures, then the British and French would use force. Foreseeing a crisis and worried about his instructions to avoid the use of force, Reed asked for further instructions, apparently hoping that if war took place he and the Americans would not be obligated to sit on the sidelines.

In February the four powers handed almost identical notes to Chinese officials at Shanghai for delivery to the emperor. By this time Count Putiatin, of Russia, and Reed had become such close friends that Putiatin sent his note in the same envelope with Reed's.

When Reed reported how closely he was associated with the other ministers, Cass gave his full approval. Concerning Reed's earlier request for instructions as to what course he should pursue in the event of war, Cass replied that the alternative of warfare might be forced upon the United States.[19]

The replies of the Chinese offered no hope of progress toward a peaceful settlement and Reed wrote: "You will observe the same tone of apparent courtesy exhibited here . . . ; the same unmeaning profession; the same dexterous sophistry; and what is more material, the same passive resistance, the same stolid refusal to yield any point of substance."[20]

Before the four ministers proceeded to the Gulf of Pechili, Putiatin received instructions not to participate in the use of force. This pleased Reed, who would not now be left in an isolated position if force were used. However, he thought it best to take along all available naval vessels so as to show the Chinese "that it is not the want of means which compels the United States to abstain from measures of hostility."[21]

What took place in the Gulf of Pechili need not be retold here. British representative Elgin and French representative Gros decided that the Chinese emissary sent to negotiate lacked proper authority. Reed charged them with mere punctilio and urged Elgin and Gros to avoid hostilities. Putiatin did the same. Their advice was rejected, and the British and French bombarded the Taku forts at the mouth of the Pei-ho.

Reed and Putiatin chose the peaceful course and entered into negotiations with the Chinese emissary. Reed was assisted by Samuel Wells Williams and W.A.P. Martin. Williams noted in his journal that what China needed was the society for the diffusion of cannonballs, but it was also Williams who showed genuine concern for Chinese interests. He undoubtedly was responsible to a great degree for the restraint shown by Reed.

In June 1858 the new treaty was completed. The United States gained the right to correspond directly with the authorities in Peking, the right of its minister to make an annual visit to the capital, the opening of two new treaty ports, and the right to acquire a residence in the treaty ports. Extraterritoriality was modified so that arrests could be made by Chinese officials as well as by American consuls. Finally, Article XXIX provided for religious toleration. This was the work of Williams, who confided that the Chinese would never have agreed to it had they grasped what it would mean. Reed, who was completely won over to the missionary cause, saw in it simply the means for protecting converts and thereby aiding the missionary enterprise. The article as applied served Chinese wrongdoers, who covered themselves by professing that they were Christians.

The treaty was almost more significant for what it did not provide than for what it did. It did not provide for residence of the American minister in Peking. Reed saw that the Chinese had reason to fear that the presence of foreign diplomats in the capital would undermine the standing of the dynasty in the eyes of the Chinese people. Nor did the treaty grant the right of American ships to navigate the inland waterways—a proposal that had been prominent in discussions prior to the negotiations and which was strongly advocated by merchants as the means to extend trade. Williams was convinced that access to the interior would have disastrous results, probably promoting endless disturbances and exposing the people of the interior to the unruly foreign miscreants who had so often wracked such evil in the open ports. Reed agreed and wrote to Secretary Cass that he owed it to candor "to say that observation of some of the results of commercial contact since I have been in China has very much abated my anxiety to open what are called new markets, and to increase the area of collision and of corruption and oppression."[22] He was fearful of the consequences of access because "the foreigner carries extraterritoriality with him—remote from consuls." There are, he wrote, after the British treaty had been completed and had opened the inland waterways to foreign shipping, "the abuses and dangers which this new system of unlimited intercourse seems to foreshadow."[23]

Reed and Williams were also concerned about the provisions in the British treaty opening eleven new ports and reducing tonnage duties. Reed correctly saw that this "will transfer most of the coasting trade of China to foreign vessels." Both American representatives were concerned about placing a heavy burden upon the central government of China by making it responsible for compliance with treaty obligations. Each Chinese province enjoyed a high degree of autonomy, and what happened in Canton gave the people in Shanghai no concern. Officials in each province depended on local revenues and, in turn, on the goodwill of the people in the area. Peking exercised limited authority in the local province, but the new treaties made it the obligation of the central government to protect the new treaty rights of foreigners, an arrangement that would arouse antagonism toward Peking.[24]

The new treaty did not, unlike the Cushing Treaty, outlaw trade in opium. Both Reed and Williams looked on the opium trade as a disgrace, but they were also chagrined by the widespread smuggling that was going on. As they saw it, to continue the unenforceable ban only served to hide the realities.

Reed left China a wiser man. The behavior of many westerners, the exploitation, and the American involvement in corruption left him distraught. In one of his final reports during the negotiation of the commercial treaty, he observed that only Samuel Wells Williams and Thomas Francis Wade, British scholar and public servant, were beyond "the prevalent influence here, by which everything is thought right which is determined adversely to the Chinese."[25] He pondered the question as to whether the gains of unrestricted commerce would overbalance the evil.

The British treaty opened eleven ports, provided that the foreign legation could be in Peking, and gave British ships the right to navigate the Yangtze. The same provisions, under the most-favored-nation clause, became the rights of Americans. Once again the United States profited by British use of force. The editor of the *New York Times* observed that Lord Clarendon had consulted merchants before drafting his instructions to Lord Elgin who, in turn, consulted the British merchants in China before entering upon negotiations. The editor concluded: "The instrument indeed smells of the warehouse." The terms "are big with mischief to the existing Chinese system precipitating a crisis in the affairs of the empire . . ."[26] The crisis was to be of long duration, but this particular note of criticism was to be drowned out by acclamations phrased in the rhetoric of the Open Door and the missionary crusade.

The opening of Japan, the most dramatic victory in American foreign relations of the 1850s, met the felt need for notification to the outside world that a new Hercules had appeared upon the scene. Not only was American society imbued with a flaming competitive spirit, but so was the western world at large. Nations, as individuals, vied with one another for glory and gold. What could offer greater reason for pride than to be the first to establish relations with the empire of Japan. Daniel Webster summed up contemporary feelings: "The moment is near when the last link in the chain of oceanic steam navigation is to be formed." He took a global view:

> From China and the East Indies to Egypt, thence through the Mediterranean and Atlantic Ocean to England, thence again to our happy shores, and other parts of this great continent; from our own ports to the southernmost part of the isthmus that connects the two western continents; and from its Pacific coast, north and southward, as far as civilization has spread, the steamers of other nations and of our own carry intelligence, the wealth of the world, and thousands of travelers.[27]

Samuel Wells Williams, who was to accompany Perry to Japan, summed up the purposes of the mission in a letter to his brother. "These are our ostensible reasons for going to this great outlay and sending this powerful squadron to Japanese waters; the real reasons are the glorification of the Yankee nation, and food for praising ourselves."[28]

Japan was the last link, the final bastion of antiquity, to be opened to the world; it also gave promise of rewards more tangible than national pride. Commercial opportunities attracted some. Those engaged in shipping saw Japan as a way station for a steamship line from San Francisco to Shanghai. Naval captains viewed it as a coaling station. Each of these influenced decision makers to some degree, but it was Japan's proximity to China, the lodestar of Far East trade, that gave Japan its importance. Just as China loomed larger on the horizon after the acquisition of California, so did Japan.

Naval officers who had sailed in the Mediterranean, off the coast of Africa, patroled the waters off Mexico and served in the Asiatic squadron, were alert to the glory to be won in strange seas. Their visions expanded with the coming of steamships. This was as true, of course, of British, French, and Russian naval officers. All were intrigued by Japan, who forbade their coming. Each of the major powers had its eyes fixed on that country, so it is little more than an accident that the Americans proved to be the first to negotiate a treaty. So intense was the rivalry that Commodore Perry, in 1853 and 1854, lived in dread that these rivals would beat him to the prize. When he finally succeeded in negotiating a treaty, he feared that Congress might delay approval and thereby yield to a rival power the honor of being first to complete a treaty. Consequently, he let the Japanese believe that his signature made it final and urged President Pierce to hasten ratification.

Americans in general admired adventure and took double pride in having one of their own countrymen lead the way. Perry, alert to the public appetite for a great sea story, employed Bayard Taylor, well-known writer and newspaper correspondent. Taylor's reports to the New York *Tribune* circulated throughout the country. Finally, Taylor told the full story in a book that served to inscribe Perry's name in the pantheon of American heroes.

Shipwrecked sailors from the large American whaling fleet in the north Pacific often found themselves stranded in Japan. Usually they were sent to Nagasaki, where one Dutch ship a year was permitted entry. News of mistreatment of these sailors, including confinement in small cages and an occasional beheading, found its way back to the United States. The Japanese later maintained that the shipwrecked sailors were only dealt with harshly when they created trouble, but whatever the facts Americans heard only the versions of the sailors. This issue was of sufficient scope that insurance companies in New York called on Congress to send a mission to Japan.[29]

In 1845 Commodore Biddle was delegated to transport to his post the newly appointed commissioner to China, Alexander H. Everett. Secretary of Navy George Bancroft included in the instructions to Biddle a commission to go to Japan and negotiate a treaty. Biddle sailed up the Bay of Yedo and made this first official request, but he was promptly refused and ordered to leave. In the course of his interview Biddle was struck by a Japanese sailor. The Japanese government offered an apology, and Biddle chose to drop the matter. Later, Americans heard the story as far away as the Loo Chuu Islands, and the story indicated that the Japanese had treated Biddle with contempt and he dared not show resentment.

In 1849 Commander James Glynn, while in port in Batavia in the Dutch East Indies, learned that sixteen shipwrecked American sailors were being held in Japan. Glynn, in the *Preble*, set sail for Nagasaki, the port open to Dutch ships. As he sailed up the Bay of Yedo a never-ending stream of Japanese boats met him, and signal guns were fired on land to give warning that a strange ship had approached. Glynn refused to be stopped and proceeded until he reached a safe anchorage. Soldiers on the surrounding hills set up artillery and pointed at his ship. The Japanese agreed to negotiate after Glynn warned that the United States knew how to rescue its citizens and that if the prisoners were not released he "would do something else." He firmly insisted on talking to an official of high rank, and after two days of negotiations with the governor of Nagasaki he secured the release of the prisoners. The first break in the wall of isolation had appeared, and Glynn concluded that Japan could be induced to open her doors.

Glynn's role in the opening of Japan has been overshadowed by what followed, but due to Glynn Perry's mission came into being. Glynn's full confidence that Japan was now on the verge of changing course, his plea that haste was necessary because the British and Russians would soon seek entry, and his stress on the need for firmness brought action. On his return to the United States he wrote a persuasive letter to President Fillmore. Access to a port in Japan, he contended, was absolutely necessary for the accommodation of a line of steamships from San Francisco to Shanghai. If the arrangement could not be brought about peacefully, then it must be done by force. The opening of Japan was a matter of right; it had been resisted by imbecility and injustice. Glynn outlined the qualities required of the naval officer to be entrusted with the assignment: "matured judgment," "a ready tact to comprehend and extricate himself from any unpleasant position he might find himself suddenly and unexpectedly placed," patience, readiness to conduct hostile operations, and firmness in insisting on his right to deliver in person the letter from the president. He himself, after learning of Biddle's failure to be firm, had engaged in brusqueness so as to convey to the Japanese an impression of strength.[30] Glynn's prescription fitted Perry.

Glynn wrote to Howland and Aspinwall, the New York shippers, proposing a steamship line, and if this were to be undertaken Japan must be opened. Coal, he wrote, was plentiful in Japan, and a port there would serve as a coaling station. The treatment of the sailors he had rescued provided a good cause for a quarrel. He wrote: "They won't willingly come to terms—make them; such an unnatural system would at the present day fall to pieces upon the slightest concussion. But it is better to go to work with them peacefully if we can."[31]

Commodore Matthew Perry, sixty years old and a veteran of long experience patroling the coast of Africa and blockading Mexico, received the assignment. On the one hand, he was able, given to the mastery of the last detail, prescient as to contingencies that might arise, a rigorous disciplinarian, wholly immune to being swayed by either friend or rival. On the other hand, his respect for others was swallowed up by respect for himself. Virtually no obstacle could distract his attention from his main goal, in this instance a treaty with Japan. When graciousness and hospitality served him, he employed them as suited the occasion. He exasperated others with his punctiliousness; he was a stickler not only with his crew but with the Japanese, magnifying the slightest departure from his demands as cause for greater rigidity. He found intimidation and threats useful. Finally, he was the grand imperialist who sought to extend American control over the Bonin Islands and would have applauded converting the Pacific into an American lake.[32]

Perry's use of threats dismayed Samuel Wells Williams, but Japan would not have responded to a sweetly phrased invitation to join the family of nations. The Japanese lived in memories of the oft-repeated tales of what had happened to them at the hands of the Portuguese two hundred years before, and they were well informed about what the British had done during the Opium War. They were especially sensitive to the threat of the intrusion of Christianity and what this would mean in terms of undermining their polity. During Perry's second visit the Tokugawa shogun consulted the several daimyos who held large feudal estates as to their views on the question of entering into a treaty. The daimyos responded with great unanimity that everything was to be feared from the well-armed westerners.

Perry's conduct and repeated threats of force placed before the Japanese the unhappy options of reversing a policy of two hundred years standing or facing an attack by vastly superior forces. Perry gave them little choice, but his success was also due in some measure to the fact that the United States appeared less dangerous because of its remoteness. The Japanese may also have felt some degree of reassurance from the president's explanations that the United States had no colonies and that the American government was wholly separate from organized religion. However, the display Perry offered to Japanese officials and thousands of onlookers was undoubtedly more impressive than the reassuring words of the president. The repeated performances of the band, the frequent firing of salutes, the drills performed on shore by the highly disciplined marines and sailors, the gifts of the latest agricultural machines and tools, and the miniature locomotive and passenger cars that whirled around the 370 feet of track gave the Japanese their first view of the miracles of modern technology. The setting up of a short telegraph line that instantaneously conveyed messages amazed the Japanese, just as did the machinery of the steamships, which scores of Japanese were invited to inspect. Impressive as these exhibitions were and as imposing an appearance as Perry made with his deliberate strategy of aloofness, his success probably owed more to the fact that the Japanese recognized that the time had come for a change. Both Glynn and Perry knew they were dealing with a highly civilized people who should be treated as equals. In spite of Perry's boldness, his requests of the Japanese were strikingly modest and free of threats of intrusion in internal affairs.

The treaty Perry negotiated opened the ports of Shimoda and Hakodate, neither of them promising of future growth. A consul was to be permitted to reside at Shimoda. Like so many other treaties negotiated by the United States, the Perry Treaty included the most-favored-nation clause. The treaty also provided for the return of shipwrecked sailors. Thanks to Samuel Wells Williams, the treaty did not provide for extraterritoriality.[33] The missionary-diplomat had seen at first hand the abuses of that privilege in China, and he persuaded Perry not to request it. Nor was there any provision for the right of residence nor for regular diplomatic representation at the capital. A more limited arrangement for access can scarcely be imagined, but Perry had opened the long closed door, which could be pushed further open in the years ahead.

It remained for Townsend Harris to open the door more. Harris, at one time a New York merchant, embarked on a new career after a failure in business. He traveled to the Far East, where he resided for short periods in Hong Kong, Manila, Penang, and Calcutta. In 1853 he was named American consul at Ningpo, one of the less important treaty ports in China. In 1856 he was named consul at Shimoda and also instructed to negotiate a treaty with Siam before taking up his new post. Shimoda, little more than an obscure and isolated village, offered him little but great loneliness and ill health, but he saw an opportunity to take on a new and challenging task when the Russians and the Dutch succeeded in negotiating far more liberal treaties with Japan than the treaty negotiated by Perry. He resolved to go to Yedo where, by dint of persuasive argument directed at Japanese self-interest, he was successful. He laid particular stress on the dangers Japan faced from the imperialistic powers of Europe, and argued that Japan could minimize the dangers by negotiating a treaty with the United States along lines favorable to Japan and then have this serve as a model when negotiating with other powers.

The new treaty, negotiated in 1858, established full diplomatic ties and opened the way to the growth of commerce. The United States received the right to station consuls at each of the treaty ports, established a detailed schedule of duties, provided for the right of residence in treaty ports, and granted freedom of travel. Yokohama, Nagasaki, and Hakodate were opened to American naval ships for obtaining supplies. The treaty also provided for extraterritoriality and included a most-favored-nation clause.

The American ventures in the far reaches of the Pacific in the 1850s placed it in the middle of the highly competitive world outside of the West. The United States joined in the line of march, eager to avoid being left in the lurch, convinced that the march meant progress, remaining blissfully unaware of where the march would lead.

NOTES TO CHAPTER XIII

    1. In 1846 an American commissioner, George Brown, wrote to Caleb Cushing that he had written over sixty despatches to Washington. About forty of these should have arrived in time for him to have received replies, but he had received only one reply to all he had written. Brown, who achieved a reputation for being extremely outspoken, portrayed a dismal scene of a highly incompetent Hawaiian government and of widespread crime in Honolulu.
    Brown to Cushing, Feb. 6, 1846. Papers of Caleb Cushing, Library of Congress.
    2. Ralph S. Kuykendall, *The Hawaiian Kingdom 1778–1854 Foundation and Transformation* (Honolulu: The University of Hawaii Press, 1947), p. 194.
    3. Ibid., p. 203.
    4. James Buchanan, minister to Great Britain at the time, had as secretary of state under Polk shown sympathy with the Hawaiians. As minister in London he wrote several letters advising against annexation on the ground that in the event of war with either England or France the United States would not be able to defend the islands.
    5. John King Fairbank, *Trade and Diplomacy on the China Coast The Opening of the Treaty Ports 1842–1854* (Cambridge: Harvard University Press, 1953), p. 177.

6. Senate Executive Documents, 28th Cong., 2nd Sess., Document No. 67.
7. Ibid.
8. Dennett's conjecture is no more than that. Cushing's attitude changed, and in a letter to the secretary of state on July 8 he stated that the harsh tone of his earlier correspondence with the governor was necessary and had served a useful purpose, for it would have been disadvantageous to make such bold statements to Ch'i-ying. It may be assumed that Cushing learned that nothing was to be gained by his brash language; it is also likely that his American colleagues so advised him.
9. Edward V. Gulick, *Peter Parker and the Opening of China* (Cambridge: Harvard University Press, 1973), p. 117.
10. Ibid., p. 121.
11. Fairbank, *Trade and Diplomacy on the China Coast*, p. 196.
12. Hosea Ballou Morse, in his three-volume work *The International Relations of the Chinese Empire* (New York: Longmans, Green, & Co., 1910), wrote concerning Yeh: "Every request of the envoys to be received as representatives of their country was peremptorily rejected: every written communication to which they were then reduced, was answered in an evasive, and yet conclusive, manner; every demand for redress of injuries or reparation for losses was brushed aside, as if he were the final arbiter; and the claim made by each in succession of the three maritime powers, and later by Russia, for a modification in the existing treaty relations, was treated as one not worthy even of discussion or consideration—the present relations were all that could be desired." See Vol. I, p. 503.

John Fairbank described Yeh as a "stubborn diehard xenophobe." See *Trade and Diplomacy on the China Coast*, p. 277.
13. Parker to United States merchants in Canton, March 8, 1856. Senate Executive Documents, 35th Cong., 2nd Sess., Vol. IX.
14. Ibid., Parker to Marcy, Dec. 12, 1856.
15. Reed to Cass, Nov. 25, 1857, Senate Executive Documents, 36th Cong., 1st Sess., Vol. X, Doc. No. 30.
16. Senate Executive Documents, 36th Cong., 1st Sess., Vol. 10, Doc. No. 30, Reed to Cass, Dec. 28, 1857.
17. Ibid., Reed to Cass, Jan. 13, 1858, and Albert Freeman, vice consul at Shanghai, to Reed, Jan. 26, 1858, and Feb. 6, 1858.
18. Ibid., Reed to Cass, Feb. 13, 1858.
19. Ibid., Cass to Reed, Apr. 28, 1858.
20. Ibid., Reed to Cass, Apr. 3, 1858.
21. Ibid.
22. Ibid., Reed to Cass, June 30, 1858.
23. Ibid., Sept. 4, 1858.
24. Ibid., Oct. 22, 1858.
25. Ibid.
26. *New York Times*, Nov. 23, 1858.
27. Senate Executive Documents, 32nd Cong., 1st Sess., Vol. IX, Secretary of State Daniel Webster to Commodore Aulick, June 10, 1851.
28. Arthur Walworth, *Black Ships Off Japan The Story of Commodore Perry's Expedition* (Hamden, Conn.: Archon Books, 1966), p. 39.
29. Dennett, *Americans in Eastern Asia*, p. 25.
30. Senate Documents, 32nd Cong., 1st Sess., Vol. IX.
31. Glynn to Howland and Aspinwall, Feb. 24, 1851.
32. Perry bought land on Peel Island in the Bonins for a future coal depot for the navy, and he wrote urging that the United States acquire a foothold in the Bonins. See Arthur Walworth, *Black Ships Off Japan*, pp. 61-62.
33. Dennett, *Americans in Eastern Asia*, p. 359.

Chapter XIV

Looking Backward on a Nation That Looked Forward

Three aims of the United States caused a deep involvement in international affairs: expansion, the ambition to promote commerce, and the prevention of Europe from promoting a balance of power system in the New World. The new nation displayed unlimited zeal in seeking to achieve these objectives and, in the years 1820 to 1860, also experienced remarkable success, catapulting itself from a weak republican experiment to dominance in North America and to second rank in world trade. These achievements owed much to the country's phenomenal internal economic growth and also to the absence of any significant restraints upon it by other great world powers.

Great Britain and France had reason to resent their new rival in commerce, to distrust the unmitigated boldness of many American statesmen, and to wonder what the new nation's future impact on foreign affairs would be. They were increasingly concerned about the absence of any checks upon the United States by other countries of the New World. Problems, both internal and external, prevented France and Great Britain, allies from 1832 to 1848, from joining to prevent the growth of the giant America that loomed on the horizon.

France was a monarchy in name only after 1830. Behind the monarchical façade the middle class ruled, but uneasily because as harbors in an area producing raw materials for foreign markets, the imposition of treaties assuring access to markets, and the establishment of spheres of influence meant security in promoting trade.

For the British particularly—due to their dependence on cotton imports and their commerce in the Pacific—Texas, California, and Central America were of justifiable concern. Control by the United States would work to British disadvantage. British foreign ministers, from Palmerston to Malmesbury, sincerely protested that Great Britain had too many colonies, but they could not proclaim an indifference to commerce and shipping nor foreswear arrangements to promote them. Nor were Americans able to take an apathetic attitude as to a dominant influence by Great Britain in an independent Texas, California, or Central America. Far from being apathetic, the United States was belligerent in opposing British predominance and by 1860 had won the battle diplomatically.

Mexico was the loser in this contest because it was unable to establish an effective government in its own provinces and faced rebellion. Nor could it manifest sufficient unity and strength to win the confidence of Great Britain. Consequently, British foreign ministers refused to intervene in its behalf and gradually resigned themselves to United States domination of North America.

National interest is the final determinant of foreign policy. It is subject to generally accepted codes of proper behavior among nations, the law of nations—a limitation that carries weight only to the extent that transgression of the code reaps resentment, fear, and hatred that can prove costly. During the early decades of its existence the United States made constant appeals to the law of nations in its quarrels with Great Britain and France. As the nation grew stronger, it relied less and less on such appeals, but it continued to lay claim to a superiority of morality in its dealings with foreign powers and justified its most aggressive acts as those of self-defense. In this it was not unique, for both the British and French indulged in a similar rationalization. Moral considerations had little, if any effect, on the conduct of foreign affairs either in the United States or in Europe, in spite of nationalistic boasts to the contrary. In this respect, the United States behaved much as did its rivals.

The political, as well as the economic, structure contributed to the degree of boldness practiced. The Democratic and Whig parties, equally balanced until the 1850s, seized on foreign affairs to strengthen themselves. During the John Quincy Adams administration the Democrats in Congress, speaking for southern farmers and Baltimore merchants, exploited the opportunity to attack the government for its rigid stand in demanding that Great Britain abandon the imperial preference system. The Whigs, in turn, attacked Andrew Jackson for his brusque demands on France at the time of the controversy over unpaid claims. In 1844 the Democrats made political capital out of the Oregon and Texas questions, and in 1845 and 1846 the Whigs united against Polk on the termination of the treaty of joint occupation and his handling of the negotiations with Mexico. Daniel Webster stooped to making political capital out of the visit of Louis Kossuth.

Party rivalries were a product of competition for office and of sectional differences on major questions such as expansion and the tariff. The Northeast generally favored a protective tariff, was less aggressive regarding expansion, and valued good relations with Great Britain. The West was strongly expansionist and hostile to Great Britain. The South demanded Texas and Cuba, took a strong stand on Central American questions, and at the same time favored free trade. However, at best, these are generalizations, for there were many exceptions. George Bancroft of Massachusetts was as strong an expansionist as Polk from Tennessee. Southern Whigs opposed Polk on both the Oregon and Mexican questions. Calhoun gave a high priority to free trade, opposed Polk on Oregon, and denounced him for his management of negotiations with Mexico. It was the Northwest, rather than the South, that pushed most vigorously for additional territory at the close of the Mexican War.

In a country so vast and with such an array of different economic interests as the United States, agreement on any one foreign policy was almost unattainable. Interest varied along sectional lines and also according to economic pursuits. These differences often disrupted party harmony within a single state. After 1840 sharp differences emerged in Massachusetts, New York, and Pennsylvania. In each of these states there were bitter contests between parties as well as struggles within parties. On occasion these arose out of personal rivalries, but they also had their origin in disputes over economic issues and slavery. These differences, too, made agreement on foreign policy difficult.

Politicians were more sensitive to changing currents of public opinion and to the necessity of marching in step on issues of major concern to their local constituencies than they were concerned about taking an olympian view and arriving at the truth regarding national interest. All this added to the confusion and to the burdens of presidents and secretaries of state in conducting foreign affairs.

An appraisal of the leadership during these years must take into account the political and economic structure, the prevailing world situation, and the forces that were sweeping the country and a large part of the western world. Domestic political considerations frequently determined decision making. Yet, historians' concern about the role played by presidents and secretaries of state testify to their faith that leaders are not mere pawns whose decisions are predetermined by the forces at work. Individuals make a difference.

John Quincy Adams hastened the acquisition of the Floridas by his dogged diplomacy. Albert Gallatin—laboring under the burden of difficult instructions, and negotiating with powerful Great Britain —managed by skill, patience, mastery of the problems under consideration, and reasonableness to turn a dismal prospect into a bright achievement. Others bungled. Daniel Webster demonstrated consummate political skill in his negotiations with Ashburton but committed something like a diplomat's felony in refusing to include the Oregon question for consideration. Had the Oregon question been dealt with before it became an explosive controversy, peace need not have been endangered.

Polk could quite probably have reached an agreement with Great Britain on Oregon, one essentially on the terms he accepted, but he persisted in appeasing extremists by appearing to demand all the territory, refused to listen to advice, and ignored dispatches from Everett that made clear a compromise settlement was within reach. As David Pletcher has so ably argued, Polk overstated his case in his inaugural, overreacted to Pakenham's rejection of his offer, and challenged the British by instructing Buchanan to prepare a legal case using threadbare arguments. Amid dangerous tensions, Polk gave no indication of being willing to enter into a negotiation and did nothing to quiet talk of war.

Again, in his negotiations with Mexico, Polk acted on the dangerous assumption that the best way to get what he wanted was to assume a bold front. With Mexico he went one better and sought not only territory across the Nueces, which Texas claimed but had not governed, but for good measure sought to buy California. The price of his bravado was an unpopular and a much longer war than he anticipated.

James Buchanan served his country well as minister to Great Britain, but as president he showed that he lacked balance and an understanding of what constituted a national interest. He was guided by whatever appeared to improve his own political fortunes and became obsessed with the necessity of acquiring Cuba. He entertained fears of black emancipation in Cuba and permitted these fears to blind him to the evils of slavery. He not only gave way to impatience and distrust of Spain but lost all touch with political realities in pushing for acquisition of Cuba after it was a lost cause. In his efforts to acquire parts of Mexico and to push treaties granting the United States the right of intervention in both Mexico and Nicaragua, he defied the great majority in Congress and identified himself with extremists in the deep South.

The political system did not elevate strong and able men to the presidency. Tyler, Polk, Taylor, Fillmore, Pierce, and Buchanan lacked stature and demonstrated a parochial unilateralism in diplomacy. Two of these six men became president when the incumbent died. Polk became the despair of some of his own early supporters. Pierce was denied nomination for a second term by his own party. Buchanan left office under a cloud of distrust. High officeholders were too often men with feet of clay. The party organizations that elevated them to power failed to show responsibility.

The excitement of the new age of railroads and steamships and the pride taken in the nation's growth had their counterpart in arrogance, boastfulness, and a subordination of moral values to national greatness measured in material terms. Cass, as secretary of state, supported the most notable filibusterer, Walker. Soulé, as minister to Spain, challenged the French minister to a duel and injured him. Some members of Congress issued blood-curdling statements. The governor of Mississippi openly planned a filibustering attack on Cuba.

Slavery seriously damaged the nation's reputation among Europeans, who labeled it barbarous. Considering the American boast that their nation was the land of freedom, the existence of slavery appeared to be a glaring paradox. The slave trade and American participation in it led to serious controversy with Great Britain. Infinitely more important was the expansionist influence of the slaveholding region. The drive for Texas and then for Cuba owed much to the conviction that the continuation of slavery was dependent upon the acquisition of these territories. Ugly racism made itself felt constantly.

Bibliography

UNITED STATES GOVERNMENT DOCUMENTS

Despatches from United States Ministers to France and Great Britain, 1820 to 1860
Instructions to United States Ministers to France and Great Britain, 1820 to 1860
Senate Executive Documents, 1830 to 1860
House Executive Documents, 1830 to 1860
American State Papers, Vols. V and VI
Annals of Congress and Congressional Globe, 1820 to 1860

PRIVATE PAPERS

George Bancroft Papers, Massachusetts Historical Society
James Buchanan Papers, Pennsylvania Historical Society
Lewis Cass Papers, Clements Library, University of Michigan
Caleb Cushing Papers, Library of Congress
Edward Everett Papers, Massachusetts Historical Society
Albert Gallatin Papers, Library of Congress
James K. Polk Papers, Library of Congress

PUBLISHED DOCUMENT COLLECTIONS

Manning, William R., ed. *Diplomatic Correspondence of the United States Inter-American Affairs, 1831–1860, Vol. XII. Texas and Venezuela.* Washington: Carnegie Endowment for International Peace, 1939.
———. Vol. III. *Inter-American Affairs, 1831–1850.*
———. Vol. VIII. *Mexico, 1831–1848.*
———. Vol. IX. *Mexico, 1848–1860.*
Richardson, James D., ed. *A Compilation of the Messages and Papers of the Presidents of the United States.* Washington: Bureau of National Literature and Art, 1897.

PUBLISHED MEMOIRS AND PAPERS

Adams, John. *The Adams Papers*. Edited by L. H. Butterfield, Vol. II. Cambridge: The Belknap Press of Harvard University Press, 1961.
Adams, John Quincy. *Memoirs of John Quincy Adams*. Edited by Charles Francis Adams. Philadelphia: J. B. Lippincott & Co., 1874–77.
Benton, Thomas Hart. *Thirty Years: or a History of the Working of the American Government for Thirty Years, from 1820 to 1850*. New York: D. Appleton and Co., 1854–56.
Clay, Henry. *The Papers of Henry Clay*. Edited by James F. Hopkins and Mary W. M. Hargreaves. Lexington, Ky.: The University Press of Kentucky, 1973.
Fillmore, Millard. *Millard Fillmore Papers*. Edited by Frank M. Severance. Buffalo, N.Y.: Buffalo Historical Society, 1907.
Jefferson, Thomas. *The Writings of Thomas Jefferson*. 10 vols. Edited by Paul Leicester Ford. New York: G. P. Putnam's Sons, 1895.
Madison, James. *The Writings of James Madison*. 9 vols. Edited by Gaillard Hunt. New York: G. P. Putnam's Sons, 1901.
Polk, James K. *The Diary of James K. Polk during His Presidency, 1845 to 1849*. Edited by Milo Milton Quaife. Chicago: A. C. McClure & Co., 1910.
Webster, Daniel. *The Papers of Daniel Webster*. Edited by Charles M. Wiltse. Hanover, N.H.: Dartmouth College by the University Press of New England, 1974.

SECONDARY SOURCES

Books

Abel, Annie Heloise, and Klingbert, Frank J., eds. *A Side-Light on Anglo-American Relations, 1839–1858 Furnished by the Correspondence of Lewis Tappan and Others with the British and Foreign Anti-Slavery Society*. Lancaster, Pa.: The Association for the Study of Negro Life and History, Inc., 1927.
Adams, Ephraim Douglas. *British Interests and Activities in Texas 1838–1846*. Baltimore: The Johns Hopkins Press, 1910.
Adler, Dorothy. *British Investments in American Railways*. Charlottesville, Va.: University of Virginia Press, 1970.
Barbour, Brian M., ed. *American Transcendentalism An Anthology of Criticism*, South Bend, Indiana: University of Notre Dame Press, 1973.
Bemis, Samuel Flagg. *John Quincy Adams and the Foundations of American Foreign Policy*. New York: Alfred A. Knopf, 1950.

Berthoff, Rowland Tappan. *British Immigrants in Industrial America.* Cambridge: Harvard University Press, 1953.
Billington, Ray. *Westward Expansion A History of the American Frontier.* New York: The Macmillan Co., 1960.
Blumenthal, Henry. *A Reappraisal of Franco-American Relations 1830–1871.* Chapel Hill: The University of North Carolina Press, 1959.
Brack, Gene M. *Mexico Views Manifest Destiny An Essay on the Origins of the Mexican War.* Albuquerque, N.M.: University of New Mexico Press, 1975.
Bradley, Harold W. *The American Frontier in Hawaii The Pioneers 1789–1843.* Palo Alto, Calif.: Stanford University Press, 1942.
Brebner, John Bartlet. *North Atlantic Triangle The Interplay of Canada, the United States and Great Britain.* New Haven: Yale University Press, 1945.
Bruchey, Stuart. *Roots of American Economic Growth 1607–1861, An Essay in Social Causation.* New York: Harper & Row, 1965.
Cole, Charles C., Jr. *The Social Ideas of the Northern Evangelists 1826–1860.* New York: Columbia University Press, 1954.
Corey, Albert. *The Crisis of 1830–1842 in Canadian-American Relations.* New Haven: Yale University Press, 1941.
Cumberland, Charles C. *Mexico The Struggle for Modernity.* New York: Oxford University Press, 1968.
Current, Richard N. *Daniel Webster and the Rise of National Conservatism.* Boston: Little, Brown and Co., 1955.
Daniels, George H. *American Science in the Age of Jackson.* New York: Columbia University Press, 1968.
———. *Science in American Society A Social History.* New York: Alfred A. Knopf, 1971.
Dawty, Alan. *The Limits of American Isolation: The United States and the Crimean War.* New York: New York University Press, 1971.
Dennett, Tyler. *Americans in Eastern Asia A Critical Study of the Policy of the United States with reference to China, Japan and Korea in the 19th Century.* New York: Barnes & Noble, Inc., 1941.
Depree, A. Hunter. *Science in the Federal Government A History of Policies and Activities to 1940.* New York: Harper & Row, 1957.
Dunbar, Willis Frederick. *Michigan A History of the Wolverine State.* Grand Rapids, Michigan: Erdmans Publishing Co., 1965.
Dunham, Arthur L. *The Industrial Revolution in France 1815–1848.* New York: Exposition Press, 1955.
Ettinger, Amos Aschback. *The Mission to Spain of Pierre Soulé A Study in the Cuban Diplomacy of the United States.* New Haven: Yale University Press, 1932.
Fairbank, John King. *Trade and Diplomacy on the China Coast The Opening of the Treaty Ports 1842–1854.* Cambridge: Harvard University Press, 1953.

Fuess, Claude M. *The Life of Caleb Cushing*. New York: Harcourt, Brace and Co., 1923.
Graebner, Norman A. *Empire on the Pacific; a Study in American Continental Expansion*. New York: Ronald Press Co., 1955.
Gulick, Edward V. *Peter Parker and the Opening of China*. Cambridge: Harvard University Press, 1973.
Hansen, Marcus Lee. *The Atlantic Migration 1607–1860 A History of the Continuing Settlement of the United States*. New York: Harper & Row, 1961.
Hidy, Ralph W. *The House of Baring in American Trade and Finance English Merchant Bankers at Work*. Cambridge: Harvard University Press, 1949.
Higham, John. *From Boundlessness to Consolidation The Transformation of American Culture 1848–1860*. Ann Arbor, Michigan: William Clements Library, 1969.
Hildreth, Richard. *Theory of Morals An Inquiry Concerning the Law of Moral Distinctions and the Variations and Contradictions of Ethical Codes*. Boston: Charles C. Little and James Brown, 1844.
Ihde, Aaron J. *The Development of Modern Chemistry*. New York: Harper & Row, Publishers, 1964.
Johannsen, Robert W. *Stephen A. Douglas*. New York: Oxford University Press, 1973.
Klein, Philip Shriver. *President James Buchanan A Biography*. University Park, Pa.: Pennsylvania State University Press, 1962.
Kuykendall, Ralph S. *The Hawaiian Kingdom 1778–1854 Foundation and Transformation*. Honolulu: The University of Hawaii Press, 1947.
Landes, David S. *The Unbound Prometheus*. Cambridge: Harvard University Press, 1969.
Leys, M. D. R. *Between Two Empires A History of French Politicians and People between 1814 and 1848*. New York: Longmans, Green, and Co., 1955.
McCormac, Eugene I. *John Forsythe Secretary of State July 1, 1834 to March 3, 1837*. Vol. IV of *The American Secretaries of State and Their Diplomacy*. Edited by Samuel Flagg Bemis. New York: The Pageant Book Co., 1958.
———. *Louis McLane Secretary of State May 29, 1833 to June 30, 1834*. Vol. IV of *The American Secretaries of State and Their Diplomacy*. Edited by Samuel Flagg Bemis. New York: The Pageant Book Co., 1958.
May, Arthur James. "Contemporary American Opinion of the Mid-Century Revolutions in Central Europe." Philadelphia: University of Pennsylvania Ph.D. thesis, 1927.
May, Ernest. *The Making of the Monroe Doctrine*. Cambridge: Harvard University Press, 1975.

Merk, Frederick. *Fruits of Propaganda in the Tyler Administration.* With the collaboration of Lois Bannister Merk. Cambridge, Mass., 1971.

———. *Albert Gallatin and the Oregon Problem.* Cambridge: Harvard University Press, 1950.

———. *Manifest Destiny and Mission in American History, a Reinterpretation.* With the collaboration of Lois Bannister Merk. New York, 1963.

Mott, Frank Luther. *A History of American Magazines 1741-1850.* New York: Appleton and Co., 1930.

Munroe, John A. *Louis McLane Federalist and Jacksonian.* New Brunswick: Rutgers University Press, 1973.

Nadel, George and Perry Curtis, *Imperialism and Colonialism.* London: The Macmillan Co., 1964.

Nevins, Allan. *Fremont The West's Great Adventurer.* New York: Harper & Brothers, 1928.

Nichols, Roy F. *Franklin Pierce Young Hickory of the Granite Hills.* Philadelphia: University of Pennsylvania Press, 1958.

North, Douglas C. *The Economic Growth of the United States.* New York: Prentice-Hall, Inc., 1961.

Nye, Russell. *Society and Culture in America 1830-1860.* New York: Harper & Row, 1974.

Paolina, Ernest N. *The Foundations of American Empire William Henry Seward and U.S. Foreign Policy.* Ithaca, New York: Cornell University Press, 1973.

Parker, Nancy Nichols, ed. *The French Legation in Texas.* Austin: Texas State Historical Association, 1971.

Perkins, Bradford. *Castlereagh and Adams England and the United States 1812-1823.* Berkeley: University of California Press, 1964.

Perkins, Dexter. *History of the Monroe Doctrine.* Boston: Little, Brown & Co., rev. ed., 1955.

Pletcher, David M. *The Diplomacy of Annexation Texas, Oregon, and the Mexican War.* Columbia, Mo.: University of Missouri Press, 1973.

Potter, E. B., ed. *The United States and World Sea Power.* Englewood Cliffs: Prentice-Hall, Inc., 1955.

Rauch, Basil. *American Interest in Cuba: 1848-1855.* New York: Columbia University Press, 1948.

Schroeder, John M. *Mr. Polk's War American Opposition and Dissent 1846-1848.* Madison, Wisconsin: University of Wisconsin Press, 1973.

Scroggs, William O. *Filibusters and Financiers.* New York: The Macmillan Co., 1916.

Seager, Robert. *and Tyler too A Biography of John and Julia Gardiner Tyler.* New York: McGraw-Hill Book Co., 1963.

Sellers, Charles. *James K. Polk Continentalist 1843-1846.* Princeton, N.J.: Princeton University Press, 1966.

Smallwood, William Martin and Mabel Sarah Coon Smallwood. *Natural History and the American Mind.* New York: Columbia University Press, 1941.
Spencer, Donald S. *Louis Kossuth and Young America A Study of Sectionalism and Foreign Policy 1848–1852.* Columbia, Mo.: University of Missouri Press, 1977.
Thistlewaite, Frank. *The Anglo-American Connection in the Early Nineteenth Century.* Philadelphia: University of Pennsylvania Press, 1959.
Thomas, Hugh. *Cuba The Pursuit of Freedom.* New York: Harper & Row, 1971.
Walworth, Arthur. *Black Ships Off Japan The Story of Commodore Perry's Expedition.* Hamden, Conn.: Archon Books, 1966.
Webster, C. K., ed. *Britain and the Independence of Latin America, 1812–1830.* London: Oxford University Press, 1938.
———. *The Foreign Policy of Palmerston 1830–1841.* London: G. Bell and Sons, Ltd., 1951.
Williams, Frederick Wells, ed. *The Life and Letters of Samuel Wells Williams.* New York: G. P. Putnam's Sons, 1889.
Williams, Mary Wilhelm. *John Middleton Clayton Secretary of State March 7, 1849 to July 21, 1850.* Vol. VI of *The American Secretaries of State and Their Diplomacy.* Edited by Samuel Flagg Bemis. New York: The Pageant Book Co., 1958.
Wiltse, Charles M. *John C. Calhoun Sectionalist, 1840–1850.* New York: The Bobbs-Merrill Co., 1951.
———. *The Papers of Daniel Webster.* Hanover, N. H.: Dartmouth College by the University Press of New England, 1974.
Wittke, Carl. *We Who Built America The Saga of the Immigrant.* Cleveland: Press of Western Reserve University, 1964.
Wood, Gordon. *The Rising Glory of America.* New York: G. Braziller, 1971.
Wright, Chester. *Economic History of the United States.* New York: McGraw-Hill Book Company, 1941.

Articles

Brown, Kenneth L. "Stephen Gerard, Promoter of the Second Bank of the United States." *Journal of Economic History*, Nov. 1942.
Cootner, Paul H. "The Role of the Railroads." *Journal of Economic History*, Dec. 1863.
Curti, Merle. "Young America." *American Historical Review*, Oct. 1926.
"De Kay's Address." *North American Review*, July 1826.
"Hildreth's Theory of Morals." *North American Review*, Apr. 1845.
Jenks, Leland. "Railroads as an Economic Force." *Journal of Economic History*, May 1944.

Jones, Wilbur Devereux. "Lord Ashburton and the Maine Boundary Negotiations." *The Mississippi Valley Historical Review A Journal of American History*, Dec. 1953.

Le Duc, Thomas. "The Maine Frontier and the Northeastern Boundary Controversy." *American Historical Review*, Oct. 1947.

May, Robert E. " 'A Southern Strategy' for the 1850's: Northern Democrats, the Tropics, and the Expansion of the National Domain." *Louisiana Studies An Interdisciplinary Journal of the South*, Winter 1975.

"Nationality in Literature." *North American Review*, July 1849.

North, Douglas C. "International Capital Flows and Development of the American West." *Journal of Economic History*, Dec. 1956.

Review of *American Notes for General Circulation*. *North American Review*, Jan. 1843.

Review of Morris Birbeck's *Notes on a Journey in America, from the Coast of Virginia to the Territory of the Illinois*. *Edinburgh Review*, June 1818.

Review of Peter S. Du Ponceau's *A Dissertation on the Nature and Extent of the Jurisdiction of the Courts of the United States*. *North American Review*, July 1825.

Review of *Recent American Literature*. *North American Review*, Oct. 1940.

Review of *The American Association for the Advancement of Science*. *Putnam's Monthly Magazine*, Sept. 1853.

Review of *The Irish in America*. *North American Review*, Jan. 1841.

Review of Stewart Dugald's *The Philosophy of the Active and Moral Powers of Man*. *North American Review*, July 1830.

Rippy, J. Fred. "Diplomacy of the United States and Mexico Regarding the Isthmus of Tehuantepec, 1848–1865." *Mississippi Valley Historical Review*, Mar. 1920.

Sharrow, Walter G. "William Henry Seward and the Basis for American Empire, 1850–1860." *Pacific Historical Review*, Aug. 1967.

Shewmaker, Kenneth E. "Daniel Webster and the Politics of Foreign Policy." *The Journal of American History*, Sept. 1976.

Sioussat, St. George L. "Memphis, The Gateway of the West." *Tennessee Historical Magazine*, Vol. III, 1932.

Urban, C. Stanley. "The Ideology of Southern Imperialism: New Orleans and the Caribbean, 1845–1860." *The Louisiana Historical Quarterly*, Jan. 1956.

Watt, Alastair. "The Case of Alexander McLeod." *Canadian Historical Review*, June 1931.

Williamson, J. G. "International Trade and United States Economic Development: 1827–1843." *Journal of Economic History*, Sept. 1961.

Index

Aberdeen, Lord (George Hamilton Gordon)
  and Central America question, 230–31
  as foreign minister, 108, 120
  and Maine boundary question, 111, 112, 114–15
  and Oregon question, 148–49, 151, 160, 164
  and slave trade, 108–109, 121–27
  and Texas annexation, 126–34, 139
  and West Indies trade restrictions, 81–82
Abolitionists, 137, 215, 228. *See also* Antislavery movement
Addington, Henry, 57, 69, 71
Adams, John, 6, 9
Adams, John Quincy
  and American claims against France, 86, 91
  on foreign alliances, 50–51, 52
  on French trade restrictions, 47
  on Greek war for independence, 51
  memoirs of, 54
  and national interests, 48–49
  noncolonization principle of, 50–51, 56, 58, 66
  and noninvolvement in Europe, 54, 56
  as president, 62, 64, 80
  on President Monroe, 49
  as secretary of state, 47, 48–59
  and South American republics, 52, 53, 55, 58
  and West Indies trade restrictions, 62–63, 64, 80
Agassiz, Louis, 36, 38
Agriculture, 22, 23, 35, 45
Alamo, 122
Alcock, Rutherford, 272, 273
Alexander I, Tsar, 49, 52, 53
Allen, William, 137, 146, 147, 156–57, 162, 163, 184
American Association for Advancement of Science, 36
Amoy, 272
Anglophobia, 120, 233
Annexation
  movement for Cuba, 138, 203, 204, 215, 216–18, 225, 226, 242–52
  movement for Hawaii, 260
  Texas, 125–26, 127, 128, 129–30, 134, 135–41
  West Florida, 5, 11–12
  See also Territorial expansion
Antislavery movement, 202–204
  British, 95–96, 103–105, 124–29, 130, 131–32, 208, 228
  and Cuban annexation movement, 208
  and Texas, 131–32, 136
Antwerp, 77
Archer, William S., 138
Arista, Mariano, 238
Aroostook valley, 102–103, 111, 112
Aroostook War, 103
Articles of Confederation, 3–4, 13
Ashburton, Alexander, 109, 110–15, 145

Astor, John Jacob, 67
Atocha, Alexander J., 182
Austin, Stephen, 121, 122

Bagot, Charles, 113
Balance of power, 21–22, 203
Bancroft, George, 30
  and Japan, 281
  and Mexican War, 174, 177, 183, 186, 188–89
  and Nicaragua, 220
  and Oregon, 158, 159
Bank of the United States, 25
Baring, House of 25
Barnburners, 145
Bartram, John, 35
Bates, Joshua, 25
Bay Islands, 223, 224, 226, 228, 229, 230, 231, 232
Baylies committee, 66–67
Beach, Moses Yale, 244
Beaumarchais, Pierre Augustin Caron de, 88
Beecher, Lyman, 8, 15
Belgium, 77
Belize, 217, 222, 223, 224, 226, 228, 230, 231
Belly, Felix, 252
Belmont, August, 247, 249–50
Belser, James, 136
Benjamin, Judah P., 237, 241, 246, 252
Bentham, Jeremy, 29, 33
Benton, Thomas Hart, 114, 139, 152, 172, 174, 185, 237
Berthoff, Rowland, 28
Biddle, James, 281
Biddle, Nicholas, 125
Bigelow Papers, 191
Bingham, Hiram, 258
Birkbeck, Morris, 17–18
Birney, James G., 136, 144
Black, James A., 148, 157
Black, John, 177, 179, 183
Black Warrior, 248, 249
Bonin Islands, 283

Borlond, Solon E., 231
Boston Atheneum, 38
Bourbons, 78, 83
Bowditch, Nathaniel, 35
Bowring, John, 265, 274
Brazil, 59
Bremmer, Fredrika, 31
Bridgman, Elijah, 269
British
  -American rivalry, 5–6, 10, 13, 46, 61–74, 81, 203, 214–35
  antislavery movement, 95–96, 103–105, 124–30, 131–32, 208, 242
  capital in U.S., 20, 24, 25–26
  immigrants, 26, 27, 28
  imperialism, 224–25
  imperial preference system, 63, 64, 80, 82
  literature, 30–34
  naval supremacy, 45
  restrictions on U.S. trade, 4, 13, 46, 61–64, 65, 68, 71, 80–83
  suppression of slave trade, 95–96, 103–110, 113–14, 115
  See also England; Great Britain
British Honduras, 224
British Immigrants in Industrial America, 28
British West Indies. *See* West Indies, British
Broglie, Achille Charles Léonce Victor de, 89, 91
Brougham, Henry Peter, 31, 165
Brown, Albert, 254
Bruchey, Stuart, 25
Buchanan, James, 203
  and antislavery movement, 203, 204
  and Central America question, 214, 217, 226–32, 252, 254
  and China, 275
  and Crimean War, 210
  and Cuban annexation movement, 208, 209, 217–18, 247, 249–50, 251–52

Buchanan, James (cont'd.)
  and Mexican War, 179, 182, 184
  as minister to Great Britain, 226, 227
  and Oregon question, 149, 150–51, 152, 154, 157, 160–61
  as presidential candidate, 154, 232
  as secretary of state, 146, 147
  and Tehuantepec route, 241
  and territorial expansion, 249–50, 251–52
  and Texas annexation, 138
Bulwer, Henry Lytton, 222–33
Burton, K. G., 126
Byron, George Gordon, 33

Caldwell, George A., 137
Calhoun, John C., 54
  and Greek war for independence, 51
  and Mexican War, 49, 180, 184, 185–86, 187
  and Oregon question, 145, 154–55, 157, 163
  and South American republics, 53, 55–56
  and Texas annexation, 130–32, 133–35
  and transcontinental railroads, 168
Calhoun-Pakenham correspondence, 130
California
  acquisition of, 189, 236
  American interest in, 118–19, 168, 172–73
  under Mexican rule, 119, 171
  and Mexican War, 168, 188–89, 192
Campbell, James, 201
Campbell, Robert Blair, 244
Canada
  -American frontier disputes, 98–102
  insurrection movement in, 95, 98
  and Maine boundary question, 64, 71, 72–73, 94–95, 102–103, 110–12, 114–15
  Maritime Provinces, 4, 80, 81, 82
Canadian Refuge Relief Association, 100
Canal projects, Central American, 217, 218–19, 220, 222, 233, 252
Canal transportation, 23, 25, 27–28
Canning, George, 51, 53, 54, 55, 57, 67
Canning, Stratford, 50, 63, 66, 68–72
Canton, China, 269, 270
Carlyle, Thomas, 31, 34
Caroline affair, 98–99, 102, 107, 108, 114
Carr, Dabney S., 146
Cartwright, Peter, 15
Cass, Lewis
  and British suppression of slave trade, 113–14
  and China, 275
  and Cuba, 225, 243
  as minister to France, 76, 113–14
  and Nicaragua, 252, 253
  and Oregon, 162
  and slavery, 204, 206
  and Tehuantepec route, 241
  and Texas annexation, 140, 147
Castillo y Lanzas, Joaquin M. de, 183, 188
Central America, 208, 214–35
Chateaubriand, François René de, 52–53
Chatfield, Frederick, 218–19
Chi'i-ying, 267–68, 269–70
China, 119, 168, 260–79
Churches, 14–16
Claiborne, John, 198
Clarendon, Lord (George William Frederick Villiers), 210, 227–30, 231, 232, 247, 279
Clay, Henry, 64, 69, 71, 91, 118, 138, 144

Clayton, John M., 187, 195–96, 219, 220, 222–33
Clayton-Bulwer Treaty, 215, 217, 222–33
Cleaveland, Parker, 37
Coal, 197
Coleridge, Samuel Taylor, 31, 32, 34
Collins, E. K., 200, 201
Collins, Perry McD., 197
Colombia, 59
Colton, Calvin, 15
Columbia River, 149, 150, 157, 159, 164
Commercial Convention of 1815, 61, 63, 72, 73
Common law, 29
Constitution, 4, 104
Constitutional Convention, 13
Convention of 1818, 70, 72
Cooper, James Fennimore, 30, 31
Copper, 197
Corey, Albert, 100
Corn, 196
Corn Laws, 24
Cornwallis, Charles, 3
Corwin, Thomas, 198–99
Costa Rica, 232
Cotton, 75, 76, 137, 198, 243
  exports, 22, 196
Cousin, Victor, 31, 34
Coxe, Richard S., 177–78, 179
Crampton, J. F. T. C., 232
Crawford, William, 49, 51, 54
Creole affair, 109
Crescent City, 246, 247
Crevecoeur, Hector St. John, 7–8
Crimean War, 203, 209–11, 227
Crittenden, William L., 244, 245
Cuba
  emancipation question in, 242, 244, 245–46, 247
  and Great Britain, 50, 70, 131, 209, 218, 229, 242
  Spanish rule of, 50, 216, 217, 229, 242
  U.S. annexation movement for, 138, 203, 204, 215, 216–18, 225, 226, 242–52
  U.S. offer to purchase, 244, 249, 251–52
Cunningham, Edward, 272
Curti, Merle, 206
Cushing, Caleb, 154, 216, 231, 247, 249, 263–64, 265, 267–70
Cushing Treaty, 269, 270, 279

Daily Picayune, New Orleans, 237, 240–41, 245
Dallas, George, 146, 204, 215, 217, 232, 233
Dana, James Dwight, 36, 39
Darwin, Charles, 38–39
Davis, Jefferson, 247, 249, 254
Dawson, William, 226
De Bow, J. D. B., 169, 242–43
De Broglie. *See* Broglie
Declaration of Rights of Man, 10
De Grasse. *See* Grasse
De Kay, James E., 37–38
Democratic Empire Club, 138
Democratic party, 144, 216, 236–37
Dennett, Tyler, 268
Dickens, Charles, 34
"Diplomatic Act," 133
Dix, John Adams, 139, 140, 163, 191
Donelson, Andrew J., 135, 175–76
Douglas, Stephen, 168–69, 200, 203, 204, 206, 210, 225–26
Douglas affair, 105–106, 107
Downs, S. W., 226
Du Ponceau, Peter S., 29
Durham, Earl of (John George Lambton), 100
Dutch, 77
Dwight, Timothy, 14

East Indies, British, 4
Economy, American, 13–14, 22–26
Egypt, 97–98
Elementary Treatise on Mineralogy and Zoology, 37
Elgin, James, 277, 279

Elliott, Charles, 124, 126, 139, 140
Emancipation question, 215, 228
  in Cuba, 242, 244, 245–46, 247
Emerson, Ralph Waldo, 34, 191
England
  domestic problems of, 79–80
  foreign trade of, 44
  industrialization of, 44, 45
  and War of 1812, 3, 14
  See also British; Great Britain
English immigrants, 27, 28
Erie Canal, 23, 24, 27
Essay on Human Understanding, 32
Eve, Joseph, 124
Everett, Alexander, 154, 281
Everett, Edward, 58, 76, 108–110, 114–15, 128–29, 145, 148–49, 159–60, 227
Expansionism. *See* Territorial expansion
Exports, 43, 45, 196

Federalist, The, 8
Federalists, 1, 9, 10
Ferdinand VII, 52
Filibustering expeditions
  against Canada, 100
  against Cuba, 244–45
  against Nicaragua, 216, 252–54
Fillmore, Millard, 197, 207, 208, 226, 239, 244
Florida, 5, 7, 11–14
Foreign investments in U.S., 20, 24, 25–26
Foreign trade, U.S., 12–14, 196
  British restrictions on, 4, 13, 46, 61–64, 65, 68, 71, 80, 83
  and China, 119, 263–65, 269
  and Cuba, 242–43
  different policy views on, 2
  exports and imports, 13, 24, 25, 43, 45, 196
  French restrictions on, 5–6, 76
  growth of, 13–14, 18, 43, 45, 76–77
  and House of Baring, 25

  zeal for, 196, 197
Forney, James, 154, 155
Forsyth, John, 96, 97, 103, 104–105, 108, 113
Fox, Henry S., 108
France
  and American spoliation claims, 48, 84–92
  and China, 272, 275, 276–77
  and Crimean War, 203, 210
  and Cuba, 208
  1848 revolution in, 204–205
  foreign trade of, 44, 45, 46, 47, 76
  and Hawaii, 258, 259
  industrialization of, 44–45
  and Louisiana Purchase Treaty, 47, 48, 86, 87, 88
  and Mexico, 119, 120, 132–33, 134, 139–40, 171
  and Texas annexation, 120, 124, 125, 127, 129–30, 132–33, 134, 139
  under Louis Philippe, 83–84, 86, 87, 120
  and U.S. trade rivalry, 46, 47
Franklin, Benjamin, 9, 35, 111
Freedom of the seas, 6, 16–17
Free trade, 12–13, 63
Fremont, John Charles, 172–73, 185
French immigrants, 26
French Revolution, 10–11
French West Indies, 14

Gadsden, James, 241
Gaines, E. P., 122
Gallatin, Albert
  on American spoliation claims, 48, 85
  and Maine boundary question, 71, 72
  and Oregon question, 65–66, 69–70, 71–73, 165
  and South American republics, 52–53
  and U.S. foreign trade, 46–47

Gallatin, Albert (cont'd.)
  on West Florida, 5
  and West Indies trade restrictions, 68–69, 70
Garay grant, 237, 238, 239, 240, 241
Gardiner, Alexander, 138–39
Gaulburn, Henry, 127
George III, 3
German immigrants, 26, 27, 28
Ghent, Treaty of, 3, 4, 6
Gilmer, Thomas, 125
Glynn, James, 281–82
G. P. *Weeks*, 101
Grasse, François Joseph Paul de, 3
Gray, Asa, 36, 38
Great Britain
  and Canada-U.S. frontier disputes, 98–102
  and Central America, 214–35
  and China, 119, 264, 265, 271, 272, 273, 275–77, 278, 279
  and Crimean War, 203, 210, 211
  and Cuba, 50, 70, 131, 209, 218, 229, 242, 247
  and Hawaii, 258, 259
  internal problems of, 119–20
  and Maine boundary question, 64, 71, 72–73, 94–95, 102–103, 110–12, 114–15
  and Mexico, 119, 120, 126–27, 132–33, 134, 139–40, 171, 192
  and Nicaragua, 217, 218–33
  and Oregon question, 64, 65–67, 69–70, 71, 72–73, 115, 118–19, 120, 148–52, 157–66
  and South American republics, 53
  and Texas annexation, 120, 124, 125–26, 127, 132–33, 134, 139–40
  and U.S. trade restrictions, 4, 13, 46, 61–64, 65, 68, 71, 80–83
  See also British; England
Greek war for independence, 51, 54, 58–59, 206

Greeley, Horace, 210
Green, Duff, 125, 126, 127–28, 129, 134
Gregg, David L., 260
Guizot, François Pierre Guillaume, 120, 124, 129, 130, 133, 134, 139, 203
Guadalupe Hidalgo, Treaty of, 192, 237

Hamilton, Alexander, 1, 10
Hamilton, James, 127, 128
Hannegan, Edward, 146, 147, 162, 206
Hansen, Marcus, 26–27
Hargous, P. A., 237, 238, 239
Harris, Levitt, 79, 88–89
Harris, Townsend, 284–85
Hawaiian Islands, 257–60
Hawthorne, Nathaniel, 31
Haywood, William, 147
Head, Francis Bond, 113
Henry, Joseph, 36, 37, 38
Herrera, José Joaquin, 181
Higham, John, 201
Hildreth, Richard, 33
Hill, Isaac, 85
Hise, Elijah, 219, 220, 225
Hitchcock, Edward, 36
Hollins, G. N., 231
Holmes, Isaac E., 137–38
Holy Alliance, 50, 51, 52, 53, 55, 56, 59
Honduras, 219, 222, 223, 232
Honolulu, 257, 258
Hooper, Samuel, 188–89
Horn, Henry, 155
House of Baring, 25
Houston, Sam, 122, 123, 126, 127, 130, 132, 134, 174, 175–76
Howard, Tilghman A., 135
Howland and Aspinwall, 282
Hudson's Bay Company, 119, 145, 164
Hughes, Charles, Jr., 63
Hughes, Christopher, 146

Index

Hungarian revolt, 207
Hunkers, 145
Hunters Lodges, 99–100
Huskisson, William, 63, 66, 67–68, 69, 70, 71, 72

Iago affair, 107
Illinois Central Railroad, 199–200
Immigration, 7–8, 20, 26–29
Imperial Maritime Customs Service, 265–66, 273
Imports, U.S., 13, 24, 25
Impressment, 6, 96, 104, 115
Industrial revolution, 27, 43, 44, 45
Ingersoll, Joseph R., 227
Irish immigrants, 27–28, 29
Irving, Washington, 30, 31

Jackson, Andrew, 80, 82, 86, 90–91, 92, 121, 126, 150, 153
Japan, 197, 279–85
Jay, John, 9
Jay Treaty, 4
Jefferson, Thomas, 5, 6–7, 10–11, 12, 16–17, 35
Jeffersonians, 1, 9
Jones, Anson, 123, 126, 132, 133, 134, 135, 140, 174–75
Juan de Fuca Strait, 149, 164

Kamehameha III, 260
Kansas-Nebraska Act, 210, 251
Kant, Immanuel, 34
Kennedy, William, 133
King, William R., 134–35
Kossuth, Louis, 205–206, 207–208

Lafayette, Marquis de, 87, 88
Lamarque, Maximilien, 78
Landes, David S., 45
Land hunger, 12, 121, 243. *See also* Annexation; Territorial expansion
Larkin, Thomas, 172, 185
Law, George, 242, 246

Lawrence, Abbott, 195–96, 202–203, 220–22, 227
Lee, Arthur, 13
Legaré, Hugh Swinton, 126
Letcher, Robert P., 238, 239
Lieven, Khristofor Andreevich de, 75
Liholiho, Alexander, 260
Lincoln, Abraham, 195
Linnaeus, Carolus, 35
Literature, 30–35
Livingstone, Edward, 75, 78, 79, 89–90, 92
Livingstone, Robert, 16
Locke, John, 32
Lopez, Narcissa, 216, 244–45
Lorcha Arrow affair, 274
Louisiana Historical Quarterly, 216
Louisiana purchase, 5, 12, 47, 48, 86, 87, 88
Louis Napoleon, 203
Louis Philippe, 77, 78, 83, 86, 87, 89, 120, 133, 134
Louis XVIII, 44, 84
Lowell, James Russell, 191
Lower California, 192, 241

McDuffie, George, 68, 146, 162
McLane, Louis, 90
  and Mexican War, 183
  and Oregon question, 145, 149, 151, 154, 157, 158, 160, 163–64
  and West Indies trade restrictions, 80–83
McLane, Robert, 273–74
McLeod case, 107–108
Maclure, William, 37–38
Madawaska settlements, 112
Madison, James, 3–4, 5, 6, 8, 10, 11–12, 16, 63
Magazines, American, 30
Mail contracts, U.S., 200–201
Maine boundary question, 64, 71, 72–73, 94–95, 102–103, 110–12, 114–15
Makenzie, William Lyon, 113

Mangum, Willie, 166
Manifest Destiny, 12, 170, 173–74, 216, 243, 254
Mann, A. Dudley, 207
Manufacturing, 24, 45, 197
Marcy, William L., 177, 206, 226, 248, 249
Maritime Provinces, 4, 80, 81, 82
Marsh, George Perkins, 207
Marsh, James, 32
Marshall, Humphrey, 273
Martin, W. A. P., 277
Mason, James, 240
Mason, John Y., 247, 249, 250
Medicine, 35
Mejia, Francisco, 184
Mercantilist policy, 24
Merchant marine, 6, 43, 45, 62, 75
Metternich, 52
Mexico
  France and, 119, 120, 132–33, 134, 139–40, 171
  Great Britain and, 119, 120, 126, 127, 132–33, 134, 139–40, 171, 192
  internal problems of, 119, 170–71
  and Tehuantepec route, 225, 226, 237–41
  and Texan war for independence, 122
  and war with U.S., 164, 165, 168–92
  See also Texas
Middle class, 21
Middleton, Henry, 48
Miguel, Don, 77, 78
Milan decree, 5–6
Mining, 28, 196–97
Missionaries
  in China, 262–63, 265
  in Hawaii, 258
Monroe, James, 47, 49, 50, 51, 53, 54, 56–59
Monroe Doctrine, 12, 56–59, 61, 233
Moralism, national, 14, 15–16, 17

Morse, Isaac, 136
Mosquito Protectorate, 218–33
Motley, John, 30
Mott, Frank Luther, 30
Murphy, Tomás, 132, 133
Murphy, William S., 126

Nanking, Treaty of, 119, 264, 265, 269, 274
Napoleon, 5, 6, 44, 78
Napoleonic wars, 5, 7
National Academy of Science, 36
National Bank, 9, 96
Nationalism, American, 11–13, 17
National Turnpike, 23
Natural Theology, 33
Navigation acts of 1818, 63
Navy, U.S., 201, 208
Netherlands, 77
Neuces River, 169, 175, 192
Neutrality act of 1818, 100, 122
Neutral rights, 6, 16–17, 57, 210
Neuville, Hyde de, 47, 48
New Brunswick, 95, 102, 103
New Mexico, 180, 189, 192
New Orleans, 215–16, 236, 237, 240
New Orleans Tehuantepec Company, 237, 239
New York Times, 210, 211
New York *Tribune*, 210
Nicaragua, 218–33, 252
Nichols, Roy F., 206
Niles, Nathaniel, 78
Noncolonization principle, 56, 57, 58, 65, 66
Noninvolvement policy, 21–22, 39, 54, 56, 214
Nootka Sound Treaty, 69, 70
North, Douglas C., 25
North American Review, 30, 31–32, 33, 38, 58
Northeast boundary question. *See* Maine boundary question
Northwest boundary question. *See* Oregon question

Northwest Fur Company, 65–66, 69–70, 72
Notes on a Journey in America, 17–18
Nullification movement, 79

Ohio, 17
Olney, John J., 253
Oregon question, 64, 65–67, 69–70, 71, 72–73, 115, 118–19, 120, 148–52, 157–66
Origin of Species, 38–39
Ostend Manifesto, 250, 251
O'Sullivan, John L., 243–44
Oswald, Richard, 114
Opium trade, 270, 276, 279
Opium War, 119, 265

Pakenham, Richard, 124, 127, 130, 131, 133, 149, 150–52, 154
Paley, William, 33
Palmerston, Lord (Henry John Temple)
 and canal projects, 220
 and China, 271
 and Maine boundary question, 114–15
 and Mosquito Protectorate, 220–23, 224
 and slave trade, 104–108
 and Texas annexation, 124
 and U.S.-Canadian border troubles, 98–99, 101–102, 103, 113
 on Webster-Ashburton Treaty, 114
Paredes y Arrillaga, Mariano, 181, 182, 184, 190
Paris, Treaty of, 71, 94–95
Parker, Peter, 263, 265, 269, 271, 274–75, 276
Parker, Theodore, 34, 191
Parrott, William, 177, 178, 179, 180, 181, 187
Patronage, party, 155
Paulding, H., 253, 254

Paulet, George, 259
Pedro I, Don, 77–78
Peel, Robert, 103, 110, 114, 120, 125, 159
Peña y Peña, Manuel de la, 179, 181, 188, 192
Perrin, Louis Emile, 259
Perry, Matthew C., 197, 200, 265, 280–81, 282, 283–84
Perry Treaty, 284
Pezuela, Marques de la, 245–46
Philosophy of the Active and Moral Powers of Man, The, 32
Pierce, Benjamin, 36, 38–39
Pierce, Franklin, 204, 206, 210, 225, 237, 260
 and Central America, 214, 226
 and Crimean War, 211
 and Cuba, 246, 247, 249
 and Kansas-Nebraska Act, 210
 and Tehuantepec route, 241
Pletcher, David, 292
Poe, Edgar Allen, 31
Poinsett, Joel Roberts, 170
Polignac, Auguste de, 86
Polk, James K., 121, 144, 146–48
 and California, 174–75, 184
 and Central America, 219
 and Cuba, 243–44
 Diary, 146, 148, 156, 157
 as an expansionist, 121, 144, 173, 174
 and Great Britain, 148
 and Mexican War, 141, 169, 177, 179, 180, 183, 184–92
 and Monroe Doctrine, 59
 and the Oregon question, 145, 148, 149, 150, 151–55, 156–66
 on protective tariffs, 156, 158
 and Texas boundary, 175
Portugal, 77–78
Pottinger, Henry, 269
Prescott, William, 30
Priestley, Joseph, 12
Privateering, 4, 210
Proclamation of 1763, 71

Protestantism, 8–9
Puget Sound, 164
Putnam's Monthly, 211–12

Quadra Island, 149, 159
Quadruple Treaty, 115
Quasi-War, 4
Quitman, John A., 244, 246
Quintuple Alliance, 50, 52, 53

Railroads, 24, 28, 198, 199, 214
  transcontinental, 168–69, 198, 209, 216, 217, 236, 237, 241
Recollections, 21
Redfield, William C., 36
Reed, William B., 275–79
Re-exports, 13–14
Reform Bill, 78, 83
Rejon, Manuel Crescencio, 133, 134
Religion, 14–16
Republicans, 9–10
Revivalism, 14–15
Rhett, R. Barnwell, 136
Rice, 22, 76
Rio Grande, 175, 176, 179, 180, 187, 192
Rives, William C., 83, 85–88, 138
Roads, 23, 25
Ruatan, 223, 224, 226, 229–30
Rush, Richard, 48, 51, 57, 58, 63, 66, 204–205, 206, 211
Russia
  and China, 276–77
  claim of, to Pacific coast, 50–51
  commercial treaty with U.S., 75
  and Crimean War, 203, 210, 211
  and Near East, 77
Rye, 196
Rynders, Isaiah, 138–39

Salas, José Mariano, 190, 237
Saligny, Alphonse Dubois de, 123, 124, 140
Sanders, George, 206
Sandwich Islands, 257

San Juan, Nicaragua, 218–19, 220, 222, 224, 225, 226, 230, 231
Santa Anna, Antonio Lopez de, 122, 126, 133, 134, 182, 190, 192
Saunders, Romulus M., 244
Science, American, 35–39
Scott, Sir Walter, 31, 33–34
Scott, Winfield, 29, 100, 103, 189, 192
Seager, Robert, 138, 139
Sebastiani, Horace Françoise Bastien, 87–88
Secession, 215
Sectionalism, 2, 13, 214–17, 236–37, 291
Self-righteousness, national, 14, 16
Sellers, Charles, 121
Sergeant, John, 25
Seward, William Henry, 108, 203, 208–209, 218, 226, 251
Shanghai, 272
Shannon, Wilson, 134, 177
Sherman, Sidney, 174
Shipbuilding, 43
Shipping, growth of, 75–76
Siberia, 197
Sickles, Daniel E., 250
Silliman, Benjamin, 36
Sir Robert Peel, 100
Slavery
  and Cuban annexation move, 204, 208, 215, 216, 251
  priority of the South, 2, 96, 215–16
  and sectionalism, 96, 195, 215
  and southern expansionists, 215–16
  and Texas, 126–27, 128, 129, 131
  See also Antislavery movement
Slave trade
  British suppression of, 95–96, 104–105, 108–110, 113–14
  and Quadruple Treaty, 115
  U.S. Congress on, 104
  U.S. efforts to curb, 80

Slidell, John, 179, 180, 181, 182, 183, 184, 186, 251, 252
Sloat, John Drake, 179, 185–86
Sloo, Albert G., 200, 240–41
Smith, Adam, 13
Smith, Ashbel, 126, 127–28, 132, 133, 140
Smith, O. J., 110
Smith, Samuel, 67–68, 79
Smithsonian Institution, 36–37, 38
Sons of Liberty, 99
Soulé, Pierre, 203, 206, 247, 248–50
South, 22–23
  and British imperialism, 224–25
  and cotton, 22–23, 243
  and Cuban annexation movement, 204, 208, 215, 216
  and expansionism, 204, 215–16
  and low tariffs, 214
  and slavery issue, 2, 80, 214, 215
  and Texas annexation, 131, 136–37, 140, 215
South American republics, 50, 51, 52–53, 55, 56–57, 58, 59
Spain
  and Cuba, 216, 217, 229, 242, 247, 249
  and Florida, 5, 11
  invaded by France, 50, 51
  and Portugal, 77–78
  possessions of, 5, 11
  and South American republics, 50, 51, 52–53, 55, 56–57, 58, 59
  trade policy of, 217, 242
Spanish-American War, 254
Sparks, Jared, 111, 112, 114
Squier, George, 219, 220, 222, 223, 225
Steamboat transportation, 198–99, 200
Stephens, Alexander, 138
Stevenson, Andrew, 76, 97, 98–99, 101–102, 103, 104–108, 115
Stewart, Dugald, 32–33
St. Lawrence River, 64, 111, 112
Stockton, Robert F., 174

Sturgis, William, 149
Sugar, 243
Superior, Lake, 112

Taipeng rebellion, 256
Tappan, Benjamin, 132
Tariff, U.S.
  against Great Britain, 67, 81
  on foreign ships, 62, 67
  low, policy, 25, 29, 214
  Polk's efforts to reduce, 156, 158
  protective, 25, 125, 156, 158
Taylor, Bayard, 281
Taylor, Zachary
  on Clayton-Bulwer Treaty, 223–24
  and Cuban annexationists, 244
  and France, 205
  and Kossuth, 207
  in Mexican War, 174, 177, 178, 180–84, 186–87, 190
  and Nicaragua, 219
  as president, 205, 207, 219, 223–24, 244
Tehuantepec, 225, 226, 236, 237–41
Tennyson, Alfred, 31
Territorial expansion, 144, 202
  and Buchanan, 249–50, 251–52
  and California, 118, 119, 168, 173
  and Canada, 95
  and Cuban annexation movement, 208–209, 242–52
  and Florida, 5, 7, 11–14
  and Hawaii, 260
  and land hunger, 12, 121, 243
  and Louisiana, 5
  and Oregon, 118–19, 144, 173
  and Polk, 153, 163, 173, 243–44
  Seward's views on, 209
  and slavery issue, 214–15, 218
  and Texas, 118–19, 123, 125, 127, 129, 144
Texas, 118–41
  American interest in, 118–19
  American settlers in, 121–22
  annexation of, 125–26, 127, 128,

Texas (cont'd.)
   129–30, 133, 134, 135–41
   application for statehood, 123
   boundary, 169, 175–76, 178, 179, 180, 187, 192
   hostilities with Mexico, 124–25, 129, 134, 170
   independence of, 170
   Mexican rule of, 119, 121–22
   as a republic, 123–40
   and slavery issue, 126–27, 128, 129, 131
   war for independence, 122
Textile industry
   in England, 44
   in U.S., 24, 197
Thomas, Richard, 259
Thompson, Waddy, 170
Thoreau, Henry David, 191
Thurston, Asa, 258
Tigre Island, 220, 222, 223
Tobacco, 22, 75, 76
Tocqueville, Alexis de, 15, 21
Toombs, Robert, 254
Transcendentalism, 31, 34–35
Transcontinental railroads, 168–69, 198, 209, 216, 217, 236, 237, 241
Trist, Nicholas P., 105, 191–92
Turner, Frederick Jackson, 202
Turney, Hopkins, 156–57
Turkey, 51, 58–59, 210
Tuyll, Baron, 50–51, 55, 56
Tyler, John
   on American claims against France, 85
   and Maine boundary question, 110
   and Oregon, 150
   and Texas annexation, 126, 129, 132, 133, 134, 135, 138

United States (steamboat), 101
United States Mail Steamship Company, 200
Upshur, Abel P., 125, 126, 128, 145

Utilitarianism, 33

Vail, Aaron, 75, 83
Van Buren, Martin, 80, 85, 100, 103, 118, 123, 191
Vancouver Island, 149, 159, 164
Vergennes, Charles Gravier, 3
Villèle, Joseph de, 52

Wade, Thomas Francis, 279
Walker, I. P., 206
Walker, Robert J., 125
Walker, William, 216, 252–54
War for Independence, 3, 12
War of 1812, 3, 4, 6, 7, 14
Ward, Thomas Wren, 25
Warren, John, 8–9, 13
Wealth of Nations, 13
Webster, Daniel
   on British suppression of slave trade, 113
   and China, 263–64
   on foreign trade, 280
   and Greek war for independence, 58–59
   and Hawaii, 258–59
   and Hungarian revolt, 207
   and McLeod case, 108
   on Monroe Doctrine, 58
   and Oregon question, 115, 145, 161
   and Tehuantepec route, 238, 239
Webster-Ashburton Treaty, 114, 118
Wellington, Duke of (Arthur Wellesley), 103, 111–12
West Florida, 5, 11–12
West Indies, British
   and Canadian Maritime Provinces, 4, 80, 81, 82
   and British antislavery movement, 104–105
   opened to U.S. trade, 82–83
   prohibition of slavery in, 96, 104–105
   and restrictions on U.S. trade, 4,

West Indies, British (*cont'd.*)
    13, 46, 61–64, 65, 68–69, 71, 80, 83
West Indies, French, 14
Westward movement, 17, 23, 24
Whaling industry, 197, 257
Wheat, 23–24, 196
Whiggery, 1–2
Whigs, 190–91, 236–37
Whitney, Asa, 168, 237
Wickliffe, Charles A., 174
Wilkes Expedition, 37
Williams, Samuel Wells, 263, 275, 277, 278, 279, 280, 283, 284
Wirt, William, 55
Wittke, Carl, 27
Woodbury, Levi, 137, 140
Woods, Lake of the, 112
Woodward, George C., 155
Wordsworth, William, 33
Wright, Chester, 23

Yankeephobia, 120
Young America movement, 206, 225
Yrisarri, A. J. de, 252

LIBRARY OF DAVIDSON COLLEGE

Books on regular loan may be checked out for **two weeks**. Books must be presented at the Circulation Desk in order to be renewed.

A fine is charged after date due.

Special books are subject to special regulations at the discretion of the library staff.

JUL -1 1982			
JAN 29 1985			
SEP 22 1986			